2-16-00

D1067825

Recipes and Remembrances

from an Eastern Mediterranean Kitchen

Recipes and Remembrances

from an Eastern Mediterranean Kitchen

A Culinary Journey through

Syria, Lebanon, and Jordan

Sonia Uvezian

UNIVERSITY OF TEXAS PRESS, AUSTIN

First edition, 1999

Requests for permission
to reproduce material from this work should
be sent to Permissions, University of Texas
Press, Box 7819, Austin, TX 78713-7819.

⊚ The paper used in this book meets the
minimum requirements of ANSI/NISO
Z39.48-1992 (R1997) (Permanence of Paper).

***Library of Congress
Cataloging-in-Publication Data***

Uvezian, Sonia.
Recipes and remembrances from an eastern
Mediterranean kitchen : a culinary journey
through Syria, Lebanon, and Jordan / Sonia
Uvezian.—1st ed.
p.   cm.
Includes bibliographical references and index.
ISBN 0-292-78535-6
1. Cookery, Mediterranean.   2. Cookery, Middle
Eastern.   3. Middle East—Social life and cus-
toms.   I. Title.
TX725.M628U94   1999
641.5956—dc21   98-47155

Frontispiece from page ii: A party at dinner.
From William McClure Thomson, The Land
and the Book, *vol. 3 (New York, Harper, 1885).*

∾

There were two hairdressers in London, the best spies Buonaparte had. A hairdresser, generally speaking, must be a man of talent—so must be a cook; for a cook must know such a variety of things, about which no settled rules can be laid down, and he must have great judgment.

—[Charles Meryon], *Memoirs of the Lady Hester Stanhope* (1845)

∾

Contents

Although only a single author's name appears on the title page, this book could not have been written without the invaluable support and assistance of my husband, David Kaiserman, who participated in every step of its creation over a period of more than twenty years and who was, in effect, a virtual collaborator.

Introduction

Beirut and Mount Lebanon. *From John Carne,* Syria, the Holy Land, Asia Minor, &c., *vol. 2 (London, Fisher, Son, 1836)*

THE TIME WAS THE 1950s, the place Beirut, Lebanon, the very heart of the eastern Mediterranean world. I had been awakened at dawn's first light by the muezzin's call to morning prayer from the minaret of the Grand Mosque, which stood on the Rue Weygand two blocks east of my family's apartment on the Rue des Capucins. Carrying my breakfast tray, I stepped out onto the balcony, where I was greeted by the sound of tolling bells emanating from the tower of the Capuchin church just to the west of our building. The sun was beginning its ascent over the towering Lebanon Mountains, which loomed in shadowy majesty above the rapidly stirring metropolis. Gradually it rose beyond their snowy summits, bathing them in a pure, radiant light that quickly extended down the mountainsides, bringing into bold relief the many villages nestled in their folds. The light spread over the terraced foothills with their orchards and olive groves and enveloped the city, which lay glistening on the coastal plain, its skyline an intriguing blend of architectural styles: Byzantine, Arab, Romanesque, Gothic, Italian, and the strikingly modern. I gazed northward toward the beautiful Bay of St. George and beheld the ever-busy harbor. It was filled with tankers and cargo ships from many lands as well as with local fishing boats and pleasure craft, and its docks were beginning to hum with activity. The sparkling blue Mediterranean and the vibrant harbor, the lush coastal plain, the picturesque foothills, and the massive overhanging mountains all combined to create a spectacular setting for the city I called home.

At this early hour the bounty of the countryside was pouring into the already bustling Arab *suq* located close to the mosque, while a short distance from the church shopkeepers in the French market were setting out their newly delivered supplies of flowers and produce along with freshly baked baguettes and other *prix fixe* items for buyers who preferred not to engage in the traditional Middle Eastern custom of haggling over prices. In the *Burj,* or old town, coffee shops with their huge trays of exotic saffron cakes and honey-drenched pastries were starting to fill up with patrons, and near the French market the European-style *pâtisseries,* with offerings as authentic as any on the Continent, were preparing to welcome an equally enthusiastic clientele. The streets were becoming crowded with cars, trolleys, peddlers, and pedestrians. Businessmen attired in tailored Western suits and secretaries and shopgirls wearing the latest French and Italian fashions contrasted sharply with visiting desert sheikhs in flowing robes and headdresses and veiled Muslim women in somber black.

This striking amalgam of old and new and East and West, which contributed in no small measure to the overwhelming appeal of Lebanon's dynamic capital, was reflected in the breakfast I was enjoying on my balcony on that magnificent, faraway spring morning: a French omelet incorporating a Middle Eastern filling accompanied with a basket of Arab and French breads, oil-cured black olives, yogurt cheese, honey and jam, a pot of spiced tea, and, to finish, a bowl of chilled strawberries and cream flavored with rose water.

Both the muezzin's call and the church bells had ceased and another sound had caught my attention: that of construction, for Beirut was experiencing a building boom. Under the Romans the city (then known as Berytus) was a major center of commerce and learning, with the most famous law school in the Empire. Now, after many centuries, it was again in its ascendancy, having become the hub of commercial, intellectual, and cultural activity not only for all of Lebanon but for the entire Middle East. In keeping with early tradition, it was also thriving as a lively and cosmopolitan pleasure port. Although Beirut would not attain the pinnacle of its "Golden Age" for several more years, tourists from all over the world were already beginning to descend on it in droves, both to savor its luxuries and to view the many impressive antiquities surrounding it.

History speaks eloquently in Lebanon, as it does in Syria and Jordan. In ancient times these three countries were part of a large territory often referred to as Greater Syria, which also encompassed Israel and portions of Turkey and Iraq. This territory was in turn part of a region known as the Fertile Crescent, where mankind first acquired the means of producing its own food and where the first great civilizations arose. Located at the crossroads of major trade routes and blessed with rich soil, Greater Syria was a prize coveted by a host of different peoples and empires, among them Egyptians, Babylonians, Canaanites, Hittites, Hurrians, Arameans, Assyrians, Persians, Greeks, Romans, Arabs, Crusaders, Mongols, and Turks. Most of them left their imprint in one way or another, not only on the landscape but on the culture in general, including the food.

Today Syria, Lebanon, and Jordan form a rich tapestry of ethnic and religious groups. Although the great bulk of the population is considered to be Arab (a term I have occasionally employed in this book to avoid complication), it is in fact extremely mixed in ancestry. Almost everyone speaks Arabic, but English and French are also widely used and many minorities, such as Armenians, Assyrians, Circassians, Greeks, Kurds, Turks, and Turkomans, continue to utilize their traditional languages (and recipes). Both Muslims (the vast majority) and Christians are divided into a number of different sects. Another important religious group are the Druze. Very few Jews now remain, although historically they were a significant and influential minority.

Cliffs and sculptured tablets near the Dog River north of Beirut. These inscriptions commemorate the military feats of conquering heroes dating back to Ramses II in the thirteenth century B.C. From Charles William Wilson, ed., Picturesque Palestine, Sinai and Egypt, *vol. 2 (New York, D. Appleton, 1883)*

Syrian gentlemen of various sects. *From William McClure Thomson,* The Land and the Book, *vol. 1 (New York, Harper, 1880)*

Perhaps the purest Arab stock are the Beduin, many of whom have abandoned their nomadic way of life in recent years in favor of a more settled existence. Not long ago Jordan's population was made up mostly of Beduin. At present, however, the Palestinians, who have emigrated from their homeland in what is now Israel, represent the majority.

Because Syria, Lebanon, and Jordan were all part of Greater Syria for nearly two thousand years and have existed as separate states for only a relatively short time, they share not only a common language and cultural heritage but a common culinary tradition as well. When differences occur, they are not necessarily between countries, but are often between urban and rural areas or one town and another. These differences can be traced to various influences, such as types of food available due to geography, local or family customs, religious dietary laws, and the degree of interaction with the West. Nonetheless, each country is known for certain specialties. Jordanians are proud of their *mansaf, musakhan,* and *maqlubi,* the last two being of Palestinian origin. In Syria, Aleppo is noted for numerous specialties, including *muhammara, lahm bi ajeen,* and *karabij halab,* while Hama is known for *halawat al-jibn.* Damascus, the capital, has long been renowned for different kinds of *fatta* and such sweets as *barazik, amardine,* crystallized fruit, and Middle Eastern ice cream. Of the many towns in Lebanon that pride themselves on their local specialties, Zahleh is famous for *tabbuleh, kibbeh* (especially raw *kibbeh*), *assafeer*, garlic-flavored grilled chicken, and *nammura;*[1] Ehden and Zgharta for *kibbeh* (particularly grilled *kibbeh*); Sidon for *al-sanyura* and *barazik;* al-Batrun for lemonade; Tripoli for ice creams, pastries, and confections, including *jazariyya, halawat al-jibn,* and pumpkin, rose petal, and orange blossom jams; al-Mina (Tripoli's port) for fried fish; and Baalbek for *lahm bi ajeen.*

Of all the factors that have shaped the culinary traditions of Lebanon, the most decisive one has been that of nature. Despite its small size, the country possesses a great diversity of terrain and microclimates, the latter ranging from subtropical to subarctic. Arab poets tell us that Mount Lebanon bears winter on its head, spring on its shoulders, and autumn in its bosom, while summer lies sleeping at its feet. This image is confirmed by the French traveler Constantin-François Volney, who made an extended visit to the region in 1784:

> Syria unites under the same sky different climates and brings together in a narrow space enjoyments that nature has spread elsewhere in great distances of time and space. In our country, for example, it has separated the seasons by months; in Syria one can say that they are but hours apart. . . .[2]

Today, of course, they are separated by only minutes.

The astonishingly varied conditions of temperature, rainfall, altitude, and soil have made Lebanon an agricultural marvel, as evidenced by the pyramids of winter and summer produce simultaneously displayed in urban markets in seeming defiance of the seasons. Only a short space of sixty miles separates the Mediterranean littoral from the arid steppes of Western Asia, a distance, however, that encompasses several different growing zones due to the position of the Lebanon Range and its great height. Vegetables, dates, sycamores, bananas, loquats, citrus fruits, and sugarcane all flourish on the coastal plain, while in the foothills olives, grapes, figs, and almonds are among the principal crops. Slightly higher up are found orchards of walnuts, hazelnuts, apricots, cherries, peaches, and plums; stone pine, mulberry, and carob trees also thrive in the salubrious air. Beginning at about 2,500 feet one enters a level of intense apple and pear cultivation. The Bekaa Valley, the nation's breadbasket, presents still another zone.

My interest in food dates back to happy times in Shtora, a small town lying east of Beirut in the central Bekaa, where my family's summer home with its extensive garden was located. Perhaps more than any other place, it is the Shtora of the 1950s that evokes nostalgia for my Lebanese childhood.[3] One of the most eagerly anticipated events of the year was the Easter holidays, which we would often spend in Shtora. To get there we would take the Beirut-Damascus road, which only a few miles outside Beirut begins to twist and turn up into the mountains, providing breathtaking vistas of the city, the coastal plain, and the shimmering Mediterranean. Continuing inland, it climbs swiftly, curving its way between deep gorges and craggy cliffs. Less than half an hour from Beirut the road passes through what used to be three of Lebanon's leading summer resorts: Aley, Bhamdun, and Sofar. Virtual ghost towns in winter, they would spring into activity

A Maronite village on the slopes of Mount Lebanon. *From Charles William Wilson, ed.,* Picturesque Palestine, Sinai and Egypt, *vol. 2 (New York, D. Appleton, 1883)*

Pietro's Hotel in Shtora, the famous halfway house on the Beirut-Damascus road, photographed in 1875. *From Henry Harris Jessup,* Fifty-Three Years in Syria, *vol. 1 (New York, Fleming H. Revell Company, 1910)*

with the arrival of warm weather, when their luxurious hotels, cabarets, and casinos would overflow with exuberant nightlife. In these resorts East and West rubbed shoulders with aplomb. A French chanteuse singing Gallic love songs could be heard in the bar of a fashionable hotel, where urbane waiters served champagne to chic Beirut women dressed in the newest Parisian designer creations, while outside only a short distance away, street vendors dispensed lemonade and licorice juice from elaborate urns strapped to their backs.

A few miles beyond the lovely tree-lined main avenue of Sofar, the highway reaches its summit at the 5,000-foot-high Dahr al-Baidar pass, which on winter weekends would be alive with skiers and fun-loving Lebanese out for an excursion in the snow. After Dahr al-Baidar the road descends abruptly into the peaceful Bekaa Valley, but not before one is rewarded with an unforgettable view of its long patchwork quilt of colorful square fields nestled between the protecting ranges of the Lebanon and Anti-Lebanon.

The excitement engendered in us by this majestic sight was due partly to our now being only a few minutes from our destination, for as soon as we came down into the valley we would be in Shtora. With its invigorating climate and pleasant surroundings, the town was a popular health resort and a favorite haven for honeymooners. Situated at nearly the midpoint between Beirut and Damascus, it had long been an ideal resting place for travelers.

Some of the fruit trees in our garden would just be bursting into glorious bloom, filling the air with an intoxicating fragrance, and all kinds of flowers, growing wild and free, bordered the path beside the sparkling stream that rushed through the town. The land was bountiful and rich, and everything seemed joyous and intensely alive.

Easter vacations were spent celebrating the outdoors with a round of picnics, tennis, cycling trips, and long walks in the countryside where the fields and hillsides bloomed with carpets of wildflowers in a profusion of colors. Although we did some cooking (mostly picnic fare), our Shtora kitchen was not yet the hub of activity it would soon become, especially during the late summer and early fall, when it would be the scene of almost continuous food preparation, not only for immediate consumption but for the whole year ahead. At that time the unending harvest from our garden would challenge the most ambitious cook, yet nothing was wasted (see Chapter 14).

The Bekaa is the agricultural heart of Lebanon and contains some of the most fertile farmland in the world. Wheat, barley, and millet have been grown in this valley since the dawn of civilization, and in the days of Rome it was a major granary of the Empire. Almost any crop can be cultivated, however. The Shtora region in particular was and still is known for its meticulous vegetable and fruit cultivation. I remember people commenting on the aroma, taste, and texture of melons and other fruit, discussing with the solemnity of wine experts not only the different varieties but the areas in which they were grown, the amount of sun they received, and the quality of irrigation.

The plain of the Bekaa is dotted with historical sites, many of which served as backgrounds for our picnics. A favorite spot was Anjar, with its poplar-shaded spring and nearby ruins of an Umayyad pleasure palace. Another was Baalbek, site of the most gigantic complex of Roman temples ever built. This awe-inspiring shrine gains an even more impressive dimension set against the splendor of the vast valley and the snow-clad Lebanon Mountains. It was spellbinding to stand near the temples and look out across the wide expanse of the Bekaa filled with the iridescent green of young wheat interrupted only here and there by a cluster of trees signifying a village or hamlet. Surrounding the town were lovely gardens, their fruit trees adorned with pink and white blossoms, where peasants in traditional dress could be seen hard at work in the invigorating air and bright sunshine.

Numerous foods and dishes described in this book remain associated in my mind with particular settings: *kibbeh* and *tabbuleh* in a park just outside Baalbek; fresh pistachios and walnuts at a charming café along the banks of the Barada River near Damascus; a rich and nourishing cinnamon-scented soup after a day's skiing at the Cedars of Lebanon; and garlic-flavored grilled chicken at a picturesque willow-shaded restaurant beside an icy mountain stream in Zahleh.

Many of the dishes eaten today have been little altered since they were invented centuries ago, for cooking in this part of the world is steeped in tradition and is handed down from mother to daughter.[4] In the past, when the majority of people were illiterate, this was the norm, but even today culinary skills continue to be acquired mainly by observation and participation rather than by following recipes in cookbooks. When I was growing up, perhaps the primary focus of a village girl's education was on learning how to cook. It was not unusual for a ten-year-old to be able to bake bread and to have mastered a basic repertoire of simple dishes.

The recipes included in this book represent only a fraction of those found in Syria, Lebanon, and Jordan. To compile a comprehensive collection would require several volumes. I have purposely limited myself to a relatively small selection here, instead devoting space to the geographical, historical, and cultural context of the region's food in an effort to present the subject in a fuller perspective.

I have suggested interesting variations for many of the recipes; however, an almost endless number of others exist owing to the diverse interpretations given to dishes in each country, with changes that occur regionally, locally, and even within a single family. I have also included my personal modernizations and adaptations of several recipes from medieval Arab culinary manuals (these are indicated by ornaments). In addition, you will encounter some of my own creations (also indicated by ornaments) that have been inspired by the Middle Eastern style of cooking.

You will find scattered throughout this volume a few stories about Joha, the legendary folk hero of the region. Also included are a number of sayings and proverbs. Some of these are of Armenian origin and are identified by the sign $\mathcal{A}$ to distinguish them from the Arab ones. Looking back on my life in Lebanon, I am struck by how frequently people resorted to proverbs to substantiate their statements and add zest to their conversations. I even remember proverbs about proverbs, such as the often-quoted "Proverbs of the common people are like salt for the food" and "A proverb never tells a lie." Indeed, the use of an appropriate proverb to make a point was usually more convincing to many villagers than the most logical argument.

Although I have endeavored to include interesting information about all three countries, I have devoted somewhat more space to Lebanon because of its reputation as a center of gastronomy and its cosmopolitan heritage; I have also wished to share some of my own memories and insights. The "eastern Mediterranean kitchen" in the title is actually that of our summer house in Shtora as well as the one in our Beirut apartment. Had I been born in Syria or Jordan, I would doubtless have approached the subject from a different perspective.

The complex and tragic events that for more than half a century have convulsed the territory covered in this book have unfortunately given rise not only to violent and intense feelings but to inaccurate and simplistic stereotypes, all of which have extended even into the realm of cookery. At long last misguided prejudices are showing signs of eroding, and Middle Eastern cuisine is now beginning to receive the widespread accolades it has always deserved. I hope that this book will convey to its readers my respect and enthusiasm for the fascinating culinary heritage of Syria, Lebanon, and Jordan, and that it will win new friends for it as well.

A Note on Transliteration

Since I have not written this book in a scholarly style, I have refrained from following any specific system exclusively in transliterating Arabic recipe titles and other words and have avoided the use of diacritical marks. The resulting spelling is therefore only approximate, as will be any attempt at pronunciation. It may be helpful, however, to note that in Arabic speech the sound of the *l* in the definite article, *al*, is suppressed before the sounds *d, n, r, s, sh, t,* and *z;* thus names such as Bayt al-Din, al-Zabadani, and al-Salt are actually pronounced *Bayt ad-Din, az-Zabadani,* and *as-Salt.* Also, in the colloquial language of the region the word ending *-a* is often pronounced *-eh,* as in *labna/labneh* and *muhallabiyya/muhallabiyyeh,* and the letter *q* is frequently enunciated only by a glottal stop, sometimes represented in English by an apostrophe or omitted entirely, for example, *mana'ish* or *manaish* for *manaqish.* Finally, I have written certain well-known names of places and personages in the way they are usually rendered in English, for instance, Beirut, Tripoli, and Saladin rather than Bayrut, Tarabulus, and Salah al-Din.

Historical Background

Roman ruins at Baalbek.

One had always known that the stone imprint of the Empire was to be found throughout the ancient world. But it was a book-knowledge, a thing understood intellectually. Here at Baalbek, with tremendous force, the known becomes the felt, and history puts on flesh.

Robin Fedden, Syria and Lebanon.

From *John Carne,* Syria, the Holy Land, Asia Minor, &c., *vol. 1 (London, Fisher, Son, 1836)*

The Earliest Civilizations

THE FOOD OF MESOPOTAMIA

Archaeologists have discovered that agriculture was first practiced by the ancestors of the Egyptians along the Nile River in Nubia as early as 12,000 B.C. Around 8000 B.C. people began to cultivate crops and domesticate animals in northern Iraq, Anatolia, and several locations in Greater Syria. During the fourth millennium B.C., highly organized societies based on large-scale agriculture made possible by canal irrigation arose in Mesopotamia, the land between the Tigris and Euphrates Rivers in what is now Iraq. In Greater Syria advanced northern Mesopotamian cultures had become established well before 2000 B.C., first at Ebla and, not long after, at Mari on the Euphrates (these had been preceded by smaller-scale non-Mesopotamian cultures). Excavations at Mari have brought to light the remains of an enormous palace that boasted a library of about twenty thousand clay cuneiform tablets, which have provided invaluable information on daily life in the region. These excavations have also revealed remarkably well-preserved domestic areas such as kitchens and pantries.

The Mari tablets, as well as information from other sources, give us some idea of the foods consumed at the palace court. These included meat (beef, mutton, and goat), game, fish, and both leavened and unleavened bread. Among the popular vegetables were cucumbers, peas, beans, cress, and garlic. Desert truffles were considered a great delicacy, and the tablets mention baskets of them being sent to the king. The cuneiform texts often refer to dates, the most common fruit, as well as to grapes and figs. Beverages included locally produced barley beer and wine imported from cooler regions to the north and northeast. Milk from sheep, goats, and, to a lesser extent, cows was also an important element of the diet.

Knowledge of the food of Mari heightens our curiosity about the cookery of the Sumerians, Akkadians, and, later, the Babylonians and Assyrians, all of whom occupied

*Mesopotamian figures on enam-
eled brick. From Georges Perrot
and Charles Chipiez,* A History of
Art in Chaldea & Assyria, *translated and edited by Walter Armstrong, vol. 2 (London, Chapman
and Hall, 1884)*

the land farther to the east and southeast. Although this area lies beyond the one being
covered in the present volume, its enormous influence, not only on Greater Syria but
on all of Western civilization, justifies some discussion of its cuisine, particularly in light
of recent important discoveries.

Despite the wealth of material unearthed about the various Mesopotamian peoples,
there seemed to be few clues as to how they actually prepared their meals. Lately, however, cuneiform symbols inscribed on tablets dating from approximately 1700 B.C. have
been found to be a documentation of numerous recipes, making them the oldest such
collection in existence. The tablets, as well as other written records, artistic depictions,
and archaeological remains, reveal that the Mesopotamians, or at least those of the upper
classes, possessed a remarkably advanced cuisine of striking richness and sophistication.

The Mesopotamian kitchen offered at least one hundred kinds of soup and no less
than three hundred kinds of bread. Meat from both domestic and wild animals was
eaten. One text mentions meat-stuffed intestinal casings, perhaps the earliest form of
sausages. Many kinds of fresh- and saltwater fish and shellfish were consumed. Millet,
wheat, and, especially, barley were staple cereal crops, while gardens yielded a wide

variety of vegetables and fruits. Herbs and spices, among them mint, juniper berries, and, possibly, mustard, cumin, and coriander, were used to flavor foods. Salt was also employed, though in moderation. Honey and the sap of the date palm were used as sweeteners, as was a molasses made from date juice (*dispu;* see *dibs,* page 73). A fermented sauce known as *shiqqu* was used extensively. Prepared from fish, shellfish, or grasshoppers, it appears to have been similar to Worcestershire sauce and the Vietnamese *nuoc mam.* Methods of food preservation included drying, salting, and smoking. A number of fruits were preserved in honey.

Sheep, goats, and cows provided milk, some of which was churned into butter; the butter in turn was clarified in order to preserve it. The Sumerian word for clarified butter, *samn,* survives in modern Arabic. Milk was also soured and made into cheese. Besides *samn,* animal fat (lard and that from the tail of the fat-tailed sheep; see *aliya,* page 70) and olive, sesame, and linseed oils were employed in cooking.

Of the many kinds of beverages imbibed by the Mesopotamians, beer was by far the favorite. It was brewed primarily by women, who not only prepared it for their families but sold it outside their houses, thus becoming history's first tavern keepers. Next to beer, the most popular beverage was grape wine, imported from cooler regions to the north.

The Mesopotamians broiled or roasted food over an open flame or glowing coals.

(top) Mesopotamian amphorae. (bottom) Mesopotamian ewer. From Georges Perrot and Charles Chipiez, A History of Art in Chaldea & Assyria, *translated and edited by Walter Armstrong, vol. 2 (London, Chapman and Hall, 1884)*

Long-simmering meat and/or vegetable stews were popular. Two types of ovens were utilized for baking: an upright clay cylinder, called *tinuru*, for unleavened bread; and a dome oven, which provided less intense heat and retained the steam produced by the foods being cooked, making it possible to prepare fermented doughs and leavened breads. The Mesopotamian method of baking unleavened bread still survives today in the Middle East, Central Asia, and India. The names for various outdoor ovens—*tannur* in the Fertile Crescent, *tonir* in Armenia, *toné* in Georgia, and *tandoor* in India—are all derived from the ancient Mesopotamian *tinuru.*

The Mesopotamian nobility and priesthood took a serious interest in gastronomy. Their meals were prepared by male master chefs (*nuhatimmu*), who exercised their skills in well-equipped kitchens, often using ingredients that were expensive and difficult to obtain. On the other hand, in ordinary households which did not have access to such ingredients, the food was prepared by women and must have been simpler and less varied.

Based on the information we now possess, it appears that Mesopotamia, long known as the "Cradle of Civilization," was also the birthplace of haute cuisine. This is not to say that the Mesopotamians' concept of good food is compatible with ours. For example, most of us would probably find their use of fats and oils excessive and that of

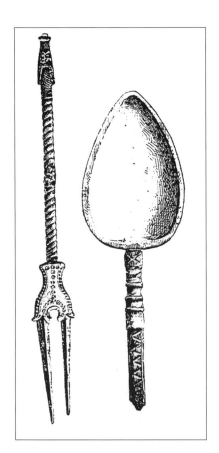

Mesopotamian bronze fork and spoon.
From Georges Perrot and Charles Chipiez,
A History of Art in Chaldea & Assyria,
translated and edited by Walter Armstrong,
vol. 2 (London, Chapman and Hall, 1884)

salt inadequate, nor would we necessarily share their obsession with every member of the onion family. Although modern Middle Eastern cooking is obviously quite different from that of ancient Mesopotamia, an unquestionable link between the two can nevertheless be clearly perceived.

∾

He who possesses much silver may be happy; he who possesses much barley may be glad; but he who has nothing at all may sleep.
(Mesopotamian proverb)

∾

THE FOOD OF GREATER SYRIA, CA. 3000–64 B.C.

The diet of the average person living in ancient Syria was largely vegetarian: bread, cereals, olives and olive oil, vegetables, fruits, and dairy products supplemented by fish where available and, on rare occasions, by meat. Wheat, barley, and millet were the chief cereal crops (rice was not introduced until the fourth century B.C.). People would pluck off the fresh, not-yet-ripe ears of wheat, rub off the husks, and eat the kernels raw, or else they would roast the grain directly over an open fire or on a hot stone or iron plate and, after it had sufficiently cooled, rub off the husks before savoring the kernels. Grain thus roasted is referred to as "parched" in the Old Testament (see *freek,* page 246). The staff of life was bread, both leavened and unleavened, made either wafer-thin or in flat, round cakes. It was baked on hot stones, convex plates made first of clay and later of iron (see *saaj,* page 308), or in various kinds of outdoor ovens, the general name for which was *tannur* (from *tinuru,* above), to whose hot walls the dough was applied, either on the inside or outside. Although wheaten bread was common, barley bread was the usual kind eaten by the poor.

Second in importance to cereals were legumes. Onions, leeks, garlic, cucumbers, radishes, lettuce, and chicory were raised extensively. Mint, wild marjoram, mustard, coriander, anise, cumin, nigella, and capers were used as condiments. Salt was employed both as a flavoring and as a preservative. Olives were an indispensable food, and olive oil, which served as the primary cooking fat, was one of the three main foodstuffs for which ancient Syria was celebrated, the other two being wheat and wine. Fruits and nuts were consumed in abundance. Grapes, figs, and dates were especially prized, as were pomegranates, whose multitudinous seeds were a symbol of fertility.

By far the greater portion of the grape harvest was turned into wine, which was universally imbibed. Certain locations, notably Lebanon and Helbon near Damascus, were renowned for their vintages. Large quantities of grape juice were boiled down into a molasses (see *dibs,* page 51), which was one of the principal sweeteners, sugar being unknown at the time. Molasses was made from figs and dates as well. Honey from wild bees was also employed as a sweetener. For tartness, the juice of sour pomegranates was commonly used.

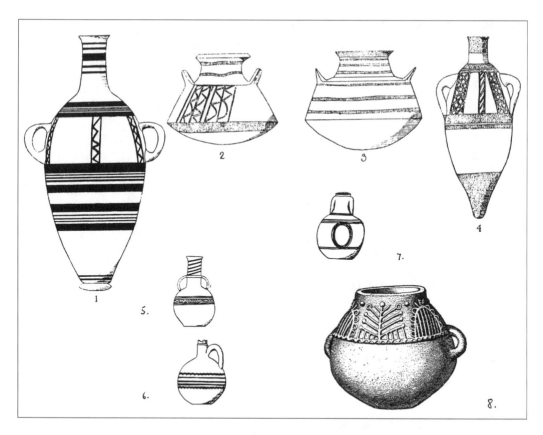

Ancient Syrian pottery. *Examples 1 through 7 from Frederick James Bliss and Robert Alexander Stewart Macalister,* Excavations in Palestine during the Years 1898–1902 *(London, Palestine Exploration Fund, 1902); Example 8 from Louis Charles Lortet,* La Syrie d'aujourd'hui *(Paris, Librairie Hachette, 1884)*

Dairy products were essential elements of the diet. Ewe's milk was esteemed, and goat's milk even more so. Milk was obtained from cows, asses, and camels as well. It was considered an especially refreshing beverage when allowed to sour slightly. In addition, milk was churned into butter, which was clarified in order to preserve it since it would otherwise spoil in the warm climate. Milk was also made into cheese.

Only the rich could afford meat on a regular basis. The flesh of cattle, goats, and sheep was eaten; that of young animals—veal, kid, and lamb—was preferred, lamb being the meat of choice for feasts. Pork, too, was consumed, though not by the Hebrews, who regarded it as unclean.

The meat of domestic animals was supplemented by that of ground game. Although chickens did not become common in Syria until the latter part of the sixth century B.C., numerous other birds and their eggs were important articles of food. Locusts, whether roasted, fried, salted, or boiled and dried, were also eaten. Fresh, dried, and salted fish were much appreciated.

The preparation of food was the responsibility of the wife or, possibly, a slave. Only the nobility possessed homes with spacious kitchens, which were staffed by professional chefs, both male and female. The usual method of cooking meat was to cut it into pieces and simmer it in water. Vegetables and crushed wheat were commonly added, and the stew was seasoned with salt and herbs. Meat was also boiled in milk; however, this practice was expressly prohibited in the Hebrew Scriptures. Other popular methods of cooking meat included baking it in an oven (which may have been sunk into the ground) and roasting, first on hot stones from which the embers had been removed and, later, on an iron or wooden spit. Fish was broiled either directly on hot coals or on a spit suspended above them.

Among the nomadic peoples food was presented in a large bowl set on a leather or plaited straw mat placed on the ground. The family sat cross-legged around the bowl and ate from it with the fingers of their right hands, using pieces of bread to scoop up morsels or to dip into the gravy as a sop, cutlery being unknown. In settled communities, at least at a later period, it was the fashion for men (but apparently not for women and children) to dine reclining on low couches. The women of the household or male servants brought the food in on trays, which were set upon low stands.

When a person of some means wished to entertain guests, he sent out his servants to convey invitations and, on the appointed day, dispatched them a second time with a reminder, a custom that was still being followed in the Lebanon Mountains as recently as the nineteenth century. Upon arriving at the host's residence, the guests were warmly welcomed. Their hands were washed, as were their feet if they had traveled some distance. After the principal guests had been assigned places of honor on the various couches, everyone sat down and the meal, which was composed of several courses, began with appetizers such as salted fish and cured olives. It was common practice for the host to offer particularly savory morsels of food to those he wished to single out for special distinction. At the conclusion of the meal everyone's hands were washed a second time, after which bowls filled with fruit made their appearance. Wine, which had accompanied the meal, was now indulged in more enthusiastically, the guests' cups being filled from large bowls in which the wine was mixed with water and perfumed with aromatic herbs and spices. Music, dancing, and such diversions as the guessing of riddles provided entertainment during this portion of the festivities.

THE PHOENICIANS, LORDS OF THE SEA

Among the many different peoples of ancient Syria it was the Phoenicians, inhabitants of the coast of what is now Syria, Lebanon, and northern Israel, who came to exercise the dominant commercial influence in the region around the twelfth century B.C. Concentrating on seafaring and trade rather than armed conquest, they supplied the entire Mediterranean area with wheat, legumes, dried fruits, and high-quality wine and olive oil. Their ships carried trees, shrubs, herbs, salt, dried fish, salted fish roe, almonds, lambs and goats, rare spices, and exotic perfumes. The Phoenicians were famous for the purple dye they produced from fluid extracted from a species of mollusk,

Murex trunculus, found in great numbers along the Mediterranean coast near Tyre and Sidon. They used this dye to color the beautiful textiles they wove and exported. They were also superb craftsmen known for their glazed pottery, translucent molded glass, jewelry, ivory carvings, and wood- and metalwork. In the course of their mercantile activities and their establishment of colonies (notably Carthage), these intrepid sailors and explorers brought the civilization of the East to North Africa and Europe. The Phoenicians' greatest gift to the world, however, was the first truly phonetic alphabet.

In the eighth century B.C. Phoenicia was conquered by the Assyrians, who were followed in turn by the neo-Babylonians, the Achaemenid Persians, and the Macedonians, the last of whom implanted and developed Greek culture in the region, thereby ushering in the Hellenistic Age (ca. 300–64 B.C.).

ROME, BYZANTIUM, AND SASSANID PERSIA

With the advent of Roman rule in 64 B.C. Greater Syria was able to enjoy a long period of relative stability and prosperity that lasted for nearly seven hundred years. Agriculture thrived, population grew apace, and the economy was stimulated to an extent previously unknown. The Bekaa Valley and the Hauran Plateau in southern Syria became major granaries of the Empire.

Roman cuisine, or local adaptations of it, was appropriated to some extent by members of the ruling class. Ordinary citizens, however, remained faithful to their own deeply rooted culinary traditions. As in previous eras, cereals, vegetables, and fruit constituted the principal nourishment of the common people, and meat was consumed on a regular basis only by the rich. One item that was immensely popular in both Rome and Syria, and indeed throughout much of the ancient world, was a fermented fish sauce called *garum* or *muria* by the Romans. This condiment possessed a long history and appears to have been related to the Mesopotamian *shiqqu.*

After the split of the Roman Empire in A.D. 395 the eastern half, more Greek than Roman, became the Byzantine Empire, which governed Greater Syria until the early seventh century, at times clashing violently with Sassanid Persia, the other major power in the Middle East. During the reign of the sixth-century emperor Justinian I and his empress Theodora, chefs at the Byzantine court turned out dishes from Greece, Cyprus, Syria, Armenia, Persia, and India. Favorite appetizers included olives, cheese, cold ham, pork sausage, fish roe, and artichokes and beans in olive oil. The Byzantines were also fond of soups and stews incorporating grains, pasta, vegetables, tripe, fish, and meatballs, often enriching them with a sauce of beaten eggs and lemon juice similar to the modern *avgolemono.* Grilled fish, duck, ham, or pork appeared as main courses. On holidays special dishes such as spit-roasted whole suckling pig and whole baby lamb were featured.

The most distinguished Middle Eastern cuisine during this period was that of the Sassanids, a dynasty that ruled Persia from 224 to 651. A number of Sassanid dishes have been mentioned by the Arab writer al-Tha'alibi (961–1038), for example "the king's dish," which was composed of hot and cold meats, rice jelly, stuffed (grape?) leaves, pickled chicken, and a very sweet date purée. A "Khorassanian dish" consisted of spit-roasted meat and meat cooked in butter and its own juices. A "Greek dish" was prepared with rice, eggs, milk, butter, sugar, and honey, while a "Dekhan dish" featured slices of salted mutton with pomegranate juice and eggs. The meat of a young kid that had been nourished on the milk of its mother as well as that of a cow was much esteemed; its intestines, rubbed with olive oil, were thought to be especially appetizing. Jellied pork, buffalo, young camel, and wild ass were also popular. Meat was sometimes marinated in curdled milk seasoned with spices. Game dishes included stews prepared with hare or gazelle. Fruits were paired with meat or poultry, while nuts were ground and used to thicken numerous dishes. Many types of sweets were concocted, including dates and pastries stuffed with nuts, candied chestnuts, and jams made from citrons, quinces, myrobalans, walnuts, and Chinese ginger. The influence of the highly developed cuisine of the Byzantines and, especially, that of the Sassanids is still evident in many present-day Middle Eastern dishes.

The Arabs

Following the death of the Prophet Muhammad in A.D. 632, Islamic armies, imbued with the revolutionary fervor of their new religion, swept up from the Arabian Peninsula into Greater Syria, forcing the Byzantines to abandon the entire province. Persia, weakened both militarily and internally, was next to fall. Gradually the Arabs appropriated all the lands of the Sassanids, including part of the Caucasus and much of Central Asia. Pushing westward, they conquered North Africa, nearly all of the Iberian Peninsula, and, for a time, Crete, Sicily, and even a portion of southern France. Most of the population of Greater Syria eventually converted to Islam, and Arabic became the official language. Change was, however, slow in areas where ancient beliefs and cultural patterns were strongly ingrained; in fact, parts of the Lebanon Mountains where Christians had entrenched themselves have remained bastions of that faith to this day.

During its first century of existence the sprawling Islamic Empire was governed by the Umayyad dynasty of caliphs, with Damascus as its capital. In 750 the seat of power was transferred to Iraq and to the Abbassids, who ruled for the next five hundred years, although the lands from Greater Syria west to Spain were lost fairly early on to Umayyad and Fatimid caliphs, and many eastern provinces became independent enough to be subjects in name only. Baghdad, founded in 762 on what had been Persian soil, became the new capital of the Empire and quickly blossomed into one of the world's most resplendent and cosmopolitan cities, imposing its cultural standards, including those relating to food, not only on Greater Syria but on even the most distant provinces. Under Harun al-Rashid (reigned 786–809) and his son al-Ma'mun (reigned 813–833) the Abbassid Caliphate achieved its pinnacle of glory. The very best of Persian civilization was retained and developed. There was a great intellectual awakening, with advances made in mathematics, medicine, and philosophy that were unrivaled in their time. Trade and commerce were conducted on an enormous scale. Arab ships sailed to China for silk and porcelain, the East Indies for spices, and Zanzibar and East Africa for ivory and gold.

ARAB COOKERY BEFORE THE CONQUEST

The food of the pre-Islamic Arabs, particularly that of the pastoral nomads, was elementary. Milk (supplied by camels, sheep, and goats) and dates formed the basis of daily sustenance. Since fresh milk (*halib*) could not be kept in a hot climate, curdled milk (*laban*) was overwhelmingly consumed. Clarified butter (*samna*) was used for cooking, and simple cheeses were made. Meat, considered a luxury, was eaten very infrequently. The usual kind was mutton, camels being slaughtered only in times of extreme scarcity. Beef and goat rarely figured in the diet, chicken was hardly known, and pork was virtually nonexistent. Sheep's tail fat (*aliya*) as well as fat from the humps of camels was greatly prized. Game such as gazelle, ibex, desert hare, bustard, and ostrich was hunted. The Beduin also consumed large desert lizards, hedgehogs, and even mice and grasshoppers. Fish was eaten both fresh and dried. The nomads supplemented their austere diet with edible wild plants, including the desert truffle, while the settled communities were able to enjoy a variety of cultivated vegetables and fruits. Bread, usually made from barley rather than from wheat, was a common food among villagers and townspeople though it was rare among the nomads. Fermented drinks prepared from honey, wheat, barley, dates, and raisins were known, as was grape wine.

Born of humble and frugal circumstances, the dishes of this period were uncomplicated and contained only a few ingredients. Little use was made of spices due to their high cost, although the Arabs were engaged in transporting them to other lands. *Sawiq,* a food of the common people, was a kind of dried barley meal mixed with water, butter, or *aliya*. Among the various types of gruels were *harira* (flour cooked with *laban*) and *khazir* (bran and small pieces of meat cooked in water). Many kinds of broth, especially those incorporating squash or strips of dried meat (*kadid*), were popular. *Tharid,* which consisted of bread crumbled into a broth of meat and vegetables, and *hays,* a mixture of dates, butter, and *laban,* were both favorites of the Prophet.

Following the Conquest the cookery of the Arabs underwent a rapid transformation as the new rulers quickly abandoned many of their old traditions stemming from nomadic life and eagerly adopted the lifestyles, foods, and culinary techniques of their more sophisticated subjects. The medieval Arab historian al-Tabari (d. 922) has related an anecdote that tellingly illustrates the swiftness of this process. When 'Amr ibn al-'Asi conquered Egypt in 641 he demonstrated the finality of the event to the Egyptians by arranging a three-day display of the Arabs' intentions. On the first day the Arab soldiers were shown having a traditional meal. A camel was slaughtered and its meat cooked in a pot of salted water. The soldiers devoured the meat straight from the pot, grabbing it with their hands and tearing at it with their teeth, and drank up the broth. On the second day, attired in Egyptian clothing, they savored Egyptian delicacies and observed Egyptian dining customs. On the third day they put on a parade to exhibit their military might, after which ʿAmr ibn al-ʿAsi summarized the lessons to be learned: "I want you to realize that the Arab warrior you saw on the third day has no intention of abandoning the lifestyle of the second day to return to the life of the first day." [1]

THE DEVELOPMENT OF MEDIEVAL ARAB CUISINE

Agricultural development was given high priority under the Umayyads and during the first century of Abbassid rule. In addition to indigenous crops, the Arabs assiduously cultivated fruits and vegetables they had encountered in the East and brought them westward to the Mediterranean, ultimately effecting a revolution in European food habits. Among the newly discovered foods were citrus fruits, originally from India and China. Citrons (known to the ancient Canaanites and Hebrews), lemons, bitter oranges (brought from India), and shaddocks were all harvested.

The great advances in agriculture and mercantile activity and the attendant expansion of available goods and services gave a massive impetus to gastronomy and ushered in a golden age of cookery. A new court cuisine was developed that blended the culinary traditions of the Near East with that of Persia. The Arabs could now afford to make use of the spices they procured from the Orient. They also practiced techniques of food preparation learned from the Orientals, such as the creation of iced desserts, a skill they had acquired from the Chinese. Although the ordinary inhabitants of the occupied territories retained many of their dishes, considerable interaction inevitably took place, and the cooking style of the entire region ultimately came to possess an underlying unity despite the presence of geographical, economic, cultural, and religious differences.

The ruling class raised its quest for dining pleasure to an extraordinary level, spending enormous sums on huge, well-equipped, and well-staffed kitchens that turned out sumptuous and elaborate concoctions based on a wide range of ingredients, many of them rare, exotic, and costly. Skilled cooks were highly sought after and were brought from India, Khurasan, Egypt, black Africa, and other lands. No matter how opulent and sophisticated the food became, however, Koranic prohibitions, specifically those regarding pork, animal blood, and wine, were strictly observed. [2]

Certain foods such as okra and raw onions were largely shunned by the affluent minority. Sugar and honey were almost always preferred to the lowly *dibs*. Although sheep's tail fat was constantly employed, after clarification it was often perfumed and enriched with pieces of quince and apple, dried coriander, dill, onion, cinnamon, and mastic. In addition, it was tinted yellow, red, or green. Dates, a Beduin staple, also figured in the court cuisine, but their humble origins were transcended by having their pits replaced with blanched almonds or pistachios.

It was not only the palace chefs who determined which foods or dishes were the most desirable. A whole group of upper-class epicures came into being who delighted in preparing and even inventing dishes, which were often named after them. One of the most important of these was the renowned singer and poet Prince Ibrahim ibn al-Mahdi (779–839), a younger half-brother of the caliph Harun al-Rashid. These gastronomes were expected to be familiar with the most esoteric culinary creations and differentiated themselves from the common people by their passion for exotic fare, adopting elements of the cuisines of prestigious foreign cultures, especially that of Persia. The search for the unusual, the explosive growth of agriculture and commerce, the lure of Baghdad, which attracted gifted and adventurous individuals from all over the Empire, and the dominance of a wealthy and powerful court whose standards were emulated by the affluent class were all factors that caused regional cooking traditions to be brought together and transformed into a highly refined and cosmopolitan cuisine, one that was not confined to the court, though it remained inaccessible to the masses.

CULINARY MANUALS

Numerous treatises were written on the cooking and serving of food as well as on its healthful (and, sometimes, harmful) properties, and collections of recipes from the court cuisine were compiled. These literary efforts considerably predate the earliest-known medieval European cookery books, which appeared in France during the fourteenth century.

In his encyclopedic work, *al-Fihrist,* the tenth-century bibliographer al-Nadim lists eleven "Books Composed about Cooked Food" by nine different early Abbassid authors, including the previously mentioned Ibrahim ibn al-Mahdi, who is believed to have written the first practical and comprehensive cookbook in the Arabic language. While directly concerned with food and its preparation, these volumes (as well as others cited elsewhere) also deal with related topics such as table manners and diet and dietetics. Only a small number of culinary manuals are known to have survived. They consist of one from the early tenth century, the *Kitab al-tabikh wa-islah al-aghdiyya al-ma'kulat wa-tayyibat al-at'ima al-masnu'at* (not mentioned by al-Nadim), attributed to Abu Muhammad al-Muzaffar ibn Nasr ibn Sayyar al-Warraq, five from the thirteenth century, and a very few others of unknown date. Those known to be from the thirteenth century are the *Kitab al-tabikh* by Muhammad ibn al-Hassan ibn Muhammad ibn 'Abd al-Karim al-Katib al-Baghdadi (d. 1239); the *Kitab al-wusla ila'l-habib fi wasf al-tayyibat wa'l-tib,* possibly by the historian and *wazir* Kamal al-Din ibn al-'Adim (1192–1262); the *Kitab wasf al-at'ima al-mu'tada,* an Egyptian work; and two other manuscripts that were written in Islamic Spain, one attributed to Ibn Razin al-Tujibi and the other anonymous. Among the undated culinary manuals is another anonymous work from Egypt, the *Kanz al-fawa'id fi tanwi' al-mawa'id.*

The Kitab al-Tabikh *(Cookery Book) of al-Warraq*

This book, three manuscript copies of which are still extant, is of particular importance in that its author was able to work from copies of earlier culinary manuals that are now lost, among them the one written by al-Mahdi during the first half of the ninth century. Its 132 chapters contain an enormous amount of information as well as recipes for an extensive variety of preparations ranging from soups, cold dishes, dairy products, omelets (see *ijja*, page 153), substantial main dishes, stuffings, and breads to condiments, syrups, preserves, pastries, puddings, sweetmeats, and beverages. The long list of ingredients described by the author cannot fail to impress the reader with both the number and types of foodstuffs utilized in Abbassid cookery. In addition to providing instruction on culinary matters, al-Warraq enumerates the beneficial and harmful properties of various foods and supplies information on kitchen utensils and their proper care, on the causes and prevention of spoiled food, and on the dining habits and table manners of the aristocracy.

The culinary art revealed in al-Warraq's work is one of considerable complexity and refinement, and it is not without justification that this earliest surviving Arab cookbook has been described as "the cornerstone of medieval urban haute cuisine" by Manuela Marín and David Waines in their 1993 edition of the *Kanz al-fawa'id fi tanwi' al-mawa'id.*

The Kitab al-Tabikh *(Cookery Book)* of al-Baghdadi

A collection of 160 recipes (plus a few variations) that dates from 1226, this book was edited and published in Mosul by the Iraqi scholar Dr. Daud Chelebi in 1934. Soon afterward it was translated into English by the British Orientalist Arthur J. Arberry, who featured it in his article, "A Baghdad Cookery-Book," published in the periodical *Islamic Culture* in 1939. In his introductory remarks al-Baghdadi declares that in his opinion food is the noblest and most consequential of all human pleasures, for it is "the body's stay, and the means of preserving life. No other pleasure can be enjoyed unless a man has good health, to which food is ancillary." Al-Baghdadi included recipes for only those dishes that were his personal favorites, noting that he had examined several other culinary manuals and rejected some of their recipes because they were for "strange and unfamiliar dishes, in the composition of which unwholesome and unsatisfying ingredients are used." In a note immediately preceding the recipes he remarks: "It is important that a cook be intelligent, acquainted with the rules of cooking, and that he should have a flair for the art." He then offers advice on such matters as keeping one's nails constantly trimmed, utilizing cooking pots made preferably of stoneware or earthenware, choosing dry firewood and avoiding sappy woods that give off much smoke, using rock salt and spices that are fresh and finely ground, and keeping pots and utensils scrupulously clean.

The note concludes with a few preparation and cooking tips, including suggestions for seasoning various types of dishes.

Al-Baghdadi's recipes, which are arranged in ten chapters, provide directions for hearty preparations rooted in peasant cookery as well as for sophisticated and subtle creations. They include meat stews containing vegetables and/or fruits; substantial productions incorporating such ingredients as meat, chicken, vegetables, grains, and pasta; dishes featuring fresh and salted fish; relishes and pickles; and desserts, breads, pastries, and confections.

The Kitab al-Wusla Ila'L-Habib (The Book of the Link with the Beloved) of Ibn al-'Adim

This culinary manual, believed to have been written in Syria during the last years of the Ayyubid Sultanate (see page 27), exists in some ten handwritten copies, each containing a number of additions and variations. The French Orientalist Maxime Rodinson described and analyzed the book in an article entitled "Recherches sur les documents arabes relatifs à la cuisine," which appeared in the Revue des études islamiques in 1949 (he also translated a few of the recipes). The Wusla is divided into ten chapters, which are preceded by an introduction wherein the author states that he has personally tested all the recipes many times. Included in the first chapter are formulas for perfumes, incense, powders, pomades, and even a remedy for perspiration. Next come sections on beverages, many of them made with fruit; the preparation of sour fruit juices (verjuice, lemon, bitter orange, and sumac) for use in cooking; directions for distilling and flavoring white vinegar; a method for clarifying, perfuming, enriching, and coloring sheep's tail fat; and the definition of the spice blend atraf al-tib (page 64). There is an extensive chapter offering approximately seventy-five recipes for chicken dishes as well as chapters containing recipes for fried and roast meats; meat stews incorporating vegetables, fruit, rice, bread, nuts, and curdled milk; breads, sweets, and pastries; preserves made with vegetables, fruit, nuts, flowers, small fish, small birds, and meat; sauces; and omelets (ijjas), relishes, and pickles. The last two chapters feature scented and colored soaps, fragrant waters for perfuming the hands, and lozenges for sweetening the breath.

Examination of the Wusla reveals it to be a work of great culinary significance. Its author was an aristocrat accustomed to court life, and as Professor Rodinson has observed, it is more representative of the haute cuisine than al-Baghdadi's volume, which contains a larger number of relatively simple recipes.

DIET AND DIETETICS

Under the Abbassids the science of dietetics assumed great importance. Each food was thought to possess positive and negative attributes, and by matching foods with the temperament of a given individual one could supposedly identify those foods that were beneficial or harmful to his or her physical and spiritual well-being.

The Abbassid caliphs, their families, *wazirs*, and even their singers owned personalized cookbooks containing recipes believed to be beneficial to their health. Both caliphs and *wazirs* often insisted that their physicians be in attendance when they took their meals. The caliph Harun al-Rashid reportedly would not touch his food unless his doctor was present; moreover this doctor was authorized to have any dish he considered injurious to the caliph's health removed from the dining table, even over the objections of the Commander of the Faithful himself!

∾

Gluttony diminishes wisdom.
(Medieval Arab proverb)
∾

ADDITIONAL SOURCES

Besides the authors of culinary manuals, there were many other writers who included valuable material on food and dietary habits in their works. One such author was the geographer and historian al-Mas'udi (d. 957). In his *Muruj al-dhahab wa-ma'adin al-jawhar* (Meadows of Gold and Mines of Gems), he describes a gathering held at the express request of the caliph al-Mustakfi (reigned 944–946) to discuss the favorite foods of the period and the poetry that had been composed in their praise. After each poem was recited al-Mustakfi bade that everything mentioned in the verses be served to the company, so far as it was possible. Among the dishes consumed were roast meat and fowl, *harisa, sanbusaj, qatayif,* and *judhaba.* In this same work al-Mas'udi informs us that he himself wrote a manual about food (regrettably lost) in which he offered a summary of culinary art, the knowledge of which could not be ignored by a well-bred man. He also states that he included information on wines, on desserts and their manner of presentation, on the art of combining spices and other ingredients for seasoning, and on how to be a cultivated and gracious dinner guest.

THE CRUSADERS, AYYUBIDS, MONGOLS, AND MAMELUKES

In 1095 European Christians mounted the first of several Crusades in an effort to reclaim the Holy Land from the Muslims. The Crusaders, or Franks as they were called by the Arabs, were surprised to come upon a civilization more advanced than their own, many aspects of which they adopted. Among the host of foods for which they developed a taste were a number previously unknown or else lost to Europeans since Roman times, including rice, spinach, dried fruits, citrus fruits, pomegranates, almonds, pistachios, cloves, nutmeg, mace, and, perhaps most important, sugar. With the last came sweetened soft drinks made with fruit juices and flower essences and many kinds of sweets.

During much of the twelfth century Greater Syria (except for areas occupied by the Crusaders) was controlled by the Seljuk Turks. They were overthrown, however, by

Crusader castle at Sidon, in southern Lebanon. *From Charles William Wilson, ed.,* Picturesque Palestine, Sinai and Egypt, *vol. 2 (New York, D. Appleton, 1883)*

Saladin (1138?–1193), the great military leader and founder of the Ayyubid dynasty, which ruled Egypt from 1169 to 1262 and most of Syria until 1260. To the east the declining Abbassid Caliphate, which had been dominated by the Seljuks for two centuries, came to an inglorious end at the hands of the Mongols, who then fell upon Syria, capturing Aleppo, Homs, Hama, and Damascus. The Mamelukes, military slaves originally from the Caucasus and Central Asia who had seized power in Egypt, drove the Mongols out of Syria, after which they proceeded to conquer all the great Frankish fortresses, thereby bringing the era of the Crusades to a close.

Soon after the Crusaders returned to Europe, recipes of Arab and Persian provenance made their appearance in European cookery books. Conversely, the influence of European cookery on that of the Arabs first became manifest during the period of the Crusades, as seen in such recipes as Frankish-style roast lamb and a highly seasoned bread called *aflaghun*. Medieval Arab cuisine had an enormous and long-lasting effect on European cookery, playing a dominant role well into the seventeenth century.

CULINARY LITERATURE DECLINES, BUT THE MODE OF COOKING SURVIVES

After the fall of the Abbassid Caliphate in 1258 gastronomy continued to claim its adherents, although not as visibly as before. There was a noticeable decline in the number of culinary manuals. An example from the fifteenth century that has been cited by Professor Rodinson is the *Kitab al-tibakha,* a manuscript of five or six pages by the Damascene legal scholar Ibn al-Mibrad (d. 1503), which consists of forty-four brief recipes arranged in alphabetical order.[3]

While it is unlikely that modern readers would share the medieval Arab fondness for perfuming dishes with camphor and ambergris, seasoning them with *murri,* a black and bitter condiment made with fermented grain and spices, or soaking foods in fat (as in *judhaba,* a pastry drowned in the melted fat of a saffron-smeared chicken suspended above it while it bakes), the surviving culinary manuals are filled with imaginative preparations that make use of a remarkable variety of ingredients. Although the recipe directions appear rather sketchy by contemporary standards, often being unspecific as to amounts and cooking times, they nonetheless possess a familiar ring to those acquainted with kitchen parlance. Many of the dishes described in these volumes are quite similar to ones encountered in the Middle East, Caucasus, and North Africa today.

The Ottoman Era

Greater Syria continued to be governed by the Mamelukes until 1517, when they were ousted by the Ottoman Turks. Originally nomads from Central Asia whose diet was limited to milk and milk products, meat, bread, and pasta (although it was much enriched as they made their way across Persia and Transcaucasia), the Turks assimilated the culinary traditions of their subjects, particularly the highly developed cookery of the Greeks and Armenians and, to a lesser extent, that of the Arabs.[4] The resulting "Turkish" cuisine exerted a considerable influence on the eating habits of the region's population, especially those of the affluent. The four-hundred-year-long Turkish domination was, by and large, a period of crushing poverty and stagnation. The common people, heavily taxed and with little or no hope for the future, felt dread rather than respect for their masters. Despite this state of affairs, it was during the Ottoman era that Europeans succeeded in greatly expanding their commercial relations with the Levant, establishing important facilities for trade not only in the major mercantile centers of Aleppo and Damascus but in smaller towns such as Acre, Beirut, and Sidon.

DINING IN ALEPPO

The Chevalier d'Arvieux, a seventeenth-century French author and epicure who served as a consul in the Levant for many years, considered Aleppo a good town for the gourmet, possessing excellent beef, mutton, honey, cheese, butter, olive oil, fruits and vegetables, and locally produced wine. In his invaluable study, *The Natural History of Aleppo,* written a hundred years later, the indefatigable Alexander Russell, physician to the English factors (business agents) who lived and worked in the Great Khan in Aleppo, has provided us with a detailed account of the contemporary dining habits of a city that was and still is celebrated for its fine cuisine. We learn that affluent Muslims partook of

Washing the hands. *From*
William McClure Thomson,
The Land and the Book, *vol. 3*
(New York, Harper, 1885)

two extensive meals daily, one differing little from the other. As in the past, food was served on a large circular tray set on a low folding stand or stool. After the diners washed their hands, they sat down on mattresses or cushions placed on the floor around the tray, and grace was said before eating. It was customary for a few saucers of pickles, salad, yogurt, and salt to be placed on the tray and, all around the edge, thin flat loaves of very white bread and wooden or tortoise-shell spoons (no knives and forks were used since the diners ate with their fingers). Russell describes a typical meal in a well-to-do household:

> The dishes are brought up covered, and set down in the middle of the table, one at a time in succession; the whole amounting to twenty or thirty: and the same service is repeated, with little variation, every day.
>
> The first dish is almost constantly soup, and the last a plain pilaw. The intermediate course consists of a variety of dishes. . . . Mutton in small bits, roasted on iron skewers, with slices of either apples or artichoak bottoms, and onions, between each piece; or mutton minced small, and beat up with spiceries into balls, and roasted also on skewers: both [of] which are called Kubab. Mutton or lamb stewed with gourds, roots, herbs, and chiches [chickpeas]; fowls, pigeons, and sometimes quails, or other small birds, boiled or roasted, but more frequently made into ragouts. Farce-meat, which is called Mahshee,[5] composed of mutton, rice, pistachios, currants, pine nutts, almonds, suet, spice, and garlic, is served up in a variety of shapes, and takes an additional name from the respective fruit which is farced or stuffed, as Mahshee of mad apple [eggplant], cucumber, or gourd. It is also enveloped in the

leaves of vine, endive, beet, or borage, and is then called Yaprak. A lamb thus farced and roasted entire, is a dish not uncommon at feasts.

... Burgle [bulgur] ... being beat up with minced meat, suet, and spiceries, is formed into large balls and either boiled or fried [kibbeh] ...

[T]hey have several sorts of pyes [sanbusak]; minced meat with pomegranate grains, spread upon thin cakes, and baked on an iron plate [lahm bi ajeen]; sausages made without blood; and a great variety of sweet dishes, and pastry;⁶ the former made with honey or dibs, and rather luscious; the latter is very well made, but retains the strong taste of the Arab butter....

A few plates of sweet flummery [baluza] are served by way of desert, for they seldom serve fruit at that time: and last of all, appears a large bowl of Khushaf, which is a decoction of dried figs, currants, apricots, cherries, apples, or other fruit, made into a thin sirup, with pistachio nutts, almonds, or some slices of the fruit, left swimming in the liquor.⁷ This is served cold, sometimes iced, and with a few spoonfuls of it, the repast concludes.

They drink nothing but water at meals, and very often do not drink till an hour after dinner....

Muslims of lesser means were served much more frugally:

Among people of middling condition, who have seldom more than three or four dishes, the whole is set down at once on the table ... but, except people of the lowest class, who live almost wholly on vegetables, the quality of the dishes is nearly the same, that is, they are highly seasoned, greasy, and generally made very acid with the juice of lemons, pomegranates, or unripe grapes....

Concerning the Christian community of Aleppo, Russell informs us that their mode of eating was essentially similar to that of the Muslims:

But the Shorba [soup] and Pilaw are less constant dishes; they eat more Burgle and less rice; and oil is often employed in their cookery, where the Turks [Muslims] use butter. Instead of Khushaf, wine and fermented spirits are substituted, of which many drink liberally. To drink a small glass of brandy [arak], immediately before sitting down to meals, is an universal practice.

On holidays Christians were apt to remain at table "for several hours" after a meal, drinking and smoking:

When the first glass is presented after dinner, a slice of apple, or other fruit, is stuck upon the edge of the glass; a custom observed also on ceremonial visits at the Festivals, when wine is served before the coffee, and is then termed the feast cup.

The Christian women do not sit at table with the husband ... Some (particularly of the Maronites) have of late deviated from this custom, and, adopting the use of tables, chairs, and service in the European style, not only make the female part of the family sit down with them at meals, but permit them occasionally to appear before the Europeans, whom they sometimes entertain at their houses....

Russell also includes some observations on the eating habits of Aleppo's Jewish population, noting that they consumed more poultry than any other animal food and that the poor among them lived chiefly on bread, pulses, herbs, and roots, all dressed with sesame oil, which was seldom used by the city's other inhabitants. Jewish women did not sit with the men except on holidays.

Commenting on the tables of the Europeans, Russell remarks:

> The cooks . . . are Armenians, but have been taught French or English cookery, and only now and then, by way of variety, serve up some of the country dishes. . . .
>
> . . . The Europeans are supplied with excellent bread made in the French manner.
>
> . . . The wines in common use are a dry white wine of the country, and a light red Provençal wine. The French present Liqueurs at the Desert. The English drink a draught of very weak punch, before dinner and supper; a custom found so deliciously refreshing, that most of the other Europeans, many of the native Christians, and some even of the Turks, have adopted it.

The wealth of information provided by Russell shows that by his time the essential character and content of the region's cuisine as we know it had been firmly established (although the dishes today tend to be lower in fat) and that some European dining habits were already being borrowed by elements of the population.

DAMASCUS, A GOURMET'S TOWN

Like Aleppo, Damascus has long been famous throughout the Arab world for its cuisine, which has earned it the nickname of *al-Matbakh* (the Kitchen). In his book, *The Holy Land* (1910), Robert Hichens has described some of the foods offered for sale in the city's bazaars:

> In front of the butchers are sheep's heads, calves' heads, and joints deftly decorated with gold paper and scarlet anemones; the confectioners display trays of biscuits, soft cakes, and various kinds of wonderfully light pastry, sticky with honey and grape syrup: at the entrances of the numberless eating-houses are skewers stuck through balls of fried and larded meat, strips of fat lambs' tails, soups of splendid colors,—the coral-red soup beloved of the Eastern is to be seen on all sides,—and bowls full of savory messes, in which rice, *cous-cous* grain, red pepper, spices, fruit, mutton, and chicken mingle in a smooth and succulent mass. Ice-cream is being eagerly bought, and on many spotlessly clean counters are arranged charmingly shaped blue-and-white bowls of sour milk and curds, ornamented with patterns of rich cream. Damascus must be the epicure's paradise. In no other town of East or West have I seen so many alluring displays of food. And butchers, bakers, and confectioners are artists, coquettishly clever in arranging their goods to tempt the most fastidious appetite. The little red anemone, be sure, is the badge of a subtle mind determined to take you captive.

KITCHEN EQUIPMENT

As in former times, the homes of the poor possessed no separate kitchens but often consisted of only a single room with a rude hearth of two or three stones set up to contain the fire and support cooking utensils. In rural areas, weather permitting, cooking was done outdoors on a similar hearth. One type of outdoor cooking would

Entrance to Damascus. *From Charles William Wilson, ed.,* Picturesque Palestine, Sinai and Egypt, *vol. 2 (New York, D. Appleton, 1883)*

surely strike us as being decidedly unconventional. Traveling in the Syrian Desert near Palmyra, the Reverend Josias Leslie Porter encountered Beduin women perched atop huge camels and surrounded with piles of cooking vessels. "In a long march," he writes, "they often prepare the food on the camels' backs, and serve it out to their husbands, brothers, or sons."[8]

In cities or towns the homes of the more prosperous usually had a kitchen with a fireplace and broad chimney, within whose arched recess was a wide bank or range constructed of brick or stone. This range was about three feet high and supplied with circular holes to receive the charcoal, which was supported by an iron grating and fanned from an opening underneath. The pots and saucepans were set on the holes or on trivets, which raised them above the fire.

Towns were provided with public ovens (*furns*) that were generally wood-burning, where people could either purchase bread or take their own to be baked. In addition, certain dishes were prepared at home and carried to the ovens for cooking. In the countryside, however, bread was baked in various types of clay ovens, upon iron plates (sing. *saaj*), or directly on hot stones or embers.

Kitchen utensils. *From Henry J. van Lennep,* Bible Lands: Their Modern Customs and Manners Illustrative of Scripture *(New York, Harper, 1875)*

A variety of tinned copper vessels was found in every well-appointed kitchen. Apparently this had been the case for hundreds of years, for according to the fourteenth-century Moroccan traveler Ibn Battuta it was the custom in Syria for a girl about to be married to receive an "outfit" from her father, the greater part of which consisted of copper kitchen utensils. Such outfits were considered prized possessions and were made the subject of special stipulations in marriage contracts.[9] Among the most common kitchen utensils was the *dist,* a two-handled caldron made of tinned copper that was used for making large quantities of food such as rice or bulgur, grape molasses, tomato paste, and *qawarma* (page 70), or even for cooking a whole sheep or goat for feasts. An essential utensil was the *tanjara,* a much smaller vessel, made of tinned copper and provided with handles and a lid. It was used for preparing everyday meals such as stews and pilafs and could also function as a serving dish. Other important utensils were a frying pan (*miqla*), made of tinned copper or iron; a large circular metal tray with raised sides (*siniyya*), used for both savory and sweet dishes such as *kibbeh* or baklava; and an earthenware kettle (*qidr*) with two large handles, commonly utilized for vegetable dishes. For grilling meat there was the *manqal,* a charcoal brazier about two feet high made of brass, copper, or clay. Preparation tools included knives, metal or wooden spoons, a wooden cutting board, a strainer, a colander, various sieves, a metal or wooden ladle, a dipper, a large stone or wooden mortar (*jurn*), a wooden pestle (*madaqqa*), a small brass mortar (*hawan*) and pestle for pounding spices and garlic, roasting skewers, and a special dish with a perforated bottom like a colander (*maftuliyya*) that was used for making round pasta pellets called *maftul.* Households also possessed breadmaking equipment (page 311) and implements for making and serving coffee (pages 394–395).

Although it is probable that virtually every kitchen in Ottoman Damascus contained at least one *tanjara,* the sight of a person wearing what appeared to be one on his head created quite a sensation, especially when Europeans attired in Western rather than Oriental dress were still a rare occurrence:

It is not a difficult matter to become the wonder of a city: and as yet unconscious of the way in which I had merited to be one, I followed the crowd . . . A little boy, struck by the singular shape of a round hat which I wore, clapped his hands and called out, "Abu-tanjier!" "Abu-tanjier!" "the father of a cooking-pot! look at the father of a cooking-pot!" This was echoed from every side; for the resemblance a hat bears to the common cooking-vessel with a rim to it, is too strong to escape, and I was pursued by the shouts of the people till I was nearly out of sight.

A woman, who had heard the uproar, came to her door, and, as I had out-walked the crowd, she could not resist the chance of gratifying her curiosity, and begged me to show her my hat. I took it off with great gravity, and put it in her hands; I believe she was disappointed to find that it was not a cooking-pot in reality: I rescued it from her in time to save it, or it might have been lodged in one of the colleges, as a perpetual puzzle to the learned of the city.[10]

WESTERN INFLUENCE DURING THE NINETEENTH CENTURY

By the nineteenth century European manners had begun to modify the lifestyle of the more affluent native Christian population. The Englishman Laurence Oliphant has left us a description of the well-to-do Christians of Haifa. In the privacy of their home,

*Household utensils.
1. Woman's wardrobe and treasure box. 2. Rough straw basket. 3. Wheat basket. 4. Vegetable basket. 5. Chair. 6. Groups of baskets. 8 and 9. On this shelf are coffee utensils, wooden spoons, a wooden lock, and a gourd bottle. 11. A cooking vessel on top of a wooden cutting board. 12. Bellows. 13. Wooden mortar and pestle for pounding coffee beans. 14. Short-handled broom. Nos. 7 and 10 are missing. (From the Hartford Theological Seminary Collection.) From Elihu Grant,* The People of Palestine *(Philadelphia, J. B. Lippincott, 1921)*

a husband and wife were apt to relax in loose Oriental garments as they sat on their *diwan* sipping morning coffee, each smoking a *narghileh* (water pipe). Yet, observes Oliphant:

> If you call upon this worthy couple as a distinguished foreigner . . . you are received in a room in which they never enter, except upon such state occasions, by the same gentleman, in a perfectly fitting black frock-coat and trousers, varnished boots, and a white waistcoat, and by the same lady, in a dress which has been made in Paris.
>
> The furniture consists of massive tables with marble tops, and handsome arm-chairs and couches covered with costly satins. The walls are resplendent with gilt mirrors and with heavy hanging curtains. The floors are covered with rich carpets. There is a three-hundred-dollar piano, on which the lady never plays . . . [Y]our host . . . has a guest-chamber . . . if you are going to stay with him, and he has so far adopted civilized habits that he sleeps on a bed himself, and not on mats on the floor, like his forefathers. His dinner is served on a table, which is spread as he had seen it spread in the houses of foreigners, but he retains the native cooking, the huge pillaw of rice, the chicken stew with rich and greasy gravy, the lamb stuffed with pistachio nuts, the leben or sour milk, the indescribable sweet dishes, crisp, sticky, and nutty, the delicious preserves of citrons, dates, and figs, the flat bread and the goat cheese, and the wine of the country.[11]

Pottery. 1. Jar for storing oil, olives, molasses, or vinegar. 2. Water jar. 3. Jar for holding water or other liquids. 4 and 5. Smaller varieties of No. 3. 6 and 7. Jars for carrying water on the head. The next jar to the right of No. 7 is the kind commonly used for yogurt. 8, 9, and 10 and the three jars suspended by cords in the middle of the picture are all drinking jars; the two having neither spouts nor handles are for cooling water. 11, 12, and 15. Clay dishes for butter, jelly, or milk. 13. Cooking vessel. 14. Charcoal braziers. 16. Missing. 17. Salad dishes. (From the Hartford Theological Seminary Collection.) From Elihu Grant, The People of Palestine *(Philadelphia, J. B. Lippincott, 1921)*

Beirut in the mid-nineteenth century. *From William McClure Thomson,* The Land and the Book, *vol. 3 (New York, Harper, 1885)*

The Ottomans had granted more autonomy to Lebanon than to adjacent provinces, allowing it to experience a greater degree of development and modernization. By 1850 Beirut had become the commercial capital of Greater Syria and boasted elegant mansions, hotels, and cafés. At Batista's Hotel a traveler could enjoy an Oriental dinner served Parisian-style and afterward indulge in a bottle of well-iced claret. Describing a dinner he attended at the home of a wealthy Beirut merchant, the Englishman James Lewis Farley writes:

> Numerous servants handed round plats, which were nearly all in the French style, a pilau, and gourds stuffed with rice and meat being the only native dishes. The wines of Cyprus and Mount Lebanon, and excellent wines from France, were in profusion.[12]

The French scholar Louis Charles Lortet mentions being invited to the home of a prosperous Beirut silk merchant, where a multitude of Arab sweets perfumed with musk and rose water were served European-style by elegantly costumed male servants. The evening was presided over by the merchant's charming fourteen-year-old wife, resplendent in diamonds, who spoke perfect French and, after the repast, amazed her distinguished guest by performing several Mozart sonatas "*avec beaucoup de sentiment*" on an excellent piano![13]

According to the British consul Frederic Arthur Neale, the town enjoyed a lively social scene:

Amongst the Europeans inhabiting Beyrout there are some first-rate musicians and pianists. Evening quadrille parties, or musical *réunions,* are of frequent occurrence; and some of the grandees occasionally give a ball, with a sumptuous supper, to which all the *élite* of every religion and costume are invited. On these occasions the Pasha's band generally attends, and right well do they execute their duties. The uninitiated stranger, arriving from Aleppo, or Tripoli, or Latachia, is astounded to hear the latest polkas and waltzes admirably performed. Nor are the dancers one whit behind; the newest steps are executed.

... To such a pitch of refinement ... has Beyrout arrived at the present day, that it is considered by the Levantines a perfect Syrian Paris.[14]

CULINARY WORKS OF THE LATE NINETEENTH AND EARLY TWENTIETH CENTURIES

This period of Western influence saw the appearance of a number of cookbooks, most of them published in Cairo. Some contained recipes for not only Near Eastern but also European dishes prepared according to "new" or "the most recent" methods. Of singular importance is a volume published in Beirut in 1885, the *Tadkirat al-khawatin wa-ustad al-tabbakhin* by Khalil Sarkis, one of the founders of the Lebanese Arab press. The sixth edition of this work, dating from 1931 and entitled *Ustad al-tabbakhin,* has been analyzed by Professor Rodinson. It is divided into two parts, the first of which contains five sections. The opening section contains information and advice on such matters as the food resources available during each month of the year, household chores and cleanliness (especially in the kitchen), buying and carving meat, using spices and herbs, cooking methods, preparation of family meals, entertaining, table manners, and cooking in tune with the seasons. The second section is devoted to Middle Eastern cuisine and is divided into fifteen chapters containing recipes for soups; rice dishes; stuffed vegetables; ground meat dishes; *kibbeh;* poultry, meat, and game dishes; variety meats; stews with and without fruit; dishes prepared with milk; and cereal dishes. Section three is composed of eight chapters that offer recipes for meatless dishes that may be served during the Christian Lent. These highlight such ingredients as fish, shellfish, snails, frogs, vegetables (including dried legumes), rice, and hors d'oeuvres. Following this section are appendices on table arrangements, on the order of courses, and on foods eaten at breakfast. The fourth section covers pastries and sweets and the fifth, jams and syrups. The second part of the book is given over entirely to European cuisine.

Professor Rodinson mentions another cookbook, the *Kitab dalil al-tabbakhin,* which used to be sold by itinerant peddlers hawking their wares in the towns and villages of Lebanon. The contents of this small volume are borrowed from various earlier cookbooks, with several recipes lifted word for word from the *Ustad al-tabbakhin.* The book includes a number of recipes for hybridized dishes labeled "Arabo-French," one example being fish and potato patties. This work, which offered the basics of simple family cooking, was still in print when I was a child, a testament to its enduring popularity.

From 1920 to the Present

Following the defeat of Turkey in World War I, the Ottoman Empire was dismantled, and Greater Syria was placed under mandate by the League of Nations, with France being given the responsibility of administering Syria and Lebanon, and Britain, the territories of Palestine and Trans-Jordan. In 1943 Lebanon became the first country to achieve full independence, followed by Syria and Jordan in 1946.

The dominant European influence in Syria and Lebanon during this period was, understandably, that of France. It was most apparent in Beirut, where French culture mingled with the Arab in a fascinating manner. With its French street names, kiosks, sidewalk cafés, and European-style villas, the city took on such a Gallic air that it was often referred to as "The Paris of the East." French became a second language for many Lebanese, who spoke it so fluently that it was often difficult to distinguish between them and the numerous tourists who flocked to the country from France. All this French influence had a positive effect on the culinary life of Beirut, making it possible not only to dine in restaurants that served outstanding French food but also to purchase French wines and liqueurs, breads, cheeses, sausages, and pastries much more easily than one can generally buy them in America today. French influence was felt in Aleppo and Damascus as well, though on a far smaller scale, and those fabled inland cities of lovely gardens and tall minarets have steadfastly remained more traditional and Oriental than the pleasure-loving metropolis by the sea.

During the French Mandate and the three decades following it, Beirut was home to many Europeans, including a number of Russians who had made their way to the Levant after the Bolshevik Revolution. One of these émigrés, a former admiral in the Czar's navy, became a waiter in a local restaurant! There was also a long-established American colony centered around the American University of Beirut, whose picture-postcard campus overlooks the Mediterranean.

My own immediate neighborhood was a microcosm of Beirut's multinational personality. Its residents included a French doctor, an Armenian dentist, a Greek professor and writer, a Maronite Christian banker, an Italian artist, a Syrian diplomat, and a stylish, cultured Czech woman who used to host literary gatherings and performances of chamber music in her fashionable salon. Her husband was rumored to be a secret agent, a plausible assumption considering the fact that Beirut, besides being the intellectual, cultural, and commercial capital of the Middle East, was a hotbed of foreign intrigue as well.

With its dazzling setting of sea and mountains, Beirut was renowned as an international playground. Millions of vacationers, enchanted with its combination of European chic and Middle Eastern hospitality, were drawn to its beaches, hotels, elegant shops, restaurants, cabarets, and casinos. Venturing beyond the environs of the city, tourists were quick to embrace the rest of Lebanon. Indeed, in 1966 *Life* magazine aptly described this jewel-like country as "a kind of Las Vegas-Riviera-St. Moritz flavored with the spices of Araby." [15] Ann Zwicker Kerr expressed the sentiments of many Westerners about the Lebanon of the 1950s when she wrote the following nearly four decades later:

> For me it was not just the Frenchness nor the Arabness nor the Armenianness that made Lebanon so appealing, but rather the collage of them all in a cultural and linguistic blend of charm and style and color. . . .
>
> Along with the appeal of the blend of cultures was the physical beauty of the country in its variety of seascapes and mountain vistas, added to the genuine warmth and hospitality of the people who lived there. In the few weeks since my arrival, I had become completely smitten with this lovely place. [16]

LEBANON, A GOURMET'S MECCA

In keeping with its status as a hub of international business and tourism, the Lebanese capital was a food connoisseur's paradise. When it came to dining out, Beirut's hundreds of restaurants afforded opportunities that were unparalleled elsewhere in the Middle East. From *paella* and Bombay curry to hamburgers and banana splits, Beirut had it all.

During the civil war some restaurants in Beirut and other towns continued to operate in the face of seemingly impossible odds. A French journalist, visiting the no-man's-land along the coast between Tyre and Sidon, was astonished to come upon a seafood restaurant with its tables immaculately set and its owner and staff ready to provide a magnificent repast for him and his colleagues. In an instant there appeared a splendid array of appetizers, followed by platters of succulently grilled and fried fish. He watched incredulously as the company was regaled with one exquisite delicacy after another amid the surrounding devastation, as if the martyred nation were trying to make amends for what had befallen it.

Fortunately, in the past few years dining out in Lebanon has made a strong comeback. The country is virtually bursting with establishments that cater to all tastes and budgets, from street vendors, open-air cafés, and fast-food eateries to plush restaurants more French than ones in Paris.

A VIGOROUS AND EVOLVING CUISINE

The cookery of Syria, Lebanon, and Jordan is considered by many to be Arab food at its best. During the past hundred years it has drawn inspiration from outside sources while retaining its age-old distinctive character. A number of Western foods have gained popularity, some dishes of foreign origin have been adapted to suit local tastes, and the cuisine has grown lighter and more digestible. In an area of the world where the art of cooking most likely had its genesis, that art remains very much alive and well today.

Markets

Scene in an Arab market. *From John Carne,* Syria, the Holy Land, Asia Minor, &c., *vol. 2 (London, Fisher, Son, 1836)*

"REGARD IT! A PITCHER OF PITCHERS! The sun and the moon of pitchers!"
"That! It is dented, worthless. But out of charity I will offer you fifty piasters."[1]
(A typical example of bargaining in Syrian *suqs* of former times.)

Markets, or *suqs*, played a vital role in the life of the Islamic Empire. The Persian traveler Nasir-i-Khusrau (1004–1088), who visited Syria in 1047, described Tripoli's bazaars as "well built, and so clean that one might take each to be a palace for its splendor. Every kind of meat, and fruit, and eatable that ever I saw in Persia is to be had here, and a hundred times better in quality."[2] Goods from Arabia, Armenia, Azerbaijan, Byzantium, Egypt, Ethiopia, Iraq, Khurasan, Transoxiana, India, and China were all to be found in the *suqs* in remarkable abundance and variety and could be purchased by anyone with the money to pay for them.

Before Vasco da Gama found the sea route to India in 1498, camel caravans were a primary way by which rice, spices, and other highly sought-after commodities were brought from the East to the bustling trading centers of the Fertile Crescent. Even after the use of overland trade routes declined, caravans remained the principal mode of transporting goods within the area.

Camel caravans held a special fascination for me as a youngster since for generations my father's family had been in the wholesale import-export business, handling both food and nonfood items and operating a caravan between southeastern Anatolia and Beirut. An important stop on my family's caravan route was Aleppo, whose immense *suq* had been the commercial mecca of the Middle East in the days of the caravan trade. Following the discovery of the maritime route to India, Aleppo remained the focal point for mercantile activity in the region, and during the sixteenth and seventeenth centuries many *khan*s were built as warehouses and residences for the European agents who were licensed to operate in the Ottoman Empire. Several of these are still found in the *suq* today. *Khan*s were also built in other trading centers such as Damascus and Sidon as well as in the countryside.

Interior of the Great Khan at Damascus. From John Carne, Syria, the Holy Land, Asia Minor, &c., *vol. 1 (London, Fisher, Son, 1836)*

Over the years some abandoned *khan*s in rural districts became the sites of weekly fairs that enjoyed great popularity among the peasantry, who flocked to them to buy, sell, and barter. Men, women, and children would arrive at these markets carrying the products of their labor in baskets, on trays, in earthen jugs and jars, in large skin bottles, and on camels, mules, horses, and donkeys. Peddlers and craftsmen all set up stalls and loudly hawked their wares. The nineteenth-century missionary William McClure Thomson has given a description of a lively Tuesday market held at the celebrated *Suq al-Khan* below the southern Lebanese town of Hasbayya:

> Cotton is brought in bales from Nablus; barley, and wheat, and sesame, and Indian-corn from the Huleh, the Hauran, and Esdraelon. From Gilead and Bashan, and the surrounding districts, come . . . cattle and flocks, with cheese, leben, curdled milk, semen [clarified butter], butter, honey, and similar articles. Then there are chickens and eggs, figs, raisins, apples, melons, grapes, and all kinds of fruits and vegetables in their season . . . .
>   . . . These fairs . . . are the daily newspaper, for there is one for every day within a circuit of forty miles. They are the exchange, the political caucus, the family gathering, the grand gala-day, and underlying the whole is the ever-present aim of making money.[3]

The *suq*s lie at the heart of all Arab communities. Whether sprawling bazaars, as in Aleppo and Damascus, or marketplaces in smaller towns, they bring together the diverse elements that form the mosaic of Middle Eastern society. The age-old custom of bargaining has practically disappeared, and while some haggling still persists, most prices are now fixed.

In a large *suq* the shops of each trade are grouped together in the manner of the medieval guild system. Artisans can often be seen at work openly practicing their time-honored skills. In the past parades were frequently held in the *suqs*, not only to provide occasions for merrymaking but also to showcase the accomplishments of local craftsmen. One such parade, held in seventeenth-century Aleppo, was witnessed by the French traveler Jean de Thévenot, who described bearers carrying elaborate floats on which bakers were rolling and shaping dough and a contingent of confectioners who marched carrying fairy-tale castles made of sugar on their heads.

There is so much to explore in an extensive *suq* that a visit can often become an all-day affair. Should hunger strike while shopping, vendors are always near at hand dispensing kebabs, *falafel*, lentil soup, *ful mudammas*, charcoal-roasted corn and chestnuts, freshly baked breads and pastries, candies and confections, and lemonade and other drinks. One can easily overeat for a song.

The *suqs* are stocked with an exceptional variety of foods: an abundance of fruits, vegetables, and herbs newly picked from nearby orchards and gardens; great mounds of dried fruits; large sacks of nuts, flour, rice, bulgur, and dried legumes; honey in the comb; barrels holding a profuse assortment of olives; tubs brimming with porcelain-white cheese; and carcasses of meat, live poultry, and, where available, fresh and saltwater fish. Perhaps most overwhelming is the plenitude of spices, many of them familiar to Americans, and others, such as *mahlab* and sumac, not well known.

Visiting the historically evocative *suqs* of Aleppo and Damascus, where anyone from Ibn Battuta to Marco Polo could stride in at any moment and not look out of place, was always an event. Nothing like them existed in Beirut, where most of the old bazaars had been torn down to make way for twentieth-century progress. Although today the remarkable range of goods has expanded to include the latest modern appliances and electronic gadgetry, many of the traditional handicrafts are still on display and the atmosphere of bygone days continues to survive, for these *suqs* have been declared National Trusts and are not to be changed.

Don't start a *khan* with one donkey.

Ingredients

Market scene in northwestern Syria. *From John Carne,* Syria, the Holy Land, Asia Minor, &c., *vol. 3 (London, Fisher, Son, 1836)*

OVER THE CENTURIES GREATER SYRIA has enjoyed a widespread repu-
tation for the high quality of its many food products. The eminent tenth-century Syrian
geographer al-Muqaddasi has left us the following valuable information:

> Unequalled is this land of Syria for its dried figs, its common olive-oil, its white bread . . .
> also for the quinces, the pine-nuts . . . raisins . . . the herb of mint . . . And further, know that
> within the province of Palestine may be found gathered together six-and-thirty products
> that are not found thus united in any other land. . . . Now the first seven are the pine-
> nuts, called "Kuraish-bite," the quince or Cydonian-apple, the 'Ainuni and the Duri raisins,
> the Kafuri plum, the fig called as-Saba'i, and the fig of Damascus. The next seven are the
> Colocasia [taro] . . . the sycamore, the carob or St. John's bread . . . the . . . jujube,
> the artichoke, the sugar-cane, and the Syrian apple. And the remaining twenty-two are the
> fresh dates and olives, the shaddock, the indigo and juniper, the orange, the mandrake,
> the Nabk fruit,[1] the nut, the almond, the asparagus, the banana, the sumach [sumac], the
> cabbage, the truffle, the lupin [lupine], and the early prune, called at-Tari; also snow, buffalo-
> milk, the honey-comb, the 'Asimi grape, and the Tamri—or date-fig. Further, there is the
> preserve called Kubbait;[2] you find, in truth, the like of it in name elsewhere, but of a different
> flavour. The lettuce also, which everywhere else, except only at Ahwaz[3] . . . is counted as a
> common vegetable, is here in Palestine a choice dish.[4]

Continuing his account, al-Muqaddasi enumerates the exports of Syrian provinces and towns. Besides many of the above-mentioned items, he lists others such as
cheeses from Jerusalem, grain, lambs, and honey from Amman, rice from Baisan, "the
treacle called *dibs*" from Baisan and Sughar, oil of violets from Damascus, dried herbs
from Aleppo, and, from Baalbek, "the sweetmeat of dried figs called Malban." He further relates that "the best honey is that from Jerusalem, where the bees suck the thyme;
and likewise from the Jabal 'Amilah."[5]

The Ottoman era saw the introduction of plants from the New World, including
potatoes, tomatoes, corn, and peppers. Numerous Western writers were greatly impressed by the exuberant fertility and rich cultivation of many districts. The British

Colonel Charles Henry Spencer Churchill describes the lower and middle regions of the Lebanon Mountains:

> [There are] large groves of olive trees teeming with the greatest fecundity and producing the finest quality of oil; while in the more sheltered valleys, where water abounds, lemons, oranges, pomegranates, sugar canes, bananas, coffee, and every possible variety of European orchard fruit may be reared in the open air, and by the commonest attention be made to attain a richness and luxuriance not to be surpassed.
>
> Nor is [the soil] less redundant in its vegetable productions. Melons, cucumbers, pine apples, everything in fact which requires the artificial aid of the hot-house in other lands, may here be matured in three or four months, by the mere effect of climate.[6]

In his account of a journey undertaken through northern Lebanon, the American missionary Henry Harris Jessup relates:

> We passed terraces of mulberry, fig and grape . . . Irish potato, Indian corn . . . beans, squashes, and eggplants were growing side by side in great luxuriance, while the hedges were covered with great clusters of ripe blackberries. . . . How I would delight to welcome you to these beautiful gardens and vineyards and show you the tempting clusters of large white and purple grapes, and the red and white figs which melt like honey on the tongue. These are the native luxuries of Syria, and the season of vintage is the jubilee of the Mount Lebanon peasantry.[7]

In the south, the Jordan Valley was considered one of the greatest garden spots imaginable:

> The abundance of water, the richness of the soil, and the warmth of the climate, wonderfully adapt it to the growth of all tropical produce. All kinds of vegetables are in season all the year round.[8]

Fed by the waters of the Barada River, the Ghuta oasis surrounding Damascus continued to be the agricultural jewel of Greater Syria, as it had been in medieval times. Dr. Edward Robinson, yet another adventurous nineteenth-century American minister, who was also a Biblical topographer, observes:

> All the species of grain . . . are raised in profusion. . . . Vegetables of all kinds are abundant and cheap. . . . Almost every species of fruit is produced . . . [9]

Today the region's geographic diversity supports an extraordinary range of foods. Indeed, with the introduction during the twentieth century of new kinds of fruits and vegetables such as avocados, cultivated mushrooms, and Belgian endive, the number and the variety of crops now far exceed those of former times.

Vegetables

The importance of vegetables in the region's cookery is borne out by such medieval Arab sayings as "Vegetables are the ornaments of the dining table" and "A table without vegetables is like an old man devoid of wisdom." Since meat has traditionally been expensive, vegetables have of necessity played a major role in the cuisine, and much inventiveness and ingenuity have been lavished on their preparation.

Various locations in medieval Syria were celebrated for the excellence of their vegetables. Damascus was known far and wide for its asparagus, which was regularly sent to the Abbassid caliph al-Muʿtasim in Baghdad via his private post. ʾAskalan (now Ashqelon), on the coast of Palestine, was famous for a particular kind of onion, *Allium ascalonicum*. The designations "shallot" and "scallion" are both derived from the name of this town. Taro was grown in the gardens of Tripoli, while outstanding cucumbers were found in the Bekaa Valley and in the vicinity of Aleppo.

The poor were greatly dependent on vegetables for much of their nutrition. One vegetable appreciated by persons of both high and low estate was eggplant, referred to as "poor man's meat" but enjoyed with equal relish at the tables of caliphs. Two others that found favor at all levels of society were beans and lentils, which could be substituted for bread when wheat was in short supply.

The population also consumed numerous wild plants that could be found free for the taking in the mountains and open country, as they still can to some extent today. Especially noteworthy in this respect were the slopes of the Lebanon Mountains, where according to the Syrian geographer al-Dimashqi (d. 1327) "more than ninety kinds of plants and herbs spring up naturally without cultivation and are therefore available to everyone, though they are of great value."[10] Desert truffles, esteemed by the ancient Egyptians and Mesopotamians, were also prized by medieval Syrians. When a leading citizen of Aleppo's Jewish community received two and a half pounds of truffles as a present, the sender apologized for the meagerness of his gift![11]

Westerners often remarked on the abundance and variety of vegetables cultivated in Ottoman Syria. Russell has enumerated those found in eighteenth-century Aleppo:

> Among the vegetables which enter into the diet of the inhabitants, the mad apple [eggplant] claims a principal place. There are three varieties of it. They [are] . . . universally in request at the tables of every class: they are even dried, or preserved in salt, so as to furnish an occasional dish throughout the winter. . . .
>
> The love apple or tomato, which used only to be raised in pots, like other flowers, has of late been cultivated, and is brought to the Bazars. . . .
>
> . . . From the beginning of November to the end of March, the markets are supplied with cabbage, rapecole [kohlrabi], spinach, beet [Swiss chard], endive, raddish, red beet, carrot, and turnip. Cauliflower comes in towards the end of January and is plentiful till the middle of March. In April and May come in [romaine] lettuce, [fava] beans, pease, artichoke, purslain, and two sorts of cucumbers, all which continue in season till July. Young cucumbers are again brought to market in September, for the purpose of pickling.
>
> From June to September there [are] . . . adder [hairy] cucumber, kidney bean, Jews mallow [*mlukhiyya*], esculent mallow [okra], orange shaped pumpion [pumpkin], and several varieties of Gourd. Squash comes in towards the end of September, and remains in season till January.
>
> The following pot herbs are also cultivated in the gardens: coriander, fennel, garlic, onions, leek, parsley, celery, caraway, cress, foenugreek, mint, and fennel flower [nigella].

. . . [T]he fields afford capers, borrage, common mallow, sorrel, dandelion, water cress, and truffles. Savory,[12] wild as well as garden, is much used by the natives to give a relish to bread; they pound it when dry, then mix a certain proportion of salt, and dip their bread in it at breakfast, or after meals. Mustard is very little used except by the Franks; it is found in abundance growing wild, but is not cultivated. . . . Wild asparagus is brought from Harem.[13]

The Colocasia [taro] is sometimes brought from the coast, but at present not in request at Aleppo. . . . It is plentiful on the coast; and, at Tripoly, the grocers employ the leaves instead of paper, for wrapping up their wares . . . [14]

In addition to fava and kidney beans, Russell lists several other legumes, including lentils, chickpeas, vetch, and mung beans. Two other vegetables mentioned by nineteenth-century writers are cardoons and potatoes. More recent arrivals are sweet potatoes and yams, which were being cultivated in northern Syria by the 1870s. The modern Lebanese even make a dessert with sweet potatoes and clotted cream (*qashta,* page 149).

Fruit

An enormous variety of exceptionally flavorful fruits ripen to perfection under the bright Mediterranean sun. According to the Chevalier d'Arvieux, the gardens of seventeenth-century Aleppo produced an abundance of wholesome and delicious fruits, among them winter and summer peaches; two kinds of apricots; seven kinds of plums; six kinds of apples; five kinds of pears; six kinds of pomegranates; white, black, and red grapes comprising nine different kinds; three or four kinds of watermelon; cantaloupes; oranges; lemons; citrons; three kinds of dates; two kinds of figs; azaroles; myrtleberries; sorbs; three kinds of mulberries; and almonds, walnuts, and five kinds of pistachios. A century later, his compatriot Volney praised the quality of Syrian fruits:

The vine growing on stakes, or climbing on the oaks, yields red and white wines that could equal those of Bordeaux. . . . Jaffa sees in its gardens . . . watermelons, preferred to those of Broulos itself.[15] Gaza has dates like Mecca, and pomegranates like Algiers. Tripoli produces oranges like Malta; Beirut, figs like Marseilles and bananas like Santo Domingo; Aleppo has the exclusive privilege of pistachios, and Damascus justly boasts of bringing together all the fruits of our provinces. Its stony soil is suited equally to the apples of Normandy, to the plums of Touraine, and to the peaches of Paris. One counts there twenty species of apricots, of which one contains an almond that makes it sought after throughout all of Turkey.[16]

In the past fruit was consumed in enormous quantities where it was plentiful. D'Arvieux tells us that more fruit was eaten in Aleppo than in any three European cities of equal size, and Charles Addison, writing in the nineteenth century, observed that the inhabitants of Damascus subsisted chiefly on fruit and bread.[17]

A common practice in Ottoman Lebanon was sending gifts of fruit. They did not, however, come in pretty packages as they often do here in America today:

A peasant arrived with an ass-load of musk grapes and *mukseysy* grapes. . . An ass-load in those happy countries is but a proof of the abundance that reigns there. A bushel-basket of oranges or lemons, a bunch of fifty or sixty bananas, ten or twelve melons at a time, were presents of frequent occurrence.[18]

Fruit, rather than pastries and other rich desserts, provides the usual conclusion to a meal. Considering its quality and variety, it is not surprising that it also constitutes a favorite breakfast food and between-meal refreshment. Fruit is used to make beverages, syrups, preserves, sweetmeats, puddings, compotes, sorbets, and ice creams. It is also combined with meat, poultry, and fish in savory dishes. This practice, a legacy of the Sassanid Persians, was especially widespread during the Middle Ages, and the culinary manuals of the period are filled with recipes for such preparations. A number of medieval dishes are named after the particular fruit featured in them, for example, *tuffahiyya* (an apple dish), *safarjaliyya* (a quince dish), and *rummaniyya* (a pomegranate dish).

People are also fond of unripe fruit, which is often eaten sprinkled with salt. I remember enjoying green almonds, oranges, grapes, and especially plums this way as a child. It was always a treat to arrive in Shtora in the spring and find greengages in our garden that were as crunchy and delightful as crisp, tart apples.

Dried fruits are greatly favored. They are traditionally incorporated into stews and stuffings, imparting to them a sense of luxury. Cooking intensifies their flavor and succulence and develops their full potential. During the winter months a bowl or compote of dried fruits and nuts is often served as dessert or as a mid-evening refreshment. Children love dried fruits and go to school with pockets full of raisins or rolls of *amardine* (page 371), and both young and old nibble on them at any time of day. Certain Aleppans even feasted on them in the middle of the night:

> Some of the voluptuous Grandees are lulled to sleep by soft music . . . or by Arabian tales . . .
> If they happen to wake in the night, and find no more disposition to sleep, they sit up in bed,
> drink coffee, or, in long nights, regale with dried fruits, and pastry. After which they smoke
> their pipe till they once more drop asleep.[19]

Today fruit is even more plentiful than in the past. The seasonal harvest of orchards, fields, and vineyards pours into city and town markets, where it is artistically displayed in a vibrant explosion of color. Vendors extol not only the taste of their fruit but also its appearance and aroma, for "fruit is first eaten with the eyes, then with the nose, and only lastly with the mouth."[20]

GRAPES

> The vine . . . is universally cultivated.
>   . . . There are upwards of thirty distinct species of grapes flourishing in [the Lebanon]
> mountains. The rocky nature of the soil, and the extreme purity of the air, no doubt tend to
> bring this delicious fruit to a perfection not attainable even in the south of Europe.[21]

Grapes have historically been the choicest fruit of Greater Syria. In former times, as now, the best grapes were grown in the Damascus area and on the sunny slopes of Mount Lebanon. "Better than those I have never tasted," wrote Thomson, "either in the Old World or the New."[22] Each variety of grape is best adapted to a special use. Some are simply eaten fresh out of hand, while others are turned into wine, *arak* (page 403), or vinegar. Certain types are prized for making raisins (*zbeeb*), and still others are utilized to make a kind of molasses called *dibs inab*, which has served as a sweetening agent for pastries and confections for thousands of years; in fact, it was not until the beginning of the twentieth century that sugar was introduced into the countryside.

When I was growing up, late summer was known as "the time of grapes." The vintage, which can last well into the fall, was for the peasantry a period of both activity and rejoicing. Thomson has quoted a colleague's description of the grape harvest as it occurred in the Zahleh region north of Shtora over a century ago:

> The Zahleh people are now in the vineyards. . . . [D]uring the hour's ride [we] were surrounded with vineyards before us, behind us, and upon either side of us . . . .The ruins of Ba'albec were in sight to the north, and toward the south Mount Hermon was towering above everything. Men, women, and children, horses, donkeys, camels, and mules, were going and coming with baskets or boxes or saddle-bags of grapes. Each person in passing politely invited us to help ourselves [from the tempting baskets], and some would take no denial.
>
> . . . In two different places companies of people were treading out the juice of the grapes to make grape molasses. In all directions people were making raisins, and some were preparing the ripe fruit to be sent to the neighboring villages for sale.[23]

Regarding the above-mentioned *dibs* (grape molasses), the English clergyman Charles Thomas Wilson has left us a detailed account of how it was usually made in Ottoman Syria:

> The grapes, which should be very ripe, are sprinkled with a little powdered clay called *howwar*, and piled up either in a sack or loose on the floor of a wine-press. . . . Where the grapes are put loose on the press, flat stones are placed over them, on which a number of men stand till all the juice is squeezed out; but where a sack is used the treaders stand directly on the bags.
>
> The expressed juice is then ladled into large caldrons, a fire is lighted beneath, and the juice carefully boiled down. The process is not so simple as might be thought. The fire needs constant attention and regulation, as should the heat be too great the Dibs will have a burnt flavour. The syrup has also to be skimmed at frequent intervals, as the lighter impurities rise to the top. After about thirty-six hours' boiling it is reduced to one-third of its original bulk, and is sufficiently cooked. It must now be left to cool and settle, when the powdered clay, already mentioned, carries down all the coarser impurities in the form of a dense precipitate, from which, when cold, the supernatant liquid must be carefully poured off; otherwise it will not keep good, but after a while ferments and becomes sour. When properly prepared it is thin syrup, of a light brown colour and of a sweet, pleasant taste. When kept for some time the water evaporates still more, and crystallization sets in. It is eaten by the natives as it is, or, mixed with flour and almonds, is made into various sweetmeats.[24]

According to Thomson, the best *dibs* was made in the Lebanese village of Bhamdun, where the grape juice was boiled down by one-half or two-thirds and then beaten until it became quite thick.[25] Many families, including mine, used to make grape *dibs* outdoors in September. I remember Shtora and other villages in the Bekaa being suffused with the sweet, irresistible scent of grape juice seething in huge copper caldrons (*dists*). The annual preparation of the *dibs* was something of a social occasion and would extend far into the night. Sitting under an indigo sky diamonded with close-hanging stars, I would feel as if I were witnessing some mysterious ancient rite, so engrossed were the grown-ups in stoking the fires and stirring the boiling grape juice in the caldrons, their figures silhouetted against the flames. Two other confections that we made with grape juice during the vintage were *bastegh* and *sharots,* both Armenian specialties (see my *Cuisine of Armenia*).

Of the several varieties of grapes in our garden, my favorite was the aristocratic *aynub shami* ("Damascus grape"), which was large, green, and extra-crisp, with a distinctive tangy-sweet flavor. I was also fond of the smaller greenish yellow, thin-skinned round grapes that grew on a trellis outside our kitchen, which in late summer would be permeated with their exquisite flowery perfume. It was great fun to be able to pluck the juicy, honey-sweet fruit by merely stretching out my arm from our kitchen window. A vine trellis is a traditional feature of many dwellings, shading porches, terraces, and roofs from the daytime heat as well as providing freshly picked fruit for eating and leaves for making *mahshi* (page 233).

In addition to those found in our garden, we grew many other kinds of grapes in our vineyard, which was located about a mile away from our house. Several times a week we would make the trip at dawn and return with baskets full of a tempting assortment of green, yellow, pink, purple, and blue-black bunches for breakfast. The path from our house wound between magnificent orchards of apple, peach, pear, and plum trees, all heavily laden with luxuriant fruit. Dotted among the orchards and set alongside glinting streams were villas and cottages, their yards filled with flowers. As the path led out from Shtora, orchards gave way to acres and acres of beautifully maintained vineyards. Our own property, which was quite extensive, was skirted at its outer edge by the tracks of a narrow-gauge railroad. Sometimes we would delay our trip to the vineyard until late afternoon to coincide with the arrival of the little train coming from Beirut, which would soon be heard winding its way among the vineyards, having triumphantly descended into the Bekaa after chugging over the high Lebanon. We would wave gleefully to the engineer as the train passed by and then watch entranced as it gradually made a sweeping curve before disappearing in the direction of the nearby Ksara vineyards on its way to Damascus. These vineyards, which covered a considerable area, belonged to the Jesuits, who operated (as they still do) the largest winery in the Middle East, producing good, well-known wines.

Lebanon's "toy train," which gave us so much delight, is now only a cherished

Scene on the Beirut-Damascus Railroad. *From* National Geographic,
January, 1911

memory. It is no longer in service, and when I learned of this recently I could not help
feeling a pang of regret.

POMEGRANATES

This fruit has been cultivated in Greater Syria since antiquity. Virtually the only type
of pomegranate available in American markets is the sweet red "Wonderful," which is
an eating pomegranate. In the eastern Mediterranean, on the other hand, there are several varieties; d'Arvieux encountered no less than six kinds in the bazaars of Aleppo,[26]
and Thomson reported that there was on Mount Lebanon "a kind perfectly black on the
outside."[27] According to the Syrian geographer Abu'l-Fida' (1273–1331), in Harim near
Aleppo a unique variety of pomegranate was cultivated that was seedless, very juicy, and
transparent, "so that you see the inside from the outside."[28]

Varieties of pomegranates differ in the acidity of their juice, which can be sweet, sour, or sweet-sour. The juice of sweet pomegranates provides a popular and refreshing beverage. Sour and sweet-sour pomegranate juices are traditionally used to make pome- granate molasses (page 57) and other syrups. They can also form the basis of excellent sauces, jellies, and ices and other desserts. Sour pomegranate juice is used much like lemon juice and vinegar to lend a tart note to savory dishes, salad dressings, sauces, and marinades. Thus when a recipe calls for lemon juice or pomegranate juice (or vinegar or pomegranate juice), what is meant is the juice of sour rather than sweet pomegran- ates.[29] If you cannot obtain sour pomegranates, you can make an acceptable substitute by souring sweet pomegranate juice with lemon or lime juice (page 56). Although bottled sweet pomegranate juice is readily available, I find it, unfortunately, unacceptable and therefore recommend that you use only fresh pomegranate juice for the recipes in this book.

Sour pomegranate seeds add delightful accents of acidity to many preparations and make a splendid garnish for dips and other appetizers, salads, baked fish with *tahini* sauce, and open-faced meat pies. Sweet pomegranate seeds are delicious eaten on their own, or they may be sprinkled with rose water or wine and sugar, decorated with blanched almonds, and served as a dessert. They are also added to fruit compotes and provide a lovely garnish for puddings and other desserts, but they are not suitable for such savory dishes as *baba ghannuj* (page 107) and Eggplant with Pomegranate Sauce (page 269), which are traditionally garnished with sour pomegranate seeds.[30] In the Middle East sour pomegranate seeds have long been sun-dried and stored for winter use. Russell informs us that both the fresh and the dried seeds were important ingredi- ents in eighteenth-century Aleppan cookery.[31] However, only fresh pomegranate seeds are called for in this book. Directions for removing the seeds from pomegranates and extracting their juice are given on pages 55 and 56.

A Tale of Sweet and Sour Pomegranates

After coming to the city of Damascus [Abu Ya'qub] . . . was engaged to keep an or- chard belonging to the king Nur al-Din. . . . When the fruit was due to ripen the sultan came to that garden, and the superintendent of the garden bade Abu Ya'qub fetch some pomegranates . . . but the superintendent, finding them sour, bade him fetch some others. He did so, and the superintendent, finding them sour also, said to him, "Have you been looking after this orchard for six months and cannot tell the sweet from the sour?" He replied, "It was for keeping that you hired me, not for eating."[32]

Fresh Pomegranate Juice

The best juice for breakfast in Shtora was stored not in a refrigerator but in the enchanting fruits that hung like ornaments from the pomegranate trees in our orchard. Using a time-honored Middle Eastern technique, I would pluck a fruit off a tree and roll

The pomegranate. From William McClure Thomson, The Land and the Book, *vol. 1 (New York, Harper, 1880)*

it on a hard surface while pressing with the palm of my hand to break the juice sacs inside without puncturing the skin. Next, I would make a hole in the side and suck out the liquid (a straw could be inserted for this purpose) while squeezing the fruit, a method that enabled me to savor the glorious juice in its pristine state. This also happens to be a good way to obtain the juice from a pomegranate. Instead of sucking it out, allow it to flow out of the hole into a nonmetallic bowl (to prevent adversely affecting both the color and flavor of the pomegranate) while squeezing the fruit. Strain the juice before using.

Here are two other ways to extract juice from pomegranates. Remove the seeds from 6 large pomegranates as directed below. Place a handful of seeds at a time in a double layer of rinsed and squeezed cheesecloth and squeeze the juice into a nonmetallic bowl. Alternatively, in a blender or food processor blend the seeds, $1\frac{1}{2}$ cups or so at a time, until liquified. Strain the blended pulp and juice through an enameled colander lined with a double layer of rinsed and squeezed cheesecloth into a nonmetallic bowl, letting the juice drip through gradually. Pour the juice into a clean bottle, seal, and refrigerate up to 4 days.

Makes about 3 cups

Note: You can freeze the juice in ice cube trays, pack the cubes in freezer bags, and store in the freezer to be used as needed. They will keep up to 3 months.

VARIATION:

Sour Pomegranate Juice

Use sour pomegranates if you can obtain them. Otherwise, use 1 tablespoon freshly squeezed and strained lemon or lime juice per cup of sweet pomegranate juice. Alternatively, you can dilute bottled pomegranate molasses with enough water to attain the consistency of fresh juice. The amount of water needed will depend on the thickness of the molasses (page 57).

HOW TO REMOVE THE SEEDS FROM A POMEGRANATE

Method I: Cut a thin slice off the blossom end of the pomegranate, being careful not to puncture the seeds inside. With the point of a small, sharp knife, carefully cut out a little of the white pith in the center (this simple, essential step will enable you to separate the seed clusters easily without splattering). Lightly score the rind lengthwise in quarters from blossom to stem end, being careful not to cut into the seeds. Place both thumbs in the center of the pomegranate in the opening where you removed the pith and, following the score lines, gently pull the fruit apart into halves, then break each piece in half again. With your fingers, bend the rind and pith back to expose the seed clusters. With a downward plucking motion of your thumb, separate the seeds, removing and discarding the pale membrane.

Method II: Here is an aquatic technique I first came across in *Sunset* magazine many years ago. Follow the directions for Method I through the scoring of the rind. Then immerse the scored fruit in a bowl or sink of cool water. Holding the fruit underwater, continue the procedure outlined in Method I. The seeds will sink to the bottom while the rind and membrane float to the top. Discard the rind and membrane. Scoop up the seeds and drain them in a colander, then gently pat them dry.

1 medium pomegranate yields about ¾ cup seeds; 1 large one, about 1 cup

A note of caution: Do not roll the pomegranate on a hard surface while pressing with your palms to soften the fruit. As I have mentioned earlier, one does this only to break the juice sacs in order to obtain the juice without removing the seeds. If the seeds are broken, you will of course lose much of the precious juice (and make a royal mess to boot) when you open the pomegranate by means of Method I; and if you employ Method II, the juice will leach out into the water. Banging the pomegranate with the back of a knife to loosen the seeds will only make matters worse. I am including this warning because both ill-advised procedures (i.e., rolling and banging the pomegranate) are recommended in another book on eastern Mediterranean cooking.

Also, pomegranate stains are difficult to remove, so take the same precautions that you would with other red fruit juices.

Note: To freeze pomegranate seeds, spread them in one layer in a shallow glass dish and freeze until firm, then pack in freezer containers. Freeze up to 4 months. To use, gently spoon out the desired amount as needed.

Pomegranate Molasses
Dibs Rumman *or* Rubb al-Rumman

This is the concentrated (boiled-down) juice of sour or sweet-sour (or a combination of sweet and sour) pomegranates. In former times it was an important preserve that households put up for the coming year. Neale lists it as one of the provisions stored by villagers in northern Syria during the Ottoman era (see *nahr bekmaze,* page 294).[33] When this molasses is made with the juice of sour pomegranates, it lends a tart note to meat, vegetable, and egg dishes, sauces, salad dressings, marinades, and stuffings. Made with the juice of sweet-sour fruit, it can be used to flavor some savory dishes and makes an excellent sauce for pork, poultry, and game birds.

Pomegranate molasses is made in various thicknesses. Although thick molasses is sometimes referred to as "*rubb,*" the two terms, "*dibs*" and "*rubb,*" are often used interchangeably. A thicker molasses will obviously be stronger, and you will therefore need less of it in a recipe than if you use a thinner molasses. Similarly, when diluting pomegranate molasses with water to substitute for fresh juice when the latter is unavailable (page 56), a thick molasses will require more water than a thin one. For this reason it is not possible to specify the exact amount of water needed. Keep in mind that the amount of pomegranate molasses and the quantity of water needed to dilute it will depend on how concentrated your pomegranate molasses is. This applies to both the homemade and commercial products; the latter can vary not only from brand to brand but from batch to batch within the same brand.

Lebanon is famous for its pomegranate molasses. A good commercial Lebanese brand, available in this country, is Cortas, which makes an acceptable substitute for the homemade product. Since bottled pomegranate molasses will not keep indefinitely, be sure to taste it before using. It should have a clean, fruity flavor.

Looking through al-Warraq's tenth-century culinary manual, I was thrilled to discover a recipe entitled "*Rubb al-rumman*" for this exotic ingredient of Middle Eastern and Caucasian cookery that is identical with one that my family used in Lebanon.[34] It is important not to confuse pomegranate molasses (also known as pomegranate syrup), which is made *without sugar* and is traditionally used to impart a degree of tartness to savory dishes, with the pomegranate syrup (*sharab al-rumman*) on page 384, which contains sugar and is diluted with water to make a refreshing, time-honored beverage.

As far as I know, my *Cuisine of Armenia* (1974) and *Best Foods of Russia* (1976) were the first publications in the West to include recipes for a Middle Eastern–style pomegranate syrup, which is not the same thing as grenadine. Following the advice of a well-meaning but misguided cook who had lived in the former Armenian Soviet Socialist Republic and who had assured me that the Caucasian version of this molasses was made with sugar, I reluctantly included some in those recipes. Further research, however, has convinced me beyond any doubt that the traditional Caucasian (Armenian, Georgian, and Azerbaijani) recipe for pomegranate molasses is in fact identical with that found in al-Warraq's manual and contains no sugar. I have therefore omitted the sugar from the recipe as it appears in the 1996 edition of *The Cuisine of Armenia.*

Unfortunately, in the years following the publication of my first two books, recipes for pomegranate molasses or syrup containing sugar have turned up in numerous works published both here and abroad featuring Russian, Georgian, Middle Eastern, eastern Mediterranean, and international cooking, with the result that I have had to live with not only my mistake but the ones found in these books as well. I must confess, however, that since none of these volumes include any of my books in their bibliographies, I feel less upset than I otherwise would about the error that has been so widely perpetuated!

Below is a recipe for pomegranate molasses. If you have access only to sweet pomegranates, add enough freshly squeezed and strained lime or lemon juice to achieve the degree of tartness desired.

In a $1\frac{1}{2}$-quart enameled saucepan bring 3 cups fresh pomegranate juice (page 54) to a boil over moderate heat. Reduce the heat and simmer, uncovered, stirring occasionally and skimming the froth, until the juice is reduced to 1 cup. Cool, bottle, and store in the refrigerator.

Makes 1 cup

Note: Since this particular molasses has been reduced by two-thirds, 1 part molasses mixed with 2 parts water can be used as a substitute for fresh juice.

VARIATION:

Thick Pomegranate Molasses

Simmer the pomegranate juice until reduced to $\frac{1}{2}$ cup. Use as above, but in smaller quantities.

～

Many will stone a fruit-bearing tree. *(A)*
(A worthy person will always be criticized.)

～

Olives

Olives are indigenous to the region, where they have been a staple for millennia. Olive trees can live to a great age; some are believed to be more than a thousand years old, yet they are still bearing fruit, making few demands but bestowing many blessings.

There is an old saying among the *fellahin* that the vine is a *sitt,* a delicate town lady who requires a great deal of attention; the fig, on the contrary, is a *fellaha,* a strong country woman who can flourish without such tender care; but the olive tree is a bold *bedawiyya,* who in spite of neglect and hardship remains a strong and useful Arab wife.

Important olive-growing areas include the Kura plateau, the Shuf, Dayr Mimas, and Hasbayya in Lebanon; the Ghuta plain surrounding Damascus, al-Zabadani, and Latakia in Syria; and parts of western Jordan. Olives are gathered in the fall, and it is a busy time when a village has many trees or when the harvest is a large one. Thomson has described the olive harvest as it occurred in Hasbayya over a century ago:

> Early in autumn the berries begin to drop of themselves, or are shaken off by the wind. They are allowed to remain under the trees for some time, guarded by the watchmen of the town. Then a proclamation is made by the governor that all who have olive-trees should go out and pick what has fallen. Previous to that, not even the owners are allowed to gather olives in the groves. The proclamation is repeated once or twice, according to the season. In November comes the general and final summons, which sends forth all Hasbeiya. No olives are then safe unless the owner looks after them, for the watchmen are removed, and the groves are alive with men, women, and children. Everywhere the people are in the trees "shaking" them to bring down the fruit. . . .
>
> The "shaking of the olive" is the severest operation in Syrian husbandry, particularly in mountainous regions. When the proclamation goes forth to "shake," there can be no postponement. The rainy season has already set in; the trees are dripping with the last shower, or

Hasbayya, in southern Lebanon. From William McClure Thomson, The Land and the Book, *vol. 2 (New York, Harper, 1882)*

bowing under a load of moist snow; but the owners must shake them, drenching themselves and those below with an artificial storm of rain, snow, and olives. No matter how piercing the wind, or how blinding the rain, that work must go on from early dawn to dark night; and then the weary laborer must carry on his aching back a heavy load of dripping berries two or three miles, it may be, up the mountain to his home.[35]

Often referred to as "the sultan of the table," this indispensable food appears at almost every meal, including breakfast. A handful of olives and a bit of white goat cheese wrapped in flatbread have made up the noon repast of farmers, shepherds, and laborers since antiquity.

A remarkable assortment of olives can be seen in markets. Depending on when they are picked, olives can be green, greenish yellow, wine-colored, brown, violet, dark purple, or black. All, however, are bitter-tasting and inedible until they have been cured. There are numerous methods of curing olives. One, described by Wilson, is still used today:

> To prepare the green olives for eating, they are usually broken slightly first, and then soaked for a while in water to remove some of the bitterness, after which they are pickled in salt and water, with a little oil, and sometimes a slice or two of lemon.[36]

A popular way of curing black olives is to salt them and leave them for several days, stirring occasionally, and then to cover them with brine and a layer of olive oil. Violet (medium-ripe) olives are often cured as follows: Two incisions are made in each olive. The olives are placed in a glass jar interspersed with lemon slices, covered with fresh lemon juice mixed with salt, and allowed to macerate for several days, during which time they are stirred frequently. They are then covered with a layer of olive oil and left for two weeks before serving. These violet olives occupy an honored position on the *mazza* (page 99).

Flavorings such as garlic, chili pepper, thyme, lemon slices, vinegar, bitter orange juice, or lemon and orange leaves are sometimes added during the curing process. Although the raw fruit absorbs flavorings more readily, you can add them to drained ready-cured olives and then cover with olive oil.

For a discussion of olive oil, see Cooking Fats (page 68).

Nuts

Nuts are enjoyed on their own as well as used in countless dishes ranging from appetizers to beverages.

ALMONDS (LAWZ)

Almond trees are thought to have been brought from their native Asia to the eastern Mediterranean by the Phoenicians. The fruits of these trees are highly prized and are eaten both fresh and dried. Very young, hand-picked green almonds are a treat. In this early, unripened stage the entire fruit is edible. Itinerant vendors peddle green almonds,

which are eaten with a light sprinkling of salt. Recipes for meat stewed with green almonds are found in al-Warraq's cookery manual and in the *Wusla*. Mature almonds are
harvested in the early fall. Since these nuts take a very long time to drop naturally, they
are knocked to the ground with long poles. I remember the colorful sight of peasant
women, clad in flowery dresses worn over tight-fitting pantaloons ruffled at the ankles,
engaged in this task in the foothills of Mount Lebanon.

For longest shelf life, purchase almonds in the shell. Store in well-sealed, airtight
containers in a cool, dry place, or freeze. If you prefer them already shelled for convenience, buy them unblanched. They will keep longer, and the skin, which is edible, will
help prevent the seed from drying out.

To blanch and toast almonds: Place shelled whole almonds in a bowl and pour
enough boiling water over them to cover. Let stand about 30 seconds or until an almond
can be slipped out of its skin easily when squeezed between the fingers. Drain the almonds, rinse them under cold running water, and slip off the skins. Pat the nuts dry
with paper towels and spread them in a single layer on a rimmed baking sheet. Toast in
a preheated 325°F oven, stirring occasionally, 10 to 15 minutes or until crisp and lightly
browned.

WALNUTS (JAWZ)

Walnut trees flourish in many parts of the region. I recall passing through one village in southern Lebanon where almost every house seemed to have at least one walnut
tree growing nearby. Long-lived and highly productive, these stately trees are greatly
valued and are included among items of inheritance in wills.

The harvesting of walnuts takes place in the fall. When I was a child, village men used
to climb the trees and knock the nuts to the ground with long poles. The women and children would then gather up the nuts and place them in baskets.

Walnuts can be consumed fresh or dried. My fondest memories of eating fresh walnuts are connected with the little village of Tanail just east of Shtora, where friends of
mine had a lovely fountained garden dominated by a magnificent walnut tree. It was
impossible to resist these once-a-year temptations even though shucking the nuts left a
deep brown stain on the hands. Those who preferred their nuts cracked and ready-to-
eat could savor them at waterside cafés in the Bekaa or in the Damascus area. Fresh
walnuts are also enjoyed in other ways. When not yet full size and before their shells
have begun to harden, very young whole ones are pickled and served on the *mazza* or
preserved in syrup and eaten as a sweet. Recipes for pickled walnuts appear in both the
Wusla and the *Kanz*.

For maximum flavor and shelf life, purchase walnuts in the shell early in the season.
If you need walnut halves, however, you may prefer to buy them already prepared this
way for convenience.

Store walnuts as you would almonds.

To toast walnuts: Spread shelled nuts in a single layer on a rimmed baking sheet. Toast in a preheated 350°F oven, stirring occasionally, about 10 minutes or until lightly browned.

HAZELNUTS (BUNDUQ)

These nuts grow particularly well near Aleppo and on Mount Lebanon. They are eaten either fresh or, more commonly, dried. Although hazelnuts are usually sold in the shell and keep longer that way, they are not easy to crack and you may prefer to buy them already shelled.

Store hazelnuts as you would almonds.

To toast and skin hazelnuts: Spread shelled nuts in a single layer on a rimmed baking sheet. Toast in a preheated 350°F oven, stirring occasionally, 10 to 15 minutes or until they are lightly browned and the skins blister. Wrap the nuts in a kitchen towel and allow them to steam about 1 minute. Rub the nuts to remove as much of the skin as possible and let them cool.

PISTACHIO NUTS (FUSTUQ HALABI)

It was the short season of fresh pistachio nuts which, in Aleppo, is almost a festival. As we sat and talked, the tables round us and the marble floors were awash with sunset-coloured skins. Our hands and breath took on a tang which was more subtle than the smell of pine.[37]

The pistachio tree flourishes on Mount Lebanon and in the Aleppo region. Aleppo pistachios were prized by the Romans, and in Russell's time they were considered the finest in the world.[38] When I was growing up, the Aleppo pistachio trade was generally in the hands of Armenian merchants, with the nuts being exported to many countries. A childhood favorite of mine was fresh pistachios in season, sold in markets and by street vendors.

Pistachios are most commonly available roasted in the shell, either salted or unsalted. Although salted pistachios are delicious to nibble on, for cooking you will need undyed, unsalted ones, which are sold at Greek and Middle Eastern groceries and at natural foods stores.

Store pistachios as you would almonds.

PINE NUTS (SNUBAR)

The seed of the fruit pine, scattered all over the country, is used, as in England in the time of Elizabeth, in every dish, sweet and savoury—to the savoury it gives mellowness, to the sweet, substance and flavour.[39]

Pine nuts are the small edible seeds found in the cones of several species of pine trees. The variety preferred for use in eastern Mediterranean cooking comes from the umbrella-shaped stone pine (*Pinus pinea*), one of the most characteristic trees of the

Beirut's **Bois des pins** *(Pine Woods). From William McClure Thomson,* The Land and the Book, *vol. 3 (New York, Harper, 1885)*

Mediterranean landscape. These creamy white nuts, which are encased in hard shells that are difficult to crack open, are most often sold already shelled and are available at Middle Eastern and Italian groceries, nut shops, natural and specialty foods stores, and some supermarkets. Since the shelled nuts can turn rancid quickly due to their high oil content, purchase them only in small amounts from stores with a rapid turnover. If possible, ask to taste one for freshness before buying.

Although pine nuts can be eaten raw, their flavor is enhanced when they are lightly toasted in a dry skillet or in an oven. If the nuts are to be sprinkled over a cake batter, this step is unnecessary since they will be toasted during baking.

To toast pine nuts: In a heavy skillet toast shelled nuts over moderate heat, stirring, about 5 minutes or until golden. Alternatively, spread nuts in a single layer in a pie pan. Toast in a preheated 350°F oven, stirring occasionally, about 5 minutes or until golden.

Spices and Herbs

Salim . . . was enveloped in an aromatic cloud that came wafting from the spice market. Star anise, cardamom, and coriander were crassly celebrating their triumph over all the other spices, though thyme from the Syrian mountains kept chiming in as well with its deep voice and a stubbornness impossible to ignore. Now and then cinnamon would whisper sweetly and seductively, when the master spices weren't paying attention. Only the saffron blossoms kept silent, preferring to rely solely on their radiant yellow to entice prospective buyers.

Lies and spices are siblings. A lie can change even the blandest occurrence into a piquant dish. The truth and nothing but the truth is something only a judge wants to hear. But just like spices, lies should be used solely to add a little flavor. "Not too little, not too much," thought Salim, "that's how they're best savored."[40]

The aroma of spices never fails to evoke in me vivid recollections of childhood trips to the bustling spice bazaar (suq al-attarin) with its heady blend of fragrances. I can still remember our spice merchant in Beirut seated in his tiny shop surrounded by shelves of carefully labeled bottles and wooden boxes containing twisted dried roots; dried leaves, berries, seeds, and stigmas; pieces of bark and wood; jewel-like resins; flower petals and essences; and a host of puzzling powders, mysterious medicinal herbs, and rare aphrodisiac mixtures. Dangling from the ceiling were branches of dried herbs, while on the counter in front of him stood his trusty mortar and pestle, ever ready for pounding cinnamon, cloves, aniseed, and pepper. During all the years we were his customers, I never once saw him leave his chair, for he could reach all of his merchandise without having to stand up!

As we have seen, Middle Eastern cuisine has made use of spices and herbs since earliest antiquity. In Biblical times the lucrative spice trade of the Mediterranean was almost entirely controlled by the Phoenicians. It was probably during the early Abbassid period, however, that spices were most extensively employed in the region's cookery. They came not only from areas within the Arab domains such as southern Arabia, Syria, Persia, and Central Asia but also from East Africa, India, the Sunda Islands, and China. Pure, top-quality spices commanded exorbitant prices, and the ability to purchase them was a mark of status. One government official boasted that in his household he ground saffron as other people ground their bread flour.[41]

Spices and herbs were essential to the medieval Arab kitchen and were valued for their alleged medicinal and aphrodisiac properties, as they continue to be today. While some recipes called for only two or three spices, most required a greater number. Various spice mixtures and seasoning blends were prepared in advance and stored to be used as needed, a practice still followed at present (see Mixed Spices, page 65, and za'atar, page 80). One frequently employed blend, known as atraf al-tib, was composed of spikenard, betel, bay leaf, nutmeg, mace, cardamom, cloves, rosebuds, the fruit (samara) of the ash tree (Fraxinus excelsior), ginger, and long pepper.[42] Another basic mixture, abzar harra ("hot grains"), consisted of pepper, caraway seeds, coriander seeds, and Chinese cinnamon.

Nowadays spices, whether whole or freshly ground, are usually purchased in small quantities and at frequent intervals from spice vendors. In this country it is best to buy them (also in small quantities) from a reputable specialty foods shop or Middle Eastern grocery with a quick turnover. Among the spices used are allspice, aniseed, caraway, cardamom, cinnamon, cloves, coriander seeds, cumin, fenugreek, ginger, mahlab, mustard seeds, nigella, nutmeg, paprika, Middle Eastern red pepper, black and white pepper, saffron, sumac, and turmeric.

Herbs are cultivated extensively and grow wild as well. Writing of the Lebanon Mountains in the mid-nineteenth century, Colonel Churchill speaks enthusiastically of "numerous medicinal herbs, growing wild in every direction, and filling the air with their fragrant exhalations."[43] Mounds of fresh herbs are heaped in the markets of cities and towns. People are so fond of herbs that various kinds are frequently served as part of a *mazza* or to nibble with certain dishes. The dining table of our summer home in Shtora was almost never without its freshly picked bouquets of herbs, especially mint, that great Lebanese favorite, which I used to gather from our garden shortly before mealtime.

Herbs most often used are parsley, mint, and coriander leaves; those less commonly employed include basil, bay leaves, dill, fennel, oregano, savory, tarragon, and thyme. Regarding mint, oregano, and parsley, it should be noted that these specifically refer to spearmint, Mediterranean oregano, and flat-leaf (Italian) parsley, the varieties preferred by local cooks.

Fresh herbs are almost always superior to dried ones. A few, however—bay leaves, marjoram, rosemary, tarragon, and thyme—are acceptable in dried form, as is oregano, which actually is best when dried. Dried rather than fresh herbs are specifically called for in certain dishes.

The amounts given for spices and herbs in the recipes in this book are meant to serve merely as guides. Use your judgment, tasting and adjusting the seasoning as you go along. If a spice or herb is unfamiliar to you, begin with only a small amount and, after tasting, add more if you wish. Do not omit seasonings entirely, however, for they play a vital role in determining the characteristic flavor of many dishes.

No matter how much care you give to weeds, they won't become basil. (*A*)

Mixed Spices
Baharat Makhluta

In Arabic the word *bahar* means "spice," and the plural, *baharat,* is most commonly used to denote spice blends. Mixed spices are employed to lend a distinctive flavor to a dish. Many households have their favorite spice blends mixed to taste and stored in airtight covered jars as a ready flavoring or condiment. There are also commercial mixtures made and sold by spice merchants. When a recipe in this book calls for mixed spices, you can either use a ready-made spice blend (available at Middle Eastern groceries) or make your own mixture and have it on hand to use as needed. Here are two combinations, each of which makes an excellent seasoning for meat soups, stews, *kafta, kibbeh,* rice or bulgur stuffings for lamb, poultry, and vegetables, and meat fillings for savory pastries.

Mixed Spices I

4 teaspoons ground cinnamon

1 teaspoon freshly grated nutmeg

1 teaspoon ground cloves

1 teaspoon ground cardamom

½ teaspoon freshly ground black pepper

In a small jar with a tight-fitting lid combine all the ingredients and mix well. Seal the jar and store in a cool, dry place away from light.

Makes 2 ½ tablespoons

Mixed Spices II

2 teaspoons ground allspice

1 teaspoon ground cinnamon

1 teaspoon ground cloves

1 teaspoon ground coriander

1 teaspoon ground cumin

¼ teaspoon freshly ground black pepper

In a small jar with a tight-fitting lid combine all the ingredients and mix well. Seal the jar and store in a cool, dry place away from light.

Makes about 2 tablespoons

Everything may be found at the spice-seller's except love.

(True love is the one thing that cannot be purchased.)

Salt

Writing nearly a century ago, the Biblical archaeologist Robert Alexander Stewart Macalister observed that a Beduin, whose love of sweets is well known, prefers salt to sugar when both are offered to him.[44] Salt has long been prized in Greater Syria, where it has been a symbol of hospitality since ancient times. To eat bread and salt with someone is to enter into a covenant of brotherhood.

Salt was an essential ingredient in medieval Arab cuisine. The kind preferred in the culinary manuals was *milh Andarani,* or rock salt from Andaran in what is now northeastern Iran. Several recipes for scented or flavored salt are found in the early Arab cookbooks. These mixtures incorporate various spices, herbs, sesame seeds, and even sour pomegranate seeds, and were used both as a seasoning and as a condiment at table.

During the Ottoman era salt formed a lucrative branch of commerce. One English-man, consumed by a desire to undertake a journey through Greater Syria but lacking the funds to do so, was able to fulfill his life's dream by purchasing two mules and two large sacks of salt and traversing the country on foot as a salt merchant, replenishing his supply as needed.[45] Great quantities of salt were gathered from saline inland lakes such as those near Palmyra and Aleppo (*Sabkhat al-Jabbul*). These lakes dry up in summer, leaving an encrustation of high-quality coarse salt. When I was growing up, salt from Jabbul was much esteemed by Aleppan cooks for its snow-white color and excellent flavor, which was devoid of any bitterness. Sea salt has been obtained from salt pans along the Lebanese coast south of Tripoli for thousands of years. It was this salt from the Mediterranean that we used in our kitchen.

Recent medical research suggests that salt is not the villain it was once believed to be. Unless you must restrict your salt intake for health reasons, there seems to be nothing wrong with using it in moderation. Since salt varies in strength and salting is very much a matter of personal taste, I have not given specific amounts in most recipes.

I have often been asked if there is a satisfactory substitute for salt. I cannot think of one, for as the medieval Arab adage goes, "Salt is as necessary in food as grammar is in speech."

Seasoned Salt

This mixture is inspired by recipes found in the medieval *Wusla* and *Kanz*.

3 tablespoons coarse salt
$\frac{1}{2}$ teaspoon ground nigella
$\frac{1}{2}$ teaspoon ground cumin
$\frac{1}{2}$ teaspoon ground coriander
$\frac{1}{2}$ teaspoon ground fennel seeds
$\frac{1}{2}$ teaspoon toasted sesame seeds
$\frac{1}{2}$ teaspoon ground aniseed (optional)

In a small bowl combine all the ingredients and mix well. Store in an airtight container. Use to season grilled fish and chicken or bulgur, rice, and vegetable dishes.

Makes about $\frac{1}{4}$ cup

When the salt blossoms.
(Used to denote improbability.)

An olive press. From
Cunningham Geikie,
The Holy Land and
the Bible *(London,*
Cassell, 1891)

Cooking Fats

OLIVE OIL

"Olive oil is the pillar of family life."

Olive oil is the principal cooking fat of Syria, Lebanon, and Jordan. The region has been a major producer of high-quality olive oil for thousands of years and has been exporting it to other lands since Phoenician times. During the Middle Ages Syrian olive oil was considered without peer in the Islamic world.

In his book, *Bible Lands* (1875), the Reverend Henry J. van Lennep observes: "The oil derived from the olive . . . may indeed be regarded as one of the indispensable necessaries of life." Families often purchase a whole year's supply, which they store in a cool, dark place since heat and light have an adverse effect on its shelf life. Olive oil is traditionally used for cooking fish, for deep-frying vegetables, and, because it does not congeal, for salads and other dishes that are served chilled or at room temperature. During their religious fasts many Christians in the region subsist largely on vegetables and grains cooked in olive oil.

The most mellow and flavorful olive oil, and the kind generally preferred, is extra-virgin. When extracted from partially ripe olives, it is deep green in color and robustly fruity, especially if unfiltered. Although many people favor this full-bodied type for all dishes that call for olive oil, some find its taste too strong except as a salad dressing or condiment and use a lighter, golden oil that is milder in flavor for frying and sautéing. It is best to experiment with different extra-virgin olive oils and choose the ones that most appeal to your palate.

Olive oil is highly regarded not only for cooking but also for possessing healthful and medicinal qualities. It is applied to sprains, strains, and earaches and is sometimes taken as a laxative. It is even used as a skin lubricant: when an American journalist asked an attendant on the terrace of Beirut's fabled Hotel St. Georges for some suntan lotion back in the 1960s, he offered her a cruet of olive oil. Indeed, olive oil is considered an all-purpose remedy from cradle to old age. The following anecdote should erase any doubts about its curative powers:

> One of the eccentric characters of Duma[46] was Hajj Ibrahim, the Egyptian doctor, the impersonation of conceited ignorance. Nothing surprised him. He had heard it all before. . . . One day in the summer of 1858, the Hajj called in his usual pompous and affable style and requested the gift of some "journalat" or American newspapers. Supposing that he wished them for wrapping-paper, we gave him some copies of the New York *Weekly Tribune,* for which he expressed great gratitude. Some three weeks later, he came again, effusive with thanks, and said he could not express his obligation to us, and insisted that we go with him to his vineyard and eat fresh grapes and figs. On passing his house he obliged us to go in and take a cup of Arab coffee. As we entered he repeated his thanks for the papers so earnestly that we asked what use he had made of them. "Look here," said he, and he led us to an earthen five gallon jar in the corner of the room, in which he had dissolved the papers into a pulp and, adding olive oil, had fed them to his patients, and, said he, "The medicine works like a charm, nothing like it, I thank you with all my heart." We looked on solemnly, and then after coffee was served, went to his vineyard, where he loaded us down with fruit.
>
> Years after, in November, 1864, I was a guest of Mr. W. E. Dodge in New York, just after the reelection of Abraham Lincoln, and the Republican glorification dinner was at the Metropolitan Hotel. Mr. Dodge took me as his guest, and in the waiting-room he introduced me to Horace Greeley, editor of the New York *Tribune.* I told him of the above incident, and of the powerful medical efficacy of the *Tribune.* He shook with laughter and at length he inquired, "Do tell me, how did it act? Was it a cathartic or an emetic?" I was unable to answer, but judging from the vigorous health of the Dumaites, it must have been a tonic.[47]

OTHER OILS

Besides olive oil, other oils used for cooking include cottonseed, corn, sunflower, and safflower oils as well as sesame oil, which enjoyed great popularity during the Middle Ages. The early Arab culinary manuals also call for walnut, almond, and pistachio oils, which lend their distinctive flavors to a number of preparations, especially pastries and other sweet dishes. Walnut oil is traditionally used in the garnish for Circassian chicken (page 115, Note).

BUTTER

Both ordinary cow's butter (sometimes called "French butter") and clarified butter (*samna,* page 148) are used in the region. Before the advent of refrigeration, most of the butter produced was clarified in order to preserve it. *Samna* is usually made from the milk of sheep, goats, or buffalo rather than from cow's milk, resulting in a rich product with a stronger and more distinctive taste than the butter Westerners are used to. When cooking with *samna,* smaller amounts are needed than if one were using ordinary butter. Also, the former does not burn as easily at high temperatures as the latter, and it keeps for months. Although *samna* has traditionally been used in the preparation of dishes that are meant to be eaten hot, in recent years it has increasingly been replaced by ordinary butter, margarine, and vegetable oils. It continues, however, to be preferred for cooking rice as well as for making pastries such as baklava and *knafi.*

SHEEP'S TAIL FAT

Aliya, the highly flavorful rendered fat from the tails of Awassi sheep (a long-fleeced Asian breed), has been a principal cooking fat in Greater Syria since time immemorial. It formerly enjoyed tremendous popularity and was extensively employed in medieval Arab recipes. According to Russell, it was very often substituted for butter in eighteenth-century Aleppan kitchens, and Wilson notes that "Failing this Semaneh, the fat of the tail of the Oriental sheep is much used for cooking."[48] Today, however, *aliya* is only occasionally encountered, having generally given way to *samna,* ordinary butter, margarine, and oil.

∾

The world is a *tmag,* the smart person a knife. *(A)*
(*Tmag* is the Armenian word for "fat tail.")

∾

Qawarma

A centuries-old custom that was still being carried on by villagers during my years in Lebanon was to buy a fat-tailed lamb in the spring and force-feed it day and night with mulberry and grape leaves, wheat hulls, and bundles of grass. In late November the animal was slaughtered. The fat from the carcass and tail was melted down in a caldron (*dist*), and small pieces of the lean meat, well seasoned with salt and pepper, were fried in the hot fat. The fried meat and the fat were packed in earthenware crocks and sealed with clay. This rural product, called *qawarma* (a Middle Eastern equivalent of *confit*), would keep a whole year without spoiling, providing villagers with an economical and versatile winter food. Only a small amount was sufficient to impart a meaty flavor to a dish, and many people actually preferred its special taste to that of fresh meat in soups, stews, pilafs, and fillings for vegetables, savory pastries, and *kibbeh. Qawarma* could be substituted for oil or butter when frying eggs.

On the day the sheep was slaughtered, relatives and neighbors joined in the annual celebration that accompanied the making of *qawarma.* I occasionally had the good fortune to be invited to these feasts by village families in Shtora. As the *qawarma* cooked,

Providing for the winter. *From* National Geographic, *January, 1911*

we sampled a number of traditional dishes made from leftover parts of the sheep such as the brains, head, intestines, kidneys, liver, and other organs (in the Middle East variety meats are not looked down upon but are the recipients of a cook's best efforts). A favorite delicacy was *krush mahshiyya,* intestines stuffed with ground mutton, rice, chickpeas, onions, and seasonings, boiled and eaten in their own broth. Another was *ghamma* (tripe), small squares cut from the stomach, stuffed with spoonfuls of the same filling, pinched together, and sewn up at the edges and boiled. Some of the best lean meat was used to make *kibbeh nayya,* which the men enjoyed with glasses of *arak.* Meat from the head and legs was used to prepare *fatta* (page 207), while the bones of the sheep imparted their flavor to *hreesi* (page 135). What with numerous families slaughtering their sheep at this time of year, villagers could look forward to one feast after another!

Although all of these dishes continue to be eaten today, most people no longer make *qawarma* in the traditional manner. Instead they purchase only enough fat lamb or mutton from the butcher to prepare a small amount at a time.

Sausages and Dried Spiced Beef

Two types of sausages, *maqaniq* and *sujuk,* and dried spiced beef (*basterma*) are produced locally. *Maqaniq* is a dense, spicy, air-dried sausage made with ground lamb, beef, or pork seasoned with salt and spices. Pine nuts or white wine and a little vinegar are sometimes added. It is delicious fried in butter or grilled on skewers over charcoal. *Sujuk* is a highly spiced, air-dried sausage made with ground beef (or, occasionally, lamb

Armenians preparing basterma *near Van in Ottoman Turkey.* From National Geographic, *October 1915*

or a mixture of lamb and beef) seasoned with salt, spices, and, usually, garlic. It is excellent sliced, fried in butter, and served with eggs. It is also delicious grilled, preferably over charcoal.

Basterma is highly seasoned, air-dried beef, thickly coated with a paste consisting mainly of fenugreek, chili pepper, paprika, black pepper, cumin, and garlic, and dried again. It is available at Armenian and Greek groceries. The best *basterma* and *sujuk* are made by Armenians, who were also specialists in their manufacture in Ottoman Turkey; indeed, there are actually Armenian families named Bastermajian, which suggests that at one time they were engaged in the production of *basterma*. Our Armenian butcher in Shtora was a past master of the art. Thinly sliced, fried with farm-fresh eggs, and accompanied with flatbread and cups of hot tea, his *basterma* provided a hearty and satisfying winter meal. Thin slices of *basterma* are also good served as an appetizer with cheese, olives, and bread.

Alcoholic Beverages

In obedience to the teachings of the Koran, strict Muslims do not drink alcoholic beverages, nor do they eat foods prepared with them. Despite this injunction, alcohol is widely consumed and readily available in much of the region. Also, wines and spirits are occasionally used in cooking. Both beer and wine are locally produced and many people, including some Muslims, regard them as aids to digestion. It is not advisable, however, even to mention alcoholic beverages unless they are first offered by the host, for they can give serious offense, especially in some villages and tribal communities.

For more information on alcoholic beverages, see Chapter 17 and Historical Background.

Additional Information on Ingredients

Bulgur *(burghul):* Wheat grains that have been boiled, drained, dried, and then left whole or crushed into fine, medium, or coarse grades. The color of bulgur varies from light to dark brown depending on the type of wheat from which it is made. Generally, fine-grade bulgur is used for *kibbeh* and *tabbuleh.* Medium bulgur is sometimes utilized in salads, *kibbeh,* pilafs, and stuffings. Coarse bulgur is the usual choice for pilafs, as it is for soups, stews, and stuffings. Recipes calling for bulgur in this book specify which grade will be needed.

Bulgur can be eaten without being cooked but it must be soaked beforehand, as when making *tabbuleh.* This nutritious and inexpensive staple is available at Middle Eastern groceries, natural foods stores, and many supermarkets.

For additional information on bulgur, see page 245.

Carob Molasses (*dibs kharrub*): A dark syrup made from carob pods that is used in cakes, cookies, sweetmeats, and drinks. It has a taste reminiscent of caramel and is often mixed with *tahini* and spread on flatbread to be eaten for breakfast, as a snack, or for dessert. Available at Middle Eastern groceries.

Chickpeas (*hummus*): Dried chickpeas are pale tan or brown in color, $\frac{1}{4}$ to $\frac{1}{2}$ inch in diameter, and shaped like wrinkled hazelnuts. They possess an earthy, somewhat nutty flavor and figure in numerous dishes, from dips, salads, and stews to stuffed vegetables and pilafs. They are also roasted and eaten like peanuts (*qudami*) or roasted, coated with sugar, and eaten as a candy (*mulabbas*). Although chickpeas are available canned, freshly cooked dried chickpeas have a superior flavor and texture. Dried chickpeas are found at Middle Eastern groceries, while supermarkets are more likely to carry canned ones. Dried chickpeas must be soaked before cooking.

Fresh green chickpeas (*khadra malani*) are also eaten when in season.

Dibs: A kind of molasses produced from carob pods, dates, grapes, or pomegranates. Available at Middle Eastern groceries.

Fava Beans (*ful*): Also called broad beans. Two varieties are used: the larger *Vicia faba megalosperma* and the smaller *Vicia faba equina.* When very young and tender, fresh fava beans (*ful akhdar*) are shelled and eaten raw or cooked complete with their pods; mature beans, however, are shelled before being cooked or dried. Frozen beans, where available, may be substituted for fresh ones.

Dried fava beans are brown unless skinned and split (*ful majrush*), in which case they are pale cream. These beans are used to make *falafel*.

The small variety of fava beans (also called horse beans, Egyptian brown beans, or, in Arabic, *ful misri* or *ful baladi*) is dried and used to make *ful mudammas*.

Dried fava beans must be soaked before cooking.

A note of caution: Some people have an enzyme deficiency that causes them to experience a mild to severe allergic reaction if they eat fava beans or even inhale the pollen of the plant.

Filo (phyllo): Tissue-thin sheets of dough used in the preparation of many-layered pastries such as baklava. Filo can be bought fresh or frozen from Middle Eastern groceries, bakeries, and pastry shops, some specialty foods stores, and many supermarkets. It is available by the pound, wrapped in clear plastic in long, narrow packages, each one containing about twenty-five or more sheets, depending on the degree of thinness. Since the size of the sheets varies from brand to brand, the amount of butter and filling called for in the recipes should be adjusted accordingly.

It is best to use filo immediately after purchasing, although it will keep in the refrigerator for about a week. If, upon opening a newly purchased package of filo, you discover that the dough has become dry, do not use it; unless it is fresh, it will crumble and flake when you try to manipulate it.

When handling filo, it is important to work quickly but carefully to prevent the delicate sheets from drying out and breaking. Any portion of the dough that will not be used for a given recipe should be kept in the refrigerator, well sealed in its plastic container. Cover the pile of sheets to be used with a lightly dampened kitchen towel. Take from the pile only the sheet you need at a particular moment; keep the rest of the sheets covered.

Freek *(freeky):* Roasted and hulled green wheat grains. For more information, see page 246.

Grape Leaves (*warak inab*): These are used fresh or preserved. Fresh leaves are eaten with *tabbuleh*. Either fresh or preserved leaves can be used to make *mahshi* (see page 233), the fresh being preferred when available. The leaves should be picked in early summer when they are tender and abundant on the vines but are not too young. Most cooks, however, will need to use preserved leaves, which are sold in jars or cans at Middle Eastern groceries, specialty foods stores, and many supermarkets.

Grape Molasses (*dibs inab*): Concentrated (boiled-down) grape juice, available at Middle Eastern groceries. It is spread on flatbread, alone or mixed with *tahini,* and is also used in the preparation of sweets. For more information, see page 51.

Kishk: A powdery cereal of bulgur fermented with milk and yogurt, *kishk* is a highly nutritious rural staple. It was apparently quite common during medieval times. Al-Warraq includes recipes utilizing *kishk* in his culinary manual (among them one entitled "Syrian *Kishk*"), while the author of the *Wusla* lists what appear to be two recipes. The first, however, turns out to be only a short comment informing the reader that the recipe is being omitted since it is so well known! Recipes calling for *kishk* are also found in the Egyptian *Kanz*.

On his journey through the Hauran region of Syria, the nineteenth-century Swiss author Johann Ludwig Burckhardt observed that *kishk* was one of the two most common dishes of the people, who usually ate it with bread for breakfast.[49] He described two local versions, one using yogurt and the other, leaven and water, the process for making both otherwise being the same.

Kishk is prepared in the early fall when the wheat crop is harvested. Villagers make it by soaking quantities of medium or coarse bulgur in milk (or milk and yogurt) in large earthenware tubs covered with clean sheepskins and blankets, which keep the contents warm and allow it to ferment. Every morning for about ten days the coverings are removed and the mixture is thoroughly kneaded by hand. When fermentation is complete, the *kishk* is spread on a clean cloth to dry, usually on the flat roof of a house or in a sheltered, sunny spot on a veranda. As it dries it is rubbed with the hands every so often to remove lumps. When completely dry, it is rubbed again and put through a sieve. The resulting powder is packed into clean canvas bags or earthenware pots and stored in a dry place.

Kishk is used to thicken sauces and soups and in the preparation of a breakfast porridge flavored with minced onion and garlic that have been sautéed in a little *qawarma* (page 70). It is also used in some peasant salads, egg dishes, and savory fillings. As a rule, townspeople do not make their own *kishk* but purchase it ready-made from stores. In this country commercially prepared *kishk* is available at Middle Eastern groceries.[50]

The importance of *kishk* in the traditional diet is illustrated by such sayings as "The ravens quarreled over the *kishk* of the neighbors" (meaning that people have fought over something that does not belong to them) and "The ravens have agreed to eat up the *kishk* of the neighbors" (said of people who have agreed on evildoing).

Knafi: A batter made of flour and water that is passed through a sieve onto a heated roller drum, where it sets immediately and is then quickly removed. The resulting soft, white strands resemble vermicelli or shredded wheat. The preparation of this dough, which is used to make a pastry of the same name and for which there is no substitute, is usually the province of professionals. *Knafi* dough can be purchased by the pound at Middle Eastern groceries and pastry shops. If frozen, defrost thoroughly before using.

Lentils (*adas*): Brown lentils are the kind most commonly encountered in American supermarkets. There are also green lentils and a smaller orange red variety, sold in

Middle Eastern groceries. Lentils need no presoaking. Whole ones should be cooked until just tender, generally 20 to 25 minutes. If you intend to purée them, however, allow 30 to 35 minutes, although split red lentils (*adas majrush*) will require only 20 to 25 minutes. Lentils are used in soups, salads, and stews and are cooked with rice, bulgur, and noodles.

Mahlab: An unusual spice derived from the fragrant kernels of pits from pea-sized wild black cherries, the fruit of the perfumed or St. Lucia cherry tree (*Prunus mahalab*). *Mahlab* is sold at Middle Eastern groceries. For best results, pound the pale brown kernels in a mortar just before using to flavor sweet yeast breads, pastries, and cookies.

Mastic (*mistki, mustaka, mastaka*): A sweet, somewhat licorice-flavored resin from the mastic (lentisk) tree (*Pistacia lentiscus*). Although this small evergreen is found in Lebanon and Jordan, most of the world's supply comes from the Greek island of Chios. Mastic is sold at Middle Eastern groceries in the form of cream-colored pellets, which must be pulverized with a mortar and pestle before using. *It should not be confused with gum arabic,* which is secreted from acacia trees found in Egypt and the Sudan. Mastic is used to flavor soups, stews, puddings, ice cream, sweet breads, candies, and preserves. Softened with a little candle wax, it has long been used as a chewing gum.

Middle Eastern (or Near Eastern) Red Pepper: This term refers to a number of dried ground red peppers, hotter than paprika but milder than cayenne, that come from such towns as Aleppo in northern Syria and Gaziantep, Maraş, and Urfa in southeastern Turkey. Aleppo pepper (*filfil ahmar halabi*), which is the mildest and very flavorful, is the kind most often carried at Middle Eastern groceries. Middle Eastern red pepper is used in appetizers, soups, sauces, stuffings, pilafs, *kibbeh,* and meat, poultry, fish, and vegetable dishes. A combination of 4 parts sweet paprika and 1 part ground hot red pepper flakes makes an acceptable substitute.

Middle Eastern red peppers, especially those from Maraş and Aleppo, as well as pistachios from both Gaziantep and Aleppo were among the foodstuffs handled by my father's family, who were engaged in the caravan trade between southeastern Anatolia and Beirut.

Mlukhiyya: A plant, Jew's mallow (*Corchorus olitorius*), whose green, slightly serrated leaves possess the viscous properties of okra but taste somewhat like sorrel or spinach. Although *mlukhiyya* is sometimes cooked and served as a vegetable dish, it is most often employed in the preparation of a gelatinous sauce for chicken or meat. When in season, fresh *mlukhiyya* is plentiful and inexpensive in the eastern Mediterranean; however, it is much harder to find here. You can grow your own *mlukhiyya* from seed. Dried and (sometimes) frozen *mlukhiyya* leaves are available at Middle Eastern groceries. For more information, see page 188.

Nigella (*habbat al-barakah, habbat al-sauda*): A small, black aromatic seed (*Nigella sativa*) shaped like a tiny teardrop. It is often mistakenly called black caraway, black cumin, black onion seed, or black sesame; however, it is unrelated to any of these save for the fact that it does resemble an onion seed. Nigella is available at Middle Eastern and Indian groceries (at the latter it may be found under the name of *kalonji*). It is used on yeast breads and as a flavoring for cheese.

Orange Flower Water (*ma' al-zahr*): Also known as orange blossom water. This is the diluted form of the fragrant essence distilled from the blossoms of the bitter (Seville) orange tree. It is used mainly to flavor and perfume syrups, beverages, confections, and pastries, puddings, and other desserts. Orange flower water is a specialty of the southern Lebanese town of Sidon, whose orange groves have been celebrated for centuries. Various brands from Lebanon and France are available here. You can buy orange flower water at Middle Eastern groceries, specialty foods stores, and some supermarkets. Concentrated orange flower essence, sold at pharmacies, is much stronger; use only drops instead of the teaspoons or tablespoons given in recipes.

Purslane (*baqla, farfahin*): A trailing plant having small yellow flowers, reddish stems, and fleshy, piquant-tasting leaves that are used in salads, stews, and in fillings for savory pastries. Purslane is often found growing wild in gardens. It is sometimes available in farmers' markets and supermarkets.

Rose Water (*ma' al-ward*): The diluted form of the fragrant essence distilled from rose petals, especially those of the highly scented pink damask rose. It is used to flavor and perfume syrups, beverages, confections, and pastries, puddings, and other desserts. Variety meats such as the head, feet, and tripe of sheep are rubbed with rose water after cleaning to eliminate odor. Good Lebanese and French brands are available at Middle Eastern groceries, specialty foods stores, and some supermarkets. Rose essence, which is far more concentrated, is sold at pharmacies; use only drops rather than the teaspoons or tablespoons specified in recipes.

Safflower (*usfur, iqdi safra*): Although this plant is best known for the oil produced from its seeds, its orange flowers are used as an inexpensive substitute for saffron, hence the names "poor man's saffron," "false saffron," and "bastard saffron," which are frequently used to describe it. Safflower lacks saffron's flavor and aroma and is therefore employed mainly for visual effect. It is used to color rice and is an ingredient in *sfuf*, a cake that often contains semolina and pine nuts.

Saffron (*za'faran*): A spice consisting of the dried stigmas of a type of crocus. It has been prized in the region since antiquity for its delicate flavor and aroma as well as for the exquisite yellow color it imparts to food. Saffron is extremely expensive; it must be harvested by hand, and several thousand stigmas are required to produce just one ounce.

When recipes call for saffron, use only the genuine article; avoid cheaper substitutes such as turmeric, Mexican safflower, or yellow vegetable coloring. Purchase the orange red threads rather than the powder; stored in a dark, dry place away from heat and cold, they can keep for several years. Pound the threads as needed in a mortar before steeping in a warm liquid. Saffron is used chiefly in fish stews, stuffings for meat, poultry, and vegetable dishes, and rice pilafs.

Salep (*sahlab*): A powder made from the dried tubers of various species of orchids. Salep has a gelatinous quality and is used in the preparation of a warming winter beverage and of ice cream. In addition to local salep (*sahlab baladi*), a Turkish import (*sahlab stambuli*), which is grayish white in color and very fine in texture, is also used in the region. Unfortunately, pure, unadulterated salep is not easy to find and is very expensive.

Semolina (*smeed*): A granulated cream-colored meal with high gluten content, made from the hearts of durum wheat berries. Fine-grain semolina flour is widely employed in the manufacture of bread and pasta, while a more coarse-textured grain is used in the preparation of cookies, cakes, and puddings. Regular (not quick-cooking or instant) farina or cream of wheat, though not made from durum wheat and somewhat different in taste and texture, may sometimes be substituted for semolina. You can find semolina at Greek, Italian, and Middle Eastern groceries and at natural foods stores; farina is available at supermarkets.

Sesame Seeds (*simsim*): The small, flat, pale cream-colored seeds of a plant known in the Middle East since earliest recorded history. Used whole, they flavor and decorate breads, cookies, and confections. They can also constitute one of the ingredients in the seasoning blend known as *za'atar*. Ground, the seeds are used to make *tahini* paste and the sweetmeat halva. Oil extracted from the seeds is also employed in cooking. Lightly toasting the seeds before using brings out their flavor. Although you can buy sesame seeds at supermarkets, they are usually less expensive at Middle Eastern and Asian groceries. They are also available at natural foods stores.

To toast sesame seeds: In a heavy skillet toast sesame seeds over moderate heat, stirring frequently, about 5 minutes or until golden. Alternatively, spread seeds in a pie pan and toast in a preheated 325°F oven, stirring occasionally, 10 to 15 minutes or until golden.

Skinless Whole-Grain Wheat (*qamh*): Whole wheat grains or kernels whose hulls have been removed. Available at Middle Eastern groceries, natural foods stores, and some supermarkets. For more information, see chapter 11.

Soapwort (*shirsh halawi, 'erq halawa, al-sabuniyya al-makhzaniyya*): A flowering plant, *Saponaria officinalis,* that is also known as "bouncing Bet." The dried root of this plant, which can occasionally be found at some Middle Eastern groceries, is a source of saponin, which foams up and expands when the root is soaked in water, boiled, and the liquid then agitated. Soapwort root is employed in the preparation of such confections as halva and snowy white *natif* cream, which is used as the topping for *karabij halab* (page 345).

Soapwort root should not be confused with soapbark (*Quillaja saponaria*), a tree of western South America. Although the latter is not indigenous to the Arab world, its bark, often referred to as *bois de Panama,* is also a source of saponin and can be used in place of soapwort.

Sumac (*summaq*): The berries that grow in clusters on a nonpoisonous Asian species of the sumac shrub, *Rhus coriaria.* Sumac has a lemony, woodsy taste. It is available dried, either whole or ground, at many Middle Eastern groceries and some spice shops. Whole dried berries, which are dark reddish purple in color, can be crushed and steeped in water to extract their essence. The resulting infusion, which has an astringent taste, is strained and the sumac water is used in cooking as a substitute for lemon juice. Ground sumac is used to lend a sour note to salads (such as *fattush,* page 122), sauces, fried eggs, fish, poultry, and meat dishes and to fillings for savory pastries, vegetables, and *kibbeh.* In addition, it is blended with other ingredients to make *za'atar.*

Tahini (also called *tahina,* from the verb *tahana,* "to grind"): An oily, nutty-flavored paste that results from crushing toasted sesame seeds. *Tahini* is used in dips and sauces as well as in the popular confection halva. It is also combined with carob, date, or grape *dibs* to make a spread for flatbread. *Tahini* is available at Middle Eastern groceries, natural foods stores, and some supermarkets. It can vary in color from beige to camel; the longer the sesame seeds are toasted, the darker the shade and the stronger the sesame flavor. Try a number of different brands and choose the one you like best.

Since *tahini* separates on standing, it will require blending before use. Placing unopened cans upside-down for several days will make blending easier. Store opened *tahini* tightly covered in the refrigerator. It will keep for a long time.

Tamarind (*tamar hindi*): A tropical tree that produces bean-shaped pods with hard, inedible seeds embedded in an edible but intensely acid-flavored pulp that tastes somewhat like an extremely sour prune. Tamarind comes in several forms: pods, compressed bricks or cakes, and, most conveniently, a pure stabilized "instant" concentrate sold in jars. Both bricks and concentrate can be purchased salted and unsalted: use the unsalted varieties. Store jars of instant concentrate in the refrigerator; freeze pods and compressed bricks.

Tamarind pods and bricks must be soaked until soft and then strained to extract their liquid for use in recipes. The concentrate can be diluted in hot water. When mixed with a little sugar, tamarind lends an appealing sweet-tart flavor to dishes. Tamarind is utilized in a number of dishes, including some meat stews and stuffed vegetables. It is also made into a tart or sweet syrup (the former can be substituted for tamarind concentrate). Tamarind can be found at Middle Eastern, Indian, and Asian markets.

Truffle (*kama*): See page 272.

Verjuice (*'asir al-hisrim*): The acidic juice pressed from unripe grapes. It is used to add tartness to stews and other dishes, salad dressings, and sauces.

Za'atar: (1) The Arabic name for thyme and other herbs such as hyssop (*Origanum maru* or *O. syriacum*) and goat's thyme (*Satureja thymbra*, a species of savory). (2) A seasoning blend that varies in its components from cook to cook and brand to brand. It is based on sumac and dried thyme, often incorporates sesame seeds, and may include hyssop or other herbs and spices. Mixed with extra-virgin olive oil, it is frequently eaten as a dip or spread on flatbread, or the bread itself may be dunked in the oil and then dipped in *za'atar*. Flatbread, olive oil, and *za'atar* are often eaten at breakfast along with olives and *labna*. Another popular choice for breakfast is *Za'atar* Bread (page 316). *Za'atar* makes a delicious seasoning for feta cheese and tomatoes and is also good sprinkled on chicken before grilling or roasting.

The quality of *za'atar* can vary greatly, some brands being so poor as to be inedible. Both Syrian and Jordanian blends are available at Middle Eastern groceries. The former is brownish in color; the latter is dark green.

When purchasing fresh thyme from an Arab grocer, one always specifies *za'atar akhdar* (green thyme).

The Modern Kitchen

A manqal, *or charcoal brazier.* *From Henry J. van Lennep,*
Bible Lands: Their Modern Customs and Manners Illustrative of Scripture *(New York, Harper, 1875)*

The ladle will bring out only what is in the pot.

In the Lebanon of my childhood kitchens were as a rule quite unpretentious. Although many city dwellers furnished their homes with modern appliances, generally speaking, kitchens throughout the eastern Mediterranean tended to contain a minimum of equipment. Electric toasters, coffeemakers, beaters, blenders, refrigerators, and ovens were often conspicuous by their absence. The lack of time- and labor-saving devices was offset by the availability of many hands to assist with the preparation of food; in those years servants were far more affordable than they are today. Also, several generations of families frequently lived together in an extended unit, with mothers, daughters, grandmothers, and aunts all sharing the cooking chores. Even in this tradition-based society, however, times have been changing. Cheap domestic help has become less easy to come by, and fewer people are willing to chop, pound, and knead for hours on end day after day. Like their Western counterparts, Middle Eastern cooks have learned to appreciate modern gadgets, simplified procedures, and utensils that require little maintenance.

For most of this century cooking was usually done on charcoal braziers and portable kerosene Primus stoves (*babur*s). It is only in the recent past that ovens have become common in homes. Even so, some dishes continue to be sent to the town oven, whose steady, intense heat produces a superior result. Such ovens were formerly heated with wood; nowadays they are more likely to be fired by gas or oil.

By the 1950s the time-honored pots and pans of tinned brass or copper were being increasingly replaced by less expensive and easier-to-take-care-of aluminum cookware imported from the West. Many urbanites, aware of the far better quality of the former, were avidly collecting them from peasant households, which were eagerly switching to the latter. Cooking pots such as the *tanjara* are now widely available in aluminum or other materials.

The introduction of new appliances and utensils has not entirely supplanted the traditional cooking equipment. The Middle East not being a society that throws things away, the old often coexists with the new, particularly in the countryside. Straw trays, mortars and pestles, and coffee mills continue to be utilized. The arrival of the refrigerator has not necessarily abolished the use of the earthenware *ibriq* (page 380) for storing drinking water, nor has it consigned its predecessor, the *namliyya* (a cupboard for preserved foods) to oblivion; this last has frequently found new life as a storage cupboard for dishware. Similarly, the venerable *dist* continues to be employed along with the pressure cooker for making preserves. In Shtora we used our *dist* for making grape molasses, tomato paste, and bulgur.

The average American kitchen will have almost all the equipment needed to prepare the recipes in this book. One appliance that will greatly reduce drudgery is a food processor. Other useful items, some of which you may already have, are listed below.

An enameled cast-iron casserole with a tight-fitting lid.

Three heavy cast-iron or tin-lined copper skillets (small, medium, and large) with covers and flameproof handles.

A glazed earthenware casserole with a tight-fitting lid.

A round or oval glazed earthenware baking dish.

A rectangular glazed earthenware baking dish.

Several wooden spoons.

A brass mortar and pestle for crushing such ingredients as nuts, spices, and garlic.

A special corer (*minqara*) for hollowing out zucchini, eggplants, and cucumbers for *mahshi.*

Metal skewers for broiling cubed meat (shish kebab) or ground meat (*kafta alla shish;* use flat-bladed skewers for ground meat).

A cylindrical coffee mill made of chased brass.

A long-handled, narrow-necked coffeepot (Arabic *rakwi,* Turkish *jezve*) made of tin-lined brass or enamelware, the four- to six-cup size being the most useful (essential for making Turkish coffee).

A set of very small cups for Turkish coffee.

Other attractive options include:

A tin-lined copper pan with several round depressions for making Arab omelets (*ijjas*).

A convex iron plate (*saaj*) for baking mountain bread.

A *falafel* scoop.

Flat or dome-shaped wooden molds with handles (*tabis*) imprinted with various designs for shaping *ma'mul* (page 342).

∾

There are many who make a jug, but few who put a handle on it. (*A*)

∾

A Tale of Cooking Pots

One day Joha borrowed a large *tanjara* (copper pot) from a neighbor. On the following day he returned it together with a brand-new smaller pot placed inside, saying, "My dear neighbor, your *tanjara* gave birth to a young one during the night." Despite the neighbor's incredulity, Joha refused to take back the small pot, declaring that it belonged to its parent and that it would be cruel to separate an infant from its mother. After much protestation the neighbor, concluding that Joha had gone mad, decided to humor him and accept the small *tanjara*. A few days later Joha borrowed a large and expensive *dist* (caldron) from his neighbor. Instead of returning it, however, he carried it off to another town and sold it. Not hearing from Joha for over a week, the neighbor went to his house to reclaim the *dist*. "Alas," said Joha, "I regret that I cannot return your pot, for it has unfortunately died and been devoured by hyenas." "What!" roared the neighbor, "Do you think I am foolish enough to fall for such a story?" "Well now, that's strange," replied Joha. "You allowed yourself to believe that your *tanjara* gave birth to a baby. Why, then, do you find it incredulous that your *dist*, which is simply a grown-up *tanjara*, should die?"[1]

A Tradition of Hospitality

A guest chamber. *From Edward William Lane,* An Account of the Manners and Customs of the Modern Egyptians *(London, John Murray, 1836)*

THERE IS A NATIVE DIGNITY in [the Arabs'] address and deportment, which will astonish those who have seen the awkward vulgarity of the lower classes in some more favored lands. Whether we enter the tent of the *Bedawy* or the cottage of the *fellah,* we are received with an ease and courtesy that would not disgrace a palace.[1]

Since very ancient times travelers in the Syrian Desert have been provided for by the laws of hospitality. It is said that anyone can stop at any Beduin's tent and be assured of a gracious reception, for its owner will automatically be obligated to furnish accommodation and protection to the best of his ability for three successive days and nights. Being a proper host is a matter of utmost honor; to be otherwise would bring shame not only upon an individual but upon his whole family. Beduin etiquette dictates that the host not dine with his guests but remain standing ready to wait on them, delaying his own meal until after they have finished. This practice is not always strictly observed, however. Rather than stand apart, a host may instead sit with his guests or share a beverage with them.

Over the centuries the spirit of hospitality has thrived in settled communities as well. During the Middle Ages hospices offered travelers free food and shelter. Both al-Muqaddasi and Nasir-i-Khusrau speak of a public guest house in the Sanctuary at Hebron where every day up to five hundred people were welcomed, each being presented with a dish of lentils cooked in olive oil, a loaf of bread weighing about three pounds, and some olives and raisins.[2] Ibn Battuta tells us of another religious house, located in the central Bekaa, "at which food is provided for all who come and go."[3]

In Ottoman times it was customary for many villages to have a guest house (*madafa* or *manzal*), maintained at public expense, where meals and bedding were provided gratis to any traveler. It was unthinkable for a visitor to have to buy food; such a breach of hospitality would have been unforgivable and would have brought disgrace upon a village. Travelers were also welcome in private homes:

If you have no tent, and be not near a khan, enter a village, choose out the best house you see, and you will hardly fail to meet with an hospitable reception at the hands of the simple

Native house on Mount Lebanon. *From William McClure Thomson,* The Land and the Book, *vol. 2 (New York, Harper, 1882)*

and kind-hearted inmates. . . . Often, as travelers pass before a garden, the children run out to them with baskets of figs or grapes, pressing them to eat of the contents, but unwilling to accept of any remuneration. When you enter a house, you will be treated, perhaps, with excellent wine of a rich flavour. . . . At any rate, they will set before you such fare as they have—bread, fruit, and the produce of their dairy, and season it with a hearty welcome. They will assist you to prepare your coffee, and to drink it afterwards, and will assign you a place where you may spread your carpet, and rest till morning blushes.[4]

To visit a home in Syria, Lebanon, and Jordan today is to bask in the full glow of Middle Eastern hospitality. Guests are met at the door with profuse welcoming greetings of "*Ahlan wa sahlan*" and are immediately made to feel that their presence is cause for happiness and celebration. When a host says "*bayti, baytak*" ("my home is your home"), he or she really means it. Visitors are never asked if they would like something to eat. Food and drink are always provided as a matter of course with as much generosity as the host can afford.[5] It is considered good manners for guests to refuse politely at first and for the host to make repeated offers; then guests should graciously accept, though with a certain show of reluctance.

An invitation to a meal usually means a lavish spread, the best the host can provide. In accordance with the well-known Arab saying, "The food equals the affection," hosts will encourage their guests to eat copiously, offering them the best morsels of food, while

The Baruk River and villages. *From John Carne,* Syria, the Holy Land, Asia Minor, &c., *vol. 2 (London, Fisher, Son, 1836)*

guests in turn will try to eat enough to satisfy their hosts, for the measure of their regard for them is equated with the amount of food they consume. Wise guests will pursue the strategy of pleasing their hosts by protesting politely *before* becoming full! That way they will still have enough room to allow themselves to be persuaded to further efforts by their hosts, who will be certain to urge them on enthusiastically.

The tradition of a host offering choice morsels of food to a guest figures prominently in one of the most far-reaching nuptial alliances in Lebanese history. During the period of the Crusades the Maʿns, masters of the Shuf region of the Lebanon Mountains, invited the Shihabs, newly arrived in the Anti-Lebanon, to a celebration honoring the latter's recent military success against the Franks. The two families and their retainers met at the source of the Baruk River, where they spent three days feasting and rejoicing. Churchill relates an incident that occurred on the second day:

> It had been intimated to the Shehaabs, that a nuptial alliance with the Maans would be a worthy consummation of their newly-sprung-up friendship and intimacy. . . . The daughter of the Emir Yoonis Maan was described to be in every way worthy of a suitor's regard. . . . Her name was Tyiby, which is the Arabic expression for "good." It was resolved, that the Emir Mahommed . . . should sue for her hand. Circumstances occurred which accelerated, and probably changed, the contemplated mode of proposal.
>
> At the festive board, the Emir Yoonis Maan, performing an act which, in Oriental manners, is a distinguished mark of honour and politeness, took a piece of meat between his

fingers, and presented it to the Emir Mahommed, who sat next to him, saying to him at the same time, "Enti tyib," or "You are good." The Emir promptly and happily retorted, "If I am good, I should have the good." The play upon the words was at once perceived, and the hint cordially and pleasantly taken. "So be it, Mahommed," said the Emir Yoonis, "the good shall be given to you." The happy suitor immediately rose and kissed the hands of his host, in grateful acknowledgment; and this act of homage and obeisance being graciously accepted, was a proof to the assembled guests, that the family compact was completed.[6]

The full consequences of this alliance were not experienced by the Shihabs for another five hundred years, when on the extinction of the Maʿn dynasty they became the rulers of Lebanon under the suzerainty of the Ottomans.

The house is small, but the heart is big.

Meals and Menus

Ablutions after a midday meal. *From Charles William Wilson, ed.,* Picturesque Palestine, Sinai and Egypt, *vol. 2 (New York, D. Appleton, 1883)*

IT IS DIFFICULT TO GENERALIZE about diet and meals in Syria, Lebanon, and Jordan since the various social classes differ considerably in the timing and composition of their daily repasts and in the manner in which they are taken. All classes eat one principal meal a day. For some people this occurs at midday, while for others it takes place in the evening. In the Beirut of my childhood, lunch, usually eaten between 12:30 and 2:00 P.M., was the main meal of the day for the majority of the population. In rural areas, however, dinner was frequently the most substantial meal. During the agricultural season it was normally eaten at sunset after the villagers returned from working in their fields. Often the evening meal was also the main one for the affluent urban class, who took it between 9:00 and 10:00 P.M. A member of this class who preferred to eat at an earlier hour would sometimes affect a tone of humility and say: "I am still a peasant; I eat at sunset."

For people of modest means the principal meal generally consists of one main dish. In well-to-do households, on the other hand, it features one or more main dishes along with several subsidiary ones, with individual tastes being accommodated. This tolerance for personal preferences in food is the reason why a mother who wants to play the game of "we are rich" will proudly enumerate all the dishes that her son dislikes, which can add up to an impressive list. It should be noted that this game involves only sons, for a daughter who is hard to please may well experience difficulty in marriage.

Although Western travelers in Ottoman Syria have described morning meals of herculean proportions, breakfast in this part of the world has usually been a simple affair consisting of bread, olives, local white cheese, yogurt cheese (*labna*) with olive oil and perhaps *za'atar*, and coffee or tea. Today many people are still content with this traditional Arab breakfast. For others the morning meal may also include such items as eggs, pancakes, raw or cooked vegetables or meat, savory or sweet pastries, honey, grape molasses, jam, butter, and fruit. In winter a warming soup is sometimes served. Breakfast can vary somewhat from region to region. For example, in Lebanon around Hasbayya, where olive trees abound, it often consists mainly of bread eaten with olives or dipped in olive oil. At Rashayya, famous for its grape molasses and dairy products, the morning meal is certain to include *dibs* and *labna*. In the Baalbek area cheese, *labna*, honey, and apricots, all local specialties, frequently appear at breakfast. Cheese and *labna*, accompanied with cucumbers and tomatoes or fresh fruit (especially grapes, melons, pears, and figs), are also popular in the Zahleh-Shtora region. Many people in Beirut and Tripoli like to stop at a *pâtisserie* on their way to work to breakfast on warm *knafi bi jibn*, perhaps enclosed in *ka'k bi simsim* (sesame bread). Another favorite is *manaqish bi za'atar*, eaten hot out of the baker's oven. Other common choices for breakfast include *hummus bi tahini* and *ful mudammas*.

A typical family lunch or dinner features a substantial dish composed of meat and grains or pasta, or of meat, vegetables, and grains. This is nearly always accompanied with a salad and, perhaps, yogurt. Bread, olives, pickles, and crudités are present on the table throughout the meal, which usually ends with fresh fruit.

A light family lunch or supper often consists of a main course of one or more vegetables cooked in olive oil, an omelet, a savory pastry, raw *kibbeh*, a hearty soup in winter, or a salad such as *tabbuleh* in summer. This is supplemented with bread, crudités, local white cheese, *labna*, and fruit.

A company meal will feature either an extensive *mazza* or, more likely, two or more main dishes such as a meat and vegetable stew, stuffed vegetables, *kibbeh*, and stuffed lamb or chicken accompanied with various appetizers and salads. For dessert there will be baklava, *knafi*, or other pastries and a basket of fruit.

It should be mentioned that cold water is present at every meal, no matter what other beverages are offered. Among the Christian population, particularly in Lebanon, wine is often served at lunch and/or dinner, and, as we have seen, coffee traditionally concludes a meal or makes its appearance following it.

∾

Have lunch and lie down; have supper and take a walk.
(An example of advice for good health.)

∾

The Manner of Serving and Eating a Meal

After pouring down the arrack and swallowing about fifty different kinds of hors d'oeuvres—for, after all, Cousin Charlotte did say that there was nothing for dinner, potluck, you know, a snack, a sandwich—you are led to a buffet which looks as though it could feed the whole population of Lebanon. And you also remember that it is going to look very bad if you don't have two helpings of everything. Finally, you have coffee and indigestion, but Cousin Charlotte says that the next time you come, she'll have a proper dinner for you.[1]

The way in which food is served and eaten varies widely, from the completely westernized at one end to the traditional Arab, which has remained essentially unchanged for many centuries, at the other. In the Beirut of my childhood, where French influence was strong, many people observed Western dining habits, as they do today. A company dinner in an affluent household would begin with cocktails and hors d'oeuvres offered in the living room. The meal itself would be served in the dining room on a conventional table spread with a cloth, with individual serving plates, cutlery, glassware, and napkins as part of the table appointments. The menu would most likely consist of both Western and Middle Eastern dishes presented in an orderly succession of courses. One or more maids would serve the food to diners, offering it first to guests. French or American coffee would often be served at the end of a meal, to be followed later in the evening by Turkish coffee or tea and pastries in the living room.

At parties the food was frequently served buffet style from a groaning table that more often than not stretched the entire length of the dining room. Guests were repeatedly urged to help themselves to the multitude of dishes and usually ate standing up, valiantly trying to do justice to the vast replenishments that would be continuously arriving.

Before partaking of a meal presented in the traditional Arab manner, guests are first received in a different room from the one in which the meal is to be served, where their hands are ceremoniously washed. Upon adjourning to the dining area everyone sits on low sofas or cushions around one or more large ornamented circular copper, brass, or silver trays set on low wooden stands or folding wooden legs. Grace is said by all before beginning to eat. Unlike the multi-course Western meal, which is served in various stages, all the dishes are placed on trays at the outset, and diners take what they wish in whatever order they prefer. There are no table implements; instead the food is eaten with the right hand, preferably with the first three fingers, although all five may be used if the food is rather soft in consistency, such as a pilaf of rice or bulgur. Pieces of folded flatbread are frequently employed to scoop food from the communal dishes and to convey it to the mouth. Certain rules of etiquette are carefully observed by both host and guests. It is usual for the host to offer particularly choice morsels of food to the most important guest and for diners to show the same consideration to their neighbors. Every effort is made to create an atmosphere of politeness, friendliness, and courtesy. The food itself is treated with respect, and many compliments are made on the excellence of its preparation. Upon the completion of the meal everyone utters "To God be thanks." Trays and their stands are then removed, and the party retires for another hand-washing ritual, after which it is time to enjoy coffee, tea, or one followed by the other along with conversation.

People, particularly in the countryside, sometimes take their meals sitting on the floor. The food is presented on a low round table (*tabliyya*), which is carried into the dining area with the various dishes already arranged on it. Alternatively, dishes of food may be brought to diners on a metal or plaited straw tray that is placed over a colorful carpet on the floor, or the dishes may be set on a large cloth spread over the

A party at dinner or supper. From Edward William Lane, An Account of the Manners and Customs of the Modern Egyptians *(London, John Murray, 1836)*

carpet. In some areas where old customs still prevail, men and women eat separately, the women often taking their meals along with the small children after the men have finished. This practice, however, is generally much less common today.

> The Lebanese would rather have a week of leftovers than think anyone wanted one more bite of anything.[2]

Menu Suggestions

BREAKFAST

Traditional Arab Breakfast

Akkawi or Other White Cheese
Middle Eastern Black Olives
Pita Bread or Mountain Bread
Tea or Coffee

Optional Additions

Yogurt Cheese
Za'atar
Extra-Virgin Olive Oil
Fried or Scrambled Eggs
Fresh Fruit

~

Cantaloupe or Persian Melon
Yogurt Cheese
Dried Fig Preserves, Quince Preserves, or
    Sour Cherry Jam
Pita Bread or Mountain Bread
Tea

~

Fresh Strawberries
Semolina Pudding
Tea

~

Grapes or Honeydew
Fried Eggs with Cheese
Slices of Pan-Fried or Broiled *Maqaniq,*
    Sujuk, or Canadian Bacon
Pita Bread or Mountain Bread
Seville Orange Marmalade or Apricot Jam
Tea

~

Chilled Fresh Orange Juice
Yogurt Pancakes
Pomegranate Syrup or Sour Cherry Syrup
Crisp Bacon
Sautéed Quinces or Sautéed Apples
Tea or Coffee

LUNCHEON

Meat or Cheese Turnovers
Lentil Soup with Swiss Chard and Potatoes
Green Cabbage and Tomato Salad with
    Lemon Dressing
Baked Stuffed Apples
Coffee

~

Yogurt Cheese and Red Pepper Dip
Kibbeh Omelet
Arugula, Cucumber, and Tomato Salad with
    Mint Dressing
Dried Fruit Compote
Coffee

~

Baked Fish with Walnut Stuffing
Rice with Spinach
Mixed Greens, Red Onion, and Tomatoes
    with Lemon Dressing
Pomegranate Ice
Butter Cookies
Coffee

~

Artichokes with Fava Beans
Chicken and Rice
Romaine, Cucumber, and Tomato Salad with
    Mint Dressing
Fresh Fruit Compote
Coffee

~

Chickpea and Tahini Dip
Eggplants Stuffed with Meat
Rice with Vermicelli
Cucumber and Yogurt Salad Variation
Quince Compote
Sesame Cookies
Coffee

~

Stuffed Apricots
Plain Rice or Bulgur Pilaf
Mixed Green Salad with Mint Dressing
Wedding Cookies
Coffee

DINNER

Filo Pastry Triangles with Cheese Filling
Baked Fish with Tomato Sauce
Saffron Rice
Spinach Salad with Lemon Dressing
Orange Coconut Cake
Coffee

~

Chickpea and Tahini Dip with Red Pepper
    Paste
Musakhan
Mixed Greens, Tomatoes, and Cucumbers
    with Mint Dressing
Fresh Fruit Compote
Coffee

~

Cheese Dip with Toasted Sesame Seeds
Lamb and Green Bean Stew
Rice with Vermicelli or Bulgur Pilaf with
    Vermicelli
Mixed Vegetable Salad Variation
Apricot Dessert
Almond Cookies
Coffee

~

Cherry or Plum Tomatoes, Cucumber Cups,
    and Romaine Hearts Filled with Tabbuleh
Meat Dumplings in Yogurt
Saffron Rice or Plain Rice
Beet Salad with Pomegranate Dressing
Stuffed Cookies with Nut Filling
Coffee

~

Damascus-Style Cheese Dip with Toasted
    Sesame Seeds and Nigella
Lamb Stew with Dried Apricots and Prunes
Saffron Rice with Nuts
Mixed Green Salad with Lemon Dressing
Stuffed Cookies with Natif Cream
Coffee

~

Yogurt Cheese and Red Pepper Dip
Lamb, Eggplant, and Rice Mold

Cucumber and Tomato Salad with Mint
    Dressing
Orange Cake with Pomegranate Syrup
Coffee

～

Herbed Yogurt Cheese
Kibbeh in a Tray
Hot Stuffed Grape Leaves or Hot Stuffed
    Cabbage Leaves
Mixed Vegetable Salad
Shredded Pastry with Nut Filling
Coffee

～

Filo Pastry Triangles with Meat Filling
Stuffed Prunes with Oranges
Plain Rice or Saffron Rice
Spinach and Red Onion Salad with Lemon
    Dressing
Shredded Pastry with Cheese Filling
Coffee

Special Occasion Dinner

Middle Eastern Black Olives
Chickpea and Tahini Dip with Red Pepper
    Paste
Tabbuleh
Cold Stuffed Grape Leaves
Eggplant with Pomegranate Sauce
Filo Pastry Triangles with Cheese Filling
Fried Stuffed Kibbeh
Stuffed Turkey
Red Cabbage with Quince or Apple
Baklava
Fresh Fruit
Coffee

A MAZZA PARTY

Toasted Almonds
Roasted Pistachios
Assorted Middle Eastern Olives
Crudités

～

Work with many, eat with few. (A)

～

Chickpea and Tahini Dip
Eggplant and Tahini Dip
Herbed Yogurt Cheese
Red Pepper and Walnut Dip with
    Pomegranate
Pita Bread
Tabbuleh
Fattush
Ful Mudammas
Cold Stuffed Grape Leaves
Falafel
Fried Stuffed Kibbeh
Spinach Pies
Meat Turnovers or Filo Pastry Triangles
Arak, Beer, Wine

BARBECUE

Chickpea and Tahini Dip
Chicken, Pepper, and Tomato Kebabs or
    Grilled Skewered Lamb and Vegetables
Roasted Corn on the Cob
Tabbuleh
Beer, Iced Tea
Watermelon Wedges
Orange Coconut Cake
Coffee

PICNIC

Assorted Middle Eastern Olives
Yogurt Cheese and Red Pepper Dip
Spicy Chickpea and Tahini Dip
Cold Stuffed Grape Leaves or Cold Stuffed
    Swiss Chard Leaves
Fried Stuffed Kibbeh
Open-Faced Meat Pies
Tabbuleh
Cantaloupe or Honeydew Wedges and
    Grapes
Stuffed Cookies with Date Filling
Sesame Cookies
Beer, Lemonade, Iced Tea

CHAPTER 1
Appetizers

Syrian ladies enjoying a leisurely afternoon. *From William McClure Thomson,* The Land and the Book, *vol. 3 (New York, Harper, 1885)*

The Cult of Leisure

I once read about a little peasant girl in nineteenth-century Syria who boldly declared that she knew where heaven was. She said that she had glimpsed it through the gate of a beautiful garden graced with waving cypresses, pines, fruit trees, and flowers that surrounded the finest house in her village. Her innocent statement no doubt elicited knowing smiles from her elders, for Arabs have long spoken rapturously of their orchards and gardens, equating them with paradise.

Over the centuries the celebrated gardens of Damascus, Sidon, and other towns have afforded the population delightful retreats where, grateful for the shade overhead, they have sat on mats and picnicked, sipped coffee, and pulled contentedly on their water pipes while taking pleasure in the songs of birds, the purling of brooks, and the mingled fragrances of fruit trees in blossom. This pursuit of leisure is also reflected in other Arab institutions such as the coffeehouse and the public bath, as well as in the traditional courtyard house with its enclosed garden. It finds expression in the Arabic word *kaif* and constitutes an integral part of eastern Mediterranean culture. In his book, *Personal Narrative of a Pilgrimage to El Medinah and Meccah* (1856), the British Orientalist, adventurer, and diplomat Sir Richard Francis Burton has given a description of *kaif*:

> [W]e were sitting silent and still, listening to the monotonous melody of the East—the soft night-breeze wandering through starlight skies and tufted trees, with a voice of melancholy meaning.
>
> And this is the Arab's *Kaif.* The savoring of animal existence; the passive enjoyment of mere sense; the pleasant languor, the dreamy tranquillity, the airy castle-building, which in Asia stand in lieu of the vigorous, intensive, passionate life of Europe. It is the result of a lively, impressible, excitable nature, and exquisite sensibility of nerve,—a facility for voluptuousness unknown to northern regions; where happiness is placed in the exertion of mental and physical powers; where niggard earth commands ceaseless sweat of brow, and damp chill air demands perpetual excitement, exercise, or change, or adventure, or dissipation, for want of something better. In the East, man requires but rest and shade: upon the banks of a

bubbling stream, or under the cool shelter of a perfumed tree, he is perfectly happy, smoking a pipe, or sipping a cup of coffee, or drinking a glass of sherbet, but, above all things, deranging body and mind as little as possible; the trouble of conversations, the displeasures of memory, and the vanity of thought being the most unpleasant interruptions to his *Kaif*. No wonder that *Kaif* is a word untranslatable in our mother-tongue!

I recall summer days when tree-shaded and vine-trellised open-air cafés would be thronged with patrons sitting by the hour making *kaif*. In the meantime, throughout the towns, gardens and courtyards with their fountains, trees, and flowers would likewise be playing their parts in an elaborate cult of ease and grace. This leisurely mode of existence, so treasured by the local inhabitants, is sometimes frustrating to Westerners, who seem to suffer from chronic activity. Americans have a saying: "Time is money." I grew up with a different one: "Time is life."

The Tradition of Mazza

Another institution associated with the cult of leisure is the partaking of appetizers, or *mazza*, which enjoy immense popularity, especially in Lebanon. The concept of appetizers is a very old one; both the ancient Greeks and Persians served nuts, vegetables, and tart fruits as hors d'oeuvres with wine. Among the medieval Arabs *nuql*—a variety of nuts, seeds, raw vegetables, herbs, and fruits (both fresh and dried)—were offered along with nonalcoholic beverages as appetizers. Many modern-day *mazza* have their origins in the *bawarid* (cold dishes) and *kawamikh* (condiments) of the Middle Ages. Regarding the derivation of the word *mazza,* according to the Lebanese author and educator Fayez Aoun, it comes from the Arabic *allumazza* (that which one tastes). There is also the word *mazmiz* (to nibble at food or enjoy at leisure).

Served in small portions on individual plates, appetizers can range from a simple assortment of raw and pickled vegetables, cheese, and olives to a spectacular collection of such variety that one can easily forget they are usually meant to be only the prelude to a meal rather than a meal in themselves. But with the number of appetizers capable of reaching a hundred or more, people often forgo lunch or dinner and make a complete meal of *mazza*.

Strictly speaking, appetizers are called *mazza* only when served with alcoholic drinks, particularly *arak,* the traditional accompaniment; otherwise they are known as *muqabbalat*. Moreover, one is invited not to a *mazza* but rather to "take a glass," it being understood that people are never expected to drink on an empty stomach. *Arak* is sometimes replaced with beer, wine, or, in pious Muslim communities, with nonalcoholic beverages. Although *mazza* are encountered in Syria and Jordan, the custom of offering them is not nearly as prevalent as it is in Lebanon.

Mazza are meant to be enjoyed in an atmosphere of warmth and conviviality; one can hardly imagine a silent or solitary *mazza!* Since most of the dishes can be prepared in advance and served at room temperature, they can be savored in a leisurely fashion. These appetizers are equally at home in a country farmhouse or at a formal reception. *Mazza* in its most sumptuous form, however, is usually the domain of restaurants.

An extensive *mazza* can include many or all of the following: nuts, seeds, and chips; olives and pickles; dips; salads; raw vegetables and fresh herbs; cooked vegetable dishes; cheeses; hard-cooked eggs; seafood, poultry, and meat dishes (often miniature versions of main courses); *kibbeh;* and savory pastries.* Some restaurants also feature charcoal-roasted small birds (*assafeer*) and quail and fried frogs' legs. Flatbread, an omnipresent accompaniment, is used to scoop up many of the appetizers. Whether offered at parties and receptions, as a preamble to a meal, or as a meal in itself, *mazza* are a hallowed tradition in the eastern Mediterranean.

*In addition to the dishes described in this chapter, many others elsewhere in this book can also be served as *mazza*. These are indicated by the letter *M*.

Zahleh, a Mazza Lover's Paradise

It is only natural that I should be so fond of appetizers since in Lebanon they come as close to perfection as is possible in this world. Perhaps another reason is that the first summers of my life were spent in Zahleh, the capital of the fertile Bekaa region and one of the most celebrated spots in the Middle East for *mazza*.

Zahleh's delightful location has earned it the appellation 'Arus Lubnan (Bride of Lebanon). Situated in an area of vineyards, this charming community is built on two mountain slopes facing each other on the gorge of the Bardawni River, which cascades down from snow-covered Mt. Sannin and flows swiftly through the town. Zahleh was known for the fine quality of its *arak* long before it became famous for its *mazza*. Shortly after World War I, outdoor cafés began to spring up by the river among willows and poplars in a picturesque setting called *Wadi al-Arayish*, or "Vine Vale." With typical Lebanese enterprise, the proprietors offered free finger foods such as toasted nuts, pumpkin seeds, and chickpeas, *labna*, olives, hearts of romaine, and fresh fava beans in hopes of selling more glasses of *arak* to their customers. Their tactic proved hugely successful, and it was not long before the number of outdoor restaurants multiplied to line the Wadi. Tourists flocked to sample the increasingly varied array of dishes, and by the time I was a small child, Zahleh was renowned throughout Lebanon and beyond for the excellence and abundance of its *mazza*.

The town's colorful open-air pavilions joined one another, and it was hard to tell where one left off and the next began. People would often while away several hours for lunch or dinner, beginning at the lower end of the Wadi at the first restaurant and proceeding up through the others one by one, having a few dishes and a little glass of *arak* at each. A sumptuous banquet could be had, however, by visiting just one of the restaurants and ordering a spread of anywhere from several dozen to 150 appetizers. The integrity of the Wadi's kitchens shone in every single dish, including several for which Zahleh was noted: *kibbeh* (especially raw *kibbeh*), *tabbuleh,* fragrant garlic-flavored grilled chicken, and roasted tiny fig-pecking warblers. For many people the Wadi, with its crystalline water, cool shade, flowers, congenial atmosphere, and superb food, was synonymous with paradise. A meal at Zahleh was more than a meal; it was a celebration of life.

Zahleh was not the only locale for *mazza.* Following the success of the Wadi, "little paradises" began to proliferate in many other towns, always offering their patrons a park- or gardenlike environment with streams, fountains, and waterfalls, shade trees, and a colorful display of sweet-scented flowers. In addition, seaside restaurants that specialized in *mazza* opened in Beirut.

The Daily Promenade in Shtora

As was the custom in Lebanese resort communities, most people in Shtora went for a stroll down the main street (the Beirut-Damascus road) after six o'clock, when the air was fresh and cool and the fading sunlight bathed the fields, orchards, and nearby mountains in a soft, mellow glow. This promenade to *shamm al-hawa* ("smell the air") was a time for pleasant socializing with local residents and tourists. On our walks we would often stop at a restaurant, which provided a good vantage point for watching the parade of passersby, whether the everyday variety or the more unusual and exotic: a peasant creaking along in his cart with a load of fruit for the town's markets; flour merchants wearing *kuffiyya*s (flowing scarf headdresses), driving mules and donkeys heavily laden with sacks of grain; a well-known Beirut musician having come to Shtora to rest his nerves and to compose in peaceful surroundings; a dark-skinned, bearded, and turbaned pilgrim from faraway Afghanistan slowly working his way to Mecca; a traveling Italian acrobat arriving in town to put on a one-man trapeze and high-wire show; an itinerant Armenian photographer carrying his box and tripod, one of those men often encountered at resort cafés who, draping a black cloth over his head, would take a picture and develop it on the spot by means of seemingly mysterious and complex operations, finally producing a postcard for posterity; starry-eyed newlyweds honeymooning at the town's big hotel; a cortège of shiny black Cadillacs occupied by the sunglassed, white-robed family of a sheikh from the Gulf States whose opulent villa was located in the vicinity; other cars bearing diplomatic license plates (Shtora was a frequent site of political conferences involving Lebanon and other Arab states); travelers pausing to shop in the remarkably well-stocked grocery stores; and a few nomadic Beduin with their camels plodding silently along, austere and dignified against the deepening twilight. Although Lebanon has no desert and no indigenous nomads, each spring thousands of Beduin would come to the Bekaa to graze their huge flocks of sheep and goats. Most of them walked there from the Syrian Desert, a seven-day trip, traveling at night to avoid the scorching sun. When fall arrived they would return to Syria, making their way through the mountain passes.

All this—the delicious air, the blissful countryside, the long walks, the animated conversations, and the people-watching—conspired to work up our appetites, and we would proceed to order *mazza*. In short order there would appear small plates of *hummus bi tahini, tabbuleh,* crisp tiny cucumbers, *labna,* stuffed cabbage and grape leaves, stuffed baby eggplants and zucchini, skewered larks, and skewered meatballs, to name only some. If, however, the show on the street did not hold out much promise, rather than settle in and order more rounds of *mazza,* we would make the ten-minute drive to Zahleh, where we would either take in a movie or go dancing to live music under the stars at the Hotel Qadri. Whatever our choice, we would never consider our mission to Zahleh accomplished unless we did a bit of *mazza*-hopping at the Wadi before calling it a night and returning home to Shtora.

The Spell of the Desert and the Spell of the Oasis

One night I visited the wooden theater . . . Among the young dandies, the merchants, the Jews, there sat a Bedouin boy, a little apart. I am certain that this was his first visit to civilization. He was clad in party-colored rags, full of lovely shades of blue and purple. On his head was the keffieh. He gazed with his desert eyes at the Jewish actresses, at the boxes, at the people about him. Between the acts a boy carried about a tray covered with small dishes of nuts, melon-seeds, oranges. "Oh! my uncles," he cried, "occupy your time! Occupy your time, my uncles! Occupy your time!"

The Bedouin uncle responded to the call. He ate from every dish, paying with coins which he disinterred from his enchanting rags. The play proceeded. He stared, violently cracked his nuts, spat out the shells among his neighbors, devoured his melon-seeds. Never did his expression change. Yet no one in that place was so marvelously expressive as he was. The desert gazed out of his eyes, which till now had always looked on the limitless spaces, on the trembling mirage, and on the shining gold of the sands.

As I watched him, I knew the essence of the wonderful charm of Damascus. It is a garden city touched by the great desert. Under its roses one feels the sands. Beside its trembling waters one dreams of the trembling mirage. The cry of its muezzins seems to echo from its mosque towers to that most wonderful thing in nature which is "God without man." The breath of the wastes passes among the poplars as that Bedouin boy passed among the merchants when he came and when he went.[1]

Toasted Pumpkin Seeds
Bizr Laqtin Muhammas

I had thought I was pretty good at eating pumpkin seeds until I read the following account of how Ann Kerr's roommates at the American University of Beirut ate theirs!

Bowls of bizr were passed, a collection of pumpkin, sunflower and watermelon seeds which had been dried and salted. The object was to eat the juicy tidbit inside without swallowing the outer seed. I had noticed my roommates' facility for doing this in a continuous process carried out so discreetly that one would hardly know anything was going on. A handful of bizr is swept into the mouth and stored on one side. The tongue then gently guides a seed

A muezzin *chanting the call to prayer from a Damascus minaret.* *From Charles William Wilson, ed.,* Picturesque Palestine, Sinai and Egypt, *vol. 1 (New York, D. Appleton, 1881)*

into cracking position. Teeth come together with just the right kind of pressure to split the seed but not splinter it. Next the tongue deftly removes the inner tidbit and simultaneously transfers the shell to a storage place on the other side of the mouth. The center seed is then eaten and enjoyed.[2]

2 cups pumpkin seeds, shells left on, fibers rubbed off

1 tablespoon vegetable oil

1 tablespoon unsalted butter, melted

1 1/2 teaspoons coarse salt, or to taste

In a small bowl toss the pumpkin seeds with the oil, butter, and salt. Spread them in a single layer on a rimmed baking sheet. Toast in a preheated 250° F oven, stirring occasionally, 30 to 40 minutes or until they are golden brown and crisp. Transfer the seeds to paper towels to drain. Cool to room temperature. Serve at once, or store in an airtight container in a cool, dry place up to 2 weeks. To eat, gently crack a seed open between your teeth and eat the center portion, discarding the shell, which is *never* consumed!

Makes 2 cups

Roasted Chickpeas
Qudami

In the streets of Ottoman Damascus roasted chickpeas were frequently purveyed with the cry, "*Umm en-naren*" ("Mother of two fires"), meaning that they were well roasted. *Qudami* have an earthy, rustic quality and make a nutritious snack favored by young and old.

Fresh green chickpeas (*khadra malani*) are also popular when in season. Their crunchy texture and refreshing flavor appealed to me as a child, and I used to delight in munching on them while tending our Shtora garden. They are sometimes stewed with lamb or used in rice and bulgur pilafs. A recipe for meat stewed with green chickpeas is given in the medieval *Wusla*. Green chickpeas are hawked in the streets with the cry, "Like almonds, my *malani*," and their ballooned, empty shells are likened disparagingly to pompous, empty-headed individuals: "Like *malani,* puffed up on nothing."

1 cup dried chickpeas

4 cups water

3 tablespoons olive oil or vegetable oil

Coarse salt to taste

In a medium, heavy saucepan bring the chickpeas and water to a boil over high heat. Cover the saucepan, remove from the heat, and let stand about 25 minutes or until the chickpeas are just tender enough to chew. Drain the chickpeas and spread them in a single layer in a rimmed pan lined with several layers of paper towels. Let them dry about 1 hour, blotting them occasionally with additional paper towels.

In a large, heavy skillet combine the chickpeas and oil and sprinkle with the salt.

Cook over moderately high heat, stirring constantly, 5 to 8 minutes or until the chickpeas are toasted and crisp. Transfer the chickpeas to paper towels to drain. Serve at once, or store in an airtight container in a cool, dry place up to 2 weeks.

Makes about 1 cup

Tahini Dip
Taratur bi Tahini

Serve this versatile dip as an appetizer or as an accompaniment to Falafel (page 113), fried or steamed vegetables, grilled or fried fish, Grilled Skewered Lamb (page 203), or grilled or fried *kibbeh*.

> 1 large garlic clove, or to taste
> 1/4 teaspoon salt, or to taste
> 1/2 cup well-stirred *tahini*
> 1/3 cup freshly squeezed and strained lemon juice, or more to taste
> Cold water as needed
> 1 tablespoon finely chopped flat-leaf parsley

In a mixing bowl, using a pestle, crush the garlic and salt to a smooth paste. Add the *tahini* and mix well. Gradually beat in the lemon juice, then enough cold water, a teaspoonful at a time, to make a thick, creamy mixture. Taste and add more salt and lemon juice if desired. Transfer the dip to a small serving bowl. Garnish with the parsley and serve with warm pita bread.

Makes about 1 cup

VARIATIONS:

Tahini Dip with Za'atar ✧

Omit the parsley and stir in 1/2 teaspoon *za'atar,* or to taste. Garnish with small Middle Eastern oil-cured black olives.

Tahini Dip with Toasted Nuts and Herbs ✧

This variation is inspired by a recipe in the *Wusla* called "*sahna kaddaba*" ("mock dish") or "*baladiyya*" ("native" or "local"). The author describes the mixture as "delicious, good for you (healthful), and light on the stomach." He also indicates that it should be thick enough to spread on bread. An almost identical recipe is found in the *Kanz*.

Substitute lime juice for the lemon juice, if desired. After adding the water, stir in 2 tablespoons ground toasted hazelnuts or walnuts, 1 to 2 tablespoons each minced flat-leaf parsley and spearmint leaves, 1/4 teaspoon minced fresh thyme leaves or crushed dried Mediterranean oregano, 1/8 teaspoon ground sumac, 1/16 teaspoon Mixed Spices

II (page 66), and ½ teaspoon extra-virgin olive oil. Omit garnishing with the parsley. Sprinkle with chopped pistachios, if desired.

∽

To change the rough sea into *tahini*.
(Meaning: To smooth out all difficulties.)
∽

Chickpea and Tahini Dip
Hummus bi Tahini

This is unquestionably the Middle Eastern dip best known outside its homeland. A fixture on the *mazza*, it also makes an excellent accompaniment to *tabbuleh* (page 127) and grilled fish, chicken, and meat.

1 cup dried chickpeas, picked over and rinsed

1¾ teaspoons salt, or to taste

⅓ cup freshly squeezed and strained lemon juice, or more to taste

⅓ cup well-stirred *tahini*

1 large garlic clove, or to taste, crushed with a pinch of salt to a smooth paste

1 tablespoon finely chopped fresh spearmint leaves (optional)

1 tablespoon extra-virgin olive oil

Fresh spearmint or flat-leaf parsley sprigs

Paprika, Middle Eastern red pepper, or ground cumin

Place the chickpeas in a bowl, add enough cold water to cover them by 2 inches, and let soak overnight. Drain the chickpeas and transfer them to a medium, heavy saucepan. Add enough fresh water to cover the peas completely and bring to a boil over high heat. Reduce the heat to low and simmer, partially covered, 1 hour. Add 1 teaspoon of the salt and simmer the chickpeas about 30 minutes more or until they are tender but still intact, occasionally replenishing the liquid with boiling water, if necessary, to keep the chickpeas covered throughout the cooking period. Drain the chickpeas and reserve the cooking liquid. Set aside 1 tablespoon of the chickpeas for garnishing the dip. Remove the transparent skins from the remaining chickpeas.

In a blender or food processor combine the skinned chickpeas, lemon juice, 2 tablespoons of the reserved chickpea liquid, *tahini,* garlic, and the remaining ¾ teaspoon salt, or to taste. Process until the mixture is thick and smooth. If it is too stiff, blend in a little more chickpea liquid, a tablespoon at a time. Stir in the chopped mint, if used. Taste and adjust the seasoning.

Spread the dip in a shallow serving dish, swirling it with the back of a spoon. Drizzle the olive oil over it and garnish with the reserved chickpeas, mint or parsley sprigs, and a light sprinkling of paprika. Serve with warm pita bread.

Makes about 2¼ cups

VARIATIONS:

The following variations are my own, the second one being an adaptation of a recipe found in the *Kanz*.

Chickpea and Tahini Dip with Red Pepper Paste ⤳

After processing the ingredients, add ¾ cup Red Pepper Paste (page 299) and mix well. Omit the chopped mint and paprika. Drizzle with the oil and, if desired, sprinkle with ground cumin. Garnish with the reserved chickpeas and mint or parsley sprigs, toasted pine nuts or chopped toasted pistachio nuts, or small Middle Eastern oil-cured black olives and parsley sprigs. This makes about 3 cups.

Spicy Chickpea and Tahini Dip ⤳

Add ½ teaspoon Mixed Spices II (page 66) with the ¾ teaspoon salt. Garnish as directed or with toasted pine nuts or chopped toasted hazelnuts and fresh spearmint sprigs.

∾

He dips his bread outside the bowl.
(Meaning that a person is astray or off track.)
∾

Serving the Right Master

In the following story Joha, who had managed to become a favorite at the court of the Sultan, uses his wits to get himself out of a tight situation.

One day the Sultan was so delighted with an eggplant dish that he ordered the palace chef to have the vegetable served every day. "Don't you agree, Joha, that eggplant is the best vegetable in the world?" asked the Sultan. "Most definitely, your Majesty," answered Joha. "The very best." By the tenth straight meal featuring eggplant, however, the Sultan had changed his tune. "Take these dreadful things away!" he thundered. "I *hate* them!" "They are indeed abominable, your Majesty," agreed Joha. "Eggplant is the worst vegetable in the world." "But Joha," protested the Sultan, "only a few days ago you said it was the very best!" "That I did," replied Joha. "But I am the servant of the Sultan, not of the eggplant." [3]

Eggplant and Tahini Dip
Baba Ghannuj

This lusty, creamy dip tastes best when the eggplant has been grilled over an open fire. Serve it as an appetizer or as an accompaniment to grilled meat or fish and grilled or fried *kibbeh*.

1 eggplant (about 1¼ pounds), stemmed and hulled

¼ cup freshly squeezed and strained lemon juice, or to taste

¼ cup well-stirred *tahini*

1 medium garlic clove, or to taste, crushed with a pinch of salt to a smooth paste

½ teaspoon salt, or to taste

2 teaspoons extra-virgin olive oil

Fresh sour pomegranate seeds (page 56), if available, or Middle Eastern black olives

1 tablespoon finely chopped flat-leaf parsley

Prick the eggplant in 3 or 4 places with the tines of a long-handled fork, then impale it on the fork and grill over charcoal or a gas flame, turning it frequently until the flesh is very soft and the skin charred. (The eggplant can instead be broiled in an oven. Pierce it, place it on a broiling pan or baking sheet, and broil 4 inches from the heat about 25 minutes, turning it to char evenly on all sides.) It is important that the eggplant be thoroughly cooked inside; otherwise, both the taste and texture of the dish will be ruined. When the eggplant is cool enough to handle, squeeze it gently to remove the bitter juices. Peel the eggplant, remove any badly charred spots, and split it open. Scoop out the seeds and discard. Chop the eggplant pulp coarsely and place it in a blender or food processor. Add the lemon juice, *tahini,* garlic, and salt. Process until the mixture is smooth and creamy. Taste and adjust the seasoning.

Spread the dip in a shallow serving dish. Drizzle the olive oil over it and garnish with the pomegranate seeds or olives and parsley. Serve with warm pita bread.

Makes about 1½ cups

Red Pepper and Walnut Dip with Pomegranate
Muhammara

This vividly flavored dip is especially popular in Aleppo, where it is known as *garmirug* among the city's Armenian residents. It is also favored in Damascus, where it sometimes includes *tahini,* olive oil being used only as a garnish; indeed, some Damascenes insist that the dish is not properly prepared unless it contains *tahini* (see Variation, below). Both the flavor and texture of *muhammara* are markedly superior when the peppers have been grilled over an open fire.

Serve this dip as an appetizer or as an accompaniment to grilled fish, chicken, meat, or *kibbeh.*

6 medium red bell peppers

2 cups shelled walnuts, ground

⅔ cup toasted pita bread crumbs

1 tiny garlic clove, or to taste, crushed with a pinch of salt to a smooth paste

1 small hot chili pepper (such as red Fresno), or to taste, seeded and chopped*

2 tablespoons Pomegranate Molasses (page 57)

1 tablespoon freshly squeezed and strained lemon juice, or to taste

¾ teaspoon salt, or to taste

¼ cup plus 1 teaspoon extra-virgin olive oil

Small Middle Eastern oil-cured black olives

Toasted pine nuts

Fresh spearmint sprigs

Prepare a charcoal grill or preheat an oven broiler. If using a broiler, set the peppers on the rack of a broiler pan. Grill or broil the peppers 3 to 4 inches from the heat, turning frequently, 10 to 20 minutes or until they are blistered and charred. Enclose the peppers in a paper bag and let them steam until they are cool enough to handle. Peel the peppers, halve them lengthwise, and remove and discard the stems, seeds, and ribs. Set aside.

In a food processor combine the walnuts, bread crumbs, garlic, chili pepper, Pomegranate Molasses, and lemon juice. Blend until the mixture is smooth. Add the bell peppers and salt and process until the peppers are puréed. With the food processor running, pour in ¼ cup of the oil in a slow, steady stream and blend the mixture until it is thick, smooth, and creamy. Taste and adjust the seasoning. Transfer the dip to a serving dish, cover, and chill several hours or overnight. Just before serving, drizzle the remaining 1 teaspoon oil over the top and garnish with the olives, pine nuts, and mint sprigs. Serve with warm pita bread or Mountain Bread (page 316).

Makes about 3 cups

A note of caution: Be careful when handling chili peppers since their volatile oils may burn your skin and irritate your eyes. Wear rubber gloves if possible and wash your hands thoroughly with soap and warm water afterward.

VARIATIONS:

Substitute toasted French bread crumbs for the pita bread crumbs, or use 4 slices French bread, trimmed of crusts, dipped in water, squeezed dry, and crumbled.

Roast the chili pepper along with the bell peppers before using.

Add a pinch of ground cumin, or to taste, with the salt.

Red Pepper and Walnut Dip with Tahini and Pomegranate

Substitute 2 tablespoons well-stirred *tahini,* or more to taste, for the ¼ cup olive oil.

Baalbek Remembered

I have seen nothing in Italy that surpasses it; indeed, I may say, nothing that equals it.[4]

An important agricultural center situated on the edge of the northern Bekaa, Baalbek has existed as a crossroads of caravan routes and human migrations since the dawn of history. In the first and second centuries A.D., the Romans erected their grandest temples in Baalbek on the site of even older Phoenician shrines. The monumental splendor of these sanctuaries still remains despite the ravages of time, nature, and man.

The Baalbek region has long been famous for its fruits and dairy products. Ibn Battuta speaks of its abundance of cherries called *"habb al-malik"* ("king's cherries") and of its "many preparations of milk." The town also produces honey, walnuts, almonds, and vegetables and enjoys an excellent reputation for its *lahm bi ajeen.*

From 1956 to 1974 Baalbek played host to an international cultural event, the celebrated Baalbek Festival featuring world-class musicians, actors, and dancers.[5] These performances attracted a cosmopolitan audience, many of whom liked to picnic at the Ras al-Ain, a parklike tree-shaded area just outside of town with waterside coffeehouses, green lawns, bubbling springs, and tranquil pools with ducks and geese. While I also used to enjoy dining alfresco in these idyllic surroundings, my most memorable meal in Baalbek was taken on the veranda of a friend's summer home overlooking the majestic ruins of the Temple of Jupiter. We dined in silent meditation as we watched the setting sun fill the sky with a fiery glow, against which the six huge Columns of the Sun stood out as if suspended in timelessness. One can never forget these columns. Once seen, they stand out forever in the memory.

> They overwhelm you by the sum total of their splendor, which is so extraordinary that it has the blotting-out power peculiar to the tremendous manifestations of man's creative genius.
>   . . . Some ruins completely satisfy as ruins. Others make one sigh for a lost perfection. The Columns of the Sun at Baalbec call up only the secret murmur, "It is enough."[6]

Baalbek: Temple of Jupiter. *From John Carne,* Syria, the Holy Land, Asia Minor, &c., *vol. 1 (London, Fisher, Son, 1836)*

Yogurt Cheese and Red Pepper Dip ❧

Muhammara Labna

The few recipes I have come across for this little-known but outstanding appetizer do not begin to do it justice. The dip described here is inspired by one that was served to me years ago in Baalbek. It has met with rave reviews from all who have tasted it.

½ cup firm Yogurt Cheese (page 143)

½ cup Red Pepper Paste (page 299)

1 small garlic clove, or to taste, crushed with a pinch of salt to a smooth paste

2 teaspoons extra-virgin olive oil

2 teaspoons freshly squeezed and strained lemon juice, or to taste

Salt to taste

Small Middle Eastern oil-cured black olives or fresh spearmint sprigs

In a bowl combine the Yogurt Cheese, Red Pepper Paste, garlic, olive oil, lemon juice, and salt, and mix well. Taste and adjust the seasoning. Cover and chill 1 hour. Transfer the dip to a small serving bowl and garnish with the olives or spearmint sprigs. Serve with warm pita bread or Mountain Bread (page 316).

Makes 1 cup

Another industry at Baʿlabakk is the making of wooden vessels and spoons that have no equal in the world. . . . Frequently they make a large dish, then make a second which fits into the hollow of the first, and another in the hollow of that, and so on to as many as ten, which anyone seeing them would imagine to be a single dish. In the same way with spoons, they make a series of ten, one within the hollow of the other, and make a leather covering for them. A man will carry this in his belt and, on joining in a meal with his friends, will take it out; those who see it think it to be a single spoon, whereupon he produces nine others from within it.[7]

Cheese Dip with Zaʿatar ❧

This is not a traditional recipe but my own and has elements in common with two others I developed for my yogurt and sandwich books.

1 cup firm Yogurt Cheese (page 143) or cream cheese, at room temperature

6 ounces feta cheese, crumbled

2 tablespoons chopped fresh spearmint leaves, or to taste

Salt to taste

Middle Eastern black olives

Tomato wedges

Cucumber slices

Good-quality imported *zaʿatar* to taste

Extra-virgin olive oil

In a food processor combine the cheeses and blend until the mixture is smooth. Add the spearmint and salt and mix well. Transfer the mixture to a bowl, cover, and chill 1 hour.

Mound the cheese mixture in the center of a platter. Arrange the olives, tomato wedges, and cucumber slices attractively around it. Sprinkle with the *za'atar* and drizzle with the olive oil. Serve with warm pita bread.

Makes about 1¾ cups

VARIATION:

Add a little minced red onion or scallion or crushed garlic with the mint and salt.

Cheese Dip with Toasted Sesame Seeds ❧

Follow the recipe for Cheese Dip with Za'atar (above) with these changes: Substitute lightly toasted sesame seeds for the spearmint leaves and, if desired, stir in a little minced scallion or crushed garlic. Omit the *za'atar.* Garnish with additional sesame seeds.

Makes about 1¾ cups

Damascus-Style Cheese Dip with Toasted Sesame Seeds and Nigella ❧

This appetizer is based on an excellent cheese spread I discovered many years ago in Damascus. I have not seen a recipe for the Damascene original anywhere.

Follow the recipe for Cheese Dip with Za'atar (page 111) with these changes: Substitute 2 tablespoons lightly toasted sesame seeds, 1 teaspoon nigella, and ⅛ teaspoon ground *mahlab,* or to taste (optional), for the mint leaves. Garnish with additional sesame seeds and nigella. Omit the olives, tomato, cucumber, *za'atar,* and olive oil. Serve with the bread and raw vegetables such as sliced fennel, bell pepper strips, and trimmed and quartered radishes.

Makes about 1¾ cups

Herbed Yogurt Cheese ❧

The nineteenth-century author Isabel Burton observed a man in a Damascus *suq* eating "a peculiar salad," one of the "most delicious things that he knows":

> The salad is made by chopping garlic, thyme, mint, watercress, sage, or any other sweet herbs, putting in a piece of salt about the size of a nut, mixing it all, and then burying the whole in Leben, sprinkling the top with chopped herbs; then dip your bread in it, and eat.[8]

Variations of this classic appetizer turn up all over the Middle East. My version, given below, is derived from a recipe in the medieval *Wusla.* When I recently served it to a Damascene yogurt aficionado, he declared it to be the best yogurt cheese he had ever tasted.

1 cup firm Yogurt Cheese (page 143)

1 medium garlic clove, or to taste, crushed with a pinch of salt to a smooth paste

$\frac{1}{2}$ teaspoon crushed dried spearmint

$\frac{1}{4}$ teaspoon crushed dried tarragon

$\frac{1}{4}$ teaspoon dried dill

$\frac{1}{8}$ teaspoon crushed dried Mediterranean oregano or thyme

Extra-virgin olive oil

1 teaspoon freshly squeezed and strained lemon juice, or to taste

Salt and freshly ground black pepper to taste

1 fresh spearmint sprig

In a bowl combine the Yogurt Cheese, garlic, dried spearmint, tarragon, dill, oregano, $\frac{1}{2}$ teaspoon olive oil, lemon juice, and salt and pepper. Mix well. Taste and adjust the seasoning, cover, and chill at least 2 hours. Just before serving, drizzle with olive oil and garnish with the fresh spearmint sprig. Serve with warm pita bread and/or raw vegetables such as cucumber and fennel slices, green bell pepper strips, and trimmed and quartered radishes.

Makes 1 cup

VARIATIONS:

If top-quality fresh spearmint, tarragon, and dill are available, you may substitute them for the dried herbs, using $1\frac{1}{2}$ teaspoons minced spearmint and $\frac{3}{4}$ teaspoon each minced tarragon and dill, or to taste.

Substitute 1 teaspoon minced fresh fennel leaves or $\frac{1}{4}$ teaspoon powdered fennel seeds for the dill.

Deep-Fried Fava Bean Patties
Falafel

The full name of this time-honored food is *umm al-falafel* (mother of *falafel*), meaning that it is the spiced dish par excellence. One of Egypt's national dishes, *falafel* is also very popular in Syria, Lebanon, and Jordan, where it is avidly consumed at all times of the day: for breakfast, for lunch, as an appetizer, or as a snack.

Some of the best *falafel* I have ever eaten came from a takeout shop in Beirut. The crunchy, skillfully seasoned patties were tucked inside the pocket of a freshly baked pita bread along with sliced pickled turnips and cucumbers and dressed with *tahini* sauce and a hot tomato relish. During the summer we used to buy delicious *falafel* sandwiches from a street vendor in Zahleh. One could always predict when the local movie theater would let out by noting the time at which he stationed himself near its entrance. Upon emerging from the cinema into the pleasantly cool, dry evening air, patrons were inevitably lured by the enticing aroma of crisply fried *falafel* wafting from his pushcart.

Falafel can be made with dried fava beans (as in the recipe below), chickpeas, or a combination of both.

1 pound skinned and split dried fava beans (*ful majrush*), soaked overnight

1 large red onion or 1 bunch scallions, very finely chopped

3 large garlic cloves, or to taste, crushed

⅓ cup finely chopped flat-leaf parsley

⅓ cup finely chopped fresh coriander leaves

2 teaspoons ground cumin

1½ teaspoons ground coriander

½ teaspoon baking powder

Salt, freshly ground black pepper, and Middle Eastern red pepper to taste

Vegetable oil for deep-frying

Fresh spearmint or flat-leaf parsley sprigs, tomato wedges, and radishes for garnish

Drain the fava beans well, and in a food processor fitted with the steel blade, grind them fine. Add the onion, garlic, parsley, coriander leaves, cumin, ground coriander, baking powder, and salt, black pepper, and red pepper, and blend the mixture to as smooth a paste as possible. Transfer the mixture to a bowl, cover, and let stand 30 minutes.

Form the fava bean mixture into round patties about 1½ inches in diameter and arrange them in one layer of wax paper. In a deep fryer heat 2 to 3 inches of oil to 375°F. Add the patties, a batch at a time, and fry them in the hot oil, turning, 1 to 1½ minutes or until they are golden brown and crisp. As each batch is done, transfer the patties with a slotted spoon to paper towels to drain. Arrange the *falafel* on a heated serving platter and garnish with the mint or parsley sprigs, tomato wedges, and radishes. Serve hot with Tahini Dip (page 105).

Serves 6

Circassian Chicken
Jarkas Tawuq

Among the region's minorities are the Circassians, who during the latter part of the nineteenth century migrated from their homeland in the western Caucasus. They are a handsome Muslim people, often with fair skin and blue eyes. Circassian women are noted for their striking beauty and were highly sought after as slaves during Ottoman times.

This famous dish is found in one form or another throughout the eastern Mediterranean.

A 3- to 3½-pound chicken, cut into 6 serving pieces

3 cups water

1 medium onion, cut into 8 wedges

1 celery stalk with leaves, coarsely chopped

1 carrot, scraped and coarsely chopped

3 sprigs flat-leaf parsley

4 whole peppercorns

Salt

1½ cups shelled walnuts

⅓ cup finely chopped onion

3 slices firm white bread, torn into small pieces

½ teaspoon Middle Eastern red pepper, or to taste

Freshly ground black pepper to taste

Good-quality paprika

1 tablespoon finely chopped flat-leaf parsley (optional)

In a large, heavy saucepan combine the chicken, water, onion wedges, celery, carrot, parsley sprigs, peppercorns, and 1 teaspoon salt. Bring to a boil over high heat. Reduce the heat to low, cover, and simmer about 30 minutes or until the chicken is tender. Transfer the chicken to a plate and reserve. Strain the broth. In a large saucepan bring the strained broth to a boil over high heat. Boil rapidly, uncovered, until it is reduced to 1½ cups. Remove from the heat and cool slightly.

Combine the walnuts, chopped onion, bread, salt to taste, red pepper, black pepper, and the reduced broth in the container of an electric blender. Cover and blend until the mixture becomes a smooth purée. Taste and adjust the seasoning.

When the chicken is cool enough to handle, remove the skin and pull the meat away from the bones. Discard the skin and bones. Cut the meat into strips about ⅛ inch wide and 1½ inches long. Place the strips in a bowl, add half of the walnut sauce, and toss gently until the strips are well coated with the sauce. Mound the chicken on a platter, mask the top with the remaining walnut sauce, and sprinkle with paprika. Garnish with the finely chopped parsley, if desired.

Serves 8

Note: A more traditional garnish for this dish is made from paprika and the oil of ground walnuts. To prepare, with a mortar and pestle pulverize ¼ cup shelled walnuts with ½ teaspoon paprika. Place a small spoonful of the mixture at a time in a garlic press and squeeze the oil over the chicken.

A Clear Choice

The second wife of the amir Bashir II al-Shihabi, ruler of Mount Lebanon from 1788 to 1840, was a Circassian slave. After he chose her, the amir, who was secretly a Christian, gave orders that she should be instructed in the doctrines of his religion. In the words of Colonel Churchill:

The favoured one rejected, with expressions of horror, all attempts to induce her to abandon the faith of Islam, in which she had been brought up. These unlooked-for scruples were reported to the Emir. "Take her to the kitchen," was his unconcerned reply.[9] The choice of prospects thus laid before the young odalisk, wonderfully influenced and furthered the process of conversion; and the Maronite Bishop, who was especially charged with the care of her spiritual interests, had ere long the gratification of announcing to the Emir that his pupil had been awakened to a sense of her religious errors. The Emir immediately conferred on her the name which she now bears, of "Husn Jahaan"; or, "Beauty of the World."[10]

∽

One hour of justice is superior to a thousand months of devotion.
(Attributed to the poet laureate of the amir Bashir II.)

∽

Red Pepper Paste Pizza with Pomegranate ♦

Long before I began writing about food, I hit upon the idea of substituting pita bread for the traditional yeast doughs used to make Middle Eastern open-faced meat pies (*lahm bi ajeen*) and Italian-style pizzas. Many years later, I included a number of my recipes on this theme in articles that were published in *Vogue, Family Circle,* and *Gourmet* as well as in two of my previous cookbooks. Although I make no claim to be the only person to have come up with the idea, it was after the appearance of these recipes that pizza made with pita began to turn up everywhere!

Pizza on pita may not be a novelty anymore, but the version described below, which also comes from my kitchen, is both novel and delicious.

⅔ **cup Red Pepper Paste (page 299)**

1 tablespoon plus 2 teaspoons extra-virgin olive oil

2 teaspoons Pomegranate Molasses (page 57)

Salt to taste

A 6-inch pita bread, halved horizontally to form 2 rounds

Small Middle Eastern oil-cured black olives, pitted and halved, or toasted nuts (pine nuts or chopped blanched almonds, walnuts, or unsalted pistachios)

In a bowl combine the Red Pepper Paste, 1 tablespoon of the oil, Pomegranate Molasses, and salt and mix well.

Arrange the pita rounds smooth side down and slightly apart on an ungreased baking sheet. Spread the red pepper paste mixture evenly on the pita rounds and drizzle it with the remaining 2 teaspoons oil. Garnish the pizzas with the olives or nuts and bake in a preheated 400° F oven about 8 minutes or until the edges are lightly browned. Transfer the pizzas with a spatula to a cutting board, cut them into wedges, and serve.

Serves 3 or 4

Bayt al-Din, palace of the amir Bashir II, with the town of Dayr al-Qamar in the distance. From John Carne, Syria, the Holy Land, Asia Minor, &c., *vol. 1 (London, Fisher, Son, 1836)*

Flatbreads Stuffed with Ground Meat
Khubz bi Lahm or ʿAraʾis

Here is a flavorful Lebanese appetizer that can also double as a luncheon sandwich. Similar stuffed breads are encountered elsewhere in the Middle East.[11] This particular recipe comes from our Beirut kitchen.

Six 6-inch pita breads

2 tablespoons olive oil

3 medium onions, finely chopped

1 pound lean ground lamb or beef

3 to 4 tablespoons pine nuts, lightly toasted (optional)

1 small hot chili pepper, seeded and finely chopped (optional)

1 $\frac{1}{2}$ teaspoons Mixed Spices I (page 66)

2 teaspoons ground sumac

Salt and freshly ground black pepper to taste

Juice of $\frac{1}{2}$ lemon or lime, or to taste, freshly squeezed and strained

1 tablespoon Pomegranate Molasses (page 57)

$\frac{1}{3}$ to $\frac{1}{2}$ cup finely chopped flat-leaf parsley

Arrange the pita breads on ungreased baking sheets. Place in a preheated 350°F oven 3 to 4 minutes or until heated. Remove from the oven. With a sharp knife, carefully slit each pita one-third of the way around to make a pocket. Set aside.

In a large, heavy skillet heat the oil over medium-high heat. Add the onions and sauté, stirring frequently, until soft but not browned. Add the meat and, breaking it up with a fork, cook until browned and crumbly. Add the remaining ingredients and cook, stirring, 3 to 4 minutes. Taste and adjust the seasoning. Divide the mixture into 6 equal portions. Fill each pita with a portion of the meat mixture, spreading it evenly to the edges, and press the pita closed. Toast in a preheated sandwich grill on moderate heat until golden brown. Transfer with a spatula to a cutting board. Cut in half and then into wedges. Serve hot, accompanied with Drained Yogurt (page 142) or with lemon or lime wedges and Tahini Dip (page 105).

Serves 12

Note: Instead of a sandwich grill, you can use a large, heavy skillet, preferably cast-iron, or a griddle. Place each filled pita in the skillet and grill over medium-high heat, pressing the sandwich down with a pancake turner and turning it once to brown on both sides.

VARIATIONS:

Brush the filled pitas with melted unsalted butter before toasting them.

Substitute Mountain Bread (page 316), good-quality store-bought soft (pliable) *lavash* or *saaj* bread, or 12 flour tortillas, each 6 inches in diameter, for the pitas. If using bread, cut as many loaves as needed to make 24 pieces, each 5 by 5 inches square, reserving the remaining bread for another use. Heat the bread squares or tortillas, one at a time, on a preheated grill. Place a rectangular mound of about 2 tablespoons of the meat mixture in the center of each bread or tortilla. Fold the bottom flap over the meat mixture, fold in the sides, then roll the bread or tortilla over snugly to secure the top flap. Brush with melted butter or extra-virgin olive oil. Toast, seam side down, and serve as above. This serves 12.

CHAPTER 2
Salads

Christian women selling olive oil. *From Louis Charles Lortet,* La Syrie d'aujourd'hui *(Paris, Librairie Hachette, 1884)*

I LONGED TO BUY A HUGE COS-LETTUCE, straight from its wash in the river, and eat it sitting cross-legged on the river bank. The Syrian way was to strip off the side leaves and then rapidly nibble it from one end to the other, like a rabbit eating a carrot.[1]

Salads are present at most meals. They appear unfailingly on the *mazza*, and during hot weather substantial salads provide main courses suitable for lunches and suppers.

A wide range of ingredients is employed in the preparation of salads, including raw and cooked vegetables, herbs, fruits, nuts, flatbread, bulgur, hard-cooked eggs, and such unusual items as *kishk*, truffles, and lambs' brains and tongues. Romaine lettuce is the favorite salad green. Butterhead lettuces, endive, spinach, cabbage, watercress, arugula, dandelion greens, and purslane are also used.

The basic dressing for salads consists of finest-quality extra-virgin olive oil, lemon juice, salt, black pepper, and (usually) garlic. Other ingredients such as sumac, pomegranate molasses, and *tahini* are sometimes added, and a mild wine vinegar, verjuice, or sour pomegranate juice may be substituted for the lemon juice. The proportion of oil to lemon juice is a matter of personal taste, but the tendency is to use a generous amount of lemon juice, often as much as oil, or more, particularly in salads made with dried legumes. Occasionally yogurt is mixed with the dressing, or yogurt flavored with crushed garlic and spearmint may replace the dressing itself. In a few instances chopped lemon pulp is added to the salad ingredients and the lemon juice is omitted from the dressing.

SALAD DRESSINGS

Lemon Dressing
Salsat al-Laymun

> ¼ cup extra-virgin olive oil
> ¼ cup freshly squeezed and strained lemon juice, or to taste
> 1 medium garlic clove, or to taste, crushed to a paste with a pinch of salt
> Salt and freshly ground black pepper to taste

In a small bowl whisk together all the ingredients until well blended. Use for green or vegetable salads.

Makes ½ cup

VARIATIONS:

Mint Dressing

Crush a few chopped fresh spearmint leaves with the garlic.

Verjuice Dressing

Substitute verjuice (page 80) for the lemon juice.

Pomegranate Dressing

Salsat al-Rumman

> We now gathered under the shade of a tree and opened our provision bag . . . having made a refreshing draught of pomegranate juice, sugar, and water, we set about preparing "a dinner of herbs." From the Arabs we obtained some tomatoes and an onion, which, with our pocket knives, we peeled and shredded into a dish, sprinkling a little salt to make the juices flow and mingle. To this we added the juice of two sour pomegranates, and the whole being well stirred, we dipped our *khubbs* ("bread") therein . . . ²

Follow the recipe for Lemon Dressing (above), substituting ¼ cup fresh sour pomegranate juice (page 56) or 3 tablespoons lemon juice and 1 tablespoon Pomegranate Molasses (page 57) for the lemon juice. Use for boiled beets, *Fattush* (page 122), or a salad of fresh thyme and onions.

Makes ½ cup

Walnut Dressing

Salsat al-Jawz

⅓ cup shelled walnuts
2 slices white bread, trimmed of crusts, soaked in water, squeezed dry, and crumbled
1 small garlic clove, crushed to a paste with a pinch of salt
¼ cup extra-virgin olive oil
Juice of 2 lemons, or to taste, freshly squeezed and strained
Salt and Middle Eastern red pepper to taste

Grind the walnuts in a food processor. Add the bread and garlic and process while adding the oil in a thin stream. Gradually add the lemon juice and beat until the mixture is smooth. Season to taste with salt and red pepper. Use to dress sliced cucumbers and tomatoes or steamed vegetables such as asparagus, beets, cauliflower, or green beans.

Makes about ¾ cup

Mixed Vegetable Salad
Salata Khudra

In Shtora vegetables and herbs for salad were picked from our garden shortly before mealtimes, an especially pleasant activity during the early evening when the Bekaa would be flooded with a golden glow and the air would turn delightfully cool. For this salad I would pluck off young, crisp romaine; plump, juicy tomatoes bursting with intense flavor; firm, glossy peppers; and slender cucumbers with a crunchy texture. I would pull up scallions with bright green tops and thin white bulbs as well as crisp, slightly pungent radishes (enormous ones grow in the Bekaa). Lastly, I would snip off fragrant spearmint and parsley, both indispensable to so many eastern Mediterranean salads.

> The tender leaves from 1 small head romaine, torn into bite-sized pieces
>
> 3 medium ripe tomatoes, seeded and diced
>
> 1 medium green bell pepper, seeded, deribbed, and diced
>
> 1 small cucumber, peeled, seeded (if seeds are large), and diced
>
> 1 small red onion, finely chopped
>
> 2 scallions, finely chopped
>
> 6 radishes, thinly sliced (optional)
>
> 1/3 cup finely chopped flat-leaf parsley
>
> 1/4 cup finely chopped fresh spearmint leaves, or to taste
>
> Lemon Dressing (page 120)

In a salad bowl combine all the ingredients except the Lemon Dressing. Pour the dressing over the vegetables. Toss gently but thoroughly. Taste and adjust the seasoning. Serve at once.

Serves 6

VARIATION:

Add 1/2 cup coarsely chopped purslane and/or arugula leaves or watercress.

Bread Salad (M)
Fattush

Like *fatta* (page 207), this rustic salad was most likely conceived as a way to use up stale flatbread that would otherwise be discarded. Today it is usually made with toasted pita bread. The word *fattush* refers to the act of breaking up or crumbling.

Prepare Mixed Vegetable Salad (above) with these changes: Omit the lettuce, or use only half the amount, and add 1/2 cup purslane leaves and 1 pita bread, split, toasted until crisp, and broken into bite-sized pieces. Add 1/2 teaspoon ground sumac to the dressing.

Serves 4

VARIATION:

Substitute Pomegranate Dressing (page 121) for the Lemon Dressing.

The satisfied man breaks bread slowly for a famished man.
(The well-to-do have no sympathy for the poor.)

Vegetable Salad with Walnut Dressing
Salata Khudra bi Jawz

> **3 medium ripe tomatoes, seeded and chopped**
> **1 medium cucumber, peeled, seeded (if seeds are large), and diced**
> **1 large green bell pepper, seeded, deribbed, and diced**
> **3 scallions, finely chopped**
> **Walnut Dressing (page 121)**
> **Romaine or butterhead lettuce leaves**
> **¼ cup finely chopped fresh spearmint leaves**
> **Middle Eastern black olives**

In a mixing bowl combine the tomatoes, cucumber, green pepper, and scallions. Add the dressing and toss gently but thoroughly. Taste and adjust the seasoning. Transfer to a serving dish lined with the lettuce leaves. Sprinkle with the mint and garnish with the olives. Serve at once.

Serves 6

The judge who takes five cucumbers as a bribe will admit any evidence for ten melons.

Cucumber and Yogurt Salad *(M)*
Salata Khyar bi Laban

> Of the dishes was one for which whilst in Syria, I always retained a great liking. It is sour milk, curdled, called leben, into which cucumber is cut, with grated mint leaves sprinkled on the surface.[3]

A universal favorite throughout the Middle East, this refreshing salad exists in many variations. At its best when made with young, crisp cucumbers, it can be served as part of a *mazza* or as an accompaniment to grilled or baked lamb or *kibbeh*. The recipe given below is based on one found in the *Wusla* called *khilat baysani* (Beisanite mixture).

Other medieval versions of this venerable classic appear in al-Warraq's manual and in the *Kanz* under the title of *jajiq,* the name by which it is known to Armenians and Turks (Greeks call it *tzatziki*). The original recipe does not give quantities and calls for goat's milk, which would make the salad even more tart.

Prepare Herbed Yogurt Cheese (page 112) with these changes: Instead of the Yogurt Cheese use 2 cups plain low-fat yogurt, drained to 1½ cups (page 142), and double the quantity of garlic and herbs. Stir in 2 small cucumbers, peeled, seeded (if seeds are large), and finely diced, and 2 tablespoons additional lemon juice, or to taste. Omit the bread and/or vegetables.

Serves 4

VARIATION:

Substitute 2 teaspoons crushed dried spearmint for the herbs. This is the version of cucumber and yogurt salad most commonly encountered in Syria, Lebanon, and Jordan.

∾

A beggar being offered a cucumber refused it, saying, "It's crooked."
∾

Beet Salad with Pomegranate Dressing (M)
Salata Shamandar

Beets transcend their humble origins in this salad. Other interesting ways of serving them include dressing them with Garlic Yogurt Sauce (page 280) or, as is often done in Tripoli, Lebanon, with Tahini Sauce (page 280).

> **1 pound beets, well scrubbed and trimmed**
> **⅓ cup finely chopped red or white onion**
> **⅓ cup finely chopped flat-leaf parsley**
> **Pomegranate Dressing (page 121)**
> **1 tablespoon toasted sesame seeds, or to taste (optional)**

In a medium, heavy saucepan cover the beets with cold water and bring the water to a boil over moderate heat. Cover and simmer the beets 30 to 40 minutes or until they are tender. Drain the beets, peel them under cold running water, and dice.

In a salad bowl combine the diced beets, onion, and parsley. Pour the dressing over the salad and toss gently but thoroughly. Taste and adjust the seasoning. Cover and chill. Serve sprinkled with the sesame seeds, if desired.

Serves 4

The "The Ladder of Tyre," south of the town. From Charles William Wilson, ed., Picturesque Palestine, Sinai and Egypt, *vol. 2 (New York, D. Appleton, 1883)*

Dried Fava Bean Salad (M)

Ful Mudammas

Ful mudammas ranks first among Egypt's national dishes and is also popular in Syria, Lebanon, and Jordan. Substantial, nourishing, and inexpensive, it is relished by rich and poor alike at home and in restaurants at all hours of the day, including breakfast. It is often accompanied with radishes, scallions, tomatoes, and fresh spearmint leaves or with a salad of mixed raw vegetables, as it was once served to me near the southern Lebanese coastal town of Tyre (Sur).

> 1 cup *ful misri* (Egyptian dried small brown fava beans), soaked overnight
>
> Lemon Dressing (page 120)
>
> Extra-virgin olive oil (optional)
>
> 2 tablespoons finely chopped flat-leaf parsley
>
> Lemon wedges

Drain the beans and place them in a heavy saucepan. Cover with fresh water and bring to a boil over high heat. Reduce the heat to low, cover, and simmer the beans about 1½ hours or until they are very tender, occasionally adding a little boiling water as needed to keep the beans moist. When done, drain the beans and transfer them to a bowl. Pour the dressing over the beans. Mashing the beans gently with a fork, stir until they absorb most of the dressing. Taste and adjust the seasoning.

Spread the mashed beans on a serving platter and drizzle a little olive oil on top, if desired. Sprinkle with the parsley and garnish with the lemon wedges. Serve hot or at room temperature with warm pita bread.

Serves 4

∾

Mallow at noon, beans at night.
(Said of a poor person.)

∾

Orange, Lemon, and Onion Salad

We have seen nothing like . . . these celebrated gardens—the glory of Sidon . . . except at Jaffa, and in many respects these are more beautiful and larger. Can anything of this kind be richer or more delightful than those orange and lemon trees, loaded with golden fruit, single or in compact clusters, decked with leaves of liveliest green, and spangled all over with snowy-white flowers of sweetest fragrance?[4]

There is a well-known eastern Mediterranean salad of oranges, onions, and olives, a recipe for which, incorporating my own addition of fresh mint, appeared in my *Book of Salads* (1977). Described below is a less familiar but equally delicious salad I first tasted

Sidon, seen from the north. From John Carne, Syria, the Holy Land, Asia Minor, &c., *vol. 3 (London, Fisher, Son, 1836)*

in Sidon (Saida), which is related to it but which includes lemon slices. Similar salads, probably of Arab inspiration, are encountered in both Sicily and Spain.

During Sidon's long and majestic history its orchards have been among the most famous in the entire Middle East. I remember walking through them on magnificent early spring days during the month of the orange and lemon harvest. Some of the trees were planted so close together that both kinds of fruits appeared to be growing on the same bough.

Whenever I make this salad, memories of the scenes, scents, and sounds of those childhood walks come flooding back to me: the nearby hills blooming with carpets of wildflowers, the intoxicating perfume of the delicate blossoms, the filtered sunlight, and the songs of birds in the highest branches.

> **4 medium navel oranges, peel and pith discarded, thinly sliced crosswise**
>
> **2 medium lemons, peel and pith discarded, thinly sliced crosswise**
>
> **1 small red onion, very thinly sliced crosswise**
>
> **12 Middle Eastern oil-cured black olives**
>
> **2 tablespoons finely chopped fresh spearmint leaves**
>
> **Salt to taste**
>
> **Ground cumin to taste (optional)**
>
> **2 tablespoons extra-virgin olive oil, or more to taste**

Arrange the orange slices on a large serving platter and place the lemon slices over them. Top with the onion slices and garnish with the olives. Sprinkle with the mint and season with salt. Sprinkle lightly with cumin, if desired. Drizzle the olive oil over the salad. Serve at once or slightly chilled.

Serves 6

Bulgur, Tomato, Parsley, and Mint Salad (M)
Tabbuleh

This unquestioned star of Middle Eastern salads has become an international favorite, and no wonder! The entire population seems to have a Lucullan appetite for salads in general and for this one in particular. When I was growing up, a *tabbuleh* mania used to overcome everyone in Lebanon during the summer, providing a standing excuse for an afternoon party or picnic. In the Qadisha region (page 182) there is a tradition among young boys and girls of trying to snatch scoops of *tabbuleh* from one another before they reach the mouth, a game that cannot fail to drive any Lebanese to heights of frustration!

According to Fayez Aoun, *tabbuleh* is descended from *saf* or *safsuf,* a meatless stuffing for grape leaves that consists of bulgur, chickpeas, dried mint, olive oil, lemon juice, salt, and pepper. In Lebanon, village women used to get together in the mornings or late afternoons to enjoy *saf,* which they scooped up with fresh tender grape leaves. Over the

Scene in Mount Lebanon above the Qadisha Valley. *From John Carne,* Syria, the Holy Land, Asia Minor, &c., *vol. 1 (London, Fisher, Son, 1836)*

years the dish was refined by omitting the chickpeas, using fresh instead of dried mint, and adding parsley, scallions, and, lastly, tomatoes.

Attractive, healthful, and refreshing, *tabbuleh* charms the palate with its earthy, tangy flavor and chewy texture. The quantities of the ingredients can vary from cook to cook, although parsley is always used very generously. *Tabbuleh* keeps well in the refrigerator, but remember not to add the tomatoes until just before serving to prevent them from diluting the dressing.

1 cup fine bulgur
3 cups finely chopped flat-leaf parsley, or more
1/2 cup finely chopped fresh spearmint leaves, or to taste
3/4 cup finely chopped red onion and/or scallions
2 large ripe tomatoes, seeded and finely chopped
1/2 cup freshly squeezed and strained lemon juice, or to taste
1/2 cup extra-virgin olive oil
Salt and freshly ground black pepper to taste
3 ripe plum tomatoes, cut into wedges
The small inner leaves from 2 heads romaine

In a medium bowl cover the bulgur with cold water and let it soak 25 to 30 minutes or until soft but still slightly chewy. Drain it in a fine sieve and squeeze out as much moisture as possible with your hands. In a salad bowl combine the bulgur, parsley, mint, onion and/or scallions, and finely chopped tomatoes. Add the lemon juice, olive oil, and salt and pepper and toss gently but thoroughly. Taste and adjust the seasoning. Garnish with the tomato wedges and romaine leaves and serve.

Serves 4 to 6

Salade Russe or Salat Olivier
Salata al-Russiyya

Mention of *salade russe* in this book is not surprising when one considers the number of Europeans, including Russians, who had settled in Beirut. Two of my piano teachers were Russian émigrés. Another Russian musician, a family friend, was the nephew of Dr. Nikolai Dahl, the celebrated Moscow physician who at the turn of the century cured the composer Sergei Rachmaninoff of his extreme depression, enabling him to resume his creative work. In gratitude Rachmaninoff dedicated his *Piano Concerto No. 2* to Dr. Dahl. When this piece was first performed in Beirut in 1928 (some years before I was born) with an expatriate Russian as soloist, this same Dr. Dahl, who was also a violist, was a member of the orchestra's string section along with my father, a European-trained violinist, composer, and conductor who made a significant contribution to the cultural life of Lebanon and Syria. When the audience was informed of Dr. Dahl's presence in the orchestra, they gave him a heartfelt ovation.

Although *salade russe* was a popular buffet dish at many Beirut parties during my years in Lebanon, I am not including a recipe for it here but am mentioning it merely for the record. Readers can find recipes for this salad in my *Book of Salads* and *International Appetizer Cookbook.*

CHAPTER 3
Soups

A party at supper. *From Edward William Lane,* An Account of the Manners and Customs of the Modern Egyptians *(London, John Murray, 1836)*

UPON LEARNING THAT A MAN wished to study the Kurdish language, Joha volunteered to teach it to him even though he himself knew only a few words of Kurdish.

"Let us begin with the word for 'hot soup'," said Joha. "In Kurdish, this is called *aash*."

"I'm afraid I'm a bit confused, Master. How would one say 'cold soup'?"

"One never says 'cold soup'," replied Joha. "The Kurds like their soup hot."[1]

Most soups eaten in Syria, Lebanon, and Jordan are substantial creations designed to appease hunger rather than stimulate the appetite. Some of them have been made in much the same way for centuries.

Although this part of the world is not associated with cold weather, there are indeed areas in each of the three countries that experience uncomfortably low temperatures. Consequently, along with a few light and cooling hot-weather soups one finds hearty and warming wintertime preparations that incorporate a variety of ingredients, including meat, seafood, grains, pasta, vegetables, fruits, and dried legumes. Among the last, chickpeas and, especially, lentils are typical of the region's soups. In the countryside a robust brisk-weather concoction called *makhluta* utilizes several kinds of dried legumes, rice and/or coarse bulgur, and, perhaps, dried green beans. Another nourishing and fortifying soup is based on *kishk*. A springtime soup, traditional in Aleppo, is made with nettles and egg whites.

Chilled Yogurt and Cucumber Soup
Shurabat Khyar bi Laban

Here comes a donkey laden with cucumbers, apparently the favourite refreshment, for almost every one stops him . . .[2]

Even calorie counters can indulge in this refreshing soup.

2 small cucumbers

4 cups plain low-fat yogurt, drained to 3 cups (page 142)

1½ cups ice water

Salt to taste

3 tablespoons finely chopped scallions

2 tablespoons finely chopped fresh dill

2 tablespoons finely chopped fresh spearmint leaves

Peel and quarter the cucumbers. Cut out the seeds if too large and discard. Slice the cucumbers crosswise into ¼-inch-thick pieces and set aside.

Spoon the yogurt into a deep bowl. Gradually add the ice water, beating constantly until well blended. Add the cucumbers and salt and stir well. Taste and adjust the seasoning. Cover and chill at least 1 hour.

Just before serving, sprinkle the soup with the scallions, dill, and mint. Serve in individual soup bowls, adding an ice cube or two to each bowl.

Serves 4

Lentil Soup with Swiss Chard and Potatoes
Shurabat Adas bi Silq

> I was sitting with [a Catholic priest] one day on a stone by the way side, in conversation, when a sayd or green turbaned Mahometan passed us on an ass, carrying before him a dish of lentils, which he apparently had bought for dinner. "El mejd lillah—(Glory be to God)"—was his salutation to us; to which the priest immediately replied, "dayman—(for ever)"—and the sayd went on, and the priest continued the conversation, both quite unconscious how strange their puritanical language appeared.[3]

1½ pounds Swiss chard

1½ cups brown lentils, rinsed and picked over

8 cups beef broth, or more if needed

2 medium potatoes, peeled and cut into ½-inch cubes

⅓ cup extra-virgin olive oil

1 large onion, finely chopped

½ cup fresh coriander leaves, finely minced with 3 medium garlic cloves

½ teaspoon ground cumin, or to taste

Salt and freshly ground black pepper to taste

3 tablespoons freshly squeezed and strained lemon juice

Lemon wedges

Wash the chard thoroughly in several changes of cold water. Cut the leaves from the stems, discard the stems, and slice the leaves into ½-inch-wide strips. Set the chard strips aside.

A cucumber vendor in Ottoman Damascus. *From* National Geographic, *January, 1911*

In a large, heavy saucepan combine the lentils with the broth and bring to a boil over moderate heat. Reduce the heat to low, cover, and simmer 5 minutes. Add the potatoes and chard, cover, and simmer about 30 minutes or until the lentils and potatoes are tender, adding more broth if necessary.

Meanwhile, in a small skillet heat the oil over moderate heat. Add the onion and sauté, stirring frequently, until soft and lightly golden. Add the coriander and garlic mixture and sauté gently, stirring frequently, for a few minutes. Add the contents of the skillet to the lentil mixture. Stir in the cumin, salt and pepper, and lemon juice and simmer about 5 minutes. Taste and adjust the seasoning. Serve hot with the lemon wedges.

Serves 6

∾

A pot has found its lid.
(Said sarcastically of a couple who have similar character.)

∾

Seafood and Vegetable Soup
Shurabat Samak

Eastern Mediterranean fish soups are a legacy not only of the Phoenicians but also of the ancient Greeks, whose influence on the Syro-Lebanese coast was especially strong during the reign of the Seleucids (312–64 B.C.). I recall sampling a dish much like this one in the Syrian port of Latakia, a city that has been in existence since the twelfth century B.C. but which first gained importance under the Seleucids. More a stew than a soup, this delicious concoction is closely related to the Greek *kakavia* and makes an excellent first course when accompanied with plenty of crusty bread. The kind of fish used depends on the day's catch, and the better the fish the better the end result.

> 3 tablespoons olive oil
> 1 medium onion, finely chopped
> 1 medium green bell pepper, seeded, deribbed, and chopped
> ½ medium red bell pepper, seeded, deribbed, and chopped (optional)
> 1 large garlic clove, finely chopped
> ½ cup dry white wine
> 2 large ripe tomatoes, peeled, seeded, and diced
> 1 large baking potato, peeled and diced
> 1 large carrot, peeled and diced
> 1 medium celery stalk, diced
> 1 tablespoon tomato paste
> 1 teaspoon Red Pepper Paste (page 299)
> 1 bay leaf
> ½ teaspoon finely chopped fresh thyme leaves, or to taste
> ¼ teaspoon powdered saffron or safflower (*usfur*) (optional)
> 3 cups water
> 6 ounces each of 2 kinds of firm white fish fillets such as sea bass, red snapper, halibut, or cod, cut into 1-inch pieces
> 12 medium raw shrimp, peeled and deveined
> ¼ cup finely chopped flat-leaf parsley
> Salt, freshly ground black pepper, and Middle Eastern red pepper to taste
> Freshly squeezed and strained lemon juice to taste

In a large, heavy saucepan heat the olive oil over moderate heat. Add the onion, green pepper, red pepper (if used), and garlic and cook, stirring frequently, until the vegetables are soft. Add the wine and cook about 1 minute. Stir in the tomatoes, potato, carrot, celery, tomato paste, Red Pepper Paste, bay leaf, thyme, saffron (if used), and water. Bring the mixture to a boil, reduce the heat to low, cover, and simmer 15 to 20 minutes or until the vegetables are tender. Add the fish and shrimp and simmer

4 to 5 minutes or until just tender. Stir in the parsley, salt, black pepper and red pepper, and lemon juice. Serve at once with crusty bread.

Serves 4

ᴄᴡ

I saved it by the spoon, I spent it by the ladle. *(A)*

ᴄᴡ

Lamb and Wheat Soup
Hreesi

The origins of this warming and fortifying dish date back to Neolithic times. During the Middle Ages *hreesi* enjoyed tremendous popularity among rich and poor alike and was even a specialty of some restaurants. In the Lebanon of my childhood it used to be prepared in the countryside whenever the annual supply of *qawarma* was made (page 70), a custom that still prevails in some villages today.

Hreesi can be made with chicken instead of lamb, and *freek* (page 246) can be substituted for the skinless whole-grain wheat. The name *hreesi* is an appropriate one, for it means "mashed" or "puréed."

This age-old specialty is traditionally eaten by Christians in the mountain villages during *'Id al-Saidi,* the Feast of the Assumption, which falls on August 15. When I was growing up many Lebanese churches would be decorated with candles and flowers on Assumption Day. The most impressive celebrations, however, were held in churches named for the Virgin Mary such as the one in Bhamdun, a charming summer resort known for its excellent grapes, raisins, and *dibs.*

The observance of this festival would commence on the night of August 14 with the long, slow cooking of *hreesi.* At Bhamdun caldrons would be set up in the churchyard, and members of the congregation would donate the necessary ingredients, which consisted mainly of pieces of mutton, sheep bones, and whole-grain wheat. First the meat and bones would be cooked to make a broth. Then the wheat, which had been sprinkled with water and slightly crushed, would be added and the whole boiled and stirred for many hours until it became the consistency of porridge. Church members would take turns stoking the fires under the caldrons and stirring the broth. As the *hreesi* cooked throughout the night, everyone would have a jolly time socializing, playing games, setting off fireworks, and enjoying a variety of snacks purchased from street stands that had sprung up nearby to provide nourishment during the nocturnal revelry. Favorite foods included various candies, syrupy fritters, and seasonal fruits such as figs, grapes, and prickly pears.

With the dawning of *'Id al-Saidi* the *hreesi* would at last be ready, and following Mass the congregation would gather in the churchyard to receive portions of it under the supervision of the priest. Standing in the sparkling sunlight of early morning and breathing in the cool, fresh mountain air, the villagers would quietly eat their *hreesi* in a spirit of pious and heartfelt thanksgiving.

> 3 pounds lean lamb shoulder, bone in, cut into 2- to 3-inch pieces
> 8 cups water
> 2 cups skinless whole-grain wheat, soaked in water overnight and drained
> Salt and freshly ground black pepper to taste
> 1/4 cup unsalted butter
> 2 teaspoons ground cinnamon or ground cumin, or 1 teaspoon of each

In a large, heavy saucepan bring the lamb and water to a boil over high heat, skimming off any foam and scum as they rise to the surface. Add the wheat and season to taste with salt and pepper. Reduce the heat to low, cover, and simmer about 3 hours or until the meat is very tender and the wheat is very soft, adding more water if necessary.

Remove the lamb from the saucepan. Bone the meat, shred it as finely as possible, and return it to the pan. Simmer the mixture, stirring and beating with a wooden spoon, a whisk, or an electric beater until it forms a coarse purée of meat and wheat. Taste and adjust the seasoning and keep warm.

In a small skillet melt the butter over moderate heat. Add the cinnamon and/or cumin and mix well. Ladle the *hreesi* into heated individual soup bowls. Form a well in the center of each serving and fill it with a spoonful of the spiced butter. Serve at once.

Serves 4 to 6

It is only the bones that rattle in the pot.
(Persons of value keep silent.)

Meat Soup with Pumpkin, Quince, Apricots, and Prunes

Since this soup is my own invention, modesty prevents me from praising it as highly as I would like to.

> 5 tablespoons unsalted butter
> 2 medium onions, finely chopped
> 1 pound lean boneless lamb or beef, cut into 1-inch cubes
> 10 cups beef broth, more if needed
> 1 teaspoon ground cinnamon or Mixed Spices I (page 66)
> Salt and freshly ground black pepper to taste
> 1/3 cup lentils (optional)
> 1 pound pumpkin, peeled and cut into 1-inch cubes
> 1 quince, scrubbed well, peeled, quartered, cored, and cut into 1- inch cubes

⅓ **cup quartered tart dried apricots**

⅓ **cup dried pitted prunes**

2 tablespoons freshly squeezed and strained lemon or lime juice, or to taste

1 tablespoon sugar, or to taste

In a large, heavy saucepan melt 3 tablespoons of the butter over moderate heat. Add the onions and sauté, stirring frequently, until soft but not browned. Add the meat and cook, turning the pieces frequently until they are evenly browned on all sides. Add the broth, ½ teaspoon of the cinnamon or Mixed Spices, and salt and pepper and bring to a boil. Reduce the heat to low, cover, and simmer 40 minutes. Stir in the lentils (if used), cover, and simmer 20 minutes or until the meat is almost tender, adding more broth if necessary.

Meanwhile, in a medium, heavy skillet melt the remaining 2 tablespoons butter over moderately high heat. Add the pumpkin and sauté, turning to brown lightly on all sides.

Stir the pumpkin, quince, apricots, prunes, lemon or lime juice, remaining ½ teaspoon cinnamon or Mixed Spices, and sugar into the soup. Cover and simmer about 30 minutes or until the meat, pumpkin, and fruit are tender. Taste and adjust the seasoning and serve hot as a main course.

Serves 6

෴

Ye who buy cheap meat will regret when you taste its broth.

෴

CHAPTER 4

Dairy Products and Dairy-Based Dishes

A peasant woman churning. The churn is made of the tanned skin of a goat stripped off whole. It is partly filled with milk and, the extremities being securely closed, suspended in any convenient place by four ropes fastened to the skin of the legs. It is then regularly moved to and fro, with a jerk, until the process is completed. From Charles William Wilson, ed., Picturesque Palestine, Sinai and Egypt, *vol. 2 (New York, D. Appleton, 1883)*

THROUGHOUT HISTORY MILK and its derivatives have formed important articles of food in Greater Syria. In medieval times Jerusalem was famous for its milk and cheese, Kaisariyya (Caesarea) for its buffalo milk, and Baalbek for its many dairy products, among them *qanbaris,* identified by Maxime Rodinson as curds and by the editors of the modern Arab scholarly edition of the *Wusla* as yogurt drained of its whey. Several recipes in the *Wusla* call for *qanbaris* from Baalbek, and a recipe for *qanbaris* is given in the Egyptian *Kanz.*[1] Today the Baalbek area continues to be known for its dairy products.

Thévenot, who visited Damascus in the late seventeenth century, described some of the dairy products of that city:

> They fasten the two ends of a stick to the two hind feet of a Vessel,[2] that's to say, each end of the stick to each foot; and the same they do to the fore-feet, to the end these sticks may serve for handles: Then they put the Cream into the Vessel, stopping it close, and then taking hold on it by the two sticks, they shake it for some time, and after put a little water into it: Then they shake it again, untill the Butter be made; which being done, they pour off a kind of Butter-milk by them called *Yogourt,* which they drink. When they would have this *Yogourt* more delicious, they heat the Milk, and put a spoonfull of sower Milk to it, which they make sower with runnet; and by that mixture all the Milk becoming *Yogourt,* they let it cool and then use it; or if they have a mind to keep it, they put it with Salt into a bag which they tye very fast, that what is within may be pressed; and let it drop until no more come out: Of that matter there remains no more in the bag but a kind of a Butter or rather white Cheese, of which when they have a mind to have *Yogourt* they take a morcel, and steep it in water, which they drink with great pleasure; they use much of it to refresh themselves, especially in the Caravans, where they have always good store. This *Yogourt* is very sharp, but especially that which remains after they have made the Butter.[3]

The Euphrates River valley east of Aleppo has long been fine pasturage country for milk, butter, and cheese. In the past all the butter consumed at Aleppo plus a large amount that was exported came from this district. According to tradition, Aleppo's Arabic name, Halab, is taken from the verb "to milk."[4] The story goes that on his migration to the land of Canaan, the patriarch Abraham resided for a time on the hill upon which the massive Citadel now stands and during his stay distributed the milk of his cattle to the poor. True to its name, the "City of Milk" has enjoyed a centuries-old reputation for the abundance and quality of its dairy products. D'Arvieux praised the butter and cheese of Aleppo, noting that both were in great demand,[5] while Russell tells us that from April to September the city was supplied with excellent milk by large flocks of goats, which grazed on the neighboring pasturelands.

> During the same season, abundance of fresh cheese, Kaimak [clotted cream], and above all Leban [yogurt], is brought to market from the villages, and from the camps of the wandering tribes of Arabs and Turkmans. . . . The Leban arrives in greatest perfection, and, while the season lasts, makes up a great part of the food of the lower people. It is served also universally at all tables, either in small bowls by itself, or mixed with sallad herbs, and is sometimes poured over the roast meat, and ragouts. . . .[6]

Russell's account reminds me of my earliest summers in Zahleh, where peasant women from neighboring villages used to arrive shortly after sunrise carrying on their heads large trays containing pails of fresh milk and yogurt, which they sold from door to door. We could also purchase rich, fresh cow's milk, creamy white cheese, and superb butter with a taste hinting of hazelnuts at the dairy of a Jesuit farm in Tanail, just outside Shtora. In addition to milk products, the farm offered pots of honey, packets of dried lime tea (lime trees grew in a secluded, flower-filled garden), and, when in season, prime-quality Argenteuil asparagus, luscious strawberries, and crisp, flavorful apples the size of grapefruits. The fathers also produced, as they still do, the famous Ksara wine. With its wheat fields, orchards, vegetable gardens, and vineyards, this property, which dated from the 1860s, could well have been a farm in France. Friesian cows grazed contentedly in clover pastures, chickens and turkeys scratched about happily, and there were even a few gazelles as well as a wondrously beautiful peacock. That such an outpost of European civilization should be situated in the Lebanese countryside is not surprising when one remembers the French mandate over Lebanon and the consequent pervasion of Gallic influence on much of the life of the country.

The Shtora area is still famous for its dairy products, and many *service* (communal taxi) drivers working the Beirut-Damascus highway make a point of stopping there so that passengers can stock up on locally produced *labna* and *hallum* cheese. Today Syria, Lebanon, and Jordan all boast modern dairy farms with herds of Friesian and Jersey cattle, and the dairy industry of the three countries has benefited from up-to-date technology and training furnished by Western experts.

Yogurt
Laban

❧

He who is scalded by hot milk blows into the *laban.*

❧

Writing about yogurt brings back memories of the statuesque Beduin beauty who used to appear at our door in Shtora carrying a large container of thick homemade yogurt on her head. Although we usually had all the yogurt we could possibly need, we could not bear to refuse her, especially since what she brought was truly exceptional. With an undulating motion of remarkable grace and control, she would remove the container from her head in order to measure out our requested amount. On one of these occasions I was practicing some Chopin when she came. She had apparently never seen or heard a piano before and was filled with amazement. After this she would sometimes shyly ask if I would "make the table sing" for her and once inquired whether the table could sing only in *Franji* (European) or whether it could sing in Arabic as well!

Although its popularity in the West is only a fairly recent development, yogurt has been a basic food in the Middle East for countless centuries. Wholesome, pleasantly tangy, and easily digestible, it is present at most meals as an accompaniment to or an ingredient in a multitude of preparations both savory and sweet. It is, however, strictly omitted when fish is served, and many people, particularly in Lebanon, never combine it with *tahini* or liver.

In Syria, Lebanon, and Jordan yogurt is made from the milk of sheep, goats, and, to a lesser extent, cows and buffaloes. American yogurt, in contrast, is made mostly from cow's milk, although sheep's and goat's milk yogurt are becoming increasingly available in specialty and natural foods stores. Sheep's milk yogurt is rich and thick; that of goat's milk is less creamy and sharper in taste. Cow's milk yogurt is milder and thinner in consistency, while yogurt made from buffalo's milk is rich, dense, and strongly flavored though not as tart as the others.

Some of the yogurt available commercially in this country is quite acceptable. Be sure to choose additive-free yogurt made with live acidophilus cultures, which are thought to be beneficial. If you wish to use this guardian of good health regularly, however, I recommend that you learn to make it at home. You can make yogurt with nonfat, low-fat, or whole milk, with half-and-half, or with a combination of milk and half-and-half. Naturally, the higher the butterfat content, the richer and creamier your yogurt will be. Using a combination of fluid milk and noninstant, nonfat dry milk will result in a smoother, thicker, and more nutritious yogurt that is low in calories (see below).

1 quart whole milk

3 tablespoons active-culture, additive-free plain yogurt, at room temperature

In a heavy 2- to 3-quart enameled casserole with a tight-fitting lid, bring the milk to a boil over moderate heat, stirring constantly to prevent any skin from forming on the surface. Remove from the heat and, stirring occasionally, allow the milk to cool to a temperature of 112°F on a candy/frying thermometer. This is the ideal temperature for the yogurt bacilli to multiply. Working quickly, place the yogurt in a small sterilized bowl, add a few tablespoons of the lukewarm milk, and beat vigorously with a fork or whisk until smooth. Stir the mixture into the remaining milk in the casserole until thoroughly blended. Cover the casserole with the lid and let the mixture stand undisturbed in a warm, draft-free spot (85° to 110°F) about 6 hours or until set. Take care not to overincubate the yogurt; otherwise it will become unpleasantly sour. After it has cooled it will thicken a little more.

Transfer the casserole to the refrigerator without shaking it or stirring its contents, and chill the covered yogurt about 4 hours or until firm. It is best used within 4 days. Remember to reserve 3 tablespoons of this yogurt to use as the "starter" for your next batch.

Makes 1 quart

VARIATIONS:

For a thicker yogurt, combine ½ cup noninstant, nonfat dry milk and ⅓ cup whole milk, at room temperature, in a blender and process just until smooth. Stir into the hot milk, let the mixture cool to 112°F, and continue as above.

Here is a reliable method for making yogurt using a thermos. Preheat a clean 1-quart wide-mouth thermos by filling it with warm water (about 115°F). Cap it and let stand while you heat the milk. Pour the water out of the container and immediately replace it with the milk mixture at 112°F. Replace the cap tightly and leave undisturbed about 4 hours. Check, and if the yogurt has not set, recap at once and check again every half hour or so. When set, remove the cap, cover loosely, and refrigerate several hours until the yogurt is cold and firm.

◌

No one says, "my *laban* is sour."
(i.e., everyone praises his own)
◌

Drained Yogurt

The yogurt I grew up with in the Middle East was thicker and creamier than that generally available here. Since yogurt used for cooking purposes should be thick, thin yogurt must be drained to remove excess liquid. The longer it drains, the firmer it will become. Yields will vary depending on the initial thickness of the yogurt. After draining 1 to 2 hours, the yogurt will lose enough of its whey to make it suitable for use in salads. After 4 to 5 hours, it will work well for dips, sauces, soups, and beverages. After several more hours, it will acquire a texture similar to that of cream cheese (see Yogurt Cheese, below). Use the freshest, best-tasting additive-free yogurt possible, because draining will intensify its character.

Drained yogurt can often be substituted for whipped cream, sour cream, *crème fraîche*, clotted cream, *mascarpone*, and cream cheese.

Set a colander or fine strainer over a deep bowl and line it with a triple layer of rinsed and squeezed cheesecloth (the bottom of the colander should be suspended at least 2 inches above the bottom of the bowl). Spoon additive-free, plain yogurt into the cheesecloth. Fold the cloth over the yogurt, cover, and let the yogurt drain in the refrigerator for 1 to 48 hours, depending on the consistency desired. Pour off the whey as it accumulates so that the yogurt can drain freely. Remove the drained yogurt from the cheesecloth. Use at once, or refrigerate in an airtight container for up to 5 days or as long as it tastes fresh and there is no sign of spoilage.

Yogurt Cheese *(M)*
Labna

This easily made cheese offers a low-calorie alternative to cream cheese. The longer it drains, the firmer it will become. As with Drained Yogurt (above), yields will vary depending on the initial thickness of the yogurt.

Labna is often eaten with fresh herbs and raw vegetables such as spearmint, cucumber, and tomatoes and is used in fillings for savory pastries and *kibbeh.* Served with olive oil, olives, *za'atar,* and flatbread, it is a standard breakfast dish. Drizzled with olive oil and sometimes dusted with paprika, it is a regular feature on the *mazza.*

1 quart additive-free plain yogurt
1 teaspoon salt or to taste

In a large bowl combine the yogurt thoroughly with the salt. Follow the recipe for Drained Yogurt (above), allowing the yogurt to drain about 24 hours for a soft cheese or up to 48 for a firmer one. Use at once, or refrigerate in an airtight container for up to 5 days or as long as it tastes fresh and shows no sign of spoilage.

Makes about 1¾ cups soft cheese or about 1¼ cups firm cheese

Yogurt Cheese Balls in Olive Oil *(M)*
Labna bi Zayt

Follow the recipe for Yogurt Cheese (above), using 1½ teaspoons salt and allowing the yogurt to drain until it is quite firm and a little dry. With lightly oiled palms, roll into 1- to 1½-inch balls and place the balls 1 inch apart on a tray large enough to hold them in one layer. Cover with plastic wrap and chill several hours or overnight. Pack the cheese balls in a sterilized glass jar and cover with extra-virgin olive oil. Seal the jar and store in a cool place up to 2 weeks. To serve, place as many cheese balls as needed in a serving dish and spoon a little olive oil over them. Sprinkle lightly with paprika, if desired. Accompany with pita bread or Mountain Bread (page 316).

Cooked Yogurt
Laban Matbukh

Many Middle Eastern dishes call for yogurt as a cooking liquid or sauce, in which case it must first be stabilized with egg white and cornstarch as directed below. This step is unnecessary if you are using yogurt made from sheep's or goat's milk; however, the yogurt usually available in the West is made from cow's milk, which will curdle if cooked for a long period rather than just heated.

Stirring the yogurt in one direction only is a traditional Middle Eastern technique deemed necessary to help prevent curdling. It is also important to keep the saucepan uncovered since any steam dripping into the liquid could have an adverse effect.

> 1 quart additive-free plain yogurt
> 1 egg white, lightly beaten
> 1 tablespoon cornstarch mixed with a little of the yogurt or cold water
> 1 teaspoon salt or to taste

In a large enameled saucepan beat the yogurt until it is very smooth. Add the egg white, cornstarch mixture, and salt, and stir thoroughly with a wooden spoon. Bring to a simmer over low heat, stirring constantly in one direction only. Reduce the heat to as low as possible and simmer, uncovered, about 10 minutes or until the sauce is thickened. It is now ready to be combined and cooked with meat or vegetables without any danger of curdling.

Makes 1 quart

Sweetened Yogurt Cream ❧

Yogurt lends a pleasant tang and slashes calories in this welcome alternative to sweetened whipped cream. A similar recipe of my own creation using vanilla, which appeared in my yogurt book (1978) served as the inspiration for this one.

> ½ cup chilled heavy cream
> 2 tablespoons confectioners' sugar, or to taste, sifted
> 1 teaspoon orange flower water or rose water, or ½ teaspoon of each
> 3 cups plain low-fat yogurt, drained to 1¼ cups (page 142) and chilled

In a chilled bowl beat the cream until it begins to stiffen. Add the confectioners' sugar and orange flower water or rose water and continue to beat until stiff. Fold in the chilled drained yogurt gently but thoroughly. Serve at once, or cover and refrigerate up to 1 hour.

Makes about 2 cups

Dried Curds

This ancient product is curdled sheep's or goat's milk drained of its whey, salted, shaped into small round cakes or balls, and dried in the sun until hard. The cakes are rubbed between the hands or grated and the resulting chalklike powder dissolved in water to make a nourishing beverage that is especially welcome in hot weather. Nineteenth-century travelers like Burckhardt and Doughty appreciated the healthful and refreshing qualities of dried curds. In his book, *The Holy Land and the Bible* (1891), Cunningham Geikie describes how they were made by the Beduin in Palestine:

> A quantity of sour milk, or "leben," is put in a goat-skin bottle, and shaken till the whey separates and can be poured out. Then more sour milk is added, and the shaking and emptying of the whey continue till cheese enough is provided. This, when afterwards dried in the sun, is much used to mix with water as a cooling and strengthening drink on journeys, or it is put into flour to make cheesecakes, in which shape it is a very concentrated form of food, easily carried about.

These cakes are known as *jameed* in Jordan, where they are traditionally used in the preparation of a sauce of the same name that is poured over *mansaf*, the country's national dish. The Beduin place the cakes on the tops of their tents to dry in the sun. *Jameed* is also used to make a Jordanian lentil and rice dish known as *reshuf* (or *rajuf*).

Cheese

> Returning one day, in Syria, from a journey, I enquired the way of a countryman in the road. It was noon;—the young man, who went by eating bread and cheese, paused and cut a piece of his girdle-cake, with a pleasant look, and presented it to the stranger: when I shook the head, he cut a rasher of cheese and put it silently to my mouth; and only then he thought it a time to speak.[7]

We learn from medieval Arab sources that a variety of cheeses was produced throughout the Islamic Empire. The culinary manuals of the period include recipes that utilize cheese (for example, several in the *Kanz* call for *jibn shami,* or Syrian cheese). Much later, Westerners in Ottoman Syria described square cakes of fresh white cheese made from sheep's or goat's milk cured with rennet. This firm, mild-flavored cheese, known as *jibna khadra, jibna bayda,* or, simply, *jibn,* enjoyed universal popularity.[8] Cheese was also produced from buffalo's milk.

Today cheeses usually made from the milk of sheep, goats, and buffaloes are consumed throughout the region, with some available only in certain localities and others found in all three countries. The fresh cheese described by writers a century ago is still produced. I remember encountering families of shepherds in the Lebanon Mountains making this kind of cheese by heating goat's milk in large, heavy pans over wood fires. They would take their cheese down to markets in nearby towns and villages, where it enjoyed a ready clientele. Fresh cheese is eaten for breakfast, as an appetizer, and as a snack. It is also used as a filling for pastries and as an ingredient in fritters. When salted, packed into sterilized glass jars, and covered with brine, it will keep at least a month. This cheese is sometimes preserved in olive oil instead of brine.

A childhood favorite of mine was *jibna majdula,* a chewy, salty white cheese flavored with nigella and, perhaps, *mahlab* that lends itself to being separated into strings. In the early spring my relatives in Aleppo, like many other residents of that city, used to make it by melting down and salting the fresh cheese brought to market in tightly packed sacks or goatskins by the Beduin camped in the surrounding countryside. Lumps of the hot melted cheese would be repeatedly stretched and looped before being twisted, braided, and, finally, placed in brine in order to last through the year. This braided cheese is delicious eaten as an appetizer or snack.

Qarisheh, a whey cheese similar to ricotta, is often eaten with sugar or honey. An unusual preparation is *shanklish,* fermented cheese balls made from *qarisheh* and coated with thyme. It is especially popular in Syria and in Tripoli, the capital of northern Lebanon, which is noted for its cheesemakers.

Feta is a crumbly white cheese that is traditionally made from sheep's or goat's milk, salted, and preserved in brine. In addition to being produced locally, as in Tripoli (*jibna tarablusiyya*), this cheese is imported from other countries such as Bulgaria (*jibna bilghariyya*) and Germany, which sends large amounts of cow's milk feta to the Middle East. Feta is often eaten as an appetizer and is used in dips, salads, and savory pastries.

Hallum is a salty, semihard white Lebanese cheese made with sheep's milk. It is matured in whey and often sprinkled with nigella. It makes a good table cheese, is excellent grilled or fried, and can be used in savory pastries. A Cypriot version of this cheese, known as *halumi,* is flavored with dried mint rather than nigella. Another salty

General view of ʾAkka (Acre, now in Israel), where akkawi cheese originated. From Charles William Wilson, ed., Picturesque Palestine, Sinai and Egypt, *vol. 2 (New York, D. Appleton, 1883)*

white cheese is *akkawi,* which takes its name from the port city of 'Akka (Acre, now in Israel). This smooth, dense cheese is eaten at breakfast and is utilized in both savory and sweet pastries as well as in semolina desserts. When used in sweet preparations it is first desalted (page 339). Still another salty white cheese employed in savory and sweet pastries is *nabulsi* or *nabulsiyya,* which comes from the town of Nabulus on the West Bank. A hard sheep's milk cheese is *kashkawan,* which is actually imported Rumanian or Bulgarian *kashkaval,* Greek *kasseri,* or Turkish *kaşer.* It is also produced in a few Druze villages in the Jaulan (Golan). *Kashkawan* makes a fine table cheese and is frequently grated like Parmesan and used on pasta. It possesses excellent melting qualities and can be utilized in fillings for savory pastries. Native cooks often create their own blends of sharp and mild cheeses for filling pastries. In this country a product known as *boerek* cheese has been developed in California by an Armenian from Lebanon and is marketed by Indo-European Foods of Glendale, California.

∾

She serves cheese on paper and bread from the market.
(Said of a bad housewife.)

∾

Butter

∾

One hand in butter, the other in honey.
(Said of a rich man.)

∾

In former times the manufacture of butter (as well as cheese) among the Beduin and the peasantry was a task usually entrusted to the women, who prepared it in much the same way as in Biblical times (indeed, some Arab women still churn butter in this manner today!). The process has been described by an English traveler in Ottoman Syria:

> Close to the milking-ground is a triangle of wood, in which hangs an ox-hide, having at each end of it two small sticks for handles. When the milk is put into this skin, two women draw it backward and forward between them, and in this manner make the sweetest butter I have ever tasted. When it is ready, they dash their long arms into the skin, and scoop it out . . . [in]to the . . . bowls.
>   . . . I made a most excellent breakfast, although a little puzzled at first which side or in what manner to butter my bread. My companions led the way by rubbing their cakes every now and then into the bowl; and, thus initiated into the mystery of eating Arab bread and butter, I made great progress.[9]

Butter was used lavishly in the kitchens of nineteenth-century al-Karak (in what is now Jordan), whose inhabitants were celebrated for their unbounded hospitality. Burckhardt writes of a custom peculiar to the town when he visited it:

It is considered at Kerek an unpardonable meanness to sell butter or to exchange it for any necessary or convenience of life; so that, as the property of the people chiefly consists in cattle, and every family possesses large flocks of goats and sheep, which produce great quantities of butter, they supply this article very liberally to their guests. . . . If a man is known to have sold or exchanged this article, his daughters or sisters remain unmarried, for no one would dare to connect himself with the family of a Baya el Samin, or seller of butter, the most insulting epithet that can be applied to a man of Kerek.[10]

Butter was also generously employed in Aleppan kitchens. Made indiscriminately from the milk of goats, sheep, cows, and buffaloes, it was supplied mainly by nomads, who transported it to town in the same goatskins in which it was churned. Since there was no refrigeration in those days, most of the butter was clarified (see below) and stored in jars or skins for future use.

Modern-day Syria produces abundant butter, much of it from sheep and goats. When I lived in Lebanon most of the clarified butter used locally was imported from Aleppo, where it was made with sheep's milk. Butter from the milk of buffaloes was also produced near Aleppo by an Armenian family of our acquaintance, who kept a herd of these animals in the swamps along the Orontes River and employed modern manufacturing techniques in their plant. Another Syrian city famous for its clarified butter as well as its yogurt is Hama, an attractive community farther south on the Orontes.

Clarified Butter
Samna

This butter, from which water and impurities have been removed, has traditionally been a preferred cooking medium and still remains so for certain dishes (see page 70). Just how great the demand for it was in Ottoman Syria is borne out by a letter in which a local amir ordered approximately 630 pounds of *samna* from a Zahleh shopkeeper in lieu of rent! [11]

1 pound unsalted butter, cut into 1-inch pieces

In a heavy saucepan melt the butter over low heat, being careful not to let it brown. Remove the pan from the heat and let the butter stand about 3 minutes. Skim the froth and strain the butter into a bowl through a sieve lined with a double thickness of rinsed and squeezed cheesecloth, discarding the milky solids in the bottom of the pan. Pour the clarified butter into a clean jar, cover the jar tightly, and refrigerate. Covered and chilled, this butter will keep indefinitely.

Makes about ¾ pound

∾

If you cook the meal with words, I'll promise you an ocean of butter.

∾

Clotted Cream

Qashta

> As soon as we had come to the west of the Belaz, we were supplied very constantly with
> clotted cream (*kymak*) and sour milk (*leben*), than which the dairy can produce nothing
> better.[12]

Cream is not a traditional cooking ingredient in the Middle East. There is, however, a
rich concentrated cream made from the milk of ewes or buffaloes that is known under
a variety of names, including *qashta* and *zubdi* in Arabic and *kaymak* in Turkish. This
voluptuous product, which is thick enough to be cut with a knife, is used as a topping
or filling for pastries and other desserts. It is also spread on bread with honey or jam.
Russell, who noted the resemblance of *qashta* to Devonshire cream, has left us a description of how it was made in eighteenth-century Aleppo:

> Kaimak, in Turkish is the name commonly used for this cream, but the proper Arabic name
> is Zubdy. The original Arabic receipt for making it is as follows; agreeably to which it has
> been made with success in England. "Into a copper pan twenty-three inches in diameter, and
> two inches and a half deep, put nineteen pints of fresh sheeps milk (in weight . . . fifteen
> pounds English) and place it over a moderate charcoal fire, made on a stone hearth. The pan
> must be raised above the hearth about six inches, by means of three stones, or a trivet, the
> fire is then to be blown gently for the space of two minutes, and for that time only. A thin
> scum will soon appear on the milk, and in about half an hour cover the whole surface. You
> will then perceive it simmer, or a small motion in the middle of the pan will show that it is
> just beginning to boil.
>
> You must now, having provided a pint mug, or the like vessel with a handle, ladle the
> milk till you bring it into an entire froth, which will require about two minutes; and as the
> froth and blubbers subside, the Kaimak will rise on the surface, covering it in the form of a
> honey comb.
>
> It is requisite at this time to be attentive to the fire. Should the Kaimak appear swelling
> in any part, immediately remove some of the fire, which if still too fierce, damp it with ashes.
> The remaining fire is then to be spread equally under the pan, and if no swellings appear on
> the surface of the milk, it may be left to thicken, and cool.
>
> The Kaimak, when cold, is to be carefully stripped off with the fingers, in the form of a
> rolled pancake, only thicker; but in this operation it is hardly possible to prevent the cake
> breaking into pieces.
>
> The Kaimak produced will be found to weigh one pound two thirds English . . . and the
> remaining milk will measure eleven pints. The milk is rich and sweet, but will have acquired
> a burnt taste.
>
> The remaining milk submitted again to the same operation, will produce a second cake
> of Kaimak, weighing one pound and a quarter English, but inferior in quality and colour to
> the first.
>
> Though goat's milk be plenty in Aleppo, sheep's milk is preferred for making Kaimak.
> Some experience is required for regulating the fire properly, and judging of the boiling, the
> honey comb scurf, &c. If the fire be made of rather large pieces of charcoal, and a little brisk
> at first, one or two minutes blowing will be sufficient; but it must not be hurried so as to

make the milk boil within the half hour. The vessel must not be moved nor the milk stirred, when left to cool.

The whole of the operation from the time of making the fire till the stripping off the Kaimak, was finished in about three hours.[13]

Here is a modern recipe for *qashta* that uses cow's milk, which will yield a cream that is milder in flavor than one made with either ewe's or buffalo's milk.

1 quart heavy cream

In a large, heavy enameled skillet $2\frac{1}{2}$ inches deep, bring the cream slowly to a gentle simmer. Reduce the heat to very low. Ladle out a portion of the cream, and with the ladle held at least 10 inches above the skillet, pour it back in a thin, steady stream. Continue to aerate the cream in this manner for 1 hour or until the surface is covered with bubbles. Transfer the skillet carefully to a warm place and let the cream stand 2 hours. Let the cream stand at room temperature 2 hours, then cover and refrigerate at least 12 hours.

With a thin, sharp knife, loosen the edges of the layer of cream and cut the cream into strips about $1\frac{1}{2}$ inches wide. With a spatula, carefully transfer the strips to a large, flat plate, discarding the liquid remaining in the skillet. Cover with clear plastic film and chill. Use the cream as directed in recipes, or cut it into squares and use as a topping for pastries and stewed fruits. Covered and chilled, it should keep at least 3 days.

Cream rises only after churning.

CHAPTER 5

Egg Dishes

Druze princesses from Mount Lebanon wearing the traditional hornlike headdress called a tantur.
From William McClure Thomson, The Land and the Book, *vol. 3 (New York, Harper, 1885)*

~

Rather the egg of today than the hen of tomorrow.

~

The best eggs for my Beirut breakfasts were delivered early on Saturday mornings by a villager clad in the traditional garb of a Lebanese mountaineer: a collarless white shirt and black *sharwaal,* full-seated baggy trousers tapering in at the ankles, which supposedly owe their design to the belief that the second Messiah will be born of man, thus preparing the wearer for this event should he be the chosen one. Extremely polite and rather shy in dealing with city dwellers, this simple peasant, the soul of punctuality and reliability, must have gathered the eggs for his Beirut customers at dawn and taken the day's first bus from his rural hamlet into the capital. One sensed he felt somewhat bewildered in the whirl of this sophisticated metropolis! There was no comparison between those country eggs, newly laid by free-ranging hens, and the ones sold in supermarkets. The eggs were so flavorful that we often prepared them with nothing more than a sprinkling of salt and pepper and maybe a fresh herb or two.

Eggs are an important part of the diet, especially in the countryside, where many people raise their own chickens. A broad range of ingredients is used in the creation of egg dishes, some of the more unusual ones being *basterma, maqaniq, sujuk, qawarma, kibbeh,* lamb's brains, fresh chickpeas, fennel, fava beans, sorrel, cardoons, truffles, *kishk,* pita bread, and pine nuts.

Hard-Cooked and Poached Eggs

Hard-cooked eggs are often simply mashed with olive oil or yogurt and seasoned with salt and pepper. They are also very good served with a yogurt, *tahini,* or walnut sauce flavored with garlic. On special occasions hard-cooked eggs are stuffed and decorated, or they are encased in *kibbeh* or *kafta.* They are dyed a deep red for Easter, when a favorite game played in Christian communities by children of all ages is to knock one's egg against that of another. The person whose egg survives intact is declared the winner.

In medieval times eggs were sometimes broken over stews shortly before the end of cooking and allowed to poach in the sauce. A popular way of preparing eggs today is to poach them in a yogurt sauce flavored with garlic and dried spearmint.

Fried Eggs

A standard method of cooking eggs is to fry them in finest-quality olive oil until golden brown and crunchy around the edges and garnish them with minced fresh spearmint or za'atar. Another common way is to fry them in butter or olive oil flavored with crushed garlic and dried spearmint and sprinkle them with ground sumac or sour pomegranate juice when nearly cooked. Eggs are sometimes fried in qawarma, particularly in rural areas.

Fried eggs have long been served by villagers to unexpected visitors. A near-heroic case in point occurred during the nineteenth century in the Shuf mountains of Lebanon:

> Fouad . . . related an incident that took place in the days of his great-great-grandmother.
>
> "Last-minute word reached the house that Sheik Basheer Jimblatt, with his five hundred riders, was passing through town. There was no time to prepare, yet he must not pass our house unfed.
>
> "'It can't be done,' the women declared. 'It can,' my grandmother decided. She called for wood, for butter, and an immense frying vat. There was a scurry for those round, flat bread-cakes, and they rounded up eggs. When the riders reached town, the fat was frying hot. In went the eggs. As fast as they rose to the top, they were clapped between the opened loaves, and each rider received his soldier's portion without dismounting. The job was done and the day was won." [1]

Scrambled Eggs and Omelets

Recipes for scrambled eggs appear in medieval Arab manuscripts. Today, eggs prepared this way are a favorite throughout the region. A simple and very popular dish is eggs scrambled with sautéed chopped onions and/or garlic and tomatoes. Sometimes eggs are scrambled with sautéed onions, ground lamb or beef, and such vegetables as zucchini, eggplants, potatoes, green beans, fava beans, and cardoons. The Lebanese are fond of herbed scrambled eggs sprinkled with minced scallions and topped with a tart pomegranate sauce.

Unlike the light, thin French omelette, the Arab omelet, or ijja, is firm and thick in texture. A flexible, multipurpose creation similar to an Italian frittata or a Spanish tortilla, it lends itself to a wide variety of fillings, the egg being the binding agent. Although the ijja is traditionally cooked in either olive oil or clarified butter (regular butter may also be used), the great Abbassid physician al-Razi (865–925) recommended using oil since it produces a dish that is lighter and easier to digest. [2]

An Arab omelet can be cooked on top of the stove or baked in the oven. When done, it is turned out onto a platter and cut into wedges, squares, or rectangles, depending on the shape of the pan used for cooking. It can also be made in small, individual-sized portions (there are special frying pans for this purpose with several depressions in the surface, into which the omelet mixture is poured). Small pieces of *ijja* can be served as hors d'oeuvres, while larger portions make excellent first courses, side dishes, and light entrées. Since this type of omelet can be eaten cold as well as hot, it is ideal fare for picnics and parties.

In her discussion of egg dishes, the author of a well-known Middle Eastern cookbook has mistakenly written that the *ijja* does not appear in early Arab culinary literature. Recipes for *ijjas* are indeed found in the early cookery manuals; for example, five are given in the *Wusla,* and both the *Kanz* and the *Kitab al-tabikh* of al-Warraq (a contemporary of al-Razi) each include a larger number. These medieval omelets incorporate such ingredients as lamb or mutton, chicken, small birds, truffles, fresh fava beans and chickpeas, onions, sorrel, leeks, olives, pistachios, almonds, walnuts, cheese, milk, *qanbaris,* sugar, honey, mint, parsley, tarragon, rue, cinnamon, coriander, caraway, cumin, saffron, sumac, salted lemons, wine vinegar, and *murri.* A curious recipe entitled "*Ujja fi qanani*" ("Omelet in a Bottle") is found in both the *Wusla* and the *Kanz.* To prepare this particular *ijja,* the egg mixture is put into a glass bottle. After being tightly sealed, the bottle is plunged into boiling water, where it remains until the omelet is cooked. The bottle is then carefully broken, leaving the omelet, which will have assumed the shape of the bottle. Lastly, the omelet is fried in a combination of olive and sesame oils. I strongly advise you *not* to try this recipe! I simply mention it here as an example of the quest for the unusual and ostentatious by the upper class of the period.

A lighter, single-serving French-type omelet is also encountered in the region. This more recent innovation makes use of indigenous fillings, which give it a Middle Eastern personality.

First lay an egg, then cackle. (*A*)

Fried Eggs with Cheese
Bayd Maqli bil Jibna

I first sampled eggs prepared in this fashion when I was barely five years old, during a visit to the scenic red-roofed village of Jazzin, known for its picturesque waterfalls and fine cutlery. Jazzin could have been equally famous for those fried eggs, judging by the very long time I raved about them to anyone with access to a skillet!

This dish is usually made in individual-sized two-handled frying pans. The cheeses called for can be found at specialty cheese shops or wherever Greek and Middle Eastern cheeses are sold. Other cheeses such as Cheddar or Gruyère may be substituted.

1 slice *hallum* (page 146) or *kashkawan* cheese (page 147), about ⅜ inch thick

All-purpose flour for dredging the cheese (optional)

1 tablespoon unsalted butter or olive oil

1 egg

Salt, freshly ground black pepper, and paprika to taste

Dredge the cheese in the flour, if desired. In a small skillet just large enough to hold the slice of cheese, melt the butter over moderate heat. Add the cheese, and when it starts to melt and blister, break the egg over it and cook until the white is firm and the yolk just slightly runny. Sprinkle with the salt, pepper, and paprika and serve at once directly from the skillet, accompanied with warm pita bread.

Serves 1

An Alfresco Dinner by the Dog River

Prince K . . . accompanied me in my boat to the "Nahr el Kelb," or Dog River; a stream that issues from a picturesque ravine about nine miles from Beyrout . . . [T]he steep hills that formed its banks were . . . crowned with a Maronite convent. . . .

[A] carpet was spread under the shade of spreading sycamores, and we were soon reposing upon it in placid enjoyment of our chibouques, while the Syrian servants bustled about preparations for dinner. . . .

We dined merrily together on kid from the mountain, and omelettes made with herbs that grew wild about us; the wine was cooled in the cascade, and the coffee mingled its pleasant perfume with that of the aromatic shrubs on which it was boiling. Pipes, coffee, mountain-breezes, wild flowers' scents, superb scenery, sparkling torrents, neighing horses, the sea's deep roar, and a joyous party, made us think that the monks might have pleasant times of it, after all, notwithstanding that this Eden of theirs was Eveless.[3]

Parsley, Mint, and Scallion Omelets
Ijjit al-Na'na' wa al-Baqdunis

This rural standby can be served as an appetizer, for lunch, or as a filling for pita bread. Omelets made with a single herb such as fresh parsley, thyme, or fennel are also popular.

4 eggs

¼ cup finely chopped flat-leaf parsley

¼ cup finely chopped fresh spearmint leaves

¼ cup finely chopped scallions

Salt and freshly ground black pepper to taste

3 tablespoons olive oil, or more if needed

In a medium bowl beat the eggs until they are well blended. Stir in the parsley, mint, scallions, and salt and pepper.

Mouth of the Dog River. *From John Carne,* Syria, the Holy Land, Asia Minor, &c., *vol. 1 (London, Fisher, Son, 1836)*

In a large, heavy skillet heat the olive oil over moderate heat. Drop the egg mixture, a tablespoon at a time, into the hot oil, being careful not to overcrowd the skillet. There should be about 1 inch of space between the omelets. Fry the omelets until golden on one side, then turn and brown the other side. Serve hot or cold.

Serves 3 or 4

A lady and two maids to fry two eggs!

Zucchini Omelets

Ijjit Kusa

Follow the recipe for Parsley, Mint, and Scallion Omelets (above) with these changes: Place 4 small zucchini, grated, in a colander, sprinkle with salt, and let stand 20 minutes to drain. Squeeze the zucchini dry and stir it into the egg mixture. Add 2 tablespoons all-purpose flour and, if desired, 1 medium garlic clove, crushed. Mix well and continue as above.

Serves 4

They fed him an egg and took from him a chicken.

Tomato Omelet with Cheese
Bayd bi Banadura wa Jibna

> Tomatoes, though comparatively new to the country, have become a favorite vegetable. . . . A cooked tomato sauce is boiled down and then evaporated in the sun until of considerable density, when it is set away as a winter seasoning for soups, stews and rice. Sliced tomatoes are dried in the sun for preservation. The fresh tomato is enjoyed in salads. The price per pound is something less than one cent.[4]

When I was growing up, some Lebanese villagers utilized an ingenious method of keeping tomatoes fresh for much of the winter: They picked them quite green and buried them underground in straw, which they maintained arrested the ripening process and made it possible for the vegetable to be enjoyed during the cold months.

This omelet is much like one I was once served near the Cedars of Lebanon, which, I was told, incorporated tomatoes preserved by the above method.

¼ cup olive oil

6 scallions, chopped

6 small ripe tomatoes, peeled, seeded, and cut into ¼-inch-thick slices

Salt and freshly ground black pepper to taste

¾ cup freshly grated *kashkawan* cheese (page 147) or Parmesan, or to taste

2 tablespoons finely chopped fresh basil or spearmint leaves

8 eggs, lightly beaten

3 tablespoons finely chopped flat-leaf parsley

In a large, heavy skillet with a flameproof handle, heat the oil over moderate heat. Add the scallions and sauté, stirring frequently, until soft. Arrange the tomato slices over the scallions and season with the salt and pepper. Cover and simmer about 10 minutes or until the tomatoes are soft, uncovering for the last few minutes of cooking, if needed, to evaporate excess liquid. Sprinkle the cheese and basil or spearmint evenly over the tomatoes. Reduce the heat to low, pour the eggs over, cover, and cook, without stirring, until the eggs are just set.

Place the skillet under a preheated broiler about 4 inches from the heat. Cook the omelet briefly until the top is lightly browned. Transfer the omelet to a heated platter and sprinkle with the parsley. Cut into wedges and serve.

Serves 6

꙳

If he gives you an egg, it won't have a yolk. *(A)*
(Used to describe a stingy person.)

꙳

Fish Omelet

Ijja bi Samak

Al-Baghdadi's thirteenth-century culinary manual includes three recipes for fish cooked with eggs, which bear an obvious kinship to dishes still eaten today in parts of the Middle East and the Caucasus. The omelet described below is of Persian provenance. Like many Persian dishes, recipes for which appear in the medieval Arab manuscripts, this one turns up in slightly varying forms in several countries, including Lebanon.

Many years ago a similar omelet was served to me, interestingly, in Sidon, which according to the ninth-century Arab geographer al-Ya'qubi, was inhabited exclusively by Persians, whose ancestors had been brought there by the Umayyad caliph Mu'awiyya (reigned 661–680). Other towns that were either largely or entirely populated with Persians by this same caliph were Beirut, Tripoli, Byblos, and Baalbek.

> **1 pound sole or flounder fillets**
> **Salt to taste**
> **1/4 cup all-purpose flour**
> **3 tablespoons unsalted butter or olive oil**
> **2 tablespoons freshly squeezed and strained lemon juice**
> **1 teaspoon Pomegranate Molasses (page 57) (optional)**
> **1 medium onion, finely chopped**
> **1 large garlic clove, finely chopped**
> **8 eggs**
> **1/4 cup finely chopped flat-leaf parsley, or 2 tablespoons each parsley and fresh**
>   **spearmint or tarragon leaves**
> **Freshly ground black pepper to taste**
> **Lemon wedges**

Wash the fish fillets under cold running water and pat thoroughly dry with paper towels. Sprinkle them on both sides with salt. Coat with the flour and shake to remove the excess. In a large, heavy saucepan melt 2 tablespoons of the butter over moderately high heat. Add the fish fillets and sauté about 2 minutes on each side or until golden brown and tender. Transfer the fillets to a plate, and when cool enough to handle remove any bones and chop the flesh finely. Mix the lemon juice with the Pomegranate Molasses, if used, and sprinkle over the fish.

In a small, heavy skillet melt the remaining 1 tablespoon butter over moderate heat. Add the onion and garlic and sauté, stirring frequently, until lightly browned. Remove from the heat.

In a large bowl beat the eggs with a fork or whisk until blended. Add the parsley, sautéed onion and garlic, and salt and black pepper and mix well. Add the fish and mix again. Pour the mixture into a well-buttered shallow baking dish about 9 inches in di-

The Bay of Sidon, seen from the south. From Charles William Wilson, ed., Picturesque Palestine, Sinai and Egypt, *vol. 2 (New York, D. Appleton, 1883)*

ameter and spread it in an even layer. Bake, uncovered, in a preheated 350° F oven about 30 minutes or until set.

Present the fish omelet in the baking dish, or turn it out onto a serving platter. Cool slightly. Cut into wedges and serve with the lemon.

Serves 6

For the sake of the omelet, they kiss the handle of the pan. (*A*)

Kibbeh Omelet
Ijjit al-Kibbeh

Here is a great way to use up leftover *kibbeh.*

2 tablespoons olive oil or unsalted butter
1 cup leftover fried, baked, or broiled *kibbeh* (Chapter 9), cut into small pieces
2 scallions, including 2 inches of the green tops, finely chopped
4 eggs
2 to 4 tablespoons finely chopped flat-leaf parsley, or a mixture of parsley and
      spearmint leaves
Salt, freshly ground black pepper, and Middle Eastern red pepper to taste

In a medium, heavy skillet with a flameproof handle heat the olive oil over moderate heat. Add the *kibbeh* and scallions and cook, stirring, until they are heated.

In a small bowl beat the eggs until well blended. Stir in the parsley or parsley and spearmint mixture and salt, black pepper, and red pepper. Pour the mixture over the *kibbeh* and scallions. Cover and cook over low heat, without stirring, until the eggs are just set. Place the skillet under a preheated broiler about 4 inches from the heat and cook the omelet briefly until the top is lightly browned. Cut into wedges and serve.

Serves 2

French Omelet with Middle Eastern Fillings

My two Istanbul-born cousins, who taught French history and literature in Beirut, introduced me to this type of omelet. Both women were ardent Francophiles who dressed elegantly in the latest Parisian fashions, cooked superbly in the French manner, and were even mistakenly thought to be French by the French themselves!

3 eggs
Pinch salt
Small pinch freshly ground black pepper
1 tablespoon unsalted butter
3 tablespoons Sausage Filling or Yogurt Cheese Filling (below)

In a small bowl beat the eggs until they are just blended. Season with the salt and pepper. Heat a 7-inch nonstick skillet over moderately high heat until it is hot. Add the butter and heat, tilting and rotating the pan to coat it with the butter, until the foam subsides. Pour in the eggs and allow them to set for 3 or 4 seconds. Stir the eggs with the back of a fork, lifting the edges and tilting the skillet to let the uncooked egg flow underneath. Cook the omelet until it is just set but still moist on top. Remove the skillet from the heat. Spoon the filling in a line across the center of the omelet. With a spatula or fork, fold the omelet in thirds and invert it onto a heated serving plate. Garnish as suggested below and serve at once.

Serves 1

SAUSAGE FILLING

Remove the casing from 2 ounces *maqaniq* (page 71) or *sujuk* (page 71). Chop the sausage and sauté in a little unsalted butter over moderate heat, stirring frequently, a few minutes or until browned. Drain off excess fat. Fill the omelet with the sautéed sausage and garnish with parsley sprigs and, if desired, thin slices of sausage sautéed in butter.

YOGURT CHEESE FILLING

Fill the omelet with about 2 tablespoons Herbed Yogurt Cheese (page 112), omitting the olive oil and fresh spearmint leaves. Garnish with fresh spearmint sprigs.

CHAPTER 6

Fish and Shellfish

Arab fishermen. *From Cunningham Geikie,* The Holy Land and the Bible *(London, Cassell, 1891)*

IN THE BEIRUT OF MY CHILDHOOD markets offered fish that had been swimming in the sea only a few hours before. Many people, however, preferred to obtain theirs directly from fishermen, who would station themselves along the southern portion of the Lebanese coastal highway and, displaying baskets brimming with the day's catch, conduct a brisk business with passing motorists.

A wide variety of food fish inhabits the waters off the Syro-Lebanese coast, some of the most popular being two species of red mullet (*Sultan Ibrahim ramla* and the redder, more highly prized *Sultan Ibrahim sakhri*), five species of gray mullet (*buri* or *abu sukn*), sea bass (*'arus*), grouper (*lukos*), sea bream (*farridi*), porgy (*baghrus*), various members of the herring family (*sardina*), dogfish (*kalb al-bahr*), drum and croaker (*muskar*), mackerel (*samak iskumri*), tuna (*tun*), flounder and sole (*samak Mussa*), wrasse (*shaliq*), rabbit fish (*zellek*), hake (*nazilli*), gurnard (*ghurnar*), halfbeak (*abu munkar*), and garfish (*kharman*). The sea also furnishes mollusks and crustaceans, among them shrimp and prawns, squillas or mantis shrimp, squill-fish or flat lobsters, limpets, oysters, several types of murex, octopus, squid, cuttlefish, and sea urchins. The Gulf of Aqaba provides Jordan with a range of seafood, including red mullet, sea bream, grouper, red snapper, small tuna, shrimp, sea urchins, and spiny lobsters.

Freshwater Fish

Over forty different kinds of fish are found in the freshwater lakes, rivers, and streams of the region. Of these the gray mullet, blenny, and the common eel (*anklis*) are marine immigrants. Trout abound in a number of rivers, including the Litani and the Orontes. Among the most common freshwater fish are numerous species of carp (*shabbut*) and barbel (*kersin*). One particular type of carp, *samak nahri* or "fish of the river," thrives in the mountain streams of Lebanon, where it leaps the cascades like a salmon en route to its spawning grounds in the higher elevations. Its pale pink flesh

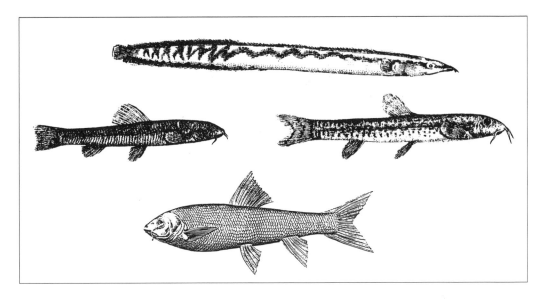

Examples of freshwater fish. Top: spiny eel; middle: two species of loach; bottom: samak nahri *(fish of the river), a type of carp. Top and middle from Alexander Russell,* A Natural History of Aleppo, *vol. 2 (London, G. G. and J. Robinson, 1794); bottom from Louis Charles Lortet,* La Syrie d'aujourd'hui *(Paris, Librairie Hachette, 1884)*

provides excellent eating. Recently carp have been successfully introduced in fish farms on Lake Assad in northern Syria.

Of the seventeen species of fish Russell identified in Aleppo's small river, the Kuwaik, the loach (*kibudi*) and the spiny eel were considered the finest.[1] When I was growing up, the Aleppo markets were further provided with fish from the Afrin, Orontes, and Euphrates Rivers and the ports of Iskenderun (Alexandretta), Latakia, and Tripoli. Eel, bleak, spined loach, carp, barbel, and catfish (*silur*), including the large sheatfish or wels (*jirri*), were among the fish sold in the markets.

Over the centuries travelers have praised the taste of fish from the Orontes, especially that of the eels, which Neale declared to be "the very best flavoured in the world," adding that picnic parties met daily along the river's banks to feast on eel pies made by a local baker.[2] Burckhardt mentions large catfish and a type of carp called *bunni,* of which the people of Homs and Hama were very fond.[3] I myself remember the marvelous taste of grilled fish prepared by the fishermen of a village on the Orontes northwest of Hama. The plentiful supply of fish and waterfowl in this area was such that the villagers never ate meat.

Among the most popular kinds of fish in the Jordan River are two types of combs (*musht*): the Nile comb (*Tilapia nilotica*) and the more abundant Galilean comb or St. Peter's fish (*T. galilea*). Other fish favored for the table include gray mullet, carp, perch, and the slender longheaded barbel (*Barbus longiceps*). After breakfasting on gray mullet that had been simply fried in oil, an English traveler exclaimed:

Examples of freshwater fish. Top: Nile comb (St. Peter's fish); bottom: slender longheaded barbel. From Henry Baker Tristram, The Survey of Western Palestine. Fauna and Flora of Palestine *(London, Palestine Exploration Fund, 1888)*

I . . . ate it from the pan, without any of the piquant aids that are commonly called in; and never was anything so delicate. What a host of recollections crowded down my throat with each delicious morsel! Richmond, thine eels!—but they are laboured by science ere they attain perfection; and ye little Blackwall fry! fairest gems of the stream! ye too are embalmed in batter with a libation of lemon-juice: and thou, *turbot à la crème et aux gratins!* sublimest productions of the *Rocher!* thou delightest by a borrowed savour. But thou, Abou Sookn, what shall I say of thee, "most rascally sweet" fish! Thou art unique!

No ketchup of fungus to deck thy corse,
Thou liest alone in thy glory![4]

Preserved Fish

In former times fish was salted and dried so that it could be taken on journeys or transported to inland areas. One kind of dried fish that enjoyed tremendous popularity all over the Abbassid Empire was the *tirrikh* (from Armenian *darekh,* "herring"), which abounds in the Lake of Van in historical Armenia (now eastern Turkey). This forearm-sized fish, which lives near the mouths of the streams feeding the lake, is still important commercially and is harvested during the spring months. Al-Baghdadi includes four recipes for *tirrikh* in his culinary manual, and the medieval geographer Yaqut (1179–1229) attests to having purchased some in faraway Balkh (in northern Afghanistan). During the Ottoman period the Orontes River was an important locale for the salt-curing of fish. From there fish were exported all over Syria and even to Cyprus for use by Christians during their fasts. Some types of fish are still salted today. They are eaten not so much out of necessity but out of preference, often as a relish with bread.

A fish product famous throughout the eastern Mediterranean since ancient times is *batarekh* or *batrakh* (French *boutargue*), the roe of the female gray mullet, which is removed from the fish in its intact membrane, washed, salted, pressed, and dried in the sun. The dried egg sacs are preserved by being encased in a thin layer of beeswax. *Batarekh* is a specialty of Lake Manzalah in Egypt, from which it has historically been exported to neighboring countries. It is cut into very thin slices and eaten with bread, olive oil, and lemon juice. Meryon, who visited Lake Manzalah in the early nineteenth century, remarked that *batarekh* was considered a great delicacy throughout the Levant by both Muslims and Christians, the latter consuming it in enormous amounts during Lent.[5]

Other Aquatic Creatures

Frogs (*dufdaa*), crabs (*ziratan*), tortoises (*silhefi*), and snails (*halazun*) are also consumed in varying degrees. It is said that the Kuwaik River takes its name from the croaking of the frogs along its banks. According to Russell, these amphibians were "so delicious, that some European Epicures have been heard to declare that it was almost worth while to make a journey into Syria, purposely to regale on them."[6] In Aleppo only the French and the native Christians took advantage of them since they were disdained as food by the Muslims. In present-day Lebanon fried frogs' legs often appear on the *mazza,* while a ragout of frogs' legs accompanied with rice is served as a main course.

Source of the Jordan, near Hasbayya in southern Lebanon. *From John Macgregor,* The Rob Roy on the Jordan, Nile, Red Sea, & Gennesareth, &c. *(London, John Murray, 1869)*

Also plentiful in the Kuwaik and even more prized than the frogs was a type of crab that attained its highest perfection during the white mulberry season. Thévenot noted how fond these crabs were of mulberries and how they "fail not to ramble about, and crawl up the Mulberry-trees, to feed on the fruit, and then it is no hard matter to catch them."[7] They were considered a great delicacy by the Europeans and were eaten by the native Christians during Lent. Although Russell states that snails were seldom consumed in Aleppo, they were sold in Syrian markets and eaten by the poor and by the Christians during their fasts preceding Christmas and Easter.[8] Today a common Lebanese way of preparing snails is to boil them and serve them with a sauce such as one based on *tahini* or pine nuts.

Syrian, Lebanese, and Jordanian recipes that call for fish often do not specify the particular variety to be used. Still, some fish, because of their size, fat content, and flavor, are more appropriate than others for certain recipes and methods of preparation.

Fish is grilled, fried, baked, braised, stewed, and made into *kibbeh*. Sauces that frequently accompany it include Tahini Sauce (page 280) and Pine Nut Sauce (page 281). Fish also goes well with Eggplant and Tahini Dip (page 104).

In parts of the eastern Mediterranean fish is never served with yogurt or with dishes that contain it. It is widely thought that the combination of fish and milk is extremely harmful and can even be fatal, but just exactly why is not clear. As far as I can tell, this belief is rooted in superstition and possesses no scientific basis. It is interesting to note that although the littérateur al-Jahiz (777–869) warned against eating the two together, al-Baghdadi included a recipe for fish with milk in his culinary manual. Unless you wish to immediately become the center of attention, it is advisable not to request fish and dairy products in the same meal when dining in Syria, Lebanon, or Jordan. Not long ago, when a Westerner ordered *shanklish* as part of a *mazza* followed by *Sultan Ibrahim* (red mullet) in a Beirut restaurant, the staff were horrified. She eventually decided not to insist when she realized that they were certain she would end up either in the hospital or the morgue! Since the proscription against eating fish with yogurt was strongly ingrained in me as well, when I was writing my *Book of Yogurt* I took a very deep breath before embarking on the fish chapter. Despite my misgivings, I bravely tried all the dishes in that chapter and, to my relief, suffered absolutely no ill effects. Nonetheless, in keeping with tradition, you will find no yogurt called for in any of the fish recipes given here!

❧

Fish, milk, and tamarind.
(Used to express the absurdity of any given situation.)

❧

Bicycling Down the Bekaa for a Meal of Trout

It is good to see . . . people ploughing, and wide stretches of browny-green earth where corn grows, and poplar groves round the villages. A broad pebbly river-bed winds south: it might be Italy, only there is a camel.[9]

Many Lebanese villages possess charming open-air cafés situated beside rushing streams, where one can dine on simple but delicious fare. What these rustic outdoor restaurants lack in opulence they more than make up for in natural scenery, and the food they serve is always fresh and well prepared. These unpretentious establishments offer such dishes as *hummus bi tahini, baba ghannuj, labna,* shish kebab, grilled chicken, and a mixed fresh vegetable salad flavored with spearmint. Flatbread and beer, wine, *arak,* or soft drinks accompany the meal. For dessert there are locally grown tree-ripened fruits and, to conclude, Turkish coffee.

Among my most enduring memories of eating freshly caught trout are those connected with late-summer cycling trips from Shtora to a café in the village of Ain Khraizat. Located near the Litani River in the southern Bekaa, this hamlet was known for its lovely spring as well as for its rich milk. My friends and I would look forward to these excursions with as much anticipation as we would to the delectable meals awaiting us at our destination. The beautiful Bekaa, checkered with fields of grain, vegetable gardens, orchards, and vineyards, was ideally suited to being seen from a bicycle, a mode of transportation that offered a perfect way to gain a full appreciation of the sights, sounds, and fragrances of the countryside, and made it easy for us to stop and chat with villagers.

One particular trip we made stands out in bold relief among all the others. As we set out from Shtora shortly after sunrise, heavy drops of dew were still on the vegetation, and a white mist rose from the stream that lay beside our path. In the distance we could hear the bleating of sheep as they were being led out to pasture. We coasted slowly by stone-built houses with pleasant gardens, inhaling the sweet perfume of roses, carnations, and honeysuckle before emerging onto the main highway that comes down from northwestern Syria. Hedges of blackberries grew along the roadside, with orchards and farms extending beyond them.

Just past Shtora the highway begins its westward ascent over the Lebanon to Beirut. We, however, turned to the left at this point and took the road that leads southward through the valley along the base of the mountains. In the spring we would gather wild tulips in the fields here while the peasants were busy working on the hillsides. Now they were equally busy reaping the benefits of all their earlier plowing and sowing. Situated only a little more than a mile down the road was the village of Qab Elias, with its brightly painted houses climbing up the side of a hill below the ruins of a medieval Druze castle. Despite its proximity to Shtora, Qab Elias seemed to belong to a different time, untouched by the contemporary world only a few minutes to the north. On the flat plain immediately outside the village lay a stretch of community-owned land dotted

View of the Bekaa from Mount Lebanon. *From John Carne,* Syria, the Holy Land, Asia Minor, &c., *vol. 2 (London, Fisher, Son, 1836)*

with ancient threshing floors and large mounds of chaff. Camels laden with sacks of grain plodded across its open expanse, and cattle drank at the nearby stream. Although some modern farm machinery is now used in the Bekaa, in those days the soil was patiently and assiduously cultivated by hand as it had been for untold centuries. With peasants at work in the fields and on the threshing floors as well as overseeing the animals, the scene here, as elsewhere in the valley, was one of intense and concentrated activity, picturesque and fascinating. Even we city-dwelling teenagers, so different in background, could not fail to sense the age-old symbiotic relationship of the villagers to their land.

Once by Qab Elias the road followed the mountainside. Springs wound down at frequent intervals, and the lush agricultural region extended before us like a long Oriental carpet, down the middle of which meandered the tree-lined Litani River. In the distance loomed massive Mt. Hermon, which straddles the border between Lebanon and Syria. The road continued by orchards and fields of grain, vegetables, and lusciously sweet, fragrant melons, for which the Bekaa is well known. We came upon people harvesting wheat and loading vegetables and fruit into crates. In this grain-growing region a common sight at the end of summer is one of peasant women washing wheat in the streams after it has been harvested and threshed. Once this arduous task is completed, the wheat is drained and spread out on large sheets on the flat roofs of houses to dry in the sun. We could see many such roofs from the road, with the grain sharing space with round straw trays filled with apricots, figs, plums, and raisins, and platters and pans of tomato paste. We trundled on past terraces of leafy mulberry trees and groves of plane trees and silvery poplars watered by springs gushing down from the mountains. Seeing the Litani now not far below us, we knew we were only a short distance from our lunch-time objective.

The café was located in a wooded area close to a limpid stream, which was channeled through a terrace shaded with awnings to provide a cool and relaxing environment for patrons. Besides the usual dishes, it offered the added attraction of trout taken directly from the nearby river and superbly grilled or fried. Prized by both anglers and epicures, this succulent and delicately flavored fish is unequalled when freshly caught and skillfully cooked in the simple and straightforward manner it was here, which provided a fitting climax to the enjoyable cycling trips taken during those carefree summers in the Bekaa.

Grilled Trout
Samak Mashwi

Grilling over charcoal or wood embers is a time-honored way of preparing fish in the eastern Mediterranean.

> 4 trout (10 to 12 ounces each), heads and tails left on, cleaned, rinsed, and patted dry
> Salt and freshly ground black pepper to taste
> Lemon and Garlic Marinade (page 288)
> Lemon wedges
> Fresh spearmint or flat-leaf parsley sprigs

Prepare a charcoal grill.

Carefully make a few crosswise incisions in the skin of the fish to prevent it from breaking during grilling. Sprinkle the cavities of the fish lightly with salt and pepper and brush the fish well on both sides with some of the marinade. Grill the fish on an oiled rack set 3 to 4 inches above glowing coals, basting occasionally with the marinade, about 5 minutes on each side or until the outside of the fish is slightly charred and the center is just opaque. (Alternatively, the fish may be broiled.)

Transfer the fish to a heated serving platter. Garnish with the lemon wedges and mint or parsley sprigs. Serve at once with Chickpea and Tahini Dip (page 106) and Tabbuleh (page 127).

Serves 4

VARIATION:

Marinate the fish in the marinade up to 30 minutes before grilling.

View of Tripoli. *From John Carne,* Syria, the Holy Land, Asia Minor, &c., *vol. 1 (London, Fisher, Son, 1836)*

Fried Fish with Oranges and Limes ⁕

Describing Tripoli around the year 1300, al-Dimashqi writes: "You get here sea-fish and birds of all varieties, such as you get in no other single place."[10] He also notes that the collection of fruit trees in the city's gardens was unparalleled. According to Volney:

> The winter on the coast is so mild, that the orange, date, banana, and other delicate trees flourish in the open air; and it appears equally extraordinary and picturesque to a European to behold at Tripoli under his windows, in the month of January, orange trees loaded with flowers and fruit, while the lofty head of Lebanon is covered with ice and snow.[11]

The glorious citrus orchards extend from the city proper to the port of al-Mina two miles away. When I was growing up, al-Mina was famous for its fried fish. Not only did local cooks have impeccably fresh fish and finest-quality olive oil at their disposal; they had a talent for frying their fish to exactly the point at which it emerged remarkably light and flavorful, crisp on the outside and succulently moist within.

This dish is based on one made with lemons rather than limes, which was served to me on a balcony overlooking the ancient city and its great sweep of citrus orchards stretching to the sea. Although lime is only occasionally encountered in Syrian, Lebanese, and Jordanian cookery, I have found that it works beautifully in many Middle Eastern preparations that are normally made with lemon, and in some (such as sauces and beverages made with pomegranate juice), it often gives superior results.

2 pounds red snapper fillets or any firm, lean white-fleshed fish fillets, about $\frac{1}{2}$ inch
 thick

$\frac{1}{2}$ cup freshly squeezed and strained orange juice

$\frac{1}{4}$ cup freshly squeezed and strained lime juice

Olive oil

1 teaspoon grated orange peel

1 large garlic clove, crushed

1 teaspoon salt, or to taste

$\frac{1}{2}$ cup all-purpose flour seasoned with 1 teaspoon Middle Eastern red pepper and salt
 to taste

Unpeeled orange slices

Unpeeled lime slices

Finely chopped fresh spearmint leaves

Wash the fish under cold running water and pat thoroughly dry with paper towels. Cut into small uniform serving pieces.

In a medium bowl whisk together the orange juice, lime juice, 2 tablespoons olive oil, orange peel, garlic, and salt. Add the pieces of fish and toss to coat thoroughly with the marinade. Cover and let stand at room temperature about 30 minutes, turning the fish a few times.

Pat the fish dry with paper towels. Coat with the seasoned flour and shake to remove the excess. In a large, heavy skillet heat about $\frac{1}{4}$ inch olive oil over moderate heat. Add the fish, a few pieces at a time, and fry, turning to brown on both sides. As each batch is done, transfer the fish to a baking pan lined with paper towels and keep warm in a preheated 250° F oven while you fry the remaining pieces.

Arrange the fried fish on a heated serving platter and surround with overlapping alternating orange and lime slices. Sprinkle the fish with the mint and serve at once with Saffron Rice (page 250).

Serves 4

∾

One fish said to another, "Move over."
"Where can I move? We are both being fried in the same pan." *(A)*
(Illustrates the futility of antagonism between fellow victims.)
∾

A Damascus Rooftop Romance

In a house near the convent, I caught an occasional glimpse of so beautiful a face, that I was tempted to seek its light oftener, perhaps, than would be wise to acknowledge. I thought I had never seen so perfectly lovely a countenance. A grated window, which looked into the centre area of the house, concealed the figure from me, and prevented my seeing in what occupation so graceful a creature was engaged. As she cast her eyes upwards through the bars—and they were the most expressive eyes in the world—I was so fascinated, that she must have been duller than Eastern ladies generally are had she not perceived it. It happened, therefore, whenever I walked upon the terrace, that accident brought the beautiful Helena, for that was her name, to the grated window, and I grew impatient to liberate her from what seemed to me a most barbarous imprisonment.

The happy moment at length arrived; I had bought a large bunch of violets in my ramble through the bazar, and, armed with so infallible an interpreter, I appeared at my post; she was busily engaged, but suspended her work a while on perceiving me, and, leaning her cheek upon her hand like Juliet, made behind her prison bars the prettiest picture imaginable. A bright instrument was in the left hand, and I thought she might have been passing her seclusion in some elegant embroidery. Now, however, I resolved to tempt her from the window, and kissing my violets threw them over the wall. She rose, and clattering on a pair of high wooden shoes, came forth, with a knife in one hand, and a fish she had been scraping in the other. My romance was at an end in a moment, and I never could recover gravity enough to return to the terrace. She was exceedingly beautiful, the daughter of a rich merchant, and had, as usual, been betrothed in her youth, but to a man who had proved false; he had gone to Alexandria, it was said, and had never since been heard of. Her unfortunate story and her beauty were equally subjects of conversation among her acquaintances. I found the misfortune, however, was not in the desertion so much, as in the necessity of remaining single until the death of the affianced husband should enable her to take another.[12]

Fish with Rice
Sayyadiyya

So extensive was the commerce of Tyre, that from Egypt and Arabia, on the south, to Armenia and Georgia, on the north, and from the frontiers of India to the utmost islands of Greece, and Spain, came the caravans by land and the ships by sea to this little spot, laden

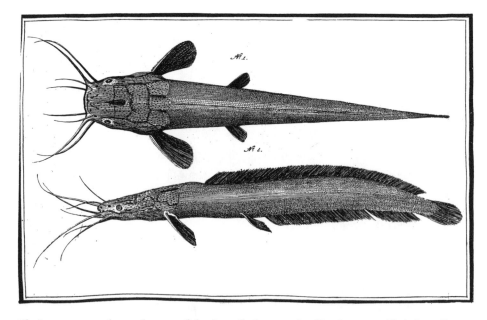

Clarias macracanthus, *a large catfish whose flesh was prized by Ottoman Christians.* From *Alexander Russell,* A Natural History of Aleppo, *vol. 2 (London, G. G. and J. Robinson, 1794)*

Tyre (Sur). From Thomas Jenner, That Goodly Mountain & Lebanon *(London, Hamilton, Adams, 1874)*

with a commerce rarely exceeded in variety and extent. No doubt her merchants were princes, and her traffickers the honorable men of the earth.[13]

Although I have enjoyed this dish on many occasions, perhaps the most memorable one was at a seaside restaurant near Tyre, where I watched fishermen edging into the waves to cast their nets as the sun sank in a ball of fire, engulfing the coast in an orange gold glow. Once the greatest city-state of Phoenicia, Tyre is today a quiet and unpretentious town of fishermen, boat-builders, and shopkeepers. Somewhere, possibly offshore under the sea, lie the remains of King Hiram's magnificent temple to the Phoenician god Melqart, and fishermen still hope that someday they will find its two huge front columns, described by the Greek historian Herodotus as one of pure gold and one of emerald.

2 pounds fish fillets (such as sea bass, cod, haddock, or halibut)

¹⁄₄ cup olive oil, or more if needed

2 medium onions, finely chopped

4 cups water

¹⁄₄ teaspoon powdered saffron, or to taste

Salt and freshly ground black pepper to taste

2 cups uncooked long-grain white rice

Pine Nut and Onion Garnish (page 289)

Lemon wedges

Flat-leaf parsley sprigs

Wash the fish under cold running water and pat thoroughly dry with paper towels. Cut into 2-inch pieces and set aside.

In a large, heavy saucepan heat the oil over moderate heat. Add the onions and sauté, stirring frequently, until lightly golden. Add the fish and cook, turning the pieces until they are evenly browned on all sides, adding more oil if necessary. Add the water, saffron, and salt and pepper and bring the mixture to a boil over moderate heat. Reduce the heat to low, cover, and simmer 10 minutes. Break the fish into small pieces with a fork and stir in the rice. Cover and simmer gently, undisturbed, about 20 minutes or until all the liquid in the pan has been absorbed and the rice is just tender, not mushy. Add a little more water during cooking if the liquid is absorbed before the rice becomes tender.

Let the *sayyadiyya* stand, covered, off the heat 5 to 10 minutes, then mound it on a heated serving platter and spread the Pine Nut and Onion Garnish over it. Decorate the platter with the lemon wedges and parsley sprigs and serve at once.

Serves 6

∾

Throw him into the sea, he comes up with a fish in his mouth.
(He is clever and avails himself even of a misfortune.)

∾

Baked Fish with Tomato Sauce (M)
Tajin Samak bi Banadura

Any firm, white-fleshed fish fillets such as red snapper, porgy, sea bass, or grouper will work to advantage in this enticing, easily prepared dish.

> 2 pounds firm, white-fleshed fish fillets
> Salt and freshly ground black pepper to taste
> 1/4 cup olive oil
> 2 tablespoons freshly squeezed and strained lemon juice
> 2 large garlic cloves, finely chopped
> 4 large ripe tomatoes, peeled, seeded, and chopped
> 1 teaspoon Pomegranate Molasses (page 57)
> Pine Nut, Raisin, and Onion Garnish (page 289)
> Lemon slices
> Flat-leaf parsley sprigs

Wash the fish fillets under cold running water and pat thoroughly dry with paper towels. Arrange in an oiled shallow baking dish just large enough to hold the fillets side by side in one layer. Rub the fish with the salt and pepper, 2 tablespoons of the olive oil, and the lemon juice. Cover the dish with aluminum foil and bake the fish in a preheated

400°F oven 15 to 20 minutes or until the flesh turns opaque and just begins to flake. Keep warm.

Meanwhile, in a large, heavy skillet heat the remaining 2 tablespoons oil over moderate heat. Add the garlic and sauté, stirring, until lightly golden. Add the tomatoes, Pomegranate Molasses, and salt and pepper to taste and cook gently, stirring occasionally, about 20 minutes or until the mixture is reduced to a thick sauce.

Arrange the fish on a large heated serving platter and spoon the tomato sauce over it. Cover with the Pine Nut, Raisin, and Onion Garnish and decorate with the lemon slices and parsley sprigs. Serve at once.

Serves 4

෴

Every fish that escapes appears great.

෴

Baked Fish with Pine Nut Sauce (M)

Samak Taratur bi Snubar

I first sampled this dish as a teenager in Juniyya, a town situated on a magnificent crescent-shaped bay just north of Beirut. Only a small red-roofed fishing port surrounded by market gardens and fruit trees in those years, Juniyya today is a cosmopolitan resort resplendent with hotels, restaurants, nightclubs, and boutiques.

> **A 3 1/2- to 4-pound whole striped bass, cleaned and scaled but with the head and tail left on, or substitute any other firm, white-fleshed whole fish**
> **Juice of 1 lemon**
> **Salt and freshly ground black pepper to taste**
> **1/4 cup olive oil**
> **2 recipes Pine Nut Sauce I (page 281)**
> **Lemon wedges or slices**
> **Flat-leaf parsley sprigs**
> **Middle Eastern black olives**
> **Toasted pine nuts**
> **Sliced fresh or pickled cucumber**
> **Radish roses**

Wash the fish under cold running water and pat it thoroughly dry with paper towels. Make 3 incisions in the skin of the fish on each side. Rub the fish inside and out with the lemon juice and salt and pepper. Cover and refrigerate 1 hour.

Brush a baking dish just large enough to hold the fish comfortably with some of the oil. Place the fish in the dish and brush the surface with the remaining oil. Bake in a preheated 375°F oven 35 to 40 minutes or until tender, basting occasionally with the pan juices. The fish is done when it is readily pierced with a fork but is still moist. Carefully transfer it to a large serving platter, cover with aluminum foil, and chill. Remove the foil and spread the Pine Nut Sauce evenly over the fish, leaving the head and tail uncovered. Garnish with the remaining ingredients. Serve cold.

Serves 6

VARIATIONS:

Baked Fish with Tahini Sauce
Samak Taratur

Substitute 2 recipes Tahini Sauce (page 280) for the Pine Nut Sauce.

Boned Fish with Pine Nut or Tahini Sauce

This version is often featured at parties. Cut the head and tail off the cooked and chilled fish. Remove the skin and bones. Place the skinned and boned fish on a serving platter, reforming it into its original shape. Put back the head and tail and spread the sauce evenly over the fish, leaving the head and tail uncovered. Garnish and serve as above.

Stone pine. *From William McClure Thomson,* The Land and the Book, *vol. 1 (New York, Harper, 1880)*

Baked Fish with Walnut Stuffing (M)
Samaki Harrah

Recipes for fish with walnut stuffing and fish with *tahini* are found in the medieval Arab culinary manuals. The handsome dish outlined below is a modern-day favorite.

A 4- to 4½-pound whole striped bass, cleaned and scaled but with the head and tail left
    on, or substitute any other firm, white-fleshed whole fish

Salt

5 tablespoons olive oil

2 medium onions, finely chopped

1 large green bell pepper, seeded, deribbed, and finely chopped

½ small hot green chili pepper, or to taste, seeded and finely chopped (see note on
    page 109)

1 cup shelled walnuts, crushed or finely chopped

3 tablespoons Pomegranate Molasses (page 57)

Freshly ground black pepper to taste

½ cup finely chopped fresh coriander leaves or flat-leaf parsley

Tahini Sauce (page 280)

2 tablespoons fresh sour pomegranate seeds (page 56), if available, or Middle Eastern
    black olives

Lemon slices

Wash the fish under cold running water and pat it thoroughly dry with paper towels. Sprinkle it inside and out with 1½ teaspoons salt and set aside.

Prepare the stuffing: In a large, heavy skillet heat 3 tablespoons of the oil over moderate heat. Add the onions, bell pepper, and chili pepper and, stirring frequently, cook about 10 minutes or until soft and lightly browned. Add the walnuts, Pomegranate Molasses, and salt and pepper to taste and cook, stirring, 3 minutes. Remove from the heat and stir in all but 2 tablespoons of the coriander or parsley leaves. Taste and adjust the seasoning.

Fill the cavity of the fish with the stuffing and skewer or sew up the opening. Place the stuffed fish in an oiled shallow baking-and-serving dish just large enough to hold it comfortably, and brush the surface with the remaining 2 tablespoons oil. Bake in a preheated 400°F oven about 45 minutes or until tender, basting the fish occasionally with the pan juices. The fish is done when it is readily pierced with a fork but is still moist. Remove the fish from the oven and spread it evenly with the Tahini Sauce. Garnish with the remaining 2 tablespoons coriander or parsley leaves, pomegranate seeds or olives, and the lemon slices. Serve hot or cold.

Serves 6 to 8

∾

While the fish is in the water, he puts the pan on the fire. *(A)*

∾

Shellfish, Tomato, and Pepper Kebabs

Whenever I make these kebabs I am reminded of the drive from Beirut up the coast to the picturesque fishing village of Jubayl (Byblos), a twenty-mile trip that is not only extraordinarily scenic but is a journey into history itself. Shortly after leaving the capital the road enters the gorge of the Dog River, where illustrious conquerors beginning with Ramses II have inscribed their conquests in stone. Nearby are the Grottoes of Ja'ita, with their stupendous stalactites and stalagmites. A few miles before Jubayl the highway crosses the Adonis River, named after the beautiful youth loved by the goddess Astarte. According to legend, when Adonis was mortally wounded by a wild boar while hunting, Astarte carried him to die at Afqa high above Jubayl. This romantic spot, where the Adonis River gushes in cascading waterfalls from a cave beneath enormous limestone cliffs, was described by the great nineteenth-century French writer and philosopher Ernest Renan as "one of the most beautiful places on earth." [14]

Jubayl, the reputed birthplace of Adonis and for many centuries a leading Phoenician commercial and religious center, is one of the oldest continuously inhabited towns in the world. When I lived in Lebanon, flat lobsters (*grandes cigales de mer*) caught off the coast of Jubayl were considered a great delicacy and appeared on the tables of the country's finest dining establishments. This dish is my re-creation of a seafood entrée featuring these crustaceans, which I enjoyed many years ago in a charming Jubayl restaurant whose vine-covered terrace overlooked a walled harbor where fishermen mended their nets as they had done for thousands of years. Lobsters (as well as shrimp) are also caught in the Red Sea and are popular restaurant specialties in Jordan's seaport of Aqaba.

> **16 very large raw shrimp in the shell**
>
> **4 baby lobster tails**
>
> **Lemon and Garlic Marinade (page 288) or Red Pepper Marinade (page 288)**
>
> **8 large cherry tomatoes**
>
> **8 $1\frac{1}{4}$-inch squares of green (or 4 each green and red) bell pepper**
>
> **Lemon wedges**

Shell the shrimp, but leave the last shell segment and tail attached to the body of the shrimp. Remove the veins. Wash the shrimp under cold running water and pat them dry with paper towels. Remove the shells from the lobster tails by cutting lengthwise through each shell.

In a large ceramic or glass bowl, toss the shrimp and lobster tails thoroughly with the marinade. Cover and let stand at room temperature about 30 minutes or in the refrigerator 1 to 2 hours, turning the shellfish occasionally.

***Source of the Adonis
River.*** *From Louis
Charles Lortet,* La
Syrie d'aujourd'hui
*(Paris, Librairie
Hachette, 1884)*

Prepare a charcoal grill.

Thread 4 shrimp, 1 lobster tail, 2 cherry tomatoes, and 2 pepper squares on each of 4 metal skewers. Grill the shellfish and vegetables on an oiled rack set about 4 inches above glowing coals, turning and basting frequently with the marinade, 6 to 8 minutes or until the shellfish are just tender and the vegetables are lightly browned. (Alternatively, the shellfish and vegetables may be broiled.) Serve at once with the lemon wedges.

Serves 4

A crab said to his son, "Walk straight." The son said, "Walk before me that I may walk as you do."

CHAPTER 7

Poultry and Game Birds

The valley of the Qadisha (Holy River). *From Charles William Wilson, ed.,* Pictur-esque Palestine, Sinai and Egypt, *vol. 2 (New York, D. Appleton, 1883)*

POULTRY RANKED AMONG THE MOST important food resources in the medieval Arab kitchen. The presence of seventy-four recipes for chicken in the *Wusla* testifies to the popularity of this bird in the court cuisine of the Ayyubids. Game birds were also much prized as food. During the spring and fall immense numbers of migratory birds passed through the region, which was home to a wealth of indigenous species as well.

Throughout the Ottoman era markets were plentifully supplied with poultry. Those in Aleppo conducted a roaring trade in chickens, turkeys, pigeons, ducks, and geese. As in the Middle Ages, Greater Syria was particularly rich in game birds. While on a visit to Aleppo in 1817, the British navy commanders Charles Edward Irby and James Mangles observed: "The cheapness and plenty of game is astonishing; every day we have had either, woodcocks, or partridges, wild-geese, or ducks, teal, the bustard, or wild turkey, joli notes, &c."[1] According to Burckhardt, the francolin (*durraj*) was regarded as the choicest of all game.[2] Neale, an avid hunter, described it as "a remarkably fine bird . . . something between a pheasant and partridge. . . . I consider it to be the most delicate game in existence."[3] Also much esteemed was the woodcock (*djaaj al-ard*). Neale writes: "In winter . . . some of the Aleppine exquisites, who are bird-killers as well as lady-killers, issue forth in pumps or slippers in search of woodcock, and return home before breakfast with dry feet, and with a dozen or more delicious birds."[4]

Today chicken as well as turkey, duck, goose, pigeon, quail, partridge, and pheasant can be purchased ready to cook in many urban markets. As in former times, however, people frequently go to the trouble of buying live poultry, which is brought cackling and squawking in crates to the *suqs* by villagers. These birds are free-ranging and have been fed a diet that often includes corn.

Age dictates the cooking method for poultry. Young, tender birds are usually grilled. Larger ones are generally stuffed with rich fillings before being boiled or roasted, or they are made into stews and casseroles redolent of herbs and spices and incorporating a variety of vegetables.

Although the stock of game birds has greatly diminished since the nineteenth century, certain parts of the region still yield a variety of unsurpassed treasures for the table. In the Bekaa, which was a hunter's paradise when I was a child, small birds (*assafeer*) were offered for sale in some markets, and restaurants used to serve them charcoal-grilled as part of the *mazza*. Among my earliest memories are those that center around summer and fall lunches featuring charcoal-grilled small birds accompanied with a selection of dips, *tabbuleh,* and mountain bread. The birds were also very good rubbed with salt, pepper, and lemon juice and fried in butter. Sharing my countrymen's enthusiasm for these little creatures, I blissfully devoured them without any inkling that they were regarded as a great delicacy. With the passage of time I stopped eating them, however, for in addition to other considerations, the visual and aural pleasures they afforded became more important to me than their exquisite taste. In any event, since small birds are protected species in this country, I have not given any recipes for them in this book.

Grilled Chicken
Farruj Mashwi

> . . . The Cedars are more than trees. . . . In the low-lying towns, everything is for sale; in a cedar-grove nothing can be bought—the worth of the man himself is all that matters.[5]

The Qadisha Valley in north-central Lebanon is a region of frighteningly deep gorges, icy streams, and waterfalls that form the heartland of the country's Maronite Christian community. Awe-inspiring scenery (including the legendary Cedars of Lebanon), deliciously piney air, picturesque villages perched precariously on the edges of cliffs, and the hauntingly lovely sound of church bells ringing up and down the valley all combine to create a magical atmosphere that casts a spell over every visitor.

I remember enjoying a wonderful meal of grilled chicken with friends many years ago in a typical mountain café on the way to the Cedars, one that remains associated in my mind with the romantic towns of Hasrun, on the gorge of the Qadisha River, and nearby Bsharri, birthplace of the celebrated Lebanese author Kahlil Gibran.

Grilled chicken is as popular in Syria, Lebanon, and Jordan as barbecued chicken in America. Countless spring chickens meet early ends on spits over charcoal or wood fires. A favorite take-out sandwich consists of spit-roasted chicken, pickles, and garlic sauce wrapped in flatbread.

> **4 *poussins* (spring chickens, available at some butcher shops) or Cornish hens (about
>   1 pound each), backbones removed and the birds flattened and patted dry**
> **Lemon and Garlic Marinade (page 288)**
> **Salt to taste**
> **½ recipe Garlic Sauce (page 283) (optional)**

Arrange the *poussins* in a shallow ceramic or glass bowl large enough to hold them in one layer. Pour the marinade over the *poussins* and turn them about to coat them

The Cedars of Lebanon. From John Carne, Syria, the Holy Land, Asia Minor, &c., *vol. 1 (London, Fisher, Son, 1836)*

thoroughly with the mixture. Cover and let stand at room temperature 1 to 2 hours or in the refrigerator several hours, turning them occasionally.

Prepare a charcoal grill.

Grill the birds, skin side down, on an oiled rack set about 4 inches above glowing coals, 8 to 10 minutes or until the skin is browned. Brush with the marinade, season with the salt, and turn the *poussins* over. Cook about 10 minutes or until the juices of the thigh run clear when pricked with a skewer. Serve at once with the Garlic Sauce, if desired.

Serves 4

Chicken, Pepper, and Tomato Kebabs
Shish Tawuq *or* Djaaj Mashwi

Chicken and meat kebabs are among the most common dishes served in local restaurants.

2 whole chicken breasts (about 12 ounces each), skinned, boned, and cut into 2-inch pieces

2 large green bell peppers, seeded, deribbed, and cut into 1-inch pieces

2 large tomatoes, cut into 12 wedges each

Thyme Marinade (page 288) or Spicy Marinade (page 288)

In a large ceramic or glass bowl combine the chicken, peppers, and tomatoes with the marinade. Toss gently until the pieces are thoroughly coated with the mixture. Cover and let stand at room temperature 1 to 2 hours or in the refrigerator several hours, turning the pieces occasionally.

Prepare a charcoal grill.

Thread the chicken, peppers, and tomatoes alternately on 4 long metal skewers. Grill on an oiled rack set about 4 inches above glowing coals, turning and basting occasionally with the marinade, 15 minutes or until the chicken is tender. (Alternatively, the chicken and vegetables may be broiled.)

With the side of a knife or fork, push the chicken and vegetables off the skewers onto heated individual plates. Serve at once with Garlic Sauce (page 283), Chickpea and Tahini Dip (page 106), or Eggplant and Tahini Dip (page 107) and Tabbuleh (page 127).

Serves 4

VARIATION:

Substitute 3 small onions, quartered and separated, for the tomatoes.

The Lebanese village of Bsharri, birthplace of Kahlil Gibran. From John Carne, Syria, the Holy Land, Asia Minor, &c., *vol. 3 (London, Fisher, Son, 1836)*

Petra. *From Charles William Wilson, ed.,* Picturesque Palestine, Sinai and Egypt, *vol. 2 (New York, D. Appleton, 1883)*

Petra through the Eyes of a Cook

Jordan's two most remarkable antiquities are Jerash, the best-preserved Greco-Roman city in southwestern Asia, and the hidden city of Petra, the capital of the Nabatean kingdom, which flourished from the fourth century B.C. to A.D. 106. Petra was famous for the magnificent Hellenistic architecture of its tombs, which are carved out of white and rose-colored sandstone cliffs. Edward Lear, a nineteenth-century writer and artist, explored Petra with his cook, who described it in unusually colorful terms:

"Oh master," said Giorgio (who is prone to culinary similes), "we have come into a world where everything is made of chocolate, ham, curry powder, and salmon"; and the comparison was not far from an apt one.[6]

Musakhan

During a visit to Jordan many years ago, the three things that most impressed me were Petra, which was incomparable; Jerash, which was memorable; and *musakhan,* which was irresistible. A famous Palestinian country dish from the West Bank, *musakhan* is a richly flavored preparation of chicken steamed in olive oil, onions, and sumac and other spices, baked on flatbread, and often garnished with pine nuts. It is a specialty of several restaurants in Amman, the capital of Jordan.

There are numerous recipes for *musakhan,* which can be made with *tabun* bread (page 310), *khubz marquq* (page 316), *khubz saaj* or *shrak* (page 313), or pita. Many Palestinians insist that the dish is not authentic unless made with *tabun* bread. In some versions the bread serves only as a base for the chicken and onions, while in others it is also used to cover the top, like a closed sandwich.

Here is an easy-to-prepare version that was taught to me by a Palestinian cook.

4 tablespoons extra-virgin olive oil, or 2 tablespoons each olive oil and unsalted butter

4 medium onions, chopped

1¼ pounds chicken breasts, skinned, boned, and cut into ¾-inch pieces

1½ teaspoons ground sumac, or to taste

1 teaspoon ground cinnamon

½ teaspoon ground cardamom

Pinch ground allspice (optional)

Salt and freshly ground black pepper to taste

Juice of 1 lemon or lime, or to taste, freshly squeezed and strained

4 pita breads, halved crosswise to form 8 pockets

In a large, heavy skillet heat the oil over moderate heat. Add the onions and sauté, stirring frequently, until soft but not browned. Add the chicken and sprinkle with the sumac, cinnamon, cardamom, allspice (if used), and salt and pepper and cook, stirring, 5 minutes. Add the lemon or lime juice and cook gently, stirring occasionally, about 10 minutes or until the chicken is tender but still juicy. Taste and adjust the seasoning. Fill the pita pockets with the chicken mixture, allowing equal portions for each sandwich. Toast the stuffed pita pockets in a preheated sandwich grill, or arrange them on a baking sheet and heat in a preheated 350°F oven about 10 minutes. Serve at once with Drained Yogurt (page 142) and a salad.

Serves 4

VARIATION:

Stir in 2 tablespoons toasted pine nuts when the chicken is tender.

Jerash. From Walter Keating Kelly, Syria and the Holy Land *(London, Chapman and Hall, 1844)*

Braised Chicken with Eggplant
Djaaj bi Batinjaan

> 2 medium eggplants, peeled and cut into 1½-by-1-by-½-inch pieces
>
> Salt
>
> ½ cup vegetable oil or olive oil, or as needed
>
> A 3-pound chicken, cut into 8 serving pieces
>
> 3 tablespoons olive oil
>
> 2 large onions, finely chopped
>
> 3 medium garlic cloves, finely chopped
>
> 1 teaspoon Mixed Spices II (page 66)
>
> 4 large ripe tomatoes, peeled, seeded, and chopped
>
> 2 teaspoons Pomegranate Molasses (page 57)
>
> 3 tablespoons freshly squeezed and strained lemon juice, or to taste
>
> Freshly ground black pepper
>
> 2 tablespoons finely chopped flat-leaf parsley

Sprinkle the eggplant pieces generously with salt and let them drain in a colander about 30 minutes to get rid of their bitter juices. Rinse under cold running water, squeeze with your hands to remove moisture, and dry thoroughly with paper towels.

In a large, heavy skillet heat the vegetable oil over moderate heat. Add half of the eggplant and sauté, turning the pieces frequently, until lightly golden. With a slotted spoon, transfer the pieces to paper towels to drain. Repeat with the remaining eggplant, adding more oil if necessary. Pour the oil from the skillet, allow the skillet to cool slightly, and wipe it clean.

Pat the pieces of chicken thoroughly dry with paper towels. In the same skillet in which you sautéed the eggplant, heat the olive oil over moderate heat. Add the chicken, skin side down, and sauté, turning to brown evenly on all sides. Transfer to a plate and set aside.

Pour off all but 3 tablespoons drippings from the skillet. Add the onions and sauté over moderately high heat, stirring frequently, until lightly browned. Add the garlic and Mixed Spices and sauté, stirring, about 30 seconds. Stir in the tomatoes, Pomegranate Molasses, lemon or lime juice, black pepper, and salt to taste. Return the chicken and any juices that have accumulated on the plate to the skillet and tuck the pieces into the tomato mixture. Bring to a boil and reduce the heat to low. Cover and simmer about 45 minutes or until the chicken is very tender. Stir in the sautéed eggplant and the parsley, cover, and simmer 10 minutes. Taste and adjust the seasoning. Serve hot with Bulgur Pilaf with Vermicelli (page 259) or Rice with Vermicelli (page 250).

Serves 4

∾

Riddle: What gives birth every day?
Answer: A chicken.

∾

Mlukhiyya with Chicken
Mlukhiyya bi Djaaj

> The luncheon was splendid, a feast of Near Eastern delicacies. I chose, because I had liked it of old, a potage of *mouloukieh:* gluey-green, garlic-drenched, the rice and the chicken slipping down, but the taste of the herbs sticking to one's teeth, nostalgically, through the afternoon.[7]

Mlukhiyya has been an Egyptian staple since Pharaonic times. Recipes calling for it appear in early Arab culinary manuals. The name *mlukhiyya* is derived from the Arabic word for "royal" because dishes made with this vegetable enjoyed the favor of kings, among them the seventh-century Umayyad caliph Mu'awiyya. For many people *mlukhiyya* is an acquired taste but, judging by the passion it engenders among countless Lebanese, Syrians, and Jordanians, once acquired it can become addictive.

This particular recipe comes from Lebanon. In Beirut sour pomegranate seeds were sometimes marinated along with the chopped onions, a splendid addition that I have not come across elsewhere.

Chicken Stock (below)

Marinated Onions (below)

3 pounds fresh or frozen *mlukhiyya,* or 12 ounces dried *mlukhiyya* leaves, picked clean and finely crumbled

Garlic and Coriander Mixture (page 287)

3 pita breads, split, toasted, and broken into bite-sized pieces

Plain Rice (page 249)

The reserved chicken meat from the Chicken Stock recipe, reheated in a little of the stock

Prepare the Chicken Stock and the Marinated Onions. Set aside.

If you are using fresh *mlukhiyya* leaves, cut off the stalks. Wash and drain the leaves and pat them dry with paper towels. Chop the leaves very finely. Frozen *mlukhiyya* only needs defrosting. If using dried *mlukhiyya,* place the crumbled leaves in a bowl and pour a little hot water over them. Allow the leaves to absorb the moisture and swell, sprinkling with a little more water if necessary.

In a large, heavy saucepan bring the Chicken Stock to a boil over high heat. Stir in the *mlukhiyya* leaves, reduce the heat to low, and simmer, uncovered, stirring occasionally, 5 to 10 minutes if using fresh *mlukhiyya* leaves, 15 to 20 minutes if using dried leaves. Add the Garlic and Coriander Mixture and simmer, stirring occasionally, about 2 minutes. Taste and adjust the seasoning. Serve at once from a heated tureen, accompanied with the toasted pieces of pita bread, the rice, the reheated chicken meat, and the Marinated Onions presented separately in individual serving dishes. Diners help themselves by first placing a layer of toasted pita bread in their soup plates, followed by a little *mlukhiyya,* then a layer of rice, some chicken, more *mlukhiyya,* and, finally, Marinated Onions to taste.

Serves 6

CHICKEN STOCK

A 3-pound chicken
8 cups cold water
2 medium onions, quartered
1 garlic clove
2 medium ripe tomatoes, peeled and quartered (optional)
1 1/2 teaspoons salt, or to taste
Freshly ground black pepper to taste

Place the chicken in a kettle and add the water. Bring the water to a boil over high heat and skim the froth. Add the remaining ingredients, reduce the heat to low, cover, and simmer, skimming the froth occasionally, 1 hour or until the chicken is tender. Transfer the chicken to a plate and strain the stock. Skin and bone the chicken. Cut the meat into small pieces and reserve.

Makes about 1 1/2 quarts

MARINATED ONIONS

2 large red onions, finely chopped
1/2 cup fresh sour pomegranate seeds (page 56), if available
1 cup wine vinegar or freshly squeezed and strained lemon juice, or to taste

In a bowl toss the onions and pomegranate seeds with the vinegar or lemon juice. Cover and let stand at room temperature 1/2 hour, stirring occasionally.

❧

Riddle: What is it that leaves its house only after breaking down the door?
Answer: A chicken.

❧

Chicken and Rice

Djaaj ma Ruz

> Mashgharah is a pretty village, with good water. . . . The Shaykh begged of us not to pitch our tents, but to go to his house, where we had a supper of rice and chickens. *We* were Captain Burton and I . . . three Begs, a deputy from the absent Kaim-makam, the priest, the Shaykh, and several others. I saw forty intrigues around the bowl of rice that night, all dipping the hand into the same dish, and silently making plans one against another.[8]

A 3- to 3 1/2-pound chicken

2 tablespoons unsalted butter, at room temperature

1 medium garlic clove, crushed to a paste with a pinch of salt

1/4 teaspoon Mixed Spices I (page 66) or ground cinnamon

Salt and freshly ground black pepper to taste

1/2 cup water

1/2 recipe Saffron Rice with Nuts (page 253), or 1/2 recipe Saffron Rice with Ground Meat
    and Nuts (page 253)

Rinse the chicken inside and out under cold running water and pat it thoroughly dry with paper towels. In a small bowl combine the butter, garlic, Mixed Spices or cinnamon, and salt and pepper and blend well. Rub the cavity and entire surface of the chicken with the mixture. Place the bird in a shallow roasting pan just large enough to hold it comfortably and add the water to the pan. Bake in a preheated 450° F oven about 1 hour and 15 minutes or until the chicken is tender and golden brown, basting frequently with the pan juices. The bird is done if the juices run clear when the fleshy part of the thigh is pricked with a skewer.

Meanwhile, prepare the saffron rice, reserving the sautéed nuts.

To serve, cut the chicken into quarters or into 8 pieces. Spoon the rice onto a large heated serving platter and arrange the pieces of chicken attractively on top. Sprinkle with the reserved nuts and serve at once.

Serves 4

Note: You may bone the chicken before arranging the pieces over the rice.

❧

A man's chicken looks to his neighbor a goose.

❧

Natural bridge over the Litani River. From Charles William Wilson, ed., Picturesque Palestine, Sinai and Egypt, *vol. 1 (New York, D. Appleton, 1881)*

Cornish Hens with Sour Plum Sauce ❧

This is my adaptation of a recipe found in the *Wusla.* Interestingly, today one associates the combination of chicken and plums not with the eastern Mediterranean but with the Caucasus.

2 Cornish hens or *poussins* (spring chickens, available at some butcher shops),
     about 1 pound each, backbones removed and the birds flattened
Salt and freshly ground black pepper to taste
3 tablespoons Clarified Butter (page 148)
Fresh spearmint or coriander leaves
Sour Plum Sauce with Mint (page 286)

Pat the hens thoroughly dry with paper towels. Rub well with the salt and pepper. In a large nonstick skillet heat the butter over moderate heat. Add the hens, skin side down, cover, and cook 15 minutes. Reduce the heat and cook 10 minutes. Turn the hens over, cover, and again cook 15 minutes over moderate heat and 10 minutes over reduced heat or until they are a deep golden brown and cooked through.

Arrange the hens on a heated platter and garnish with the spearmint or coriander leaves. Serve at once with the Sour Plum Sauce with Mint and Saffron Rice (page 250).

Serves 2

VARIATION:

Cornish Hens with Sour Cherry Sauce ❧

Chicken with sour cherries, a specialty of my Aleppan relatives, served as the inspiration for this variation.

Substitute Sour Cherry Sauce (page 285) for the Sour Plum Sauce with Mint.

A Picnic by the Dog River

Last week . . . M—[gave] a pic-nic, or perhaps I ought to call it a *fête champètre,* at the Nahr-el-Kelb. After an early breakfast we started in boats . . . and in an hour and a half we arrived at the Dog River.

. . . The cook and other servants had been sent on previously in another boat, and that important functionary was soon in the midst of the utensils of his profession, surrounded by slaughtered fowls, turkeys, English hams, and other delicacies. It is astonishing how expert these Arab cooks are in fitting up their culinary apparatus. A few stones placed over one another, with holes for the charcoal, appear to suffice for enabling them to prepare their pilaus and other delicious little plats. Our cook is an Arab Soyer,[9] and orders about his subordinates with the air of a gastronomic potentate. On this occasion he, if possible, exceeded his former achievements. The roast turkey, stuffed with truffles, was worthy of the most famous *maître de cuisine* of London or Paris, and would have set Apicius and Darteneuf longing in the shades below, could they have known of it. The epicurean R—signified his unqualified approbation of this *chef-d'oeuvre* of what he seems to consider the first of the arts.

Smyrna, Aleppo, Damascus, and Jaffa supplied us with our dessert, and the wines of Cyprus, France, and Spain were cooled with the pressed snow from the peaks of Lebanon. . . .[10]

Stuffed Turkey
Habash Mahshi

In the Lebanon of my childhood turkey was the traditional centerpiece of the Christmas meal. In some households chicken was preferred, while in others, both were featured. Immediately preceding the holiday season, it was possible to buy live turkeys from sellers who made the rounds of the residential streets, shepherding their gobbling

View of Beirut from north of the Dog River. From Charles William Wilson, ed., Picturesque Palestine, Sinai and Egypt, *vol. 2 (New York, D. Appleton, 1883)*

flocks ahead of them with long guiding sticks. Although traffic would often be brought to a halt as the birds made their leisurely way across a busy intersection, motorists would remain uncharacteristically patient, even smiling, as the turkeys passed. Since virtually all Lebanese consider themselves gourmets, they undoubtedly regarded the few minutes' wait as a small price to pay for the epicurean pleasures these birds would soon provide.

When I was growing up, turkeys were allowed to range freely and as a result their meat was quite tough; hence, stewing was the usual method of cooking them. To prepare this dish with American turkey, you may roast the bird by any preferred method or as directed below.

> 1 turkey, about 12 pounds
> Salt and freshly ground black pepper to taste
> Meat and Rice Stuffing with Nuts and Raisins (page 289)
> 1/2 cup unsalted butter, at room temperature
> 1 cup water
> Parsley or watercress sprigs

Rinse the turkey under cold running water and pat thoroughly dry with paper towels. Season it inside and out with salt and pepper. Pack the neck cavity loosely with some of the stuffing, fold the neck skin under the body, and fasten it with a skewer. Pack the body cavity loosely with the remaining stuffing and truss the bird.

Rub the turkey with the butter and place it breast side up on the rack of a roasting pan. Roast in a preheated 425°F oven 30 minutes. Reduce the heat to 325°F and baste the turkey with the pan juices. Add the water to the roasting pan and roast the turkey, basting it every 20 minutes, about 2 1/2 hours or until the juices run clear when the fleshy part of a thigh is pricked with a skewer and a meat thermometer inserted in the same spot registers 180°F. Transfer the turkey to a heated platter and discard the trussing string. Cover the bird loosely with aluminum foil to keep it warm and let it rest 15 minutes before carving. Garnish with the parsley or watercress sprigs.

Serves 10

Note: The turkey may be presented whole, or it may be sliced onto a large serving platter with the stuffing heaped in the center.

Duck with Quinces and Pomegranate Sauce ✦

Whenever I prepare duck I am reminded of the celebrated Baron Hotel in Aleppo, where I first tasted it. The Baron was built in 1909 by two brothers, the Mazlumians, who were among the thousands of Armenian refugees from Cilicia in southern Anatolia who fled the Ottoman pogroms of the 1890s and settled in Syria and Lebanon. From Crusader times well into the fourteenth century, Cilicia was an independent kingdom established by Armenians who had emigrated there after their country, centered on Lake Van in eastern Anatolia, was incorporated into the Seljuk Empire in 1071. The Cilician Armenians acquired so many titles that the kingdom soon became full of barons, and the term (pronounced "bah-*rone*" in Armenian) eventually came to mean simply "mister" or "sir." The Mazlumians bestowed their honorific title from Cilicia on their hotel.

The Baron quickly established itself as one of the premier hotels in the entire Middle East, offering Western comfort coupled with Eastern hospitality. It catered to the rich and famous, many of whom traveled on the Orient Express, which used to terminate in Aleppo: Theodore Roosevelt, T. E. Lawrence, Charles Lindbergh, and Agatha Christie were only a few of its illustrious guests. Back in the 1920s the hotel's terrace was a favorite place for shooting wild ducks in the adjacent swamps. Today it overlooks the Rue Baron, the main street of downtown Aleppo, and is a popular spot for sipping a drink and watching the world go by. The well-stocked bar inside calls to mind a set out of *Casablanca,* where one half-expects to run into Humphrey Bogart! Although the hotel's dining room no longer features wild boar, pheasant, and caviar on its menu, the food is still well prepared. Filled with nostalgia and character, the Baron possesses a certain aura of personality achieved by only a few hotels around the world.

The dish described below draws its inspiration from several recipes in the *Wusla* rather than from the Baron. Although the medieval recipes call for chicken, I have found that duck works at least as well with the quinces and pomegranate sauce. As for the Baron's duck, all I can recall is that it was a marvel of succulence and flavor, audibly crisp on the outside and meltingly tender within.

> **2 pounds boneless duck breasts, trimmed of excess fat**
> **Salt and freshly ground black pepper to taste**
> **Fresh spearmint sprigs**
> **Sautéed Quinces (page 276)**
> **Pomegranate Sauce with Ginger and Mint (page 284)**

Pat the duck breasts dry with paper towels and season with the salt and pepper. Heat a large, heavy ovenproof skillet over moderate heat until hot. Add the duck breasts, skin side down, and cook about 15 minutes or until the skin is crisp. Turn the duck breasts and transfer the skillet to a preheated 400° F oven. Roast the breasts 10 to 15 minutes for medium-rare or to desired doneness. Let the duck breasts stand about 5 minutes and cut into 1/3-inch-thick slices. Arrange the slices on a heated platter and garnish with the spearmint. Serve at once with the Sautéed Quinces, the Pomegranate Sauce with Ginger and Mint, and Saffron Rice (page 250).

Serves 4

Note: Duck breasts are available at some butcher shops. If you cannot find them in your area, purchase two large ducks and have the butcher remove the breasts for you. Freeze the leg-thigh portions for another use.

VARIATIONS:

Duck with Apples and Sour Cherry Sauce ❧

Substitute Sautéed Apples (page 277) for the Sautéed Quinces and Sour Cherry Sauce (page 285) for the Pomegranate Sauce with Ginger and Mint.

Duck with Sour Plum Sauce ❧

Omit the Sautéed Quinces and substitute Sour Plum Sauce with Mint (page 286) for the Pomegranate Sauce.

Hunting in the Shuf

Among my most exhilarating excursions into the Lebanese countryside were those to the Shuf, a region of great scenic beauty and historical interest in the south-central part of the Lebanon Mountains, whose sweeping panoramas provided inspiring backgrounds for hikes and picnics. Inhabited primarily by Druze, the Shuf is dotted with picturesque towns and villages, including three former mountain capitals of Ottoman times: Baaqlin, Dayr al-Qamar, and Bayt al-Din, site of the Alhambra-like fairy-tale palace of the amir Bashir II al-Shihabi.

Small game birds, especially partridge and quail, were plentiful in the Shuf and were enthusiastically pursued by both peasants and sportsmen. One could also purchase recently caught live birds in village markets, where they were offered for sale in little cages. I still savor the memory of perfectly grilled partridge and quail that were served to me on one of my visits to the Shuf. The birds, which had been marinated in a tart pomegranate sauce and cooked over an open fire, were accompanied with grilled small tomatoes, green peppers, and onions as well as freshly baked mountain bread, making a simple yet utterly delicious meal.

The Shuf was the favorite hunting ground of the Shihab amirs, who in their days

Dayr al Qamar, with Bayt al-Din in the distance. *From John Carne,* Syria, the Holy Land, Asia Minor, &c., *vol. 1 (London, Fisher, Son, 1836)*

Partridges. *From Louis Charles Lortet,* La Syrie d'aujourd'hui *(Paris, Librairie Hachette, 1884)*

of power and glory pursued their quarry with falcons and trained dogs. The practice of falconry, which had been introduced into Europe by the Crusaders on their return from the Levant, was a popular pastime in Syria, but only the amir Bashir kept it up in the old feudal manner. Accompanied by a retinue of family, area nobles, and attendants, he would go out in great state to the neighboring mountains, where he would pitch his tent on an elevated spot commanding a view of several valleys. As he sat on his *diwan* and smoked his pipe, some fifteen hundred to two thousand peasants, recruited for the task, would shout and beat the woods in every direction. Once a partridge was raised, the amir would release the falcon perched on his fist, and fifty or sixty horsemen and as many dogs would dash over the hills and vales in hot pursuit. Every day this sport lasted the amir would bag from 150 to 200 partridges. To quote one European who witnessed the chase:

> Let the reader picture to himself as the theatre where this magnificent spectacle was dis-
> played, all he can conceive of wild and beautiful in mountain scenery; let him imagine the
> multitude of the actors in the scene, their varied and picturesque costumes, their endless and
> ever-changing diversities of position, attitude, gesture, and grouping; the many riders, the
> beauty of their steeds, the thundering tramp of man and horse, the crashing of the rocks
> hurled from the cliffs, the baying of the dogs, and the shouts and yells bursting from a

Gorge of the Barada River near Damascus. *From Charles William Wilson, ed.,* Picturesque Palestine, Sinai and Egypt, *vol. 1 (New York, D. Appleton, 1881)*

thousand throats, and tossed to and fro by all the mad echoes of the mountains;—let him try to conjure up in his mind such a picture of intense life and movement; and he may have some faint idea of a scene unlike anything beheld in Europe.[11]

Grilled Quail
Firri Mashwi

Quail migrate twice a year between Europe and Africa. When they reach Syria and Lebanon, the exhausted birds stop to rest and are easily caught.

It was always a treat to find grilled quail on the luncheon menu in Lebanon. My most lasting memory of savoring these little birds, however, is connected with a meal I had in Bludan, a popular Syrian summer resort located near Damascus in a scenic region of purling brooks, vineyards, and gardens. The mountain panorama I looked out on during that meal was truly impressive: To my right rose the snowy summit of Mount Sannin, monarch of the Lebanon; to my left stood Mount Hermon, king of the Anti-Lebanon; and in the foreground lay the verdant plain and village of al-Zabadani.

Mention of Bludan also summons up memories of delightful meals at the town's hotel after excursions to the nearby Barada valley with its wild and romantic gorge of Suq Wadi Barada, where after falling over a ledge of rocks in a series of beautiful cascades the river becomes a torrent, roaring tumultuously between lofty and perpendicular cliffs barely more than a hundred and fifty feet apart. Today the Grand Hôtel de Bludan is a favorite spot for lunch or *mazza*.

> **8 quail, split down the backbone and flattened**
> **Thyme Marinade (page 288)**

Arrange the quail in a shallow ceramic or glass bowl large enough to hold them in one layer. Pour the marinade over the quail and turn them about to coat them evenly with the mixture. Cover and let stand at room temperature about 30 minutes.

Prepare a charcoal grill.

Grill the quail skin side down on an oiled rack set 3 to 4 inches above glowing coals 2 to 3 minutes per side or until the skin is crisp and browned and the juices of the thigh run clear when pricked with a skewer. Do not overcook. (Alternatively, the quail may be broiled.) Serve hot with Tabbuleh (page 127).

Serves 4

VARIATIONS:

Grilled Quail with Garlic Sauce

Omit marinating the quail. Simply brush them with the marinade and grill or broil as above, basting as needed. Serve with ½ recipe Garlic Sauce (page 283) and a salad.

Grilled Quail with Pomegranate Sauce ⋄

Omit marinating the quail. Sprinkle them with salt and freshly ground black pepper to taste, brush with olive oil, and grill as above, basting with oil as needed. Serve with Pomegranate Sauce with Ginger and Mint (page 284) and Saffron Rice (page 250).

Grilled Quail with Sour Cherry Sauce ⋄

Follow the recipe for Grilled Quail with Pomegranate Sauce (above), substituting Sour Cherry Sauce (page 285) for the Pomegranate Sauce with Ginger and Mint.

CHAPTER 8

Meat

Ferry over the Orontes River in northwestern Syria. *From John Carne*, Syria, the Holy Land, Asia Minor, &c., *vol. 2 (London, Fisher, Son, 1836)*

MEAT HAS TRADITIONALLY BEEN a high-status food in the eastern Mediterranean, desired by almost everyone but enjoyed with regularity only by the affluent. Because most cooks have been forced to utilize meat sparingly, they have made it go far by cutting it into small pieces or grinding it and combining it with various ingredients to create a wide-ranging repertoire of dishes. Consequently, in addition to the recipes in this chapter, you will find many others elsewhere in the book that make use of meat.

In former times the preferred kind of meat was mutton, followed by lamb, veal, and beef. Rabbit and young camel were also eaten, while the consumption of pork was confined to the Christians. Because Greater Syria did not produce a sufficient number of sheep for its inhabitants, vast flocks were brought in annually from historical Armenia, Kurdistan, and northern Mesopotamia. According to van Lennep, who often watched them as they passed on their long journey, the shepherds always walked in front, armed with a knife and a pistol and engaged in spinning woolen yarn with a ponderous spindle.[1] The flocks would gradually be decreased by sales to townspeople and villagers as they made their way south. In the spring the shepherds and their unsold sheep would find repose and refreshment in the rich pastures and abundant waters of the Lebanon Mountains. Local sheep dealers would buy up thousands of animals and sell them to the Druze and Maronite peasants, who themselves bred very few sheep but subsisted largely on bulgur, not consuming meat in quantity except on major holidays and other important occasions. It was only in the largest towns that flesh was brought daily to market.

The most common breed of sheep in the region was and still is the fat-tailed variety, which affords excellent meat and has traditionally been valued for the accumulation of fat in its caudal appendage. This fat (*aliya*) was much used in cookery, often being preferred to butter. Goat meat, especially that of kid, was also eaten, mainly by the less well-to-do. Beef was rarely consumed by the native population, not so much out of prejudice but because cows and oxen were considered too valuable to be slaughtered for food. Veal was seldom offered for sale, and pork was a rarity eaten only by Europeans. Camel meat was not normally found in markets except in Homs and Hama, which bordered on the great plains occupied by the Beduin, who regarded meat from the hump of young camel as a delicacy.

While lamb and mutton continue to be the staple meats, veal and beef are increasingly being substituted in recipes that traditionally called for the former. Other kinds of meat that are eaten include kid and goat, rabbit, camel (consumed mainly by the Beduin), and pork (occasionally eaten by Christians).

Meat is eaten either raw or well-done (though in the latter case still full-flavored, tender, and juicy) and virtually never rare. Only the freshest meat is consumed raw. Seasoned cubed fillets of raw lamb or mutton (*lahma nayya*) garnished with parsley, spearmint, and onions sometimes appear at breakfast, especially as part of morning picnics in the vineyards during the season of the grape harvest. *Kafta nayya* is made with lean raw lamb or mutton (either fillet or leg) pounded to a paste and mixed with onions, herbs (parsley, basil, or spearmint), and seasonings and garnished with lemon wedges, mint sprigs, and, perhaps, olive oil, pine nuts, and scallions. Raw meat is also combined with bulgur and seasonings to make *kibbeh nayya,* a great favorite. All of these dishes may be accompanied with a salad of sliced tomatoes and cucumbers or may appear on the *mazza.*

Ground Game

In former times Greater Syria was a hunter's paradise. Gazelle, deer, ibex, wild boar, hare, and porcupine were all abundant. According to Irby and Mangles, many types of game were brought to Aleppo's butcher shops, which were admirably neat, clean, and "equal to those of London."[2] Russell notes that gray gazelle, antelope, roebuck, and ibex were especially prized and that the flesh of wild boar was delicious.[3] When I was a child wild boars were still seen in the Lebanon Mountains, and friends from Aleppo used to rave about the kebabs of wild boar meat they would roast on picnics in the countryside. Although less plentiful than in the past, ground game still exists in considerable supply in parts of the region.

Grilled Skewered Lamb or Shish Kebab
Lahm Mashwi *or* Shish Kebab

> We dismounted for breakfast at the Khan of Dahr-el-Beider . . . Hanging in the archway of the famous inn were part of a carcass of a sheep and a goatskin full of thick leben. . . . We . . . ordered broiled meat and *leben* for our breakfast. The innkeeper instantly obeyed; he cut off a chunk of meat, cut it up in small squares, strung the same on slender iron rods, broiled them over a charcoal fire, and served the breakfast, apparently with as much laudable pride as, on similar occasions, thrills the heart of the most elegant housekeeper.[4]

The preferred meat for making this celebrated dish is lamb; however, beef, veal, pork (among Christians), and even camel may also be used. The practice of interspersing pieces of vegetables and, perhaps, fruit between cubes of meat is not a recent innovation, as is sometimes believed. Russell mentions slices of apples or artichoke bottoms and onions being threaded on skewers along with pieces of mutton in eighteenth-century Aleppo,[5] and Addison was served a similar dish at the palace of Bayt al-Din in 1835.[6]

> **2 pounds lean leg of lamb, trimmed of excess fat and cut into 1-inch cubes**
> **Spicy Marinade (page 288)**
> **Lemon wedges**
> **Flat-leaf parsley or spearmint sprigs**

In a large ceramic or glass bowl toss the cubed lamb thoroughly with the marinade. Cover and let stand at room temperature 1 to 2 hours or in the refrigerator 3 to 4 hours, turning the meat occasionally.

Prepare a charcoal grill.

Remove the lamb from the marinade and thread the cubes on long four-sided metal skewers. Grill on an oiled rack set about 3 inches above glowing coals, turning and basting frequently with the marinade, 8 to 12 minutes or until the outside of the meat is richly browned and the inside is pink and juicy. (Alternatively, the lamb may be broiled.)

Arrange the skewers on a heated serving platter and garnish the platter with the lemon wedges and parsley or mint. Serve the kebabs nestling in pita bread that has been squeezed around the skewers of meat toward the end of cooking to soak up the flavorful juices and used to pull the meat off the skewers. Tahini Dip (page 105) and Tabbuleh (page 127) make good accompaniments.

Serves 6

VARIATION:

Grilled Skewered Lamb with Vegetables

Thread 12 large cherry tomatoes, 12 small white boiling onions (raw or parboiled), and 12 one-inch squares of green bell pepper on separate skewers and grill alongside the meat, turning the vegetables occasionally and basting with the marinade, until they are lightly browned.

∾

Like parsley, grown in dung and thrust into shish kebab.
(Said of a social climber.)

∾

Shawarma

This specialty is usually made in restaurants, food shops, and stalls to serve large numbers of people and is impractical to prepare at home. A long vertical spit is threaded with marinated lamb slices, the largest being placed at the top with gradually smaller ones toward the bottom to form a huge cone-shaped kebab. Pieces of fat cut the same size and shape as the meat are occasionally interspersed between the slices to impart moistness. The meat is then trimmed and grilled in front of a charcoal fire arranged in vertical tiers. As the spit slowly turns automatically, the outside of the meat cooks deliciously. When the meat is done, it is sliced off thinly with a very sharp knife and is caught in a pan at the bottom. The cooking and slicing process is continued until the center is reached; thus there are always crisp and flavorful outside pieces to tempt diners.

Shawarma is eaten piping hot in pockets of pita bread as a *sandweech*. Its popularity is comparable to that of the hamburger in America. The assembling of a *sandweech* usually offers the cook an opportunity to exercise a bit of showmanship. With great flourish and much knife sharpening and waving, the cook slices off the meat, dips the bread into the fat that has dripped off the meat, holds it against the flame so it flares, and then fills the pocket with the meat and sliced tomatoes, onions, and pickles, parsley or spearmint leaves, and, perhaps, *tahini* sauce or yogurt. In restaurants *shawarma* is often served as a main course, accompanied with Chickpea and Tahini Dip (page 106) and various salads. In recent years *shawarma* sandwiches made with chicken have also become popular.

Mansaf

The traditional festive dish of the Beduin and Jordan's national dish par excellence is *mansaf,* which takes its name from a word that means "big dish" or "large tray." In tent communities as well as in towns and villages, it is served to honor distinguished guests and to celebrate special occasions, from weddings to official state banquets. The best *mansaf*s are reputedly found in the towns of al-Salt and al-Karak.

A vast communal dinner, *mansaf* consists of an enormous tray lined with sheets of flatbread (*shrak,* page 313), which are covered with a layer of rice surmounted by chunks of boiled lamb. The whole is flavored with *jameed,* a sauce made from the juices of the lamb into which dried sheep's or goat's milk yogurt has been crumbled and dissolved. The rice and lamb are cooked in huge caldrons, and the tray itself can be more than six feet in diameter. Both nomads and villagers consider it a mark of honor to own such large trays, as they are supposed to indicate the extent of a host's generosity. One gigantic tray, which belongs to a tribal chieftain who resides in a palatial villa in Amman, is capacious enough to hold the meat of two dozen sheep on a bed of nearly five hundred pounds of rice! Some years ago a *mansaf* of gargantuan proportions was held in southern Jordan in honor of a visiting monarch. It consisted of a whole baby camel that had been stuffed with sheep, inside which were turkeys, which in turn enclosed chickens! The stuffed camel lay on a bed of rice so immense that it could have covered the floor of a small room.

Whole Roast Lamb
Quzi

> There was an excellent dinner on a large scale in the Amir's tent that night, lambs and kids roasted whole, stuffed with pistachios and rice, bowls of Leben, unleavened bread, honey, and butter of their own making. Bowls of clear, sparkling water stood for us to drink.[7]

Whole roast lamb is a festive dish reserved for weddings and other important ceremonies, family gatherings, and very special guests. Although it can be prepared in several different ways, it tastes best roasted outdoors on a spit turned slowly over a smoldering charcoal or wood fire. Some cooks rub it with herbs and spices, while others prefer to season it simply with salt and freshly ground black pepper. The lamb is basted with melted butter or its own fat as it cooks, until it becomes well-done and browned. It is served with platters of rice enriched with raisins, nuts, and spices and accompanied with assorted salads. Sometimes the lamb is stuffed with a mixture of ground lamb, rice, and various nuts and spices and roasted outdoors as above or in a large oven. Another method is to cook the stuffed lamb in water until tender and then transfer it to a roasting pan, coat it with melted butter or plain yogurt, and roast it in the oven until browned and glazed, basting frequently with butter and some of the lamb broth. Stuffed whole lamb is traditionally served on a large tray decorated with parsley or spearmint sprigs and is accompanied with cooked vegetables and salads.

Crown Roast of Lamb
Kharuf Mahshi

> At a dinner of some pretensions there will be, of course, the great dish *kibby*, and meat cooked with beans, and squashes stuffed with rice and meat, the two sides (the ribs) of a lamb tied together and filled with rice, minced meat, and spice; and for dessert, dried apricots, stewed oranges, and fresh apricots, and cucumbers, which the natives eat just as they would apples or any other fruit.[8]

A 16-chop frenched and trimmed crown roast of lamb (about 4 pounds)
Salt and freshly ground black pepper to taste
Saffron Rice with Ground Meat and Nuts (page 254, Note)
Fresh parsley or spearmint sprigs

Rub the lamb well with the salt and pepper and cover the ends of the bones with foil to prevent burning. Put the lamb in an oiled shallow roasting pan just large enough to hold it comfortably. Roast in a preheated 425°F oven about 30 minutes or until a meat thermometer inserted into the thickest part of the meat inside the crown registers 135°F for rare meat. If you prefer your meat to be more done, continue to roast until the internal temperature reaches 145°F for medium-rare and 165°F for well-done.

Transfer the lamb to a large platter and let stand, covered loosely, about 10 minutes. Remove the foil from the bones. Fill the hollow of the crown with as much of the saffron rice mixture as it will hold and serve the remaining rice separately. Garnish the platter with the parsley. Carve at table, allowing 2 chops per person.

Serves 8

VARIATIONS:

Mix 1 tablespoon olive oil with 2 teaspoons Mixed Spices I (page 66) and the salt and pepper. Rub the lamb with the mixture and continue as above.

Substitute 2 recipes Rice Stuffing with Dried Fruits and Nuts (page 260) or Bulgur Stuffing with Dried Fruits and Nuts (page 260) for the saffron rice above. Do not cool the stuffing. Serve while still hot.

∾

Your eyes have made roast meat of my heart.
(from *The Arabian Nights' Entertainments*)
∾

Lamb and Spinach Fatta
Fattet Sabanikh

*Fatta*s are wholesome layered dishes that were probably invented to use up stale flatbread that would otherwise be thrown out. The word *fatta* denotes crumbling or breaking into pieces. All *fatta*s have a bottom layer of toasted bread soaked in flavorful broth, another consisting most often of meat, chicken, or vegetables, a topping of creamy yogurt, and, perhaps, a garnish of toasted nuts (usually pine nuts). *Fatta*s make excellent family dishes that are popular in both urban and rural areas.

The recipe outlined below is closely related to one that appeared in an article I wrote on pita bread that was published in *Vogue* magazine nearly twenty years ago.

2 pounds spinach

2 tablespoons olive oil or unsalted butter

2 medium onions, finely chopped

1 pound lean boneless lamb, cut into 1-inch cubes

1/2 teaspoon Mixed Spices I (page 66)

Salt and freshly ground black pepper to taste

1 1/2 cups water

Juice of 1/2 lemon, or to taste, freshly squeezed and strained

2 tablespoons unsalted butter

1/3 cup pine nuts

1/2 teaspoon paprika or Middle Eastern red pepper to taste

2 six-inch pita breads, toasted and broken into bite-sized pieces

Minted Garlic Yogurt Sauce (page 280)

Wash the spinach thoroughly under cold running water. Remove and discard the stems and bruised leaves. Drain the spinach leaves, chop them coarsely, and set aside.

In a heavy casserole heat the oil over moderate heat. Add the onions and sauté until soft but not browned, stirring frequently. Add the lamb and sauté, turning to brown on all sides. Add the Mixed Spices, salt and pepper, and water and bring to a boil. Reduce the heat to low, cover, and simmer 1 hour or until the meat is tender and most of the liquid in the casserole has been absorbed. If it is not, uncover the casserole and boil until the liquid is reduced. Stir in the spinach, cover, and simmer 10 minutes. Stir in the lemon juice, taste and adjust the seasoning, and turn off the heat.

In a small skillet melt the butter. Add the pine nuts and sauté gently until golden brown, stirring frequently. Stir in the paprika or red pepper and remove from the heat.

To serve, spread the pieces of toasted pita in the bottom of a serving dish. Spoon the lamb and spinach stew over them. Cover with the yogurt sauce. Garnish with the sautéed pine nuts and dribble the paprika or red pepper butter remaining in the skillet over the top.

Serves 4

The Sanctified Hog

Muslims have traditionally rejected the flesh of swine, an abhorrence illustrated by the following anecdote concerning an event that took place in nineteenth-century Tripoli:

> One day a Maronite from [Mount] Lebanon was driving a hog to the Maronite quarter of the city, when it broke away and ran into the court of the Great Mosque around the corridors, by the minbab (pulpit) and the quiblab or mihrab (niche towards Mecca) and thence out into the street. Sheikh Aali[9] was horror-struck. The sacred mosque had been defiled, polluted beyond remedy, by an unclean animal whose very name could not be mentioned without using the word "Ajellak Allah," may God exalt you above the contamination of so vile a subject. A council was called. The mufti came and the kadi, and the chief sheikhs and Ulema. They sat around in solemn silence, until at length Sheikh Aali cautiously broached the awful subject, concluding with, "the holy place has been polluted and must be closed and never used again for prayer to Allah." Then silence, until the mufti cheerfully reassured the desponding faithful as follows: "My children, no harm has been done. When that creature, Ajellakum Allah, entered the mosque, the great holiness of the place at once transformed it into a lamb, and it remained a lamb until it went out at the gate when it resumed its original character." All exclaimed, "El Hamdu Lillah, Sabhan El Khalik. Praise to Allah. Praise to the Creator." Mutual congratulation followed. That mufti should have been made an honorary member of the Philadelphia bar.[10]

Grilled Skewered Pork with Sour Plum Sauce ⌀

Unlike Muslims, Armenians, being Christians, eat pork and drink wine, which apparently astonished the Persian traveler Nasir-i-Khusrau as he passed through Armenia in the year 1046:

*Convent of the Dancing
Dervishes, Tripoli, with
the Qadisha River in the
foreground.* From Charles
William Wilson, ed.,
Picturesque Palestine, Sinai
and Egypt, *vol. 2 (New York,
D. Appleton, 1883)*

We came to Van and Vastan, where they sell pork in the bazaar as well as lamb. Men and women sit drinking wine in the shops without the slightest inhibition.[11]

This recipe, my own, is inspired by both Armenian cuisine (the grilled pork) and the *Wusla* (the sauce).

1½ pounds boneless lean loin of pork, cut into 1½-inch cubes
Salt and freshly ground black pepper to taste
2 scallions, finely chopped
Sour Plum Sauce with Mint (page 286)

Prepare a charcoal grill.

Season the pork cubes with the salt and pepper and thread them on long four-sided metal skewers. Grill on an oiled rack set 3 to 4 inches above glowing coals, turning frequently, about 15 minutes or until the meat is well browned and cooked through. (Alternatively, the pork may be broiled.)

With the side of a knife or fork, carefully slide the pork off the skewers onto individual heated plates and sprinkle with the scallions. Serve at once with the Sour Plum Sauce with Mint and Rice Pilaf with Dried Fruits and Nuts (page 260) or Saffron Rice (page 250).

Serves 4

VARIATION:

Grilled Skewered Pork with Pomegranate Sauce ❧

Substitute Pomegranate Sauce with Ginger and Mint (page 284) for the Sour Plum Sauce with Mint.

MEAT STEWS

A large tray was brought in and set down, and the whole contents transferred to the table . . . from a deep round copper dish of the size of a wheelbarrow's wheel, rose a pile of pilaff; but twice as large must have been the tray that bore the whole sheep. Around this were placed the dishes, like the planets round the sun; the thin scons were rolled up and laid on the ground all round under the table. . . . They eat the pilaff, not at the end of the meal, but with every dish, pouring spoons full of the sauce of the dish they like best on the part of the pilaff they dig in. There was a dish before each; they were all different, and each skipped about to his neighbour's mess. I did not vary my attentions, chancing in that before me . . . It was a ragout of mutton, the meat soft as butter without losing its flavor. There was a green vegetable, wild herb, with an agro dolce sauce, the sweet and the acid of which were slightly touched, and its soupçon of richness embellished the simplicity of the pilaff when poured over it.[12]

Stews, known as *al-yakhnat*, have been a mainstay of the region's cookery for many centuries. During medieval times meat stews incorporating vegetables and fruits were frequently named after the ingredient highlighted in them, for example *isfanakhiyya* (a spinach dish), *saljamiyya* (a turnip dish), *mishmishiyya* (an apricot dish), and *safarjaliyya* (a quince dish). The balance, harmony, and textural interest of these ancient preparations, which were often achieved by the mingling of seemingly disparate elements in exciting and unexpected ways, is echoed in the stews of today, some of which are their direct descendants.

Lamb and Green Bean Stew
Yakhnit al-Lubiyya

In our house the cook gets tired of this stew, but the diners never seem to.

2 tablespoons unsalted butter or olive oil

2 medium onions, finely chopped

2 medium garlic cloves, finely chopped

1 pound lean boneless lamb, cut into 1-inch cubes

4 large ripe tomatoes, peeled, seeded, and coarsely chopped

1/2 cup water or beef broth

1/2 teaspoon Mixed Spices I (page 66) (optional)

Salt, freshly ground black pepper, and Middle Eastern red pepper to taste

2 pounds green beans, trimmed and halved lengthwise and then crosswise

In a large, heavy saucepan melt the butter over moderate heat. Add the onions and sauté, stirring frequently, until soft but not browned. Add the garlic and lamb and cook, turning the pieces of meat frequently until they are evenly browned on all sides. Stir in the tomatoes, water or beef broth, Mixed Spices (if used), and salt, black pepper, and red pepper and bring the mixture to a boil. Reduce the heat to low, cover, and simmer 30 minutes. Stir in the beans, cover, and simmer 45 minutes to 1 hour or until the meat and beans are very tender and the sauce is thickened, adding more water during cooking if necessary. Taste and adjust the seasoning. Serve hot with Plain Rice (page 249) or Bulgur Pilaf (page 257).

Serves 4 to 6

Note: As mentioned on page 266, cutting the beans in the manner suggested above enables them to better absorb the sauce. Some people, however, prefer the look and texture achieved by cutting the beans crosswise into approximately 2-inch lengths.

Lamb and Okra Stew
Yakhnit al-Bamiyya

Although okra is widely appreciated in the eastern Mediterranean, it is relatively neglected in this country outside of the South. Here is one delicious way to remedy the situation.

Follow the recipe for Lamb and Green Bean Stew (page 210) with these changes: If desired, stir in $\frac{1}{4}$ cup finely chopped fresh coriander leaves when the meat is browned. Substitute $1\frac{1}{2}$ pounds okra, rinsed and trimmed, for the green beans, and add 1 tablespoon Pomegranate Molasses (page 57) and 2 tablespoons freshly squeezed and strained lemon juice, or to taste.

Serves 4

VARIATIONS:

Pat the okra dry with paper towels and sauté it in a little olive oil before adding it to the saucepan.

Substitute 1 tablespoon tamarind concentrate diluted in a little water for the Pomegranate Molasses.

Lamb Stew with Yogurt
Laban Ummo *or* Shakriyya

Here is a venerable classic that bears some relationship to the Abbassid dish known as *madira*. The name *laban ummo* conveys the idea that the lamb has been cooked in its mother's milk.

3 tablespoons olive oil or unsalted butter

2 medium onions, finely chopped

2 pounds lean boneless lamb, cut into 1-inch cubes

$\frac{1}{2}$ teaspoon ground cinnamon (optional)

Salt and freshly ground black pepper to taste

$1\frac{1}{2}$ cups water

Cooked Yogurt (page 144)

2 tablespoons unsalted butter

2 medium garlic cloves, crushed

1 tablespoon crushed dried spearmint or $1\frac{1}{2}$ teaspoons ground coriander

In a large, heavy flameproof casserole or Dutch oven heat the oil over moderate heat. Add the onions and sauté, stirring frequently, until soft but not browned. Add the lamb and cook, turning the cubes frequently until they are evenly browned on all sides. Sprinkle with the cinnamon (if used) and salt and pepper. Stir in the water and bring to a boil. Reduce the heat to low, cover, and simmer 1 to $1\frac{1}{2}$ hours or until the lamb is very tender, adding more water during cooking if necessary. Stir in the Cooked Yogurt and cook gently, uncovered, 10 to 15 minutes.

Meanwhile, in a small skillet melt the butter over moderate heat. Add the garlic and mint or coriander and cook gently, stirring, until the garlic just turns lightly golden. Add the contents of the skillet to the lamb and yogurt mixture. Serve hot with Rice with Vermicelli (page 250), Saffron Rice (page 250), or Bulgur Pilaf with Vermicelli (page 259).

Serves 6

Lamb Stew with Plums
Yakhnit al-Khawkh

> The dinner was really excellent. Different kinds of meat cut in small pieces were mixed with chopped vegetables or sauces, so that nothing required to be separated with the fingers. One dish—a stew of meat, damsons, and onions—I am ashamed to say, pleased me much. . . . Pastry, stewed apricots, and other sweets were served without any perceptible order in the middle of the repast, and last of all came a pilau of mutton and rice.[13]

3 tablespoons unsalted butter

2 medium onions, finely chopped

$1\frac{1}{2}$ pounds lean boneless lamb, cut into 1-inch cubes

1 cup water or beef broth, or more if needed

Salt and freshly ground black pepper to taste

1 pound damson or other sour plums

$\frac{1}{4}$ cup finely chopped fresh spearmint leaves, or to taste

Court and liwan *of a private house in Damascus.* *From William McClure Thomson,* The Land and the Book, *vol. 3 (New York, Harper, 1885)*

In a large, heavy saucepan melt the butter over moderate heat. Add the onions and sauté, stirring frequently, until soft but not browned. Add the lamb and cook, turning the cubes frequently, until they are evenly browned on all sides. Add the water or broth and salt and pepper and bring the mixture to a boil. Reduce the heat to low, cover, and simmer about 1 hour and 10 minutes or until the meat is tender, adding more water if necessary. Stir in the plums, cover, and simmer about 20 minutes or until they are tender. Taste and adjust the seasoning. Sprinkle with the mint and serve hot with Saffron Rice (page 250).

    Serves 6

VARIATIONS:

Add ½ teaspoon Mixed Spices I (page 66) or ground cinnamon with the salt.

Add ¼ cup chopped fresh herbs (spearmint, summer savory, and coriander leaves) with the plums.

Lamb Stew with Dried Apricots and Prunes

Add ½ teaspoon Mixed Spices I (page 66) or ground cinnamon and the peel and freshly squeezed and strained juice of ½ lemon with the salt. Substitute ⅔ cup each dried tart apricots and dried pitted prunes plus 1 tablespoon sugar, or to taste, for the damson plums, and toasted pine nuts for the mint.

GROUND MEAT DISHES

Ground Meat on Skewers
Kafta alla Shish *or* Kafta Mashwiyya

These kebabs are often presented nestling in pita bread that has been squeezed around the skewers of meat toward the end of cooking to soak up the flavorful juices and then used to pull the meat off the skewers.

> **Kafta (below)**
> **³/₄ cup finely chopped flat-leaf parsley**
> **¹/₂ cup finely chopped scallions**
> **Lemon wedges**

Prepare a charcoal grill.

Moisten your hands with cold water and form portions of the *kafta* into 3¹/₂- to 4-inch-long sausages around flat-bladed metal skewers, pressing and molding the *kafta* to the skewers and leaving about ¹/₄ inch between each sausage. Grill the meat on an oiled rack set 2 to 3 inches above glowing coals, turning frequently, about 10 minutes or until it is evenly browned on all sides and cooked through. (Alternatively, the meat may be broiled.)

With the side of a knife or fork, carefully slide the *kafta* off the skewers onto heated individual plates. Combine the parsley and scallions and sprinkle the mixture evenly over the meat. Garnish with the lemon wedges and serve at once with warm pita bread, Chickpea and Tahini Dip (page 106), and Tabbuleh (page 127).

Serves 6

VARIATIONS:

Instead of sprinkling the grilled *kafta* with the parsley and scallions, sprinkle them with a mixture of 1 cup minced parsley, 2 mild onions, very thinly sliced, and 2 teaspoons ground sumac, or to taste.

Grilled Ground Meat Patties

Omit the skewers. Form the *kafta* into 18 oval or round patties and grill, turning to brown on both sides, until done to your taste. Serve with fried potatoes and a salad.

Kafta

This mixture is usually made to order at meat markets. Our Armenian butcher in Shtora, whose *basterma* was unsurpassed, was equally expert at making *kafta*. The speed with which he handled his huge knife to chop and blend together the ingredients was remarkable, and I used to watch his virtuoso performances with as much fear as amazement!

2 pounds lean boneless lamb or beef, ground 2 or 3 times

2 medium onions, grated

1 cup finely chopped flat-leaf parsley

2 teaspoons Mixed Spices I (page 66), or 1 teaspoon each ground cinnamon and ground allspice

Salt, freshly ground black pepper, and Middle Eastern red pepper to taste

In a large bowl combine all the ingredients. Pound or knead the mixture vigorously until it is well blended, very smooth, and pasty. (Alternatively, blend the ingredients to a smooth paste in a food processor.) Cover and chill 1 hour.

Note: If you plan to grill the *kafta* over charcoal or wood embers, grind a little fat with the lean meat. The fat will protect the meat from drying as it cooks and will melt and drip out, leaving the *kafta* pleasantly moist but not greasy.

VARIATION:

Substitute minced fresh spearmint for 1/4 cup of the parsley.

Ground Meat Kebabs with Sour Cherry Sauce
Kabab bi Karaz Hamud

Variations of this dish are encountered in Lebanon and Syria, especially around Aleppo. This particular recipe comes from our Shtora kitchen. We used to make it with tart, juicy, black cherries from our orchard and serve it with warm flatbread, plain or saffron rice, or bulgur pilaf.

1 1/2 pounds lean boneless lamb or beef, ground twice

1 medium onion, grated

1 teaspoon ground cinnamon

Salt and freshly ground black pepper to taste

2 scallions, finely chopped

Fresh coriander or spearmint sprigs

Sour Cherry Sauce (page 285)

In a bowl combine the lamb or beef, onion, cinnamon, and salt and pepper and knead the mixture vigorously until it is well blended and smooth. Cover and chill 1 hour.

Prepare a charcoal grill.

Divide the meat mixture into 36 balls. Moisten your hands with cold water and form the balls into 1 1/2-inch-long sausages around flat-bladed metal skewers, pressing and molding the meat mixture to the skewers and leaving about 1/4 inch between each sausage. Grill the meat on an oiled rack set 2 to 3 inches above glowing coals, turning frequently, 10 to 12 minutes or until it is evenly browned on all sides and cooked through. (Alternatively, the meat may be broiled.)

With the side of a knife or fork, carefully slide the kebabs off the skewers onto heated individual plates. Sprinkle with the scallions and garnish with the coriander or spearmint sprigs. Serve at once with the Sour Cherry Sauce.

Serves 4 to 6

VARIATIONS:

Add 2 tablespoons pine nuts to the meat mixture.

When the kebabs are done, remove them from the skewers and add them to the Sour Cherry Sauce. Cook gently about 5 minutes and stir in the scallions, if desired. Omit the coriander sprigs. Serve over a bed of pilaf or pieces of warm flatbread.

Meatballs with Pine Nuts in Tomato Sauce
Da'ud Basha

Da'ud Basha (1816–1873) was the first governor general (*mutasarrif*) of autonomous Lebanon. An Armenian whose real name was Karapet Davud (Davudian), he was not only a career Ottoman diplomat and high government official but also the author of a French work on old German jurisprudence that earned him international recognition as a scholar. The sultan of Turkey, the emperor Napoleon III of France, and the pope were among the personages who bestowed honors on him. Da'ud's wise and just rule in Lebanon (from 1861 to 1868) won him the respect and admiration of his subjects, and this dish, of which he was reportedly very fond, is named in his honor.

> 2 pounds lean boneless lamb or beef, ground 2 or 3 times
>
> 1½ teaspoons ground cinnamon or Mixed Spices I (page 66)
>
> Salt and freshly ground black pepper to taste
>
> ¼ cup unsalted butter or olive oil, or more if needed
>
> 3 medium onions, cut lengthwise in half and thinly sliced
>
> ⅓ cup pine nuts
>
> 2 tablespoons tomato paste
>
> 4 large ripe tomatoes, peeled, seeded, and chopped
>
> 2 teaspoons Pomegranate Molasses (page 57)
>
> 1 tablespoon freshly squeezed and strained lemon juice
>
> Finely chopped flat-leaf parsley or crushed dried spearmint to taste

In a large bowl combine the lamb or beef, 1 teaspoon of the cinnamon or Mixed Spices, and salt and pepper. Pound or knead the mixture vigorously until it is well blended and very smooth. With hands moistened in cold water, form the mixture into 1-inch balls.

In a large, deep, heavy skillet heat the butter or oil over moderate heat. Add the onions and sauté, stirring frequently, until soft and lightly golden. Add the meatballs and sauté, turning to brown on all sides. Add the pine nuts and sauté gently, stirring, about 2 minutes. Mix the tomato paste with a little water and add it along with the

Da'ud Basha, the first governor of autonomous Lebanon, 1861–1868.
From Henry Harris Jessup, Fifty-Three Years in Syria, *vol. 1 (New York, Fleming H. Revell Company, 1910)*

tomatoes to the skillet. Add the Pomegranate Molasses, lemon juice, and remaining ½ teaspoon cinnamon and season to taste with salt and pepper. Stir the mixture well, partially cover the skillet, and simmer over low heat about 45 minutes or until the meatballs are well done and the sauce is thickened. Taste and adjust the seasoning. Sprinkle with the parsley or mint and serve hot with Plain Rice (page 249).

Serves 6 to 8

VARIATION:

Add 1 small onion, grated, to the meat mixture.

Braised Rabbit with Eggplant
Arnab bi Batinjaan

Follow the recipe for Braised Chicken with Eggplant (page 187), substituting a 3-pound rabbit for the chicken.

Serves 4

෴

He who runs after two hares will catch neither. *(A)*

෴

CHAPTER 9

Kibbeh

The monastery of St. Anthony near Ehden, in northern Lebanon. *From John Carne*, Syria, the Holy Land, Asia Minor, &c., *vol. 2 (London, Fisher, Son, 1836)*

KIBBY IS THE ARAB PLUM-PUDDING and mince-pie and roast-beef, all in one.[1]

Of the many Christian feast days observed in Lebanon, one of the most exciting is '*Id al-Salib* (Sign of the Cross Day or St. Helena's Day), which falls on September 14. According to legend, Queen Helena, mother of the Roman emperor Constantine, found the True Cross of the Crucifixion on a basil-covered hill in Jerusalem early in the fourth century. She is said to have commanded that a succession of signal fires be lit in a line of watchtowers from Jerusalem to Constantinople to communicate the joyful news of her discovery to her subjects. The picturesque ruins of a tower, known as the Tower of St. Helena, still guard the northern side of the beautiful Bay of Juniyya north of Beirut.

During my years in Lebanon a stirring commemoration of this event would take place on the eve of '*Id al-Salib,* when mountain villagers celebrated with fireworks and lit hundreds of bonfires in fields, gardens, and on the flat roofs of houses, churches, and monasteries. The many rooftop fires certainly lent credence to the old fire tower legend! From the coast the flames twinkling on the mountainsides were a dramatic sight to behold. Church bells tolled and people stayed up late into the night until the last light of the fires was extinguished and all the fireworks were used up. Often a few drops of rain would fall, adding a touch of the supernatural to the evening's events, for most of the spring and all of summer until then would normally be completely dry. The illumination festivities celebrating St. Helena's legend would be followed by equally memorable gastronomic festivities, the star attraction of which was *kibbeh*. With the first hint of cool weather already in the air, the robustly gratifying character of this specialty made it an ideal choice as the favorite food for such a holiday.

Both the Lebanese and Syrians claim *kibbeh* as their national dish. The Jordanians, who call it *kubba,* are also very fond of it, as are the Armenians, among whom it is known as *keufteh*. A culinary triumph that enjoys immense popularity throughout the Fertile Crescent, *kibbeh* is a special-occasion dish par excellence and a standard blues-chaser for homesick expatriates of the region. The epitome of honest country cooking, it satisfies deep down as few other foods can. Preparing and eating this perennial favorite is not only a hallowed tradition; it is a universal addiction!

A versatile creation with seemingly endless variations, *kibbeh* is most often a blend of ground lamb, bulgur, grated onion, and seasonings. It can be eaten raw or cooked, hot or cold. The dish itself is extremely old and may well have originated in ancient Mesopotamia. It appears to have existed in Biblical times, for its method of preparation is alluded to in the Book of Proverbs (27:22). The word *kibbeh* is derived from an Arabic verb meaning "to form into a lump or ball," one of the steps involved in making the dish.

Kibbeh can be molded into various shapes, stuffed with a filling, broiled, fried, poached, or baked. Although lamb is the meat most often used, top-quality beef and, among Armenians, pork sometimes find their way into *kibbeh* dishes. There also exist meatless types of *kibbeh* that incorporate fish or vegetables such as potatoes, pumpkin, and lentils as well as versions that utilize ground rice instead of bulgur.

Different fillings are used for *kibbeh*, a classic one being a mixture of ground lamb, minced onion, spices, and pine nuts, walnuts, or pistachios. Pomegranate seeds, pomegranate molasses, or yogurt cheese are occasionally included; or pomegranate seeds are combined with yogurt cheese, chopped onion, and chopped walnuts for a meatless filling. *Kibbeh* balls are sometimes cooked in a sauce made with yogurt, *kishk*, sour pomegranate juice, or *tahini* and the juice of bitter oranges, or they are added to soups and stews. They may also be cooked with fruits such as sour cherries, quinces, and dried apricots.

In addition to the recipes and variations in this chapter, I have published some three dozen others elsewhere, the majority of them in my *Cuisine of Armenia*. There are, however, so many versions of this popular dish that a comprehensive collection would require a volume all its own.

In Syria, Lebanon, and Jordan, a woman's culinary skill is often measured by the quality of her *kibbeh*. The shaping of *kibbeh* requires practice, and women who are adept at it are respected and even envied, especially if they are blessed with a long forefinger, around which the *kibbeh* can be molded into a thin shell, a crucial step in the preparation of torpedo-shaped *kibbeh* (page 226).

The basic *kibbeh* is traditionally made by pounding lean meat from the leg with salt in a stone mortar (*jurn*). This utensil is placed on the floor and the cook, sitting on a low stool facing it, pounds the seasoned meat with metronomic precision, using a heavy wooden pestle (*madaqqa*). A grated onion that has been pounded with salt and pepper is blended with the meat. The mixture is pounded again, with the addition of a little ice water (or lumps of ice), until it is very soft and smooth in texture. Next, rinsed and drained fine bulgur is kneaded in vigorously along with additional salt and pepper and other desired seasonings, and the whole is further pounded diligently until a very refined and moist paste is formed. This method of preparing *kibbeh* is obviously quite a

Mortar and pestle for pounding **kibbeh.**
From Louis Charles Lortet, La Syrie
d'aujourd'hui *(Paris, Librairie Hachette, 1884)*

test of a cook's strength and character. The lengthy and tedious procedure can be greatly simplified by the use of a food processor.

Just how important a role *kibbeh* has played in the lives of Christian Lebanese villagers is illustrated by a quaint tradition of former times. As the hour drew near for the bride to leave her home for the wedding ceremony, custom decreed that she pretend to be grief-stricken at the prospect of parting from her parents and to act as if she had decided not to go through with the marriage. The groom's family would come to her door fully prepared for this, however, having brought along the village strongman to give the impression that he would carry her bodily to the church if she refused to come of her own volition! He would proceed to lift high the family *jurn,* which in those days weighed a hundred pounds. This formidable show of strength would put an end to the bride's feigned wailing and second thoughts and "persuade" her to proceed to the ceremony without further protestations.

If you have a good wife, do not go to weddings; you have one every day in your house.
If you have a bad wife, do not go to funerals; you have one every day in your house. *(A)*

A French Pianist's Introduction to Kibbeh

When I was a child the rhythmic pounding of *kibbeh* was a familiar sound heard from house to house in communities both large and small. It was always in the background in Zahleh's restaurants, where the finest *kibbeh* (especially raw *kibbeh*) was, and still is, made. The measured thump of *madaqqa* against *jurn* is music to the ears of the people, an aural foretaste of the pleasures awaiting their palates. What brings an anticipatory smile to the lips of a Beiruti, however, may evoke a very different response from a Parisian, who, upon observing so many cultural similarities between his own city and what was considered the Paris of the East, could be quite unprepared for manifestations of the deeply rooted indigenous traditions that lay beneath the latter's glittering Western surface.

I recall the visit to Beirut of a French pianist, who had come to give a concert. He was the guest of a cultured family whose son, an excellent pianist himself, was a friend of mine. On a bright Sunday morning the family took off for an outing, leaving the young man alone to practice undisturbed on their fine grand piano in preparation for his upcoming performance. Well aware of the problems of apartment living, he had expressed concern before they departed about annoying the neighbors, especially with everyone's windows being open on such a beautiful day. His hosts assured him that the neighbors, far from being annoyed, would actually enjoy hearing him practice since they were greatly fond of classical music. Besides, my friend would drop by after a while to see how he was getting along. Thus reassured, the young man seated himself at the instrument, and all went well for about two hours. Then, without warning, he began to hear a thumping sound of monotonous regularity coming from the windows at the rear of the apartment, where the kitchen and balcony overlooked a courtyard. After investigation revealed nothing that seemed hostile in intent, he returned, a bit tentatively, to the keyboard, but within minutes the thumping began to multiply, not only from outside but from what seemed to be within the building until he was engulfed in a mad, unceasing chorus of pounding from all sides that filled him with terror. It seemed as if everyone within earshot had banded together by some mysterious means of mass telepathy to express displeasure over his practicing and to warn him that he faced dire consequences unless he ceased at once. As the cacophony was rising to a climax the doorbell rang. The bell continued to ring, there were anxious knocks on the door, shouts in French and Arabic, and, finally, my friend burst into the apartment to find the fellow hiding behind a sofa, white as a sheet. Upon hearing the pounding noises in the background, he immediately grasped what had been taking place and broke into a fit of laughter, which did not sit too well with the Frenchman, who was in a state of near shock. My friend had to explain that what had frightened him was only the pounding of *kibbeh* as it was being prepared by all the cooks in the neighborhood for its traditional inclusion on the Sunday luncheon menu! This explanation held little credulity for the French pianist, who had never heard of *kibbeh*. Eventually, however, he calmed down and in due time was even able to sample and enjoy this timeless classic. In the end everyone had many a long and hearty laugh over the experience, and the concert itself was a huge success.

Kibbeh

You can use this basic mixture for all the meat *kibbeh*s in this chapter.

Purists notwithstanding, many cooks prepare excellent *kibbeh* in the following manner, even though it differs from the traditional time-consuming method described on page 220. The proportion of bulgur to lamb can vary from recipe to recipe and from cook to cook.

1⅓ to 1½ cups fine bulgur

1 medium onion, quartered

1 pound very lean boneless leg of lamb, cut into small cubes and chilled

1 teaspoon ground cinnamon

1 teaspoon ground allspice

2 teaspoons salt, or to taste

½ teaspoon freshly ground black pepper, or to taste

¼ teaspoon Middle Eastern red pepper, or to taste

Ice water (approximately ¼ cup)

Rinse the bulgur thoroughly in a fine sieve under cold running water. Squeeze out as much moisture as possible by handfuls and place the bulgur in a large mixing bowl. Purée the onion in a food processor and add to the bulgur. Add half of the cubed lamb to the processor and blend to a paste. Add to the bulgur and onion mixture. Repeat with the rest of the lamb. Combine the remaining ingredients except the ice water with the lamb, bulgur, and onion and divide the mixture into 3 equal batches. Process each batch in the food processor until the ingredients are well blended, adding ice water as necessary to facilitate processing. Combine the batches in a large bowl and, with hands moistened in ice water, knead the mixture until it is thoroughly blended and smooth. Cover and chill until ready to use.

Note: If you do not have a food processor, you can make *kibbeh* as follows: Substitute 1 pound very lean boneless leg of lamb, ground 3 times, for the cubed lamb and 1 medium onion, finely grated, for the quartered onion. Rinse and squeeze out the bulgur as above. Combine all the ingredients in a large bowl. With hands moistened by occasionally dipping them into a bowl of lightly salted ice water, knead the mixture about 10 minutes or until it is well blended and smooth. Cover and chill until ready to use.

The choice and quantity of spices vary according to personal taste. More or less cinnamon or allspice may be used, or both spices may be omitted or replaced with 2 teaspoons Mixed Spices (page 65), or to taste.

Raw Kibbeh (M)
Kibbeh Nayya

Hadj Aly assured me that his wife, who was a Metoualy woman, made no scruple of eating raw meat; and that, when mincing mutton to make a farce called *cubby,* she often ate so much as to spoil her dinner.[2]

It is important to use very fresh, extra-lean, tender lamb, trimmed of all fat and gristle, for this enduring favorite. The usual ratio of bulgur to lamb is 1 cup to 1 pound; however, the proportion can vary widely according to personal preference.

A note of caution: Do not make this recipe unless you are certain that the raw meat you are using is absolutely safe to consume.

> Kibbeh (page 222), using 1 to 1 ½ cups bulgur
> Extra-virgin olive oil
> Chopped scallions
> Lemon wedges
> Fresh spearmint or flat-leaf parsley sprigs
> The small inner leaves from 1 head romaine lettuce

Divide the *kibbeh* into 8 equal parts and, moistening your hands with cold water, shape each part into a round flat cake about ½ inch thick. Place the cakes on individual serving plates and, with your thumb, make an indentation in the center of each. Pour a spoonful of the oil, or to taste, in each indentation. Garnish the *kibbeh nayya* with the scallions, lemon wedges, and mint or parsley sprigs. Serve at once, accompanied with the lettuce leaves and pita bread. Eat the *kibbeh* by scooping it up with the lettuce leaves and pieces of bread.

Serves 8

Kibbeh on Skewers
Kibbeh alla Shish

This dish was just one of a dozen varieties of *kibbeh* that formed the main attraction of a spectacular picnic I attended in Aleppo, despite competition from an orchestra, singers, storytellers, jugglers, sword dancers, and belly dancers!

A natural for dining alfresco, this *kibbeh* tastes best when grilled over an open fire. In the Middle East a little fat, usually from the tail of a sheep, is ground with the lean meat, making it unnecessary to brush the skewered *kibbeh* with oil or butter during cooking. The fat protects the meat from drying out as it cooks and drips out after melting from the heat of the fire.

Follow the recipe for Ground Meat on Skewers (page 214), substituting Kibbeh (page 222) for the *kafta*. Brush the skewered *kibbeh* occasionally with olive oil or melted Clarified Butter (page 148) or unsalted butter while it is being grilled or broiled. The *kibbeh* are done when they are golden brown on all sides and cooked through. Serve hot with Tahini Dip (page 105), Eggplant and Tahini Dip (page 107), or Minted Garlic Yogurt Sauce (page 280) and a salad.

Serves 4

Kibbeh in a Tray
Kibbeh bi Saniyya

> **Kibbeh (page 222)**
> **Filling (below)**
> **6 tablespoons Clarified Butter (page 148) or unsalted butter, melted**

Divide the *kibbeh* into 2 equal parts. With hands moistened occasionally in cold water, press down 1 part smoothly over the bottom of a buttered 9-by-9-by-1½-inch baking dish. Spread the filling evenly over it. Cover with the remaining *kibbeh* by flattening small portions between your palms and placing them over the stuffing, patting them down firmly and covering it completely. Smooth the top with moist hands. With a sharp knife dipped frequently in cold water, cut the *kibbeh* into diamond shapes or squares. Brush the entire surface with butter and bake in a preheated 375° F oven about 45 minutes or until golden brown and crisp on top. Serve hot or cold with Cucumber and Yogurt Salad (page 123) or with Drained Yogurt (page 142) and Mixed Vegetable Salad (page 122).

Serves 4 to 6

FILLING

> **3 tablespoons olive oil or butter**
> **⅓ cup pine nuts**
> **1 large onion, finely chopped**
> **½ pound lean boneless leg or shoulder of lamb, ground**
> **½ teaspoon ground cinnamon**
> **½ teaspoon ground allspice**
> **Salt, freshly ground black pepper, and Middle Eastern red pepper to taste**

In a small, heavy skillet heat 2 tablespoons of the oil or butter over moderate heat. Add the pine nuts and sauté, stirring, until they are golden. Transfer the nuts with a slotted spoon to a plate and reserve. Add the remaining 1 tablespoon oil to the skillet and heat. Add the onion and cook, stirring frequently, until it is soft but not browned. Add the lamb and cook, stirring and breaking it up with a spoon, until browned. Stir in the reserved pine nuts, cinnamon, allspice, and salt, black pepper, and red pepper and mix well. Taste and adjust the seasoning.

VARIATIONS:

Substitute lean ground beef or veal for the lamb.

Substitute ¾ teaspoon Mixed Spices I (page 66) for the cinnamon and allspice.

Omit the pine nuts. Add ¼ cup chopped blanched unsalted pistachio nuts with the spices (an Aleppan variation).

Add 1 teaspoon ground sumac and/or 2 teaspoons Pomegranate Molasses (page 57) or fresh lemon juice with the spices, and, if desired, stir in 2 tablespoons minced flat-leaf parsley.

Fried Stuffed Kibbeh (M)
Kibbeh Qrass Maqliyya

The very mention of this *kibbeh* unleashes a rush of childhood memories, among them a delightful day spent in the scenic fruit-growing Diniyya region of northern Lebanon, with the town of Sir at its center. Set between two verdant valleys amid lovely waterfalls, Sir lay in a veritable Garden of Eden, the productivity of which was nothing short of amazing. It being the height of the fruit season, whole families were out in their orchards from dawn to sunset picking crisp mountain apples, plums, pears, and luscious red- and purple-skinned peaches, all of which they loaded into crates for the trucks that made their way up and down the mountain road.

In addition to the abundance of fruit and water, flowers bloomed everywhere—in the courtyards of homes, in the picturesque cafés beside the rushing millstream, and on the grounds of the town's stately hotel, which was resplendent with thousands of dahlias, begonias, and fuchsias as well as sweet-scented roses, carnations, and jasmines.

The day was rendered even more memorable by a superb dinner in nearby Tripoli highlighted by *kibbeh qrass maqliyya,* one of the city's many culinary specialties. Although it takes a certain degree of skill to make this most popular of *kibbeh*s, it takes absolutely none at all to become addicted to it!

> **Kibbeh (page 222), using 1 ½ cups bulgur**
> **Filling (page 225)**
> **Olive or vegetable oil for deep-frying**

Moisten your hands with cold water. Pinch off a lump of *kibbeh* the size of a small egg and hold it in the palm of your left hand. With your right forefinger, make a tunnel-like pocket lengthwise up the center, gradually enlarging the pocket with your forefinger all around the inside wall while rotating the *kibbeh* in the palm of your left hand until you have as thin as possible a shell without its falling apart. Seal any cracks in the shell with a finger dipped in cold water. Fill the pocket with about 1 tablespoon of the filling. Pinch the ends of the shell to seal securely and, with moistened hands, form the stuffed *kibbeh* into the shape of a small torpedo, sealing any cracks that may appear in the shell. Repeat this procedure with the remaining *kibbeh* and filling.

In a large, heavy skillet heat 2 inches oil over moderate heat. Add the stuffed *kibbeh* and fry, turning them, until they are richly browned on all sides. Transfer with a slotted spoon to paper towels to drain. Arrange the *kibbeh* on a platter and serve hot or at room temperature as part of a *mazza* or with a salad and yogurt as a main course.

Serves 4 to 6

Grilled Stuffed Kibbeh

Kibbeh Qrass Mahshiyya

Some of the best *kibbeh* in Lebanon is reputedly made by Maronite Christian cooks, especially those in the northern towns of Ehden and Zgharta, both Maronite strongholds.[3] Although these communities excel in the preparation of several types of *kibbeh*, it is the grilled version for which they are most renowned.

The following passage by Thomson may explain at least in part why both Ehden and Zgharta are well known for their *kibbeh*.

> Our road from the Cedars, though rough and rocky, has been endlessly diversified by distant views of mountain scenery, combining every element of beauty, grandeur, and sublimity. We have had glimpses of the profound gorge of the holy river Kadisha; have seen, far below and above us, several villages and convents; have crossed green valleys and purling streams; have been refreshed by the waters of cold and sparkling fountains; and have, at last, after a pleasant

A mule-driven streetcar in Tripoli. From National Geographic, *January, 1911*

Village of Ehden. *From John Carne,* Syria, the Holy Land, Asia Minor, &c., *vol. 1 (London, Fisher, Son, 1836)*

ride of three hours, arrived at this pretty village of Ehden, embowered in verdure, and surrounded by vineyards, mulberry terraces, and pine, fig, and walnut trees.

In the winter this place is buried in deep snow, and those of the inhabitants who can do so then descend to Zugharta, a large village on the south side of a fertile valley between the foot-hills of the mountain and the city of Tripoli.[4]

Local tradition has it that the Garden of Eden was located here. This assertion is, of course, highly improbable, for although Ehden is undeniably situated in an area of great scenic beauty and enjoys a salubrious climate for much of the year, it lies at far too high an altitude for Adam and Eve to have been comfortable in the middle of January!

Prepare stuffed *kibbeh* as directed in the recipe for Fried Stuffed Kibbeh (page 226), but instead of forming the *kibbeh* into torpedo shapes, form them into hamburger-shaped patties. Place a heaping tablespoon of filling between two patties, sandwich-style. Gently press the edges together with your fingertips to seal completely. Hold the sealed patties in the palm of your left hand (or your right, if you are left-handed). Cup the palm of your right (or left) hand over the *kibbeh*, giving it an arched top and a flat base. Pat the surface smooth with your fingers dipped in ice water. Brush the *kibbeh* with melted Clarified Butter (page 148) or unsalted butter or olive oil and grill or broil as directed for Grilled Ground Meat Patties (page 214). The *kibbeh* are done when they are golden brown on all sides and cooked through. Serve hot with Tahini Dip (page 105) or Eggplant and Tahini Dip (page 107).

Serves 4 to 6

Note: Other fillings for this *kibbeh* include seasoned butter or chopped sheep's tail fat (*aliya*) and onion; and yogurt cheese, chopped onion, and nuts.

Skiing in Lebanon

When French officials arrived in Lebanon after World War I to set up their mandate, they were struck by the sight of snow on the mountains looming nine thousand feet above, which immediately reminded them of the Haute Savoie. Pairs of skis were ordered from France, and soon a small group of aficionados were eagerly anticipating the annual December snows. Their strange and incomprehensible antics were looked upon with incredulity by the Maronite peasants. Eventually, however, the facile Lebanese took up skiing with great enthusiasm, and by 1935 it had become launched as a winter sport. The first Lebanese ski school was located in Kahlil Gibran's native village of Bsharri. Now one can choose from nearly a dozen modern ski resorts in the Lebanon Mountains, the one near the Cedars being the most famous.

What made skiing on Mount Lebanon so fascinating were the unexpected contrasts: the proximity of the alpine location to the seacoast, the banana and citrus orchards, and the olive groves below; the sight of pretty Lebanese girls on the slopes in fashionable, brightly colored ski clothes next to the occasional Arab in traditional dress, his long gown billowing in the breeze and his flowing *kuffiyya* held in place by a pair of goggles; a squad of Lebanese army ski troopers in fur-lined white uniforms on maneuvers; and the Arabic language being spoken in such an uncharacteristic setting. These contrasts were rendered even more dramatic in some areas of the Mountain such as Lakluk (a

Camels on Mount Lebanon. From Walter Keating Kelly, Syria and the Holy Land *(London, Chapman and Hall, 1844)*

popular ski area) during the early summer, when migrating Beduin from the desert pitched their tents beside snowdrifts and their camels grazed among alpine flowers.

Stuffed Kibbeh in Yogurt

Kibbeh bi Laban *or* Kibbeh Labaniyya

This warming and comforting wintertime favorite was especially welcome after a day's skiing at the Cedars.

Prepare stuffed *kibbeh* as directed in the recipe for Fried Stuffed Kibbeh (page 226), but do not fry the *kibbeh*.

Prepare 2 recipes Cooked Yogurt (page 144). Gently lower the stuffed *kibbeh* into the yogurt and simmer over low heat, uncovered, about 20 minutes. Meanwhile, prepare Garlic and Mint Mixture (page 288). Pour the sauce over the yogurt and stir thoroughly. Taste and adjust the seasoning.

Using a slotted spoon, transfer the *kibbeh* into individual soup bowls and ladle the yogurt over them. Serve hot with Plain Rice (page 249).

Serves 4 to 6

Fish Kibbeh

Qrass Kibbeh Samak

> 1⅓ to 1½ cups fine bulgur
> 1 medium onion, quartered
> 1 pound white fish fillets, skinned and coarsely chopped
> ⅓ cup finely chopped fresh coriander leaves, or to taste
> 1 tablespoon freshly squeezed and strained lemon juice
> Grated peel of ½ orange
> Salt and freshly ground black pepper to taste
> ½ cup olive oil

Rinse the bulgur thoroughly in a fine sieve under cold running water. Squeeze out as much moisture as possible by handfuls and place the bulgur in a large mixing bowl. Purée the onion in a food processor and add to the bulgur. Add half of the chopped fish to the processor and blend to a paste. Add to the bulgur and onion mixture. Repeat with the rest of the fish. Combine the coriander, lemon juice, orange peel, and salt and pepper with the fish, bulgur, and onion and divide the mixture into 3 equal batches. Process each batch in the food processor until the ingredients are well blended and smooth.

Moistening your hands occasionally with cold water, form the fish *kibbeh* into small hamburger-shaped patties. In a large, heavy skillet heat the oil over moderate heat. Add the patties and cook, turning them, until they are golden brown on both sides. With a slotted spatula, transfer the *kibbeh* to paper towels to drain briefly. Serve hot or cold with a salad.

Serves 4

Potato Kibbeh
Kibbeh Bataata

According to one tradition, potatoes were first introduced into Lebanon from Italy in the early seventeenth century during the reign of Amir Fakhr al-Din Ma'an, who had spent some time at the court of the Medici in Florence. Today they are a major crop in the Bekaa Valley and are an important article of diet in the three countries.

Here is an unusual way of serving potatoes.

Filling (page 225)
4 medium potatoes
1 cup fine bulgur, rinsed and squeezed dry
¼ cup all-purpose flour
¼ teaspoon Mixed Spices II (page 66) (optional)
Salt, freshly ground black pepper, and Middle Eastern red pepper to taste
¼ cup olive oil

Prepare the filling and set aside. Cook the potatoes in boiling salted water to cover until they are tender. Drain, and as soon as they are cool enough to handle, peel them.

In a large bowl mash the potatoes with the bulgur. Add the flour, Mixed Spices (if used), and salt, black pepper, and red pepper and knead until the mixture is thoroughly blended.

Moistening your hands occasionally with cold water, form the mixture into 1½-inch balls and stuff each as follows: Indent with your forefinger, pressing gently to make a hollow. Fill the hollow with a little of the filling, and with moistened hands reshape the potato mixture around the filling to enclose it securely. Gently flatten the ball into a patty.

In a large, heavy skillet heat the oil over moderate heat. Add the *kibbeh* and cook, turning them, a few minutes until they are golden brown and crisp. With a slotted spatula, transfer the *kibbeh* to paper towels to drain briefly. Mound the *kibbeh* on a platter. Serve hot or cold with a salad.

Serves 4

CHAPTER 10

Stuffed Vegetables and Fruits

Bayt al-Din. *From Charles Henry Spencer Churchill,* Mount Lebanon: A Ten Years' Residence from 1842 to 1852, vol. 3 *(London, Saunders and Otley, 1853)*

[T]HE DINNER . . . CONSISTED OF a great profusion of rice, boiled fowl, different kinds of boiled and minced meat and rice mixed together, forming a kind of sausage, enclosed in the skin of a gourd, resembling a cucumber, and several other trifling articles, all of which were so admirably seasoned, that having tasted of one, we had no disposition to quit it for another, and when we had done so, were as little inclined to return or change it for a third or fourth; yet most of us, I believe, were induced to try a little of each of them, and became such proselytes to Arab cookery, that we protested in good earnest, we should wish to dine so every day of our lives . . . though neither roast beef nor plum-pudding was among the dishes.[1]

Throughout the eastern Mediterranean a favorite method of preparing most vegetables and some fruits is to stuff them with savory mixtures. Often several stuffed vegetables of various shapes and colors are cooked and served together. Stuffed vegetables and fruits, known as *mahshi* (from the Arabic verb *hasha*, "to stuff") make economical, nutritious, and satisfying family meals as well as inviting company fare, and a good cook is expected to excel in their preparation. Although they take a bit of time, they are well worth the effort.

Stuffed vegetables are known to have existed in Sassanid Persian cuisine. They are also mentioned in medieval Arab cookery manuals; for example, recipes for cucumbers stuffed with meat appear in the *Wusla,* and both the *Wusla* and al-Baghdadi's *Kitab al-tabikh* include recipes for eggplants stuffed with meat.

There are basically two kinds of stuffed vegetables. The first contains a filling incorporating meat and is served hot as a main course. The meat is normally lamb or mutton, although beef or a combination of lamb and beef may be used. The second has a meatless filling usually based on rice and olive oil. It is served cold or at room temperature and makes an excellent appetizer. Although some people like to use long-grain rice for fillings, others prefer the medium- or short-grain varieties. When cooked, the long-grain becomes fluffy and its kernels remain separate, while the others become sticky and more absorbent.

When I was growing up, and to a lesser extent today, eggplants and zucchini were hollowed out and dried in the sun for use during the winter. They were soaked overnight, drained, and stuffed before being cooked. Pickled zucchini were also soaked, drained, and stuffed before cooking. Now that fresh vegetables are obtainable year-round, this practice has been largely abandoned, although many villagers still continue to preserve grapevine leaves. In former times stuffed vegetables used to be fried in oil or clarified butter before being stewed, which gave them a richer flavor. Nowadays, in keeping with the current preference for lighter foods, this step is generally omitted.

FILLINGS FOR VEGETABLES

Meat Filling

> 2 tablespoons unsalted butter or olive oil
> 1 medium onion, finely chopped
> ½ pound lean ground lamb or beef
> 3 tablespoons lightly toasted pine nuts
> ½ teaspoon Mixed Spices I (page 66), or ¼ teaspoon each ground cinnamon and
>   ground allspice
> Salt and freshly ground black pepper to taste

In a medium, heavy skillet heat the butter or oil over moderate heat. Add the onion and sauté, stirring frequently, until soft but not browned. Add the meat and cook, stirring and breaking it up with a fork, until lightly browned. Stir in the pine nuts, Mixed Spices, and salt and pepper and cook gently 2 to 3 minutes. Taste and adjust the seasoning. Remove from the heat and set aside.

VARIATIONS:

After the meat has browned, stir in 1 medium tomato, peeled, seeded, and finely chopped, and cook a few minutes before adding the remaining ingredients.

Add 2 tablespoons minced flat-leaf parsley with the seasonings.

Meat and Rice Filling

> ½ pound lean ground lamb or beef
> ½ cup medium- or short-grain white rice, washed and drained
> 1 medium ripe tomato, peeled, seeded, and finely chopped
> 1 medium onion, very finely chopped
> 3 tablespoons finely chopped flat-leaf parsley
> ½ teaspoon Mixed Spices I (page 66), or ¼ teaspoon each ground cinnamon and
>   ground allspice
> Salt, freshly ground black pepper, and Middle Eastern red pepper to taste

In a large bowl combine all the ingredients and knead until the mixture is well blended.

VARIATION:

Substitute coarse bulgur for the rice.

Rice Filling

⅔ cup medium- or short-grain white rice, washed and drained

2 medium onions, finely chopped

1 medium ripe tomato, peeled, seeded, and finely chopped

2 tablespoons pine nuts

⅓ cup finely chopped flat-leaf parsley

2 tablespoons finely chopped fresh spearmint leaves

¼ teaspoon ground cinnamon

¼ teaspoon ground allspice

Salt, freshly ground black pepper, and Middle Eastern red pepper to taste

⅓ cup olive oil

1 tablespoon freshly squeezed and strained lemon juice

In a medium bowl combine all the ingredients and mix well.

VARIATIONS:

Add 1 teaspoon minced fresh dill, or to taste.

Substitute ½ recipe cooked split and skinned dried chickpeas (page 270) for the pine nuts and use only ½ cup rice. Alternatively, instead of chickpeas use ¼ cup brown or green lentils, cooked until barely tender.

Substitute coarse bulgur for the rice.

Cold Stuffed Grape Leaves (M)
Mahshi Waraq Areesh (*or* Inab) bi Zayt

A classic appetizer of which one never tires.

Rice Filling (above)

60 fresh, tender grape leaves, or 60 preserved grape leaves (about 10 ounces)

2 tablespoons olive oil

1 cup water

Juice of ½ lemon, or to taste, freshly squeezed and strained

Lemon wedges

Prepare the Rice Filling and set aside.

If using fresh grape leaves, soak them in boiling salted water about 2 minutes or until they soften, then rinse under cold water. Rinse preserved grape leaves in hot water to remove brine. Spread the washed leaves on paper towels to drain.

Line the bottom of a heavy 3-quart casserole with about 10 of the leaves (torn or imperfect ones are fine) to prevent the stuffed leaves from burning during cooking. Stuff each of the remaining 50 leaves as follows: Remove the stem, if any, and spread the leaf on a plate, stem end toward you, dull side up. Place about 1 heaping teaspoon (more for larger leaves) of the filling near the stem end. Fold the stem end over the filling, then fold over the sides to enclose the filling securely. Beginning at the stem end, roll the grape leaf firmly away from you toward the tip, forming a cylinder.

Layer the stuffed leaves, seam side down and close together, in neat rows in the casserole. Combine the oil, water, and lemon juice and pour the mixture over the leaves. Gently place an inverted heatproof plate that is a little smaller in diameter than the casserole over the top to keep the stuffed leaves from unrolling while they cook. Bring to a simmer, cover, and cook over low heat about 1 hour or until the stuffed leaves are tender, occasionally adding more water, a little at a time, if necessary. Remove from the heat and cool to room temperature.

Remove the plate and carefully transfer the stuffed leaves to a serving platter. Serve at room temperature or slightly chilled, garnished with the lemon wedges.

Makes about 50

Hot Stuffed Grape Leaves
Mahshi Waraq Areesh (*or* Inab)

If there were sausages in Paradise, they would be of this kind.[2]

This popular dish can also be made with Swiss chard leaves that have been prepared for stuffing as directed in the recipe for Cold Stuffed Swiss Chard Leaves (page 237).

60 fresh, tender grape leaves, or 60 preserved grape leaves (about 10 ounces)
2 recipes Meat and Rice Filling (page 234)
2 medium garlic cloves, slivered
Juice of 1 lemon, or to taste
Salt to taste

Prepare and stuff the grape leaves as directed in the recipe for Cold Stuffed Grape Leaves (above), using 1 tablespoon of the filling (or a little more or less, depending on the size of the leaf) for each leaf.

Line the bottom of a heavy 3-quart casserole with 10 of the leaves to prevent the stuffed leaves from burning during cooking. Layer the stuffed leaves, seam side down and close together, in neat rows in the casserole, occasionally placing pieces of garlic between them. Sprinkle with the lemon juice and salt. Gently place an inverted heatproof plate that is a little smaller in diameter than the casserole over the top to keep the stuffed leaves from unrolling while they cook. Add enough water to reach the plate. Bring to a simmer, cover, and cook over low heat about 1 hour or until the stuffed leaves are tender, occasionally adding more water, a little at a time, if necessary. Serve hot with a bowl of plain yogurt on the side.

Serves 8

Cold Stuffed Swiss Chard Leaves (M)
Mahshi Silq bi Zayt

Some people like these even better than cold stuffed grape leaves.

Follow the recipe for Cold Stuffed Grape Leaves (page 235), substituting about 25 large, unblemished Swiss chard leaves for the grape leaves. Wash the chard thoroughly. Place the wet leaves in a steamer over moderate heat and steam a few seconds or until they are just limp enough to be rolled, or dip the leaves briefly, a few at a time, in boiling salted water. Cut the chard leaves from the ribs. Reserve the ribs to line the bottom of the casserole. Cut the leaves into about 3-by-5-inch pieces. Stuff and cook as directed in the recipe.

Makes about 50

Hot Stuffed Cabbage Leaves
Mahshi Malfuf

Zacklé has a style of its own.

. . . There was an activity of life . . . Every open door exhibited some work in progress— the anvil, the loom, the distaff. There was an abundant supply of all necessaries and luxuries. Magnificent sheep hung in the shambles, gigantic cabbages and grapes, large, clear, and clean, as if just selected from the vintage, or gathered from a canvass of Van Eke. The people, too, were a fine race.[3]

The above description of nineteenth-century Zahleh brings back memories of childhood meals I used to enjoy in that bustling market town at the home of a friend, whose mother excelled in the preparation of *kibbeh* (a local specialty) and stuffed vegetables, including this dish. These wonderful repasts often concluded with luscious grapes for which the Zahleh region was, and still is, famous.

Follow the recipe for Hot Stuffed Grape Leaves (page 236), substituting a 3½-pound head green cabbage for the grape leaves. Prepare the leaves as follows: Remove the thick core, loosening the leaves without detaching them. Drop the cabbage into a large pot of boiling salted water and cook about 6 minutes or until the leaves are pliable. Transfer the cabbage to a plate. Using a fork, loosen the outer leaves and remove them, being careful not to break them. Place the leaves in a colander to drain and cool. Return the cabbage to the boiling water, cook a few minutes more, and again remove the outer leaves as they become pliable. Continue this process until you come to the heart of the cabbage. Reserve the inner leaves.

Stuff each of the remaining leaves as follows: Cut out the hard rib end and spread the leaf on a plate, cut end toward you. Place about 1 tablespoon (more for larger leaves) of the meat and rice mixture near the cut end. Fold over the sides to enclose the filling securely. Beginning at the cut end, roll the leaf firmly away from you toward the tip, forming a cylinder.

Cover the bottom of the casserole with the reserved inner leaves and proceed as directed in the recipe.

Serves 6

Eggplants Stuffed with Meat
Shaykh al-Mahshi Batinjaan

This famous dish is called the *shaykh*, or "chief," of stuffed vegetables because its filling features only meat rather than meat and rice. A medieval version is found in the *Wusla*.

> 12 small eggplants, each about 4 inches long
> 2 tablespoons Clarified Butter (page 148) or olive oil, or more if needed
> Meat Filling (page 234)
> 3 tablespoons tomato paste
> 1½ cups water
> 2 teaspoons Pomegranate Molasses (page 57)
> 1 tablespoon freshly squeezed and strained lemon juice
> Salt and freshly ground black pepper to taste
> Crushed dried spearmint (optional)

Remove the stems and hulls from the eggplants and discard. Peel each eggplant lengthwise in ½-inch strips, leaving ½-inch strips of skin in between, making a striped design.

In a large, heavy skillet heat the Clarified Butter or oil over moderate heat. Add the eggplants and fry, turning to brown on all sides, adding more butter or oil if necessary. Transfer the eggplants to a shallow baking dish just large enough to hold them comfortably. Carefully slit each eggplant to within 1 inch of both ends on one side only and stuff the pocket with some of the Meat Filling. Arrange the stuffed eggplants next to one another in the dish with the slit sides up.

Dilute the tomato paste with the water. Stir in the Pomegranate Molasses and lemon juice, season to taste with salt and pepper, and pour the mixture over the eggplants. Bake in a preheated 350°F oven 35 minutes, basting the eggplants occasionally. Sprinkle with the mint, if desired. Serve hot with Plain Rice (page 249).

Serves 4

VARIATION:

Omit the tomato paste, water, lemon juice, and salt and pepper. Prepare Tomato Sauce with Pomegranate (page 287), simmering it for only 5 minutes. Spoon it evenly over the stuffed eggplants and continue as above.

Musayliha Castle, south of Tripoli. *From John Carne,* Syria, the Holy Land, Asia Minor, &c., *vol. 1 (London, Fisher, Son, 1836)*

Stuffed Zucchini

Kusa Mahshi

> Our dinner . . . consisted of a pilau, a dish of sour milk mixed with olive oil, and certain gourds like our cucumbers, stuffed with hashed mutton and boiled rice. This is, in fact, the most desirable and savory food that one can eat in the East.[4]

8 zucchini (each 4 to 6 inches long), or as many as needed

Meat and Rice Filling (page 234)

2 medium ripe tomatoes, peeled, thinly sliced, and seeded

2 tablespoons tomato paste, or to taste

1 cup water

4 tablespoons freshly squeezed and strained lemon juice, or to taste

Salt to taste

2 large garlic cloves, or to taste

1 teaspoon crushed dried spearmint

Cut about ¾ inch off the stem ends of the zucchini. Shape these into corklike lids by cutting a little off all around the bottom of each "lid." Using a *minqara* (page 83) or a vegetable or apple corer, carefully scoop out the zucchini pulp and discard (or save for another use), leaving a ¼-inch-thick shell all around. Spoon the Meat and Rice Filling into the shells and cover with the reserved lids.

Cover the bottom of a large, heavy casserole with the tomato slices. Arrange the stuffed zucchini side by side on top of the tomatoes. In a small saucepan mix the tomato paste with the water, 3 tablespoons of the lemon juice, and salt. Bring the mixture to a boil and simmer a few minutes. Pour over the zucchini, cover, and simmer gently about 50 minutes or until tender, adding more water if necessary.

Crush the garlic with a pinch of salt. Mix with the mint and remaining 1 tablespoon lemon juice and sprinkle the mixture over the zucchini. Tilt the casserole, baste the zucchini with the pan juices, and simmer a few minutes more. Serve hot.

Serves 4

VARIATION:

The stuffed zucchini are also good cooked in Spicy Tomato Sauce (page 287). Add the zucchini to the sauce after it has simmered for 5 minutes. Pour in enough water to barely cover the zucchini and bring to a boil. Reduce the heat, cover, and simmer until done.

Stuffed Apricots

Nestled in the curving valley of the Orontes River is the lovely old city of Hama, famous for its huge groaning antique waterwheels. Two of the most renowned medieval Arab geographers, Yaqut and Abu'l-Fida', were natives of Hama.

Among the many kinds of fruit grown in the environs of the city is the *hamawi* or almond apricot (*mishmish lawzi*), much praised by Arab poets. As Ibn Battuta wrote long ago, "when you break open its kernel you find a sweet almond inside it."[5] There are several recipes in the *Wusla* that call for this type of apricot, which was also found in the Bekaa, especially around Baalbek as well as in our own orchard.

Here is my version of an Armenian dish that we used to make in Shtora. The pomegranate molasses and herbs are my personal additions. Try this recipe if you are fortunate enough to find really good apricots.

> 20 large, firm ripe apricots
> Meat Filling (below)
> Unsalted butter
> $\frac{1}{2}$ cup water
> 3 tablespoons sugar, or to taste
> $\frac{1}{2}$ teaspoon Pomegranate Molasses (page 57) (optional)
> Finely chopped fresh spearmint, thyme, or coriander leaves

Cut the apricots in half lengthwise, leaving them attached at one side. Remove and discard the pits. Using a small spoon, scoop out some of the pulp from each apricot half to make room for the filling. Chop the pulp and reserve.

Stuff the apricots with the filling. Bring the halves together to return the fruits to their original shape. Arrange the stuffed apricots side by side in a buttered shallow baking dish just large enough to hold them comfortably in one layer. Put a shaving of butter on top of each apricot.

In a small saucepan combine the water, sugar, Pomegranate Molasses (if used), and reserved apricot pulp. Bring to a boil, stirring constantly until the sugar is dissolved. Pour the mixture around the stuffed apricots. Cover the dish with a lid or aluminum foil and bake the apricots in a preheated 350°F oven about 45 minutes or until the stuffing is cooked and the apricots are tender but still intact, basting occasionally with the liquid in the dish. Serve hot, sprinkled with the mint, thyme, or coriander leaves and accompanied with Plain Rice (page 249) or Bulgur Pilaf (page 257).

Serves 4 to 6

MEAT FILLING

½ pound lean ground lamb or beef

1 small onion, grated

3 tablespoons chopped toasted blanched almonds, unsalted pistachio nuts, walnuts, or
     pine nuts

1 tablespoon finely chopped fresh spearmint leaves

½ teaspoon ground cinnamon or Mixed Spices I (page 66)

Salt and freshly ground black pepper to taste

In a medium bowl combine all the ingredients and knead until the mixture is well blended.

∾

Tomorrow with the apricots.

(Meaning "never" or "fat chance!")

∾

Stuffed Prunes with Oranges

Here is another exquisite Armenian dish, which I first tasted in Beirut years ago. On that occasion it featured outstanding oranges from the nearby village of Antelias.

2 tablespoons unsalted butter

1 large onion, sliced

1 pound large, moist pitted prunes

Meat Filling (see Stuffed Apricots, above), using walnuts or pine nuts

⅓ cup freshly squeezed and strained orange juice

Unpeeled orange slices, halved

Fresh spearmint or coriander sprigs

Water wheel and house in Hama. *From* National Geographic,
January, 1913

In a small, heavy skillet melt the butter over moderate heat. Add the onion and sauté,
stirring frequently, until soft but not browned. Spread the onion in an oiled shallow
baking dish large enough to hold the prunes comfortably in one layer. Set aside.

With your forefinger, enlarge the opening of each prune and stuff the pocket with a
little of the filling. Arrange the prunes stuffed side up over the sautéed onion and sprinkle with the orange juice. Cover the dish with a lid or aluminum foil and bake the prunes
in a preheated 350°F oven 30 minutes or until the filling is cooked and the prunes are
tender.

Arrange the stuffed prunes in the center of a serving platter, discarding the onion.
Surround with the orange slices and garnish with the mint or coriander sprigs. Serve hot
with Plain Rice (page 249) or Saffron Rice (page 250).

Serves 4

၄

Eat one apricot, two apples; but of prunes, as many as you can take. *(A)*

၄

CHAPTER 11

Grains and Pasta

The Wadi Barada from the village of Bessima, northwest of Damascus. *From Charles William Wilson, ed.,* Picturesque Palestine, Sinai and Egypt, *vol. 1 (New York, D. Appleton, 1881)*

∾

When wheat and oil are provided, then the family's provisions are insured.

∾

Ever since wheat first began to be cultivated in Greater Syria about ten thousand years ago, it has been the region's principal grain crop and remains the staff of life to this day. During medieval times enormous quantities of wheat were exported from the Bekaa Valley, the Jaulan (Golan), and, most notably, the Hauran, whose exceptional productivity had made it one of the principal granaries of ancient Rome. Although it never equalled the prosperity it attained under the Romans, the Hauran continued to be a major source of wheat well into the modern era. In her memoir, *Legacy to Lebanon* (1984), Grace Dodge Guthrie recalls a familiar procession she used to observe from the balcony of her family's summer home above the Lebanese resort town of Dhur Shuwayr during the 1920s:

> Their bells ringing melodiously in the mountain air, trains of camels laden with wheat from the Hauran, always led by a driver on a donkey, lumbered down the road below our house.

This passage reminds me of harvest time in the Bekaa, where I used to watch trains of camels plodding stoically along, each animal bearing huge sacks of wheat balanced on either side of its hump. At the conclusion of the harvest, a symbolic figure plaited from sheaves of wheat was placed over the doorway of each peasant family's house to confer a blessing on its occupants and on the fruit of their labors.

Rice

Unlike wheat, rice is a relative newcomer, having been introduced into the Levant during the fourth century B.C. Al-Muqaddasi speaks of rice plantations on the plain of Baisan and in the vicinity of the former Lake Hulah in tenth-century Palestine,[1] and the medieval culinary manuals contain recipes for both sweet and savory rice dishes.

During Ottoman times the demand for rice was so great that most of the supply had to be imported, the long-grain variety from India and the short-grain from Egypt.

Just how highly rice was regarded is borne out by the following account of a meal prepared for Lady Hester Stanhope and her party by the wives of Abu Ghosh, an infamous nineteenth-century sheikh-turned-brigand who was said to hold the keys to Jerusalem. The old chief extracted heavy tolls from Christian pilgrims coming from Jaffa, who had to pass through his village in order to reach the Holy City. He was, however, so charmed by her ladyship that he treated her as an honored guest.

> The supper sent from his kitchen was prepared, as he told us, by the hands of his four wives, who vied with each other in cooking some delicacy . . . From one it was a dish of rolled vine leaves, containing minced meat. From another, kusas (known in England as the vegetable-marrow) stuffed with rice and minced meat. From the third, a lamb roasted whole. From the fourth, an immense dish of boiled rice, surrounding and covering four boiled chickens. Besides these, there was the pilaw of the country, with morsels of meat stirred up among it.[2]

Today this favorite grain, which is still largely imported, serves as an accompaniment to meat, poultry, and seafood dishes, forms a bed for stews, and is combined with any number of ingredients to create main courses. Rice can be tinted gold with saffron or pink with tomatoes. Often it is served in a mound or molded and decorated with sautéed nuts or topped with a sauce.

Although rice is simple enough to prepare, no two people seem to agree on what constitutes the ideal method of cooking it. Despite the controversy, the recipe given for Plain Rice on page 249 is a basic one that is easy to execute and produces a successful outcome.

The amount of liquid needed to cook rice can vary slightly depending on the grain's age and quality, but usually 2 cups liquid are used for each cup of rice. When the rice is cooked, some people remove the lid, place a folded kitchen towel over the saucepan to absorb excess moisture, replace the lid, and allow the rice to rest, off the heat, 10 to 15 minutes before fluffing and serving.

For the rice recipes in this chapter it is important to use long-grain white rice, which remains firm and separate when cooked. American-grown long-grain rice, readily available in supermarkets, needs no cleaning, washing, or soaking and yields excellent results. *Basmati*, an aromatic long-grain rice from India, is preferred by many cooks; however, should you choose to use it, you will need to treat it somewhat differently. It will require cleaning, washing, and soaking and will take a little less time to cook since the grains are thinner and will have absorbed water from having been soaked, and thus will be softened.

Bulgur

An earthy and delicious alternative to rice is bulgur (*burghul*). The high nutritional value and excellent keeping qualities of this wheat product have long been appreciated in the Middle East. Bulgur was a principal element in the diet for thousands of years and was upstaged by rice only in comparatively recent times. According to Burckhardt, in the early nineteenth century bulgur was the primary source of nourishment for the Druze and Maronite peasants of Mount Lebanon. He also reports that it was one of the two most common dishes eaten in the Hauran, the other being *kishk* (page 75).[3] It is still a staple food of the region. Economically appealing and just as versatile as rice, bulgur makes a wholesome base for meat, poultry, and seafood dishes and combines well with many vegetables, fruits, herbs, and spices. *Tabbuleh* and *kibbeh* are but two examples of the gastronomic heights bulgur can attain.

Bulgur should be distinguished from skinless whole-grain wheat and what is often sold under the name of cracked wheat, both of which, unlike bulgur, are uncooked. Skinless whole-grain wheat (*qamh*) is whole wheat grains or kernels whose hulls have been removed. The grains require prolonged cooking and are used in soups, stews, and puddings. Cracked wheat (*jarisha*) is simply wheat grains that have been crushed. Bulgur, on the other hand, is prepared by boiling the grains and then drying them, after which they are either left whole or crushed into fine, medium, or coarse grinds. I remember well the age-old method of preparing bulgur in Shtora, which would take place following the harvest. The hulled wheat was washed and the grains carefully separated from stones and other foreign matter. Next, the wheat was boiled in caldrons to the point of splitting the grain. It was then drained, spread on large sheets, and placed on the flat roofs of houses to dry in the sun. When thoroughly parched, the wheat was taken to the town mill to be crushed into the three different sizes. In some areas of Lebanon, bulgur used to be crushed at home by a traveling miller with a rotary crushing machine.

The subject of bulgur also brings back memories of a trip I made to Aleppo one autumn that included a visit to a public square near the Citadel, where the preparation of this historic cereal food was in progress. The wheat was being boiled in numerous gigantic caldrons placed over enormous fires. Around each caldron stood a group of Beduin women, some of whom were stoking the flames, while others were stirring the wheat with long-handled ladles. Another group was busy spreading the boiled wheat on muslin sheets to dry in the sun, and several men were packing the thoroughly dried bulgur into large sacks for transport to the city's mills.

Today the process by which bulgur is made commercially under industrial conditions still adheres to the same basic steps that have been followed in the Middle East since Neolithic times. For more information on bulgur, see page 73.

Freek

Whole wheat grains can be eaten when not yet ripe but still somewhat green. One method of preparation has been described by Thomson, who refers to green wheat by its biblical name:

Natives of Hama washing wheat in the Orontes River. The wheat is then processed into
bulgur. From National Geographic, *January, 1913*

Harvest is the time for parched corn. It is made thus: a quantity of the best ears, not too ripe,
are plucked with the stalks attached. These are tied in small parcels, a blazing fire is kindled
with dry grass and thorn bushes, and the corn-heads are held in it until the chaff is mostly
burned off. When the grain is sufficiently roasted, it is rubbed out in the hand, and eaten as
there is occasion. When traveling in harvest-time, my muleteers have very often thus prepared parched corn in the evenings after the tent has been pitched. Nor is the gathering of
the green ears for parching regarded as stealing. Parched corn is referred to in the Bible, and
it is a favorite article all over the country.[4]

Sometimes green wheat was roasted in a pan or on an iron plate. When roasted while not yet fully ripe and then either left whole or coarsely cracked, this wheat is called *freek* or *freeky* (from the verb *faraka*, "to rub") and has a greenish brown hue and a smoky, nutlike flavor. Recipes calling for *freek* are found in the medieval Arab culinary manuals. This delicious product, which takes much less time to cook than skinless whole-grain wheat, is often combined with or served alongside meat, poultry, and game birds. It is also used in stuffings for poultry, pigeon, grape leaves, and chard leaves. *Freek* can be obtained at Middle Eastern groceries.

In former times whole wheat grains were also roasted when they were fully ripe, in which case they were known as *kaliyya*.

Couscous and Pasta

Couscous, the pale-colored pellets processed from semolina flour (*smeed*) that constitute the basis of many North African preparations of the same name, has also found a home in Lebanon, where it is combined with chicken and lamb or beef, chickpeas, and small onions in a local specialty called *mughrabiyya*, a designation derived from the Maghreb, the region of North Africa in which couscous reigns supreme. A recipe for Maghrebi couscous is found in the *Wusla*, thus establishing the fact that the dish was known in the Levant as early as the thirteenth century. Lebanese couscous, however, differs from the North African in that the semolina grains are considerably larger and shaped into small pellets.

Pasta has been popular in the Middle East for well over a thousand years, possibly even longer. It formed part of the ancient Persian cuisine that was assimilated by the conquering Arabs. Various kinds of pasta are encountered in the medieval culinary manuals. Al-Warraq gives a recipe for fresh noodles,[5] which he calls *lakhsha*, a Persian word. He also refers to a dry noodle purchased from markets, known as *itriyya*, a word of Greek origin that passed into Aramaic, from which it was borrowed by the Arabs. By the thirteenth century the word *lakhsha* had been replaced by another, *rishta*, also of Persian provenance. Besides *rishta*, other types of fresh pasta are mentioned in the *Wusla*, such as *tutmaj*, dough that has been rolled out and cut into rounds or squares. The word *tutmaj* is Turkish; its presence in a work written in thirteenth-century Syria can perhaps be attributed to the fact that the Seljuk Turks had controlled most of the country during the greater part of the previous century. Another noodle product was *sha'iriyya*, identified in the modern scholarly edition of the *Wusla* as dough shaped either like hair (vermicelli) or like grains of barley.

Middle Eastern pasta dishes have a distinct character, often being flavored with such ingredients as cinnamon, allspice, coriander, spearmint, and yogurt. Not surprisingly, many Italian pasta dishes have become widely appreciated in Syria, Lebanon, and

A dinner party. From Cunningham Geikie, The Holy Land and the Bible *(London, Cassell, 1891)*

Jordan. Their tastes are similar enough to impart a comforting familiarity to the Arab palate while being different enough to intrigue it.

Plain Rice
Ruz Mufalfal

> **2 to 3 tablespoons unsalted butter**
> **1 cup long-grain white rice**
> **2 cups hot water, chicken broth, or beef broth**
> **Salt to taste**

In a heavy saucepan melt the butter over moderate heat. Add the rice and sauté, stirring, about 1 minute or until the grains are thoroughly coated with butter but not browned. Add the water or broth and salt and bring to a boil, stirring constantly. Reduce the heat to low, cover, and simmer undisturbed 20 minutes or until all the liquid has been absorbed and the rice is just tender, not mushy. Let the rice stand, covered, off the heat 5 to 10 minutes. Fluff with a fork before serving.

Serves 4

VARIATIONS:

Rice with Vermicelli
Ruz bil Sha'iriyya

Use ¼ cup butter. Sauté 1 medium onion, minced, in the butter, stirring frequently, until barely golden. Add ½ cup vermicelli, broken into 1-inch lengths, and sauté, stirring, until it is lightly colored. Add the rice and proceed as directed.

Rice with Spinach
Ruz bi Sabanikh

Substitute ¼ cup olive oil for the butter. Sauté 1 large onion, minced, in the oil, stirring frequently, until soft. Add 1 pound spinach, stemmed, washed, dried, and cut into small pieces, and sauté, stirring, until it wilts. Add the rice and proceed as directed. Serve hot or at room temperature, accompanied with lemon wedges, if desired.

Saffron Rice
Ruz bi Za'faran

Stir in ¼ teaspoon powdered saffron just before adding the water.

Saffron Rice for Fish
Ruz li Samak

Substitute 2 tablespoons olive oil for the butter and stir in ¼ teaspoon powdered saffron just before adding the water. While the rice is cooking, prepare ½ recipe Pine Nut and Onion Garnish (page 289). Serve the rice in a mound topped with the garnish.

Recollections of Aleppo

Her husband's to Aleppo gone.
(William Shakespeare, *Macbeth*)

Aleppo, Syria's second-largest city, is not as familiar to Westerners as Damascus, the nation's capital. Both cities date from the third millennium B.C. and have been rivals almost from the beginning, with Aleppo frequently overshadowing Damascus as a commercial and cultural center. Their spirited competition extends into the kitchen as well. I have heard Aleppans dismiss the food of Damascus as bland and uninteresting, and Damascenes in turn reject Aleppo's as heavy and overspiced. Speaking for myself, I have enjoyed excellent meals in both cities and have no wish to become embroiled in the controversy!

Trade has historically been the lifeblood of Aleppo. For many centuries it was the key destination of great caravans from the East and the point from which goods were

View of Aleppo, circa 1919. From National Geographic, *November, 1919*

distributed to markets lying to the north, west, and south. The city's great *suq* is the largest covered bazaar in the Middle East.

Aleppo has long had trading connections with the West, beginning with the Venetians in the thirteenth century and followed by the Dutch, French, and English (hence Shakespeare's reference above as well as the memoirs of d'Arvieux and Russell). Today this "Chicago of the Near East" remains a prosperous merchant city with a certain air of cosmopolitanism.

Aleppo has a heterogenous population of Arabs, Turks, Assyrians, and Armenians. Although the largest influx of Armenians occurred during the First World War, when tens of thousands fled the Turkish massacres, Armenians have resided here and elsewhere in Greater Syria since the sixth century B.C. During the Middle Ages the Arab occupation of historical Armenia and the devastation of the country by the Seljuk Turks forced a mass exodus of its inhabitants both to Greater Syria and to Cilicia on the southern Anatolian coast. Cilicia soon became the Kingdom of Little Armenia, whose nobility intermarried with the rulers of the Crusader states, with the result that almost all of the Latin queens and many of the princesses were either Armenian or of Armenian blood. Under the Crusaders, Armenians were found nearly everywhere from the Taurus Mountains to Egypt. After the fall of the Latin states and Little Armenia, substantial numbers of Armenians in Greater Syria gradually became Muslims or were assimilated into the native Christian population. A significant percentage of those who took refuge in the Lebanon Mountains became Maronites. Small enclaves of Armenians survived in towns and villages of northwestern Syria, some of which were exclusively Armenian. Today most villagers in that part of the country are of Armenian descent.

In early Ottoman times, more than a few enterprising and prosperous Armenians occupied a prominent position in Aleppo's international trade, and many émigrés from historically Armenian towns distinguished themselves as commercial magnates, business agents, and bankers, as well as artisans who developed their crafts as hereditary family occupations. These émigrés included a large contingent from the Armenian town of Sasun near Lake Van who, over a period of nearly three centuries, virtually monopolized the wheat and flour trades as well as the baking and sale of bread and pastry. It is not surprising that Armenian became the second language of Aleppo. Moreover, the city's culinary scene owes much to the longstanding contribution of the Armenian community, which brought its age-old cuisine from its native land.

Among the Armenians of Aleppo were some cousins of mine who owned a rice plantation. Visiting these relatives was always an event, not only because the city and its environs presented a great contrast to Beirut but also because I would be able to feast on such local specialties as braided cheese, several kinds of *kibbeh, lahm bi ajeen, karabij halab, ma'muniyya,* numerous preparations enlivened by the area's celebrated pistachios

An Armenian merchant of the early nineteenth century. *From Henry J. van Lennep,* Bible Lands: Their Modern Customs and Manners Illustrative of Scripture *(New York, Harper, 1875)*

and, last but not least, a myriad of temptations based on rice, all prepared to perfection by the talented cooks in this branch of my family.

Saffron Rice with Nuts

Here is a dish that is very similar to one I was served by my Aleppan relatives, who took great pride not only in their rice fields but in their rice recipes as well.

2 tablespoons unsalted butter or olive oil
⅓ cup pine nuts
¼ cup coarsely chopped blanched almonds
¼ cup coarsely chopped blanched unsalted pistachio nuts
2 recipes Saffron Rice (page 250)

In a small, heavy skillet melt the butter over moderate heat. Add the nuts and sauté gently, stirring frequently, until they are golden brown. With a slotted spoon, remove the nuts to a plate and set aside.

Mound the rice on a heated serving platter and top with the nut mixture. Alternatively, pack the rice firmly into an oiled smooth-sided mold just large enough to hold it. Put a heated platter over the mold, invert the mold onto the platter, rapping the mold to release the rice, and remove the mold. Top the rice with the nut mixture. Serve at once as an accompaniment to roast chicken or lamb.

Serves 8

It is better to carry stones with a wise man than to eat pilaf with a fool. *(A)*

Saffron Rice with Ground Meat and Nuts
Ruz bi Lahm

The table . . . was soon covered with steaming, yellow mounds of rice, crowned with limbs of fowls and morsels of lamb. A large wooden bowl—containing a medley of rice, minced mutton, raisins, pine-seeds, and butter, stood in the centre, and was surrounded by plates of vegetables.

. . . Flat cakes, or loaves of bread, were distributed, and we ate in primitive style, for neither knives, nor forks, nor spoons appeared. Deep impressions were soon made in the mounds of rice, and by degrees the dishes were carried away, and replaced by others, containing sweet starch and creams, stewed apricots, and preserves.[6]

Follow the recipe for Saffron Rice with Nuts (above), with these changes: Sauté the nuts and remove them to a plate as directed. Add 1 tablespoon unsalted butter or oil to the skillet and heat. Add ½ pound lean ground lamb, beef, or veal and cook, stirring and breaking it up with a fork, until browned and crumbly. Add 2 to 3 tablespoons water,

¾ teaspoon Mixed Spices I (page 66), or to taste, and salt and freshly ground black pepper to taste and cook, stirring, a few minutes. Stir in the sautéed nuts. Taste and adjust the seasoning. Top the rice with the meat and nut mixture.

Serves 8

Note: If using this recipe as a stuffing for Crown Roast of Lamb (page 206), toss the rice gently but thoroughly with the meat and nut mixture, reserving some of the sautéed nuts to garnish the top.

VARIATIONS:

Add 2 tablespoons raisins or currants to the nuts when they are barely golden.

Substitute 2 recipes Plain Rice (page 249) or Bulgur Pilaf (page 257) for the Saffron Rice.

Rice with Lentils   (M)
Mujaddara

This dish, also known in some communities as *mudardara*, is supposedly a descendant of the "mess of pottage" for which Esau is said to have sold his birthright to his brother Jacob. Medieval versions that include meat are found in both the *Wusla* and in al-Baghdadi's culinary manual. *Mujaddara* has long been a traditional Lenten staple among the Christian population.

The name *mujaddara* comes from the Arabic word for smallpox because the lentils in the rice look like a pockmarked face. Despite the black humor of its title, the dish is beloved by rich and poor alike. The proportion of lentils to rice can vary greatly from family to family. The cooked lentils may be puréed before adding the onions and rice, in which case the dish is sometimes called *mujaddara musaffayya.*

> 1 cup large brown lentils, picked over and rinsed
> 3 cups water
> 6 tablespoons olive oil
> 1 medium onion, finely chopped
> 1 cup long-grain white rice
> Salt and freshly ground black pepper to taste
> 2 medium onions, sliced

In a medium, heavy saucepan combine the lentils and water and bring to a boil over moderate heat. Reduce the heat to low, cover, and simmer about 30 minutes or until the lentils are almost tender.

Meanwhile, in a heavy skillet heat 2 tablespoons of the oil over moderate heat. Add the finely chopped onion and sauté until golden brown, stirring frequently. Add it to the lentils and mix well. Stir in the rice and enough hot water to make the liquid in the pan

2 cups. Season to taste with the salt and pepper, cover, and simmer undisturbed about 20 minutes or until the liquid in the pan has been absorbed and the rice is tender. If the liquid is absorbed before the rice is done, add a little more hot water.

While the rice is cooking, add the remaining 4 tablespoons oil to the skillet and heat. Add the sliced onions and sauté, stirring frequently, until deeply browned.

Spoon the *mujaddara* in a mound on a serving platter and garnish with the sautéed onion slices. Serve warm or cold with Mixed Vegetable Salad (page 122) or Cucumber and Yogurt Salad (page 123).

Serves 4

VARIATIONS:

Substitute 1 cup coarse bulgur for the rice.
Add ½ teaspoon Mixed Spices II (page 66), or to taste, with the salt and pepper.

∽

Onion and bread, but an open heart. *(A)*
∽

Chicken and Rice and Tomatoes
Ruz bi Djaaj wa Banadura

> A 3-pound chicken, cut into 8 serving pieces
> 3 tablespoons olive oil, or more if needed
> 2 medium onions, finely chopped
> 3 medium carrots, peeled, quartered lengthwise, and sliced
> 2 large ripe tomatoes, peeled, seeded, and finely chopped
> 1 tablespoon tomato paste
> 1 tablespoon Pomegranate Molasses (page 57)
> 2 teaspoons Mixed Spices I (page 66), or to taste
> Salt and freshly ground black pepper to taste
> 1 cup boiling chicken broth, or more if needed
> 1 cup long-grain white rice
> 1½ tablespoons unsalted butter
> ¼ cup blanched almonds
> ¼ cup pine nuts
> ¼ cup dark raisins

Pat the pieces of chicken thoroughly dry with paper towels. In a large, heavy casserole heat the oil over moderate heat. Add the chicken, a few pieces at a time, and sauté, turning to brown evenly on all sides. Transfer to a plate and set aside.

Add the onions and carrots to the casserole and sauté, stirring frequently, until golden brown. Stir in the tomatoes, tomato paste, Pomegranate Molasses, Mixed Spices, salt, black pepper, and chicken broth and bring the mixture to a boil. Return the chicken to the casserole and baste with the sauce. Reduce the heat to low, cover, and simmer, basting occasionally, 30 minutes. Stir in the rice, cover, and simmer about 25 minutes or until the chicken and rice are tender and all the liquid is absorbed, adding more broth if the mixture seems dry. Remove from the heat and keep warm.

In a small, heavy skillet melt the butter over moderately low heat. Add the nuts and sauté, stirring frequently, until lightly golden. Add the raisins and cook, stirring, until they are heated through. Remove from the heat.

Spoon the rice onto a large heated serving platter and arrange the pieces of chicken attractively on top. Sprinkle with the sautéed nuts and raisins and serve at once, accompanied with a green salad.

Serves 4

VARIATIONS:

Chicken and Bulgur with Tomatoes

Substitute 1 large red or green bell pepper, seeded, deribbed, and chopped, for the carrots, if desired, and 1 cup coarse bulgur for the rice. Omit the almonds. Serve with Cucumber and Yogurt Salad (page 123).

Chicken and Freek with Tomatoes

Substitute 1 large red or green bell pepper, seeded, deribbed, and chopped, for the carrots and 1 cup *freek* (page 246) for the rice. Omit the almonds and raisins. When the chicken and *freek* are tender, stir in 2 to 3 tablespoons minced fresh herbs (spearmint, dill, and parsley). Sprinkle with the pine nuts and serve with Cucumber and Yogurt Salad (page 123).

Lamb, Eggplant, and Rice Mold
Maqlubi

This Palestinian specialty is encountered throughout Syria, Lebanon, and Jordan and can be made with vegetables other than eggplants, such as carrots and cauliflower. Its Arabic name, which means "turned over," is an apt one, for the mold is inverted just before serving so that the rice layer ends up on the bottom and the meat layer forms the top.

   $\frac{1}{4}$ cup unsalted butter or olive oil
   2 large onions, finely chopped
   $\frac{1}{4}$ cup pine nuts
   $1\frac{1}{2}$ pounds lean boneless lamb, cut into $\frac{1}{2}$-inch cubes
   $\frac{3}{4}$ teaspoon Mixed Spices II (page 66)

Salt and freshly ground black pepper to taste
Beef broth or water
Fried Eggplant (page 268)
1 cup long-grain white rice
Pinch powdered saffron dissolved in 2 tablespoons hot water
Vegetable oil for brushing the casserole or skillet

In a large, heavy saucepan melt the butter over moderate heat. Add the onions and sauté, stirring frequently, until soft but not browned. Add the nuts and sauté, stirring, 2 minutes. Add the meat and cook, stirring, until it is evenly browned on all sides. Add the Mixed Spices, salt and pepper, and 1½ cups beef broth or water and bring to a boil. Reduce the heat to low, cover, and simmer 1 hour or until the meat is tender, adding more broth or water if necessary.

Meanwhile, prepare the Fried Eggplant and set aside.

Place the rice in a medium bowl, cover with boiling salted water, and let soak 10 minutes. Drain and return to the bowl. Add the dissolved saffron, toss well, and set aside. When the meat is done, drain and measure the liquid in the saucepan and add enough broth or water to make 1½ cups. Reserve.

Brush vegetable oil on the bottom and sides of a large, heavy flameproof casserole or saucepan with sloping sides. Arrange the meat in an even layer in the pan, cover with the fried eggplant slices, and spread the rice evenly over the eggplant. Carefully pour the reserved 1½ cups broth over the rice. Cover and cook over moderate heat about 5 minutes. Reduce the heat to low, cover, and simmer undisturbed about 25 minutes or until all the liquid in the pan has been absorbed and the rice is just tender, not mushy. Add a little more broth during cooking if the mixture seems dry. Remove from the heat and let stand, covered, 5 to 10 minutes in a warm place.

To serve, run a sharp knife around the inside edges of the pan to loosen the *maqlubi*. Place a heated serving platter upside down over the top and, grasping the pan and the platter together firmly, invert them. Carefully remove the pan to allow the *maqlubi* to retain its molded shape.

Serves 6

Bulgur Pilaf
Burghul Mufalfal

It may appear extraordinary that this dish should have escaped the observation of travellers, yet it is easily accounted for. I might have reached thus far without once seeing it, unless I had known it beforehand; and I knew of it merely from the habit of examining the contents of shops. Having seen it in a shop at Beyrout, I ordered it at my hotel. They smiled and looked shy; and positively the order had to be thrice repeated and enforced, before I got it. Everywhere it was the same struggle. That curse of our age, the aping of things from other lands, has made them ashamed of their own dish; besides it costs one-third less than rice.

Gleaners. *From William McClure Thomson,* The Land and the Book, *vol. 2 (New York, Harper, 1882)*

> This of course would not have sufficed to keep travellers in ignorance of its existence, but gentlemen travellers, however fond they may be of the kitchen, do not add cookery to their acquirements; and travelling ladies are more given to political than domestic economy.[7]

Although bulgur pilaf may not be as glamorous as rice pilaf, it has just as many uses, is at least as delicious, and is even more nutritious. This basic dish provides an excellent bed for stews and can also be served with grilled or roasted meats and poultry.

3 tablespoons unsalted butter or olive oil
1 medium onion, finely chopped
1 cup coarse bulgur
1 ½ cups boiling chicken or beef broth
Salt and freshly ground black pepper to taste

In a medium, heavy saucepan melt the butter over moderate heat. Add the onion and sauté, stirring frequently, until soft and lightly golden. Add the bulgur and cook, stirring, 1 to 2 minutes. Add the broth and salt and pepper and bring to a boil, stirring. Reduce the heat to low, cover, and simmer about 15 minutes or until the liquid in the pan has been absorbed and the bulgur is tender. Let the pilaf stand, covered, off the heat about 5 minutes. Fluff with a fork before serving.

Serves 4

VARIATIONS:

Stir in ¾ teaspoon Mixed Spices (page 65) before adding the broth.

Bulgur Pilaf with Vermicelli

Sauté ½ cup vermicelli, broken into 1-inch pieces, in the butter until lightly browned before adding the bulgur.

Honor to rice; let *burghul* go hang itself!

(This saying originates from the time when rice was considered superior to bulgur, a staple food of the peasants and poorer classes. It means that modern things have eclipsed good old things.)

Bulgur Pilaf with Dried Fruits and Nuts ⌁

This recipe, inspired by Armenian cuisine, is not traditional but my own idea and is related to one I developed for my *Best Foods of Russia* (1976). Garnishing bulgur in this manner seemed such a natural concept, yet I had never encountered it before. It was after the publication of *Best Foods* that recipes clearly derived from the one in that book began to show up elsewhere.

2 tablespoons unsalted butter
⅓ cup slivered blanched almonds
⅓ cup dried apricots, thinly sliced
⅓ cup raisins
½ teaspoon ground cinnamon
⅛ teaspoon Mixed Spices I (page 66) or allspice
Bulgur Pilaf (page 257)

In a large, heavy skillet melt 1 tablespoon of the butter over moderately low heat. Add the almonds and sauté, stirring frequently, until barely golden. Add the remaining 1 tablespoon butter to the skillet and heat. Add the apricots and raisins and sauté, stirring, until the almonds are lightly browned. Sprinkle with the cinnamon and Mixed Spices or allspice and stir to mix. Remove from the heat.

Mound the pilaf on a heated serving platter and spoon the fruit and nut mixture over it. Serve at once as an accompaniment to meat, poultry, or game.

Serves 4

VARIATIONS:

Use 1 tablespoon butter, omit the almonds, and add ⅓ cup unsalted pistachios, toasted and chopped, with the spices.

Rice Pilaf with Dried Fruits and Nuts

Substitute Plain Rice (page 249) or Saffron Rice (page 250) for the Bulgur Pilaf.

Bulgur Stuffing with Dried Fruits and Nuts

In a large bowl combine the Bulgur Pilaf and the fruit and nut mixture. Toss gently but thoroughly. Taste and adjust the seasoning. Let cook briefly, cover, and refrigerate until ready to use. This is an excellent stuffing for roast turkey, chicken, Cornish hen, or duck. It also goes well with crown roast of pork or lamb.

Rice Stuffing with Dried Fruits and Nuts

Follow the directions for Bulgur Stuffing with Dried Fruits and Nuts (above), substituting Plain Rice (page 249) or Saffron Rice (page 250) for the Bulgur Pilaf.

Freek Pilaf

Freek

Follow the recipe for Bulgur Pilaf (page 257) with these changes: Replace the bulgur with 1 cup *freek* (page 246), rinsed thoroughly and picked over to remove any husks and foreign matter. Use 2½ cups broth and simmer the pilaf about 30 minutes or until the liquid in the pan has been absorbed and the *freek* is tender. Serve hot as an accompaniment to meat, poultry, or game.

Serves 4

Baked Noodles and Eggplant with Tomato Sauce

This hearty meatless entrée will please both vegetarians and nonvegetarians alike.

12 ounces ¼-inch-wide noodles or tagliatelle, cooked al dente and drained
1 tablespoon butter
Spicy Tomato Sauce (page 287)
Fried Eggplant (page 268)
½ cup freshly grated *kashkawan* cheese (page 147) or Parmesan

In a large bowl toss the noodles with the butter. Add 1 cup of the tomato sauce and toss again.

Arrange alternate layers of noodles and eggplant in an oiled large, shallow baking dish, beginning and ending with a layer of noodles and sprinkling each layer with some of the cheese. Pour the remaining tomato sauce on top, sprinkle evenly with the rest of the cheese, and bake in a preheated 375° F oven about 30 minutes. Serve hot.

Serves 4

Meat Dumplings in Yogurt
Shish Barak bi Laban

This dish has an extremely long history, having passed into Arab cookery from pre-Islamic Persia, where it was known as *joshpara,* the source of its Arabic name. A recipe entitled *shushbarak* is found in the fifteenth-century Damascene cookbook, *Kitab al-tibakha.*

1½ cups all-purpose flour
½ teaspoon salt
½ to ⅔ cup cold water
Meat Filling (page 234)
3 tablespoons melted Clarified Butter (page 148) or unsalted butter, or as needed
Cooked Yogurt (page 144)
Garlic and Mint Mixture (page 288) or Garlic and Coriander Mixture (page 287)

Sift the flour and salt into a mixing bowl. Make a well in the center and pour in the water. Blend the mixture until it forms a soft dough and knead lightly until smooth. Cover and let rest 30 minutes.

Gather the dough into a ball and transfer to a lightly floured surface. Roll out thinly and cut into 2-inch circles. Place about 1 teaspoon of the filling on one half of each circle. Dip a finger lightly in cold water and moisten around the edges. Fold over the other half to make a half-moon and press the edges together to seal. Gently bend the half-moon so that the two ends meet and pinch them together with barely dampened fingers.

Arrange the dumplings on a baking sheet brushed with some of the melted butter and brush them with the remaining butter. Bake the pastries in a preheated 350°F oven 10 to 15 minutes or until very lightly browned but not completely cooked. Prepare the Cooked Yogurt and add the dumplings. Cook, uncovered, over moderately low heat about 10 minutes or until the dumplings are cooked through, stirring gently twice. Add the Garlic and Mint or Garlic and Coriander Mixture, stir, and cook 2 to 3 minutes more. Serve hot as a main course with Plain Rice (page 249) or Saffron Rice (page 250), if desired.

Serves 4

VARIATION:

Omit brushing the dumplings with the melted butter. Arrange them on a baking sheet and place them in a preheated 275°F oven to dry 10 to 15 minutes, or leave them uncovered at room temperature while you prepare the Cooked Yogurt.

CHAPTER 12

Vegetables and Fruits

Palmyra. *From Charles William Wilson, ed.,* Picturesque Palestine, Sinai and Egypt, *vol. 1 (New York, D. Appleton, 1881)*

ONE OF THE UNFORGETTABLE SIGHTS of the region's markets is the colorful displays of spectacular produce newly arrived from nearby gardens and orchards. Should a housewife be unable to go to the market, the market comes to her on the pushcarts of vendors, who hawk their vegetables and fruits throughout the residential neighborhoods, extolling the price and quality: "Almonds as big as cucumbers!" "Figs as white as jasmine—as fresh as the cold morning's dew!" "Tender cresses from the mountain springs! If an old woman eats them, she will be young again next morning!" "Come down and have a taste before I sell out!" Those who cannot come down can do almost all their shopping from their apartment balconies or windows by lowering baskets on ropes to the morning parade of pushcarts.

Even though our summer house in Shtora was surrounded by the seemingly inexhaustible bounty of the Bekaa Valley, we still grew a large assortment of produce in our own garden, which provided us with an abundance of vegetables and fruits, almost all of which tasted better than any others I have ever had or expect to have. This wonderful place was the product of the vision and perseverance of my father, who, though a musician, lavished the same dedication on its planning as he did on his art, personally choosing every tree and plant after painstaking research and long discussions with our gardener Ara about which species and varieties would be best suited to our particular locale.

Our garden was a never-ending source of joy to me. I loved to tend the flowers and to gather herbs, vegetables, and fruits for the family table. Keeping an eye out for just what was ripening and what would soon be ready to pick, I would seek out small zucchini, slender eggplants, young, tender green beans, and crunchy green chickpeas, which I munched on as I went along. The multitude of vegetables we grew provided us with ample incentive to prepare these blessings from the earth in many artful ways. We would often make a complete meal of vegetables, not because we were vegetarians but because the gifts from our garden were simply too tempting to resist.

An event I used to find especially exciting was the watering of the garden, which would take place every few days. Since rainfall is sparse in the Bekaa, with none falling at all during the summer, the valley's productivity is made possible by a carefully planned system of irrigation. For strictly specified periods we would be allowed to divert water from the stream that flowed past our house; then our neighbors would take their share in turns. The water would be carried off into the garden by little channels, through which glistening rivulets made their way along the rows of plants and fruit trees. This operation was expertly conducted by Ara, who with the aid of his long-handled hoe (a ubiquitous implement in the Lebanon) directed the water this way and that as needed. I too had a hoe, much smaller in size though almost as tall as I was, and under his good-natured supervision I was allowed to "help" by diverting some of the water toward a particular tree or plant.

While it may have been a source of sheer delight to me as a child, irrigation was a matter of utmost concern to farmers. The equitable sharing of water was deliberated upon very seriously by village communities and their *mukhtar*s (headmen), who were fully aware of the potential for feuding, vandalism, and misuse of water rights that this delicate issue could engender. Clashes did indeed occur, and I recall hearing about a dispute in one mountain village where the local *mukhtar,* unable to adjudicate the matter to the satisfaction of both parties, was forced to call upon the district *gendarmerie,* which fared no better and had to summon the army for assistance!

Returning to vegetables: Unlike Americans, who only recently have begun to appreciate their virtues, eastern Mediterraneans have long had a love affair with vegetables, many of which originated in this area. Cooks have elevated their preparation to an art, devising an array of inspired creations. Even dried legumes are coaxed into exciting and wholesome dishes that are savored by rich and poor alike. Vegetables are marinated, steamed, braised, sautéed, deep-fried, baked, grilled, or simply eaten raw. They are stuffed or added to fish, poultry, and meat stews or casseroles. Cooked in butter and served hot, they function as side dishes; cooked in olive oil and served at room temperature or slightly chilled, they make excellent appetizers. Vegetables such as okra, green beans, peppers, eggplants, zucchini, and tomatoes are often dried for winter use.

Besides vegetables, fruits such as quinces, apples, and prunes are occasionally served as side dishes to meat, poultry, and game. For a discussion of fruits, consult pages 49–58.

Artichokes with Fava Beans (M)
Ardishawki wa Ful Akhdar bi Zayt

These two vegetables are often paired in the eastern Mediterranean. Please be warned that some people are allergic to fava beans.

5 tablespoons freshly squeezed and strained lemon juice
6 medium artichokes

½ cup extra-virgin olive oil

6 scallions, finely chopped

¼ pound pearl onions, peeled and trimmed

1 pound fresh fava beans, shelled and, if necessary, skinned

2 medium carrots, diced

¼ cup finely chopped fresh dill, or a mixture of dill, flat-leaf parsley, and spearmint leaves

Salt and freshly ground black pepper to taste

1½ cups water

Fill a large bowl with cold water and add 2 tablespoons of the lemon juice. Prepare each artichoke as follows: Break off and discard the stem. Bend back the outer leaves until they snap off close to the base. Remove several more layers of leaves in the same manner until the pale inner leaves are reached. With a sharp stainless steel knife, trim the base and sides of the artichoke. Cut through the artichoke 1½ inches above the base, discarding the top. Pull out the thorny pinkish leaves from the center. With a spoon, scrape out the fuzzy choke underneath, being careful not to puncture the meaty part. Drop the artichokes into the bowl of acidulated water.

In a large, shallow enameled or stainless steel casserole heat the oil over moderate heat. Add the scallions and cook, stirring frequently, until lightly browned. Add the pearl onions, fava beans, and carrots. Sprinkle with the dill or herb mixture and season with the salt and pepper. Cook the mixture, stirring frequently, 2 to 3 minutes. Sprinkle with the remaining 3 tablespoons lemon juice. Drain the artichokes and add them to the casserole. Pour in the water and bring the mixture to a boil. Reduce the heat to low, cover, and simmer about 45 minutes or until the artichokes and fava beans are tender, adding more water if necessary. Remove from the heat and let cool. Serve at room temperature.

Serves 6

The apple and the pomegranate trees disputed which was the fairer, when the thistle exclaimed, "Brethren, let us not quarrel!"

Green Beans in Olive Oil (M)
Lubiyya bi Zayt

Without the diligent labor of our gardener Ara, our summer place in Shtora would never have been as well maintained as it was. The bounty of produce yielded by our garden, orchard, and vineyard was due in large part to the expertise and dedication he brought to their care. He was assisted in this endeavor by his cheerful and energetic wife,

Arminé, who would often join us on our terrace and lend a hand as we prepared freshly picked vegetables and fruits for cooking. Many a pleasant hour was spent in that delightfully light and airy setting snapping beans, shelling peas, shucking corn, stemming and pitting fruit, and scooping out vegetables for *mahshi*. The terrace was partially shaded by a row of tall, silvery poplars that bordered a little stream, which ran alongside our property before curling pleasantly away through groves of fruit trees and vegetable gardens. This much-used area, really an extension of our kitchen, was enhanced by brilliantly colored flowers growing in pots and in the adjacent garden so that one sat enveloped in a delicate fragrance, with the gentle murmur of water providing a soothing background of sound.

Just as Ara's life's work was to tend the soil, that of Arminé was to excel in culinary skill. She was one of those talented, unsung cooks frequently encountered in the Lebanese countryside, a woman with little formal education but with a deep knowledge and appreciation of good food. Both she and her husband were of peasant stock and belonged to a generation that still retained many traditional folkways at a time when they were fast disappearing. As a child from the city, I found her descriptions and explanations of old customs and habits, recorded only in the memories of people like her, fascinating and enlightening. Kind, wise, shrewd, and practical, she was also a gifted storyteller, and I used to listen enthralled as she recounted tales of Joha, the folk hero of the Middle East.

Like many eastern Mediterraneans, Arminé was very fond of green beans, and the ones in our garden gave her ample incentive to create wonderful salads, omelets, stews, and pickles. She also dried a quantity of beans and stored them for the colder months ahead, when she would use them to make the hearty soup and winter mainstay *makhluta*. The recipe outlined below as well as Lamb and Green Bean Stew (page 210) were among her favorites, and whenever I make them I recall the happy and instructive hours I spent at her side on our terrace in Shtora.

When preparing this and similar dishes, Arminé always recommended that the beans be slit lengthwise (French-cut) in order to better absorb the tomato sauce in which they were to be simmered. If, however, the beans were to be cooked in water for use in a salad or omelet, she would advise their being either left whole or cut crosswise to keep them from becoming water-soaked and thus tasteless and unattractive.

¼ cup extra-virgin olive oil

1 large onion, finely chopped

2 large garlic cloves, or to taste, finely chopped

2 large ripe tomatoes, peeled, seeded, and chopped

2 tablespoons finely chopped flat-leaf parsley (optional)

1 pound green beans, trimmed and halved lengthwise

Salt, freshly ground black pepper, and Middle Eastern red pepper to taste

1 cup water

In a medium enameled or stainless steel saucepan heat the oil over moderate heat. Add the onion and garlic and sauté, stirring frequently, until barely golden. Add the tomatoes and cook, stirring, 1 to 2 minutes. Add the remaining ingredients and bring the mixture to a boil. Reduce the heat to low, cover, and simmer, stirring occasionally, 30 to 40 minutes or until the beans are very tender. Remove from the heat and let cool. Serve cold or at room temperature.

Serves 4

Red Cabbage with Quince or Apple

I was introduced to this outstanding dish by Armenians who had spent many years in the Caucasus before settling in Lebanon. We used to make it with quinces from our Shtora garden.

1 head red cabbage (about 2 pounds)
6 to 8 tablespoons unsalted butter, melted
$3/4$ teaspoon ground cinnamon, or to taste
Salt and freshly ground black pepper to taste
Juice of 1 lemon or lime, freshly squeezed and strained
1 teaspoon Pomegranate Molasses (page 57)
2 large quinces or tart apples, peeled, cored, and cut into $1/4$-inch-thick slices
2 tablespoons sugar, or to taste
$1/4$ cup chopped walnuts

Remove the outer leaves from the cabbage. Quarter the cabbage, core, rinse, and chop coarsely. Brush a large, shallow baking dish with a little of the melted butter and arrange the cabbage in the dish. Sprinkle with $1/2$ teaspoon of the cinnamon and salt and pepper. Mix the lemon or lime juice with the Pomegranate Molasses and pour over the cabbage. Drizzle the remaining melted butter evenly over the top. Cover and bake in a preheated 350°F oven 1 hour. Arrange the quince or apple slices over the cabbage and sprinkle with the sugar, walnuts, and remaining cinnamon. Cover and bake, stirring occasionally, about 40 minutes or until the cabbage is tender. Serve hot.

Serves 4 to 6

Swiss Chard in Olive Oil (M)
Silq bi Zayt

Largely overlooked in America, this highly nutritious vegetable is prepared in a variety of tempting ways in the eastern Mediterranean. The leaves appear in soups, stews, pilafs, stuffings for savory pastries, and as an appetizer or side dish. Sliced and steamed chard stems, dressed with Tahini Sauce (page 280), Garlic Yogurt Sauce (page 280), or Lemon Dressing (page 120), are often served as an appetizer or salad.

> 2 pounds Swiss chard
> ¼ cup extra-virgin olive oil, or more if needed
> 2 large onions, finely chopped
> 2 large garlic cloves, or to taste, finely chopped
> ¼ cup cooked dried chickpeas (optional)
> Salt and freshly ground black pepper to taste
> Juice of 1 lemon, or more to taste, freshly squeezed and strained

Wash the chard thoroughly in several changes of cold water. Cut the leaves from the stems and tear them into large pieces. Reserve the stems for another use.

In a large covered pot steam the chard leaves with the water that clings to them a few minutes or until almost tender. Drain well, pressing the leaves to remove as much liquid as possible. Set aside.

In a large, heavy skillet heat the oil over moderate heat. Add the onion and sauté, stirring frequently, until lightly golden. Add the garlic and cook, stirring, 1 to 2 minutes. Stir in the chard, chickpeas (if used), and, if necessary, more oil, and season to taste with the salt and pepper. Cook gently, stirring frequently, about 5 minutes or until the chard is tender. Sprinkle with the lemon juice and taste and adjust the seasoning. Remove from the heat and let cool. Serve at room temperature.

Serves 4

VARIATION:

Dandelion Greens in Olive Oil

Substitute young dandelion greens for the Swiss chard and omit the chickpeas.

Fried Eggplant (M)
Batinjaan Maqli

The popularity of eggplant in the eastern Mediterranean is comparable to that of the potato in the West, and local cooks boast of being able to prepare this substantial and filling vegetable in as many as a thousand ways. During Abbassid times the common people were so fond of eggplant that anyone who made negative comments about the vegetable was sure to get into trouble! The caliph al-Wathiq (reigned 842–847) was addicted to eggplant and used to consume no less than forty at one sitting. The social historian al-Hamadani mentions fried eggplant as being one of the important dishes in a feast.

If eggplant is to be fried, salting and weighing down the slices or cubes beforehand helps to extract the juices, which are sometimes bitter. Moreover, salting, draining, and drying eggplant will cause it to absorb much less oil during the frying process.

Fried eggplant is eaten as an appetizer or as an accompaniment to such dishes as baked *kibbeh* and Rice with Lentils (page 254).

> 1 large unpeeled eggplant or 1½ pounds long, narrow unpeeled Japanese eggplants, stemmed and hulled
>
> 2 to 3 teaspoons salt
>
> 6 to 7 tablespoons extra-virgin olive oil, or as needed

Cut the eggplant crosswise into ⅜-inch-thick slices. Arrange the slices in a single layer on paper towels. Sprinkle both sides of the slices with the salt. Weigh the slices down with a heavy object such as a board or plate with a weight on top and let stand 1 hour, turning them after 30 minutes. Rinse and pat dry with fresh paper towels.

In a large, nonstick skillet heat 2 tablespoons of the oil over moderate heat. Add 3 or 4 slices of the eggplant (more if using Japanese eggplants) and fry about 2 minutes on each side or until golden brown and tender. With a slotted spatula, transfer the fried eggplant slices to paper towels to drain. Fry the remaining slices in the same manner, adding more oil as necessary.

Arrange the eggplant slices overlapping one another on a large serving platter. Serve hot or at room temperature as an appetizer or side dish with Garlic Yogurt Sauce (page 280), Pine Nut Sauce (page 281), Walnut Sauce with Pomegranate (page 282), or Pomegranate Sauce with Garlic and Mint (page 284).

Serves 4 to 6

Grilled Eggplant   (M)
Batinjaan Mashwi

Follow the recipe for Fried Eggplant (above) with these changes: Omit salting and weighing down the eggplant slices. Instead of frying them, brush them on both sides with extra-virgin olive oil and arrange them on an oiled grill or broiler rack. Grill or broil about 3 inches from the heat source, turning to brown on both sides. Serve as directed with one of the above sauces or with Pomegranate Sauce (page 284).

Serves 4 to 6

Eggplant with Pomegranate Sauce   (M)
Batinjaan bi Rubb al-Rumman

It was only after recipes for Eggplant with Pomegranate Sauce appeared in my first two books, *The Cuisine of Armenia* (1974) and *The Best Foods of Russia* (1976), that this superb combination began to be written about and discussed by the food establishment in the West.

This Lebanese version is traditionally garnished with seeds from sour, not sweet, pomegranates. If unavailable, use toasted nuts, as suggested below. Serve as an appetizer or as an accompaniment to grilled or fried fish or chicken and grilled, baked, or fried *kibbeh*.

> Fried Eggplant (page 268)
> Pomegranate Sauce with Garlic and Mint (page 284)
> Fresh sour pomegranate seeds (page 56), if available, or toasted pine nuts or chopped
>   toasted walnuts
> Fresh spearmint sprigs

Arrange the eggplant slices slightly overlapping one another on a large serving platter. Spread a little of the pomegranate sauce on each eggplant slice and sprinkle with the pomegranate seeds. Cover and chill 1 hour. Just before serving, garnish with the mint.

Serves 4 to 6

Baked Eggplant, Tomato, and Chickpea Casserole

Musaqaa

This popular dish, also known as *mnazzala,* can be made with eggplants, zucchini, or a combination of both. In some communities it is called *musaqaa* only when made with zucchini. Do not confuse this vegetarian casserole with the famous Greek *moussaka,* which contains meat.

Musaqaa was a specialty of a family friend from Homs (the ancient Emesa), a city described by medieval Arab geographers as having a healthful climate, attractive gardens and vineyards watered by the Orontes River, excellent markets, and handsome inhabitants of noble and generous character. Today Homs is a distribution center for produce grown in the region and is known for its handicrafts.

> Spicy Tomato Sauce (page 287), adding cooked split and skinned dried chickpeas
>   (below) with the tomatoes
> Fried Eggplant (page 268)

Spread half the tomato sauce and chickpea mixture in a 9-by-13-inch baking dish and cover with the eggplant slices. Spread the remaining tomato sauce and chickpea mixture over the eggplant. Bake, uncovered, in a preheated 350°F oven 15 to 20 minutes. Serve at room temperature, accompanied with warm pita bread and, if desired, Minted Garlic Yogurt Sauce (page 280).

Serves 6

To Cook Split and Skinned Dried Chickpeas

Place ½ cup dried chickpeas, picked over and rinsed, in a large bowl and add enough cold water to cover them by 2 inches. Let soak at room temperature overnight.

The Orontes River at Homs. From National Geographic, *January, 1913*

Drain the chickpeas and spread them in a single layer on a kitchen towel. Press the chickpeas with the palms of your hands or with a rolling pin until the skins loosen and the chickpeas split, being careful not to crush them. Transfer the chickpeas to a large bowl and cover with water. Discard the loose skins as they rise to the surface. If necessary, rub between your hands any chickpeas whose skins do not come off readily.

Drain the chickpeas and combine them in a saucepan with enough fresh cold water to cover them by 2 inches. Cover and simmer about 25 minutes or until just tender. Drain the chickpeas and let them cool to room temperature before using.

Makes about 1 cup

Okra in Olive Oil   (M)
Bamiyya bi Zayt

> Bammey, a mucilaginous pod, which when cooked with butter and the juice of the lemon or pomegranate, forms a very pleasant article . . . [1]

A common vegetable in the Middle East, okra merits more attention than it generally receives in much of this country. Although this dish is usually served at room temperature, it can also be prepared with butter rather than oil and eaten hot with rice or bulgur pilaf or as an accompaniment to chicken or meat. If you wish to use pomegranate juice in this recipe, it must be sour rather than sweet.

¼ cup extra-virgin olive oil

12 small white boiling onions, peeled, or 2 medium onions, finely chopped

3 medium garlic cloves, finely chopped, or to taste

1½ pounds small young okra, stem ends trimmed without piercing pods

3 large ripe tomatoes, peeled, seeded, and chopped

¼ cup chopped fresh coriander leaves, or to taste

Salt and freshly ground black pepper to taste

½ cup water, or more if needed

3 tablespoons freshly squeezed and strained lemon juice or sour pomegranate juice
     (page 56), or to taste

Lemon wedges

In a large enameled or stainless steel saucepan heat the oil over moderate heat. Add the onions and sauté, stirring frequently, until lightly golden. Add the garlic and okra and cook, stirring, until the okra is soft but not browned. Add the tomatoes and cook, stirring, about 2 minutes. Add the coriander and season to taste with the salt and pepper. Add the water and bring to a boil. Reduce the heat to low, cover, and simmer about 30 minutes or until the okra is tender, adding more water if necessary. Sprinkle with the lemon or pomegranate juice, cover, and simmer 5 to 10 minutes longer. Remove from the heat and let cool. Transfer the okra to a serving dish and garnish with the lemon wedges.

Serves 4 to 6

VARIATION:

Dilute 2 teaspoons tamarind concentrate or Pomegranate Molasses (page 57) in the water and use 1 tablespoon lemon juice, or to taste.

When you arrive in a new town eat of its onions.
(There is a widespread belief that if people eat onions upon coming to a new place, they will be protected from colds and stomach disturbances.)

Truffles
Kama

There is a wonderful and bountiful provision of nature for supplying food to the Bedouin Arabs in the spring. After the heavy rains, a species of vegetable somewhat similar to the mushroom grows in immense quantities in different districts of the desert. The whole desert country between Damascus and the Euphrates is in places celebrated for its abundant produce of these mushrooms; the Bedouins collect them at the stated season, and for weeks subsist on them; they are boiled, and eaten either with buttermilk or melted butter. Loads of them are, I am told, collected in sacks and brought home on the dromedaries. Many are dried in the sun and sold in the towns and villages. They are esteemed a great delicacy by the Arabs.[2]

People do not ordinarily associate truffles with the Middle East, yet these "diamonds of the table" have been harvested in Syria for many centuries. Unlike European truffles, which grow only under certain kinds of trees, a large percentage of the truffles consumed locally come from the Syrian Desert. One of the best places to find them growing in profusion is around the oasis of Palmyra, where the thunder and lightning connected with the seasonal storms are said to account for the great number of truffles. This oasis, which lies halfway along the ancient caravan route that runs northeast from Damascus to the Euphrates River, is the site of the breathtaking ruins of Palmyra (the Biblical Tadmor), a remarkable city of antiquity that attained an extraordinary degree of wealth and culture as well as a military power which for a time rivaled that of Rome itself. The modern town of Tadmur is located on this oasis.

Major Thomas Skinner writes enthusiastically about the truffles he encountered in the Syrian Desert:

Among the vegetables of this day's journey is a root resembling a truffle . . . it is a serious affair to miss them, for they make, I find, one of the chief articles of food: they are in great plenty, however; the earth is a little broken, and raised above them. The Arabs descry this appearance from a long distance, and jumping off their camels, race towards the spots, and with their sticks dig up the roots. They are sometimes larger than good-sized potatoes,

Palmyra: The Triumphal Arch. *From Karl Baedeker, ed.,* Palestine and Syria. Handbook for Travellers *(Leipzig, Karl Baedeker, 1876)*

and, burnt in the ashes, are exceedingly nice. My friend Mohammed hunts for me and himself too, and has promised to give me a handful every day. He brought me this afternoon one finely roasted, upon his usual donation of bread.[3]

The medieval Arabs were fond of truffles, and recipes that call for them appear in al-Warraq's *Kitab al-tabikh* and in the *Wusla*. The truffles are boiled, seasoned with salt, and tossed with olive oil and crushed dried thyme; cooked with eggs; or stewed with meat. In addition, the *Wusla* gives instructions for drying truffles.

The Syrian truffles of my childhood were far more affordable than their European cousins or those offered for sale in the region's markets nowadays. Although similar in appearance to European ones, Middle Eastern truffles are less pungent in taste and aroma. Of the two kinds of truffles, black and white, the former are considered superior. These fungi appear in markets still encrusted with the desert sand in which they grew and must be carefully cleaned before using. They are first soaked in water, then scrubbed thoroughly with a stiff brush. Any sand remaining in the cracks is pried out with the tip of a knife, after which the truffles are washed in several changes of water. Whether they should be peeled or not before cooking is a matter of personal preference (the *Wusla* recommends peeling the large ones only).

A favorite way of preparing truffles is to cube, marinate, and broil them on skewers over charcoal or in an oven (grilled truffles rank among the most luxurious dishes of the *mazza*). Another popular method of cooking truffles is to slice and sauté them gently in melted butter with seasonings. Truffles are also sliced, boiled, and dressed with olive oil and lemon juice; sliced and cooked with eggs; and cubed and stewed with meat.

Mixed Vegetable Casserole
Khudra bil Furn

Here is a meatless version of a popular dish that often incorporates lamb. Serve it as a light vegetarian entrée or as an accompaniment to roasted or grilled meats, poultry, or fish.

  3 large ripe tomatoes, peeled and thinly sliced

  6 small boiling potatoes, peeled and quartered

  4 small zucchini, cut crosswise into 1-inch-thick slices

  2 medium onions, each cut into 6 wedges

  2 medium green or 1 each green and red bell peppers, seeded, deribbed, and cut into
      1-inch pieces

  $1/4$ cup finely chopped flat-leaf parsley

  1 tablespoon finely chopped fresh spearmint leaves

  1 tablespoon finely chopped fresh basil leaves or dill

Salt, freshly ground black pepper, and Middle Eastern red pepper to taste

¼ to ⅓ cup extra-virgin olive oil

2 garlic cloves, crushed and finely chopped

Cover the bottom of a large, oiled shallow baking dish with half of the tomato slices. Top with the potatoes, zucchini, onions, and peppers. Spread the remaining tomato slices over the vegetables. Sprinkle with the parsley, mint, basil or dill, and salt, black pepper, and red pepper. Mix the oil with the garlic and drizzle over the vegetables. Bake, uncovered, in a preheated 400° F oven, stirring 2 or 3 times, about 1 hour or until the vegetables are tender. Serve hot or at room temperature.

Serves 6

Stuffed Prunes in Pomegranate Sauce
Khawkh bil Rumman

> Damascus, and the region about it is . . . celebrated for its fruit of various kinds. The grapes are fine—the apricots good, and abundant—the plums the largest and finest, I ever saw, being nearly as large as a hen's egg.[4]

Here is my re-creation of a dish I first tasted in Damascus. It makes a splendid accompaniment to meat, poultry, or game.

12 ounces pitted dried prunes

As many walnut halves as there are prunes

2 tablespoons unsalted butter

1½ cups full-bodied dry red wine

¼ cup sugar, or to taste

3 tablespoons Pomegranate Molasses (page 57)

1 slice lemon peel, about ½ inch wide and 3 inches long

2 tablespoons freshly squeezed and strained lemon juice

1 cinnamon stick, 2 inches long

2 whole allspice or the seeds from 2 cardamom pods, crushed

2 whole cloves

Stuff each prune with a walnut half. In a medium enameled saucepan melt the butter over moderate heat. Add the stuffed prunes and turn them in the butter 4 or 5 minutes. Add the remaining ingredients and simmer gently, uncovered, stirring occasionally, 15 to 20 minutes or until the prunes are tender. Serve warm or at room temperature.

Serves 6

Courtyard of a house in Salahiyya, near Damascus. *From John Carne,* Syria, the Holy Land, Asia Minor, &c., *vol. 2 (London, Fisher, Son, 1836)*

Sautéed Quinces

Armenians like to serve these with poultry, pork, or game.

2 large quinces
2 tablespoons unsalted butter, or more if needed
2 tablespoons sugar, or to taste
Ground cinnamon to taste

Scrub the quinces well. Peel if desired, quarter, core, and cut into 1/4- to 1/3-inch-thick slices.

In a large, heavy skillet melt the butter over moderate heat. Add the quince slices and cook, turning them occasionally, until the fruit begins to brown, adding more butter if necessary. Sprinkle with the sugar and cinnamon and cook a few minutes more, turning the slices carefully, until they are tender, golden brown, and glazed on both sides. Serve hot.

Serves 4

Sautéed Apples

Although the apple trees in our Shtora garden produced excellent fruit, we would walk a considerable distance to the neighboring village of Tanail to obtain yet another kind. Despite the fact that they were not from the seaward side of the Lebanon, where the best apples are said to grow, the Tanail apples were absolutely the finest I have ever tasted—crisp, tart-sweet, and intensely flavorful.

The path we used to take lay through lush orchards and rich farms stretching out to the horizon. In the early twilight an extraordinary tranquillity enveloped the countryside. Occasionally we would meet a little shepherd boy returning from the pasture with his flock of sheep. He never spoke but, smiling shyly, would play on his flute instead as he walked with us part of the way. No one had taught him and no one ever would, yet his playing was sensitive and remained with you long after he had departed.

This is just one of the many ways we used to prepare apples from Tanail.

Follow the recipe for Sautéed Quinces (above), substituting 4 medium Granny Smith or other tart apples for the quinces.

Serves 4

CHAPTER 13

Sauces, Marinades, Garnishes, and Stuffings

Village of Brummana in the Lebanon Mountains. *From John Carne,* Syria, the Holy Land, Asia Minor, &c., *vol. 2 (London, Fisher, Son, 1836)*

GENERALLY SPEAKING, in Syrian, Lebanese, and Jordanian cookery a sauce is an integral part of a dish rather than an independent creation that is spooned over it. There are, however, several sauces that are made and served separately, one of the most common being yogurt. Plain or flavored with garlic and perhaps spearmint, yogurt complements a multitude of dishes, although it is strictly omitted when fish is served. A great favorite is *tahini* sauce, which is an invariable accompaniment to many dishes, particularly fish. Two other sauces for fish that also go well with fried or steamed vegetables are pine nut sauce and garlic sauce.

In examining medieval culinary manuals, I came across a number of recipes for sauces in the *Wusla* and the *Kanz* that are clearly related to ones in use today, not only in the eastern Mediterranean but also in the Caucasus. In fact, the manuals contain recipes for many dishes that are more closely related to modern Caucasian (eastern Armenian, Georgian, and Azerbaijani) ones than to those found in present-day Arab, western Armenian, and Turkish cooking.[1] Both the *Wusla* and the *Kanz* include a section devoted entirely to sauces; however, al-Warraq's *Kitab al-tabikh,* a much earlier work dating from the tenth century, does not. The explanation for this lies in the fact that the sauces described in the *Wusla* and the *Kanz* did not exist in Arab cookery before the time of the Crusades and are examples of Western influence on the food of the East. The name the Arabs gave to this new preparation was *sals,* an obvious borrowing from the Latin/Italian *salsa.* Although the word itself was European, the Arab sauces were created from ingredients already in use in the indigenous cuisine. The recipes utilize such ingredients as yogurt, bread, *tahini,* nuts, raisins, garlic, herbs, spices, vinegar, and the juice of sour fruits. About half of the sauce recipes in the *Kanz* contain *tahini,* and a majority in both books include nuts—walnuts, almonds, hazelnuts, and pistachios. Also, al-Baghdadi's *Kitab al-tabikh* lists an almond-based sauce flavored with vinegar, mustard, and *atraf al-tib* (page 64). As a rule, the modern *tahini-* and nut-based sauces make use of fewer ingredients than their medieval predecessors, which are often more imaginative and exciting.

In this chapter you will also find some recipes for marinades and stuffings. Marinades are used both to tenderize and to add flavor. Marinating meat, fish, poultry, or game before grilling and basting them during cooking will improve their taste and texture and keep them from drying out. There are a few basic rules to keep in mind that apply to stuffings. To help prevent spoiling, chill stuffing before putting it into the cavity of a bird or cut of meat. Fill the cavity just before cooking time, packing the stuffing in loosely to allow room for it to expand. If you have made more stuffing than the cavity can hold, spoon the excess into a saucepan, add a little chicken broth or water, cover, and simmer until the liquid is absorbed and the stuffing is heated through. Serve in a bowl for second helpings. As soon as dinner is over, remove any leftover stuffing from the cavity, cool it quickly, and store in a covered container in the refrigerator.

Garlic Yogurt Sauce
Laban bi Tum

This venerable classic is a direct descendant of the recipe that opens the sauce section of the *Wusla*.

> 1½ cups plain low-fat yogurt, drained to 1 cup (page 142)
> 1 medium garlic clove, or to taste
> ¼ teaspoon salt, or to taste

Spoon the yogurt into a small bowl. Crush the garlic with the salt to a smooth paste. Mix with a few tablespoons of the yogurt, then add to the remaining yogurt in the bowl. Mix well. Taste and adjust the seasoning. Cover and chill.

Makes 1 cup

VARIATION:

Minted Garlic Yogurt Sauce

Stir in 1 to 2 tablespoons minced fresh spearmint or 1 teaspoon crushed dried mint leaves.

Tahini Sauce
Taratur bi Tahini

Prepare Tahini Dip (page 105), using a little more water to achieve a light, creamy consistency. Serve as a sauce for *Falafel* (page 113); hard-cooked eggs; boiled snails; vegetables such as fried cauliflower and steamed beets, cauliflower, potatoes, green beans, and chard stems; grilled, baked, or fried fish; grilled meats; and grilled or fried *kibbeh*.

Makes about 1 cup

VARIATION:

Tahini Sauce with Parsley

Stir in ¼ cup finely chopped flat-leaf parsley, or more to taste, and omit the parsley garnish. Taste and adjust the seasoning. Serve as an accompaniment to grilled, baked, or fried fish and grilled lamb. This makes 1¼ to 1½ cups.

Pine Nut Sauce I
Taratur bi Snubar

Although the tree associated with Lebanon is the cedar, for me the beautiful umbrella-shaped stone pine unleashes at least as many fond memories, including those of Beirut's *Bois des pins,* a thickly planted forest of stone pines that was a popular spot for promenades.

Stone pines figure prominently in the breathtaking scenery of the Shuf and Matn regions of the Lebanon Mountains. The hills that surround such charming resort towns as Brummana, Bayt Meri, Salima, Baabdat, and Dhur Shuwayr are crowned with these lofty trees, which fill the air with a distinctive fragrance. Hunting for *snubar* pine cones in the woods is a favorite summertime activity of many Lebanese children, who crack open the hard shells of the nuts with stones in order to enjoy the delicious kernels inside.

This sauce always reminds me of Brummana, where it was served to me as an accompaniment to a platter of perfectly fried vegetables on a pine-scented balcony overlooking Beirut and the Mediterranean.

> **1 cup pine nuts**
> **1 thick slice white bread, trimmed of crusts, soaked in water, squeezed dry, and crumbled**
> **1 medium garlic clove, or to taste, crushed to a paste with a pinch of salt**
> **⅓ to ½ cup freshly squeezed and strained lemon juice**
> **Water as needed**
> **Salt to taste**

Grind the pine nuts in a food processor. Add the bread and garlic and process until the mixture is well blended. With the machine running, gradually add the lemon juice and enough water to make a smooth, creamy sauce. Season to taste with salt. Serve with baked or fried fish; boiled snails; fried eggplant, zucchini, or cauliflower; or boiled beets.

Makes about 1 cup

Pine Nut Sauce II

Unlike the previous sauce, this one does not contain bread and is similar to a sauce in the *Wusla* called *Abyad* (White), which uses walnuts or almonds rather than pine nuts. In addition to *Abyad,* a number of other sauces in the *Wusla* are named for the color imparted to them by one or more of their ingredients; for example, *Ahmar*

A view in Lebanon on the road between Aley and Beirut. From Henry Harris Jessup, Fifty-Three Years in Syria, *vol. 1 (New York, Fleming H. Revell Company, 1910)*

(Red, for sumac juice), *Akhdar* (Green, for parsley), *Aswad* (Black, for toasted bread soaked in vinegar), and *Banafsaji* (Violet, for pomegranate juice).

Follow the recipe for Pine Nut Sauce I (above), omitting the bread and water. Serve with fish.

Makes about 1 cup

Walnut Sauce with Pomegranate ❖

A recipe for this sauce, which is popular with both Armenians and Georgians, appeared in my *Best Foods of Russia* (1976). Years later, I was pleasantly surprised to find in the *Wusla* a medieval version of it entitled *Banafsaji* (Violet), which calls for a mixture of walnuts and almonds and substitutes ginger for the herbs and spices. Besides this sauce, there are a number of other medieval Arab nut sauces that bear a striking resemblance to the present-day nut sauces of Armenia and Georgia, not only in their ingredients but also in the fact that, unlike the modern eastern Mediterranean and western Armenian *taratur/tarator,* they do not contain bread.

The nut sauces in the early cookery manuals make use of various souring agents, including vinegar, lemon juice, sour pomegranate juice, verjuice, and sumac juice. Modern Caucasian recipes for this sauce often call for vinegar or pomegranate juice. What is meant in the latter case is the juice of *sour* pomegranates; in fact, *this applies to any recipe that gives a choice of vinegar or pomegranate juice* (in Shtora we used to make this type of sauce with sour pomegranates from our orchard). If sour pomegranates are unavailable, you can substitute ⅓ cup sweet pomegranate juice mixed with 1 teaspoon strained fresh lemon or lime juice.

Like the recipe in my *Best Foods,* this one is a personal interpretation of the Caucasian original.

> 1 cup shelled walnuts
> 1 medium garlic clove, or to taste, crushed
> Salt and Middle Eastern red pepper to taste
> ⅓ cup sour pomegranate juice (page 56)
> 2 tablespoons finely chopped fresh coriander leaves, or 1 tablespoon each finely chopped
>   flat-leaf parsley and spearmint leaves
> Fresh sour pomegranate seeds (page 56), if available

In a food processor combine the walnuts, garlic, and salt and red pepper. Process until a paste is obtained. Add the pomegranate juice and blend until the mixture is smooth. Stir in the coriander or parsley and spearmint leaves. Taste and adjust the seasoning. Transfer the sauce to a small ceramic or glass serving bowl. Cover and refrigerate until ready to use. Just before serving, sprinkle with the pomegranate seeds, if available. This sauce complements poultry and fish as well as vegetables such as beets, green beans, and grilled or fried eggplant.

Makes about 1 cup

Note: For a thinner sauce, add a little more pomegranate juice. If fresh pomegranates are not available, substitute pomegranate molasses diluted with water (page 56).

Garlic Sauce
Salsa bi Tum

This sauce, known in Greece as *skordalia,* is also popular in Lebanon. It is sometimes made with bread instead of potatoes and goes well with grilled chicken or quail, fried fish, or fried, steamed, or crisp raw vegetables.

> 2 large russet potatoes
> 6 to 8 tablespoons freshly squeezed and strained lemon juice, or ⅓ cup white wine
>   vinegar
> ⅔ cup extra-virgin olive oil
> 5 or 6 medium garlic cloves, or to taste
> ½ teaspoon salt, or to taste
> Fresh spearmint or flat-leaf parsley sprigs

In a large, heavy saucepan boil the potatoes in water to cover about 30 minutes or until tender when pierced. Drain and peel while still warm. In a bowl mash the potatoes with a potato masher or a fork. Transfer 2 cups of the mashed potato to the bowl of an electric mixer, reserving any remaining potato for another use. Beat until smooth. With the mixer on low speed, gradually beat in the lemon juice or vinegar, then the oil until the mixture is well blended. Crush the garlic and salt to a smooth paste, add to the potato mixture, and blend well. Taste and adjust the seasoning. Transfer to a serving bowl. Garnish with the mint or parsley and serve at room temperature.

Makes about 3 cups

Pomegranate Sauce with Garlic and Mint

Salsat al-Rumman

> 1 medium garlic clove, or to taste
> Salt
> ½ cup Pomegranate Molasses (page 57)
> 2 teaspoons finely chopped fresh spearmint leaves
> A tiny pinch of ground sumac (optional)

In a mortar crush the garlic with ¼ teaspoon salt to a smooth paste. In a small non-metallic bowl combine the garlic paste with the Pomegranate Molasses, spearmint, sumac (if used), and salt to taste. Mix well. Serve with Fried Eggplant (page 268).

Makes about ½ cup

VARIATION:

Pomegranate Sauce

Substitute ¼ cup Thick Pomegranate Molasses (page 58) for the ½ cup Pomegranate Molasses and add ⅙ cup extra-virgin olive oil and 2 tablespoons freshly squeezed lime or lemon juice. Serve with Grilled Eggplant (page 269) or grilled trout.

Pomegranate Sauce with Ginger and Mint ❧

This recipe, my own, is influenced by the medieval *Wusla*. It is important to use fresh, not bottled, pomegranate juice for this or any other pomegranate sauce.

> 3 cups fresh pomegranate juice (page 54)
> 6 tablespoons sugar, or to taste
> 2 tablespoons freshly squeezed and strained lime or lemon juice
> ¼ teaspoon finely grated peeled fresh gingerroot
> 2 tablespoons finely chopped fresh spearmint leaves
> 1 tablespoon finely chopped toasted blanched almonds, hazelnuts, or walnuts (optional)
> Salt to taste

In a medium enameled saucepan combine the pomegranate juice, sugar, lime or lemon juice, and gingerroot. Bring to a boil over moderate heat, stirring until the sugar is dissolved. Reduce the heat and simmer, uncovered, stirring occasionally and skimming the froth, until the mixture is reduced to 1 cup. Stir in the mint, nuts (if used), and salt. Serve hot with pork, poultry, or game birds.

Makes about 1 cup

VARIATIONS:

Stir in a pinch of ground cinnamon 1 to 2 minutes before the end of cooking.

Substitute 1½ teaspoons minced scallions for the nuts.

Substitute a pinch of crushed dried Mediterranean oregano for the mint and omit the nuts.

Sour Cherry Sauce

Salsat al-Karaz al-Hamud

> The gardens [of Aleppo] produce . . . [t]he common red cherry, the white heart, and the visna cherry: the latter of which is more common than the others, and much used in confection.[2]

Sour cherries are used in both sweet and savory dishes in Syria and Lebanon, particularly in the Aleppo region. We used to make this sauce with tart, juicy black cherries from our orchard in Shtora.

1 tablespoon unsalted butter
1½ pounds sour cherries, stemmed and pitted
½ cup water
3 tablespoons sugar, or to taste
¼ teaspoon ground cinnamon, or to taste
Salt to taste

In a medium enameled or stainless steel saucepan melt the butter over moderate heat. Add the cherries and cook, stirring, about 1 minute. Add the water and bring to a boil. Cook the mixture, uncovered, a few minutes or until the cherries have softened and given off most of their liquid. Stir in the sugar and cinnamon and simmer, stirring occasionally, until the sauce thickens. Season with the salt. Serve hot with ground lamb or *kibbeh* kebabs or with poultry or game birds.

Makes about 1¾ cups

Note: If sour cherries are unavailable, substitute Bing cherries and add ¼ cup freshly squeezed and strained lemon or lime juice along with the sugar and cinnamon. Do not use canned cherries for this recipe.

VARIATIONS:

These are not traditional but come from my kitchen.

Sour Cherry Sauce with Herbs ๛

Just before serving, stir in 1½ tablespoons minced fresh spearmint or coriander leaves and, if desired, 2 teaspoons minced scallions. Alternatively, add 1 teaspoon minced fresh thyme, or to taste.

Sour Cherry Sauce with Nuts ๛

Just before serving, stir in 2 tablespoons finely chopped toasted blanched almonds or hazelnuts.

Sour Plum Sauce with Mint ๛

Recipes in the *Wusla* served as my inspiration for this sauce.

1½ pounds sour red or purple plums, pitted and chopped
⅓ cup water
4½ to 5 tablespoons sugar, or to taste
2 tablespoons finely chopped fresh spearmint leaves, or to taste
Salt to taste

In a medium enameled or stainless steel saucepan bring the plums and water to a boil over high heat. Reduce the heat, cover, and simmer, stirring occasionally, 15 minutes or until the plums are soft. Put them through a food mill and return to the saucepan. Add the sugar and bring to a boil over moderate heat, stirring until the sugar dissolves. Simmer, uncovered, stirring occasionally, about 10 minutes or until the sauce thickens. Stir in the mint and salt. Serve hot with pork, poultry, or game birds.

Makes about 1½ cups

VARIATIONS:

Substitute 1½ tablespoons minced fresh coriander leaves and 2 teaspoons minced scallions for the mint. Serve as above.

Sour Plum Sauce with Ginger and Nuts ๛

This variation is inspired by a recipe in the *Kanz* that also calls for rose water and honey. Add ½ teaspoon finely grated peeled fresh gingerroot, or to taste, with the sugar and substitute 2 tablespoons finely chopped toasted blanched almonds or hazelnuts for the mint. Serve with chicken or duck.

Tomato Sauce
Salsat al-Banadura

$\frac{1}{4}$ cup extra-virgin olive oil

2 medium onions, finely chopped

2 medium garlic cloves, finely chopped

2 pounds ripe tomatoes, peeled, seeded, and chopped

2 tablespoons finely chopped flat-leaf parsley

Salt and freshly ground black pepper to taste

In a large enameled or stainless steel saucepan heat the oil over moderate heat. Add the onions and sauté, stirring frequently, until soft but not browned. Add the garlic and sauté, stirring, until lightly golden. Stir in the tomatoes, parsley, and salt and pepper. Reduce the heat to low, partially cover, and simmer, stirring occasionally, about 30 minutes or until the sauce is thickened. Taste and adjust the seasoning.

Makes 1 $\frac{1}{2}$ to 2 cups

VARIATIONS:

Add 2 tablespoons tomato paste with the tomatoes.

Add 1 $\frac{1}{2}$ teaspoons crushed dried Mediterranean oregano with the tomatoes.

Spicy Tomato Sauce

Add $\frac{1}{2}$ teaspoon Mixed Spices I (page 66) with the tomatoes.

Tomato Sauce with Pomegranate

Prepare Spicy Tomato Sauce (above), adding 1 tablespoon Pomegranate Molasses (page 57) with the tomatoes.

Garlic and Coriander Mixture
Taqlia

More a condiment than a sauce, this enhances such dishes as Mlukhiyya with Chicken (page 188) and Meat Dumplings in Yogurt (page 261).

2 large garlic cloves, or to taste

$\frac{1}{4}$ teaspoon salt

2 tablespoons unsalted butter

2 teaspoons ground coriander, or to taste

Crush the garlic with the salt. In a small skillet melt the butter over moderate heat. Add the crushed garlic and cook gently, stirring, until it is pale gold. Add the coriander and cook, stirring, about 1 minute. Use at once as directed in recipes.

Note: For some recipes, a pinch of Middle Eastern red pepper is added with the coriander.

Garlic and Mint Mixture

Like Garlic and Coriander Mixture (above), this too is more a condiment than a sauce. It is added to some soups, stews, stuffed vegetables, Stuffed Kibbeh in Yogurt (page 260), and Meat Dumplings in Yogurt (page 261).

> 2 large garlic cloves, or to taste
> $\frac{1}{4}$ teaspoon salt
> 1 to 3 teaspoons crushed dried spearmint
> 2 tablespoons unsalted butter

Crush the garlic with the salt and mint. In a small skillet melt the butter over moderate heat. Add the crushed garlic and cook gently, stirring, until the garlic just turns lightly golden. Use at once as directed in recipes.

Lemon and Garlic Marinade

> $\frac{1}{2}$ cup olive oil
> $\frac{1}{2}$ cup freshly squeezed and strained lemon juice, or to taste
> 2 large garlic cloves, crushed
> Salt, freshly ground black pepper, and Middle Eastern red pepper to taste

In a glass or stainless steel bowl combine all the ingredients and mix well. Use as a marinade for seafood, poultry, or game birds.

Makes 1 cup

VARIATIONS:

Thyme Marinade

Add 2 teaspoons minced fresh thyme. Use as a marinade for lamb or chicken.

Spicy Marinade

Add $\frac{1}{2}$ teaspoon Mixed Spices I (page 66). Use as a marinade for lamb or chicken.

Red Pepper Marinade

Add 2 teaspoons Red Pepper Paste (page 299), or to taste. Use as a marinade for chicken or seafood.

Za'atar Marinade

Add 1 tablespoon *za'atar,* or to taste. Use as a marinade for lamb, chicken, or fish.

Pine Nut and Onion Garnish
Snubar wa Basal Maqli

> 5 tablespoons olive oil
> ½ cup pine nuts
> 4 medium onions, cut lengthwise in half and thinly sliced
> Salt to taste

In a large, heavy skillet heat 1 tablespoon of the oil over moderate heat. Add the pine nuts and sauté, stirring constantly, until golden brown. Transfer the nuts with a slotted spoon to a plate. Add the remaining 4 tablespoons oil to the skillet and heat. Add the onions and sauté, stirring frequently, until deeply browned. Remove from the heat, stir in the pine nuts, and salt to taste. Use as a topping for Raw Kibbeh (page 223), Saffron Rice for Fish (page 250), or Fish with Rice (page 172).

VARIATION:

Pine Nut, Raisin, and Onion Garnish

Use only ⅓ cup pine nuts. When the nuts are lightly golden, add 3 tablespoons raisins and sauté the mixture, stirring, until the nuts are lightly browned and the raisins puff up. Transfer the nuts and raisins to a plate and continue as above. Use as a garnish for Baked Fish with Tomato Sauce (page 174).

Meat and Rice Stuffing with Nuts and Raisins
Hashwit al-Lahm wa'l-Ruz

A traditional stuffing for poultry and lamb.

> 3 tablespoons unsalted butter or olive oil
> 1¼ pounds lean ground lamb or beef
> ½ cup chopped blanched almonds
> ½ cup pine nuts
> ¼ cup chopped shelled and blanched unsalted pistachio nuts
> 1½ cups long-grain white rice
> ½ cup raisins or currants (optional)
> 1 teaspoon Mixed Spices I (page 66)
> Salt and freshly ground black pepper to taste
> 2½ cups chicken broth or water

In a large, heavy skillet melt the butter over moderate heat. Add the lamb or beef and cook, stirring and breaking it up with a fork, until it is no longer pink. Add the nuts and cook, stirring, about 3 minutes. Add the rice and cook, stirring, until the grains are well coated with fat. Add the raisins or currants (if used), Mixed Spices, and salt and pepper and mix well. Stir in the broth and bring the mixture to a boil. Reduce the heat to low, cover, and simmer 15 to 20 minutes or until all the liquid in the pan is absorbed. Taste and adjust the seasoning. Let cool briefly, cover, and refrigerate until ready to use.

Makes about 9 cups

VARIATIONS:

Sauté 1 large onion, finely chopped, in the butter until soft but not browned, before adding the meat.

Substitute ½ teaspoon ground cinnamon and ¼ teaspoon powdered saffron for the Mixed Spices.

Meat and Bulgur Stuffing with Nuts and Raisins

Substitute coarse bulgur for the rice.

Meat and Freek Stuffing with Nuts and Raisins

Replace the rice with *freek* (page 246), rinsed thoroughly and picked over to remove any husks and foreign matter.

Bulgur Stuffing with Dried Fruits and Nuts ❧

See page 260.

Rice Stuffing with Dried Fruits and Nuts ❧

See page 260.

CHAPTER 14

Pickles and Preserves

Mount Hermon from Rashayya. *From Charles William Wilson, ed.,* Picturesque Palestine, Sinai and Egypt, *vol. 1 (New York, D. Appleton, 1881)*

∾

Lucky is he who did his autumn sowing, laid in his provisions of molasses, and filled his house with dry firewood.

∾

The Lakluk region in Lebanon is the setting for a legend that involves two kings: Nimrod, the great-grandson of Noah, and his brother Hafrun, both of whom had summer palaces in the mountains. As the weather began to turn colder, King Nimrod warned his brother that it was time for them to descend to the coast, for the roads would soon be closed and it would be impossible to receive supplies. King Hafrun refused to leave, however, saying that according to tradition, they could perish only from the wind during a storm and that he would be well protected in his palace, which was situated atop a six thousand-foot-high mountain that still bears his name. He therefore remained in the mountains while Nimrod departed to the coast to spend the winter as a guest of the king of Byblos. Eventually a terrible blizzard arose, forcing King Hafrun and his court to flee to a great chamber underneath his palace, but they could not escape the cold and were frozen to death.

With the coming of spring King Nimrod returned to Lakluk, where snow still covered the summit of Jabal Hafrun. When his men climbed up to the palace they found it empty. Continuing their search, they discovered the entrance to the underground chamber, and inside they came upon the frozen bodies of King Hafrun and his court together with all their treasure. The king was still seated on his golden throne, with the crown of the kingdom on his head.

"Let my brother reign thus through all time," declared King Nimrod, and with a heavy heart he commanded that the chamber and its entranceway be sealed up, forever enclosing the unfortunate monarch, his retinue, and the precious possessions that surrounded them.

The tale of King Hafrun has endured through the ages in the verbal tradition of the inhabitants of the Lakluk plateau. Since the area is under snow for most of the winter, the story serves as a grim reminder of the need to be prepared for the hardships imposed by the mountain climate.

A Time-Honored Tradition

There was a time not so long ago when almost all households in Greater Syria practiced the rites of "putting by." It was the fear of scarcity caused not only by harsh weather but also by such calamities as plague and political instability that originally prompted people to preserve foods. Before the advent of the automobile and a network of well-paved roads cleared by snowplows during the winter, mountain villages in Lebanon might be isolated for weeks or even months at a time, and the population would be unable to travel to the towns for supplies. Once cars, buses, and trucks became common and a modern highway system was in place throughout most of the country, villagers were no longer compelled to put by several months' worth of provisions for wintertime survival. They, like many others in Syria, Lebanon, and Jordan, have continued the practice, however, because they remain faithful to their traditions of independence and self-sufficiency and consider their way of life worthy of perpetuation. Moreover, many of the time-honored preserved foods have come to possess deep emotional significance for these mountaineers, who refuse to give them up, especially if they have moved to the coast or to distant lands, as so many have. Some of these foods are true delicacies enjoyed not only by country folk but also by city dwellers, who often obtain them from relatives in rural areas or seek them out, thus encouraging the creation of cottage industries among the villagers.

Preserving in Former Times

Medieval Arabs inherited their knowledge of food preservation from the civilizations of Greece, Rome, and the East. Milk was preserved by transforming it into cheese, yogurt, and *qanbaris*. Various formulas existed for keeping fruit fresh; one for grapes is found in the *Wusla*. Other ways of preserving fruit included drying, crystallizing in sugar or honey, and turning it into syrups or molasses (*dibs*). Drying and salting were common methods of preserving meat and fish. The most popular method of food preservation, however, was pickling: vegetables, fruits, nuts, small fish and birds, chicken, and even whole kid and lamb were all pickled.

The British consul Frederic Arthur Neale has recorded how the typical peasant in northwestern Syria prepared for the approach of winter in Ottoman times:

> He knows to a measure how much wheat is required for his household, and adds a little more for the purposes of hospitality or charity. The women are busy making burgull, boiled wheat dried in the sun, and then ground to a substance like grits. Men are gathering olives, and extracting oil from some, and preserving the rest in salt and water. The sour pomegran-

ate is boiled down into a substance, called nahr bekmaze [pomegranate molasses],[1] an acid much resembling the Indian tamarind, and made to serve for very much the same purposes. Enter a peasant's hut about the middle of November, and you see him in the midst of all these preparations: a mountain of onions is in one corner, round which are jars of various dimensions and ages, containing the household supply of oil, vinegar, wine, spirit, salt, butter, [grape] molasses, nahr bekmaze, olives in salt and water, and dried cream-cheese. On strings that are stretched all across the room, are hung festoons of dry red chilies, garlic, and mint. In a huge deal-box, with a monster padlock, the raisins and dried figs are safely stowed, beyond the reach of the children; and half the cottage is blocked up with firewood. In uncouth-looking baskets, covered with mud and lime, and which, in the dark, look like so many stout men, wrapped up in sheets, the wheat and barley, &c., are kept. The space left to be occupied by the family is not very extensive . . . [2]

Mary Eliza Rogers, a contemporary of Neale's who resided for some time in Haifa, relates how she stocked her storeroom:

It soon contained provisions for the winter: a case of macaroni, a basket of Egyptian rice, two sacks of wheat, one of which I sent to be ground, by mill-stones moved by cattle. Afterwards I had the meal sifted at the house, the smeed [semolina] was set apart for white bread, &c. and the remainder was stored for making Arab loaves for the servants.

  The large terra cotta jars, glazed inside, and rough without, ranged round the room, often made me think of Ali Baba and the forty thieves. One held the smeed, another held flour, another bran, a fourth oil, and some rather smaller ones contained olives and goats'-milk cheese preserved in oil, and a store of cooking butter. Oranges and lemons garnished the shelves; dried figs strung on thin cord, and pomegranates tied one by one to ropes, hung in festoons from the rafters, and the bundles of dried herbs of Carmel smelt sweetly. . . . My kind neighbor taught me how to add to my stores at the right seasons, to make fruit preserves, to concentrate the essence of tomatoes, and to convert wheat into starch (by steeping it in water, straining it, and drying it in the sun) for making sweet dishes, as well as for the laundry.[3]

Preserving Time in Shtora

During the years I lived in Lebanon many a household, including ours, would set itself to the task of preserving freshly picked produce. Among the first items to be preserved were grape leaves, which we would gather from our vineyard in late spring and early summer while they were still young and tender. The leaves were carefully washed, stacked, rolled up, and tied with string. The bundles were dropped into boiling salted water for a minute or so, cooled slightly, and then tightly packed into sterilized jars, covered with the boiling brine, and sealed. These preserved leaves would be used to make *mahshi* when fresh leaves were not available.

Another necessary task was the preservation of herbs, including thyme, oregano, rosemary, and, especially, spearmint, an indispensable ingredient in so many dishes. The herbs were left on their stems since they held their flavor best that way. Loosely bunched and tied together securely with string, they were hung to dry in a shaded, well-ventilated area, after which they were stored in a cool, dry place away from sunlight.

Although some preserving was done at intervals throughout the summer, most of it occurred at the end of the season, when the pace quickened dramatically, for great quantities of produce had to be processed without delay. Much of this activity took place outdoors. Fruits—apples, apricots, cherries, figs, grapes, mulberries, peaches, pears, and plums—were dried as they became ripe. In addition, we dried green beans, fava beans, peas, tomatoes, okra, peppers, eggplants, and zucchini.

Like many families, we used to dry our fruits and vegetables in the hot sun on the flat roof of our house, where they were spread on large circular straw trays. It would take several days for each batch to dry. Every morning I would be dispatched to the roof to set out trays in the sun, and from time to time during the day I would check to make sure that the loosely woven protective cloths that covered the fruits and vegetables were not touching them and had not been blown out from under the stones that were placed at the edges of the trays. At sunset I would go up to the roof one last time to bring the trays inside overnight so that their partially dried contents would not be dampened by the heavy dew of the Bekaa.

A small portion of our tomato crop was sliced and dried, while a much larger part was turned into tomato paste.[4] Puréed fresh tomatoes were simmered with salt until thick, spread on flat platters, and dried in the sun for a few days, being stirred periodically. The concentrated, aromatic paste was then spooned into sterilized jars. This method was also used to prepare a paste from red peppers (see page 299). Today few families make their own tomato paste or dry green beans, tomatoes, eggplants, zucchini, and grapes, although many continue to dry their own okra and to preserve grape leaves in brine.

The view from our roof made my task of looking after the drying of fruits and vegetables an enjoyable one. From there I could look out on orchards and vegetable gardens, with the homes of villagers and summer residents nestled among them. Somewhat farther, on two sides, stretched acres of vineyards on gently climbing terrain, followed by the towering Lebanon Mountains. To the east I could see the Anti-Lebanon not far off in the distance. In the morning everything would be brilliantly clear in the crisp, dry air, but as the day wore on and the sun beat down relentlessly, the sharpness of colors would be lost in the pallor of heat. A soft golden glow would bathe the valley in late afternoon, and when the sun began to set over the Lebanon in the west, its lingering rays would dye the slopes of the Anti-Lebanon first pink and then violet.

At summer's end and into early fall the tantalizing aromas of preserving pervaded the kitchen and backyard of our house. The pungent scent of vinegar and spices and the sweet fragrance of fruit would fill the air as fires raged under the preserving kettles. We used to pickle a wide variety of vegetables and fruits (see page 297 for information on pickling). Although all sorts of bottled jams were available in shops, many families preferred to make their own, priding themselves not only on their excellent garden produce but also on the special recipes they used. Wonderful jams and other preserves were concocted with apples, apricots, azaroles, sour cherries, citrons, fresh dates, baby eggplants, fresh and dried figs, grapefruit, grapes, nectarines, bitter orange blossoms, oranges, peaches, pears, plums, pumpkins, quinces, rose petals, strawberries, tangerines, and green walnuts (to name only some!). We ourselves made a goodly number of these, more often than not using fruits and vegetables from our garden. Jams were frequently left to finish cooking in the hot summer sun. I recall the full flavors and bright, attractive colors of apple, apricot, cherry, peach, and plum jams prepared in this manner. Rich with nuts, flavored with rose or orange flower water, cinnamon, cloves, mastic, or aniseed, and with a touch of lemon juice to prevent them from being overly sweet, many of these homemade preserves were served to guests. We also made various confections with apples, apricots, cherries, figs, grapes, peaches, pears, prunes, and quinces and transformed apricots, sour cherries, mulberries, pomegranates, and quinces into syrups.

Although it took considerable time and effort, all of this activity gave us a deep sense of satisfaction. As it approached a climax, friends and neighbors would drop by to help us prepare the vegetables and fruits, stoke the fires, stir the contents of the kettles, inform us of the day's events, change the phonograph records (Basie, Sinatra, Piaf, and many others were always in the background), and partake of a continuously replenished spread of *mazza* that kept up our strength and spirits.

A Well-Stocked Larder

At the end of the preserving season our storeroom was an awe-inspiring sight to behold. Virtually all homes had a special storeroom or, at the least, a small pantry for food. Allowing for slight regional variations, a well-stocked storeroom would boast an impressive array of barrels brimming with bulgur, skinless whole-grain wheat, rice, and dried legumes, bins of flour, sacks of potatoes, and glazed earthenware crocks of *qawarma* and *kishk*. Shelves along the walls would be lined with row upon row of glistening jars and bottles containing preserved fruits, jams, and syrups that captured the essence of fresh summer flavors. Nearby would be jars of pickled vegetables and fruits along with home-cured olives, tomato paste, and red pepper paste. In addition, there would be bottles of grape and pomegranate molasses as well as (in some Christian households) crystal-clear homemade *arak* and jewel-like brandies and liqueurs. No storeroom would be considered complete without its jars of nuts, spices, herbs, herbal teas, and home-ground salt and its bottles of vinegar, verjuice, rose water, and orange flower water. Olive oil would be stored in large glass bottles or glazed earthenware jars, while glass jars would hold *samna*, white cheeses in brine, and yogurt cheese balls in olive oil. Even the ceiling would be hung with edibles: sausages in various shapes; festoons of dried chili peppers, okra, onions, and garlic; and garlands of dried apricots, figs, and other fruits. Long twists of orange peel would also be hung to dry, to be used for flavoring teas and starting fires.

I strongly suspect that it is not only the desire to make use of what would otherwise be wasted or to evoke the sunny memories of a summer past that continues to motivate many eastern Mediterraneans to carry on the tradition of preserving foods. This practice enables cooks to select ingredients of the finest quality and to determine how they will be prepared. Homemade preserves possess a character and individuality rarely matched by store-bought products. You will find that putting by even a few preserves is well worth the effort. Once these treasures are tasted, any backsliding to supermarket standbys will be certain to raise a chorus of protest at your table!

PICKLES

> A supper was brought in on a round tray. In the center was a huge pilaff of rice, and around it several small dishes of stewed meats, grilled bones, sour clotted milk called yaoort, bits of meat roasted, with slices of apple and artichoke, pickles, and boiled fowl, &c., and round the edge thin cakes of unleavened bread, and ivory spoons.[5]

Pickling is an especially important method of food preservation in the eastern Mediterranean. In the days before refrigeration, canning, and rapid transport, it was often the only way (besides drying) that vegetables and fruits could be available for people in remote areas where the climate and terrain were inhospitable to agriculture. Even where produce was grown, it could be enjoyed fresh only in season; therefore, as necessary as pickling was in hot and arid regions, it was scarcely less so in agricultural areas. Although today pickling is no longer really a necessity, the results are so savory that it continues to be a widespread practice, and pickles remain extremely popular both as *mazza* and as accompaniments to main courses.

Vegetables most commonly pickled, singly or in combination, include green beans, beets, cabbage, carrots, cauliflower, tiny cucumbers, eggplants, okra, onions, peppers, green tomatoes, turnips, and zucchini. When added to other vegetables, a few slices of peeled beets will turn them a lovely pink—for example, beets and turnips, a traditional combination. Another frequent pairing is cauliflower and red cabbage, the latter imparting a purplish hue to the former. Green walnuts are also pickled, as are fresh thyme leaves and fruits such as grapes and lemons.

It is important to use very fresh, unblemished vegetables and fruits and a good-quality red or white wine vinegar for pickling. In recipes that use vinegar and water as a pickling solution, the proportion of one to the other may be changed to suit individual taste. More or less than or as much vinegar as water may be used. Some recipes call only for vinegar; others employ a salt and water brine, omitting vinegar entirely. The pickling solution for vegetables is often flavored with such seasonings as garlic, chili peppers, and coriander seeds; that used for fruits is commonly flavored with spices, among them cinnamon, cloves, and allspice. The solution is mixed in a clean glass container and poured over the vegetables or fruits, covering them completely, or it is first brought to a boil before being poured. Some vegetables, for example, eggplant and cauliflower, are preserved in olive oil.

Seal pickles in sterilized canning jars, and, once opened, store them in the refrigerator.

∾

What is sweeter than honey? Free vinegar!

∾

Pickled Turnips (M)
Kabees Lift *or* Lift Makbus

> Many kinds of vegetables are pickled in vinegar or salt-water and carried through the streets for sale in wooden tubs. The commonest are beetroot (*shawender*), turnips (*lift*), and cucumbers (*khiyar*).[6]

Pickled turnips have been popular for many centuries, and recipes for them appear in the medieval culinary manuals.

> 2 pounds small, firm white turnips, trimmed, peeled, and quartered
>
> 2 large garlic cloves, sliced (optional)
>
> 1 medium raw beet, trimmed, peeled, and sliced
>
> 3 cups water
>
> 1 cup white or red wine vinegar
>
> ¼ cup salt

Pack the turnips in 2 sterilized 1-quart canning jars with the garlic (if used) and the beet, dividing equally.

In a medium enameled or stainless steel saucepan combine the water, vinegar, and salt. Bring to a boil over moderately high heat. Pour over the vegetables, filling the jars to within ½ inch of the tops. Seal the jars and store them in a cool, dark, dry place. The turnips will be ready to eat in about 10 days.

Makes 2 quarts

Stuffed Eggplants in Olive Oil (M)
Batinjaan Makdus

> This is usually eaten as an appetizer.

> 3 pounds baby eggplants (3 to 4 inches long)
>
> 1 cup finely chopped walnuts
>
> 2 tablespoons finely chopped flat-leaf parsley
>
> 2 medium garlic cloves, crushed and finely chopped
>
> ½ cup fresh sour pomegranate seeds (page 56), if available
>
> 1 tablespoon salt
>
> Olive oil

Remove the stems and hulls from the eggplants and discard. Make a small lengthwise incision on one side of each eggplant. Poach the eggplants in boiling salted water about 5 minutes or until slightly softened. Drain and cool under cold running water. Gently squeeze to remove excess water.

In a small bowl mix together the walnuts, parsley, garlic, pomegranate seeds (if used), and salt. Stuff the eggplant pockets with this mixture. Arrange the stuffed eggplants compactly in layers in 2 sterilized 1-quart canning jars. Pour in enough olive oil to cover the eggplants completely. Seal the jars and store in a cool, dark, dry place. The eggplants will be ready to eat in about 3 weeks.

Makes 2 quarts

PRESERVES

Red Pepper Paste

In parts of the eastern Mediterranean one often sees shallow pans of this paste set out on the flat rooftops of houses to dry in the sun. Hot, dry weather that promises to hold for a few days would be the ideal time to make this paste; otherwise, you can use an oven. Another method is simply to simmer the peppers until they are reduced to a paste (see the variation, below).

Red pepper paste is used to flavor dips, sauces, marinades, stews, *kibbeh*, and fillings for vegetables and savory pastries. It is also very good spread on bread with a drizzle of olive oil. In Shtora we used to make it with sweet red peppers and a variety of hot pepper from our garden that I have not seen here. Red Fresnos make an acceptable substitute.

> 4 large red bell peppers, seeded, deribbed, and cut into small pieces
> 2 small red Fresno chili peppers, or more to taste, seeded, deribbed, and finely
>   chopped*
> 1 teaspoon salt
> Olive oil

Purée the peppers in a food processor, or grind them in a food chopper, using the fine blade. Transfer them to a large, heavy skillet and stir in the salt. Bring to a boil over high heat. Reduce the heat and simmer gently, uncovered, stirring occasionally, 45 minutes. Turn the pepper pulp into a shallow foil-lined baking pan and spread it out evenly. Cover the pan with cheesecloth to protect the contents from insects and dust while drying, fastening the cloth to the pan with tape to prevent it from touching the peppers. Set the baking pan outdoors in full sunlight for a few days, or as needed, stirring the pepper pulp from time to time. Bring the pan indoors at sunset and return it to the sun the next morning. The amount of time needed for drying will depend on the sun's heat.

Leave the pepper pulp outdoors until it is reduced to a thick paste; do not expose it to the sun longer than necessary. Alternatively, place the pan in a preheated 200°F oven about 5 hours or until the paste reaches the desired consistency, stirring occasionally. Spoon into a sterilized jar, cover the top with a film of olive oil, close tightly, and refrigerate.

   Makes about 1 cup

Note: To store in the freezer, drop tablespoonfuls of the paste onto a baking sheet lined with waxed paper and freeze. Once frozen, quickly wrap the dollops individually in clear plastic film, place them in an airtight container, and return them to the freezer.

VARIATION:

Instead of simmering the pepper pulp 45 minutes, simmer it, stirring frequently toward the end of cooking, 2 hours or until it is reduced to a thick paste. Store and use as above.

*A note of caution: Be careful when handling chili peppers since their volatile oils may burn your skin and irritate your eyes. Wear rubber gloves if possible and wash your hands thoroughly with soap and warm water afterward.

> Jellies . . . are often served to guests, in such cases being offered before the coffee, which must always be the last of any number of refreshments. A dish of jelly or jam, with several spoons and a tumbler of water, is passed around. Each guest takes a spoon and helps himself to a taste of jelly, then puts the soiled spoon into the vessel of water.[7]

Quince Preserves
Murabba al-Safarjal

As lovely as the Bekaa was in summer, spring and autumn were truly magical times. With the arrival of spring the many kinds of fruit trees in our orchard would burst into bloom. It would have been difficult for me to single out any particular tree as my favorite. Our picturesque quince trees held a special fascination, however, and as children we used to enjoy playing under their flowering branches, enveloped in the delicate scent of their pale pink and white blossoms. Months later, when the leaves turned and began to fall, the fruit, now golden and ripened to perfection, was ready to enrich a myriad of dishes and to be turned into exquisite syrups, candies, and, not least, preserves, which captured in jars the memory of autumn in the Bekaa.

   1 ½ **pounds quinces**
   3 cups sugar

3 cups water

1 cinnamon stick, about 3 inches long

3 whole cloves

1½ tablespoons freshly squeezed and strained lemon or lime juice

¼ cup slivered blanched almonds, lightly toasted (optional)

Scrub the quinces well. Peel, quarter, core, and cut into ¼-inch julienne strips. In a large enameled or stainless steel saucepan combine the sugar and water. Bring to a boil over moderate heat, stirring constantly until the sugar dissolves. Stir in the quinces, cinnamon stick, and cloves and bring to a boil. Reduce the heat and simmer, stirring occasionally, 45 minutes. Remove the saucepan from the heat, cover with a clean kitchen towel, and let the mixture stand at room temperature several hours or overnight.

Bring the mixture to a gentle boil and simmer, stirring occasionally to prevent scorching, about 20 minutes or until it is thickened and translucent and a small amount jells when spread on a chilled plate. Discard the cinnamon stick and cloves, stir in the lemon or lime juice and almonds, if desired, and simmer 2 minutes. Remove the saucepan from the heat and skim off any foam. Ladle the preserves into sterilized canning jars and seal the jars with the lids. Store them in a cool, dark place.

Makes about 2 pints

VARIATION:

Omit the cinnamon and cloves. Add 1 tablespoon rose water or 1½ tablespoons each rose water and orange flower water with the lemon juice.

Sour Cherry Jam
Murabba al-Karaz al-Hamud

Cherries evoke a rush of childhood memories: The drive from Aleppo to the Mediterranean coast, which passes through uplands, green mountains, and the orchards of Idlib with their plump, sweet cherries famous throughout Syria and beyond; the lonely, romantic villages of the Kisrawan region in Lebanon, where Maronites plant cherry and apple trees; and the picturesque village of Biskinta in the Matn amid its cherry orchards and cascading streams of pure mountain water. Most of all, I am reminded of the Bekaa in springtime with tulips in the fields, violets in home gardens, and dazzling displays of cherries assembled to look like bunches of grapes at roadside stands and farmers' markets. There were several kinds of cherry trees in our Shtora garden. Some of them produced sweet fruit, others sour, and still others, fruit that tasted somewhere in between. All of the cherries gave us much pleasure, whether eaten fresh off the trees or at table, dried and enjoyed during the winter, incorporated into a host of poultry, meat, and game dishes, or used to create sauces, syrups, beverages, confections, and jams such as the one described below.

Sour cherry jam is especially popular in the Aleppo region, where it is often set outdoors to finish cooking in the sun. I remember seeing enormous pans of this jam lined up on rooftops and terraces on one of my visits to that city.

> **3 pounds sour black cherries, stemmed and pitted**
> **5 ½ cups sugar, or to taste**
> **1 tablespoon freshly squeezed and strained lemon juice**

Place the cherries and sugar in alternate layers in a large, heavy enameled saucepan, ending with a layer of sugar on top. Let the mixture stand overnight. The next day bring the mixture slowly to a boil, stirring frequently. Simmer gently about 30 minutes or until the cherries are very tender, adding a little water only if absolutely required. Stir in the lemon juice and simmer 2 minutes. With a slotted spoon, transfer the cherries to sterilized canning jars. If the syrup is still a little thin, let it simmer a few minutes more until it is thick enough to coat the back of a spoon. Pour the syrup over the cherries. Seal the jars with the lids and store them in a cool, dark place.

Makes about 2 pints

Dried Fig Preserves
Teen bi Sukkar

Muhammad is reputed to have said that if any fruit has really come from Paradise it must have been the fig.

I first tasted this jam in Marjayun, the principal town in the southern Bekaa, which overlooks a fertile plain irrigated by many springs. Marjayun (Plain of Springs) is celebrated for its fresh and sun-dried figs and for its busy and colorful weekly Friday market, which takes place on its great cobblestoned square. Here one can find the famous terracotta pottery of nearby Rashayya al-Fukhar proudly displayed for sale.

Enjoy this richly flavored preserve on toast spread with *labna* or cream cheese, or offer it as a spoon sweet with Turkish coffee.

> **2 cups sugar**
> **2 cups water**
> **1 tablespoon freshly squeezed and strained lemon juice**
> **2 pounds dried figs, coarsely chopped**
> **2 rose geranium leaves, tied together (optional)**
> **1 teaspoon ground aniseed, or to taste**
> **¾ cup coarsely chopped, lightly toasted walnuts**
> **¼ cup lightly toasted pine nuts**
> **¼ cup toasted sesame seeds**
> **¼ teaspoon pulverized mastic (optional)**

A pottery at Rashayya al-Fukhar. Due to its long history of pottery making, the town has had the word al-fukhar *(pottery) appended to its name. From Charles William Wilson, ed.,* Picturesque Palestine, Sinai and Egypt, *vol. 1 (New York, D. Appleton, 1881)*

In a large enameled or stainless steel saucepan combine the sugar, water, and lemon juice. Bring to a boil over moderate heat, stirring constantly until the sugar dissolves. Simmer, uncovered and undisturbed, about 5 minutes. Add the figs and geranium leaves (if used) and simmer gently, stirring frequently, until the figs are tender and the mixture is thick. Add the aniseed, walnuts, pine nuts, and sesame seeds and simmer gently, stirring, about 3 minutes more. Remove from the heat and discard the geranium leaves. Add the mastic, if desired, and mix well. Ladle the preserves into sterilized canning jars and seal the jars with the lids. Store them in a cool, dark place.

Makes about 2 pints

VARIATION:

Substitute 2 tablespoons orange flower water for the aniseed and omit the geranium leaves and mastic.

Orange Peel Preserves
Murabba Qishr al-Abu Sfayr *or* Narinj

> Oranges from Tripoli are shipped in feluccas to all parts of Syria. Their delicious smell is only to be equalled by the taste; and the Tripolitans pride themselves much upon their excellent method of candying, not only the fruit, but also the blossom.[8]

We used to make these preserves with bitter oranges from Tripoli or Sidon, but since this variety is not readily available in the United States, I offer here a recipe that calls for sweet oranges.

6 large, thick-skinned oranges
Water
3 cups sugar
1 tablespoon freshly squeezed and strained lemon juice

Lightly grate the surface of each orange. Score the peel deeply from stem end to base into 6 segments and remove the peel carefully, leaving the fruit intact for another use.

Tightly roll up each segment of peel. Pass a large needle and heavy thread through 12 segments to form a necklace and tie the ends of the necklace together. Repeat this procedure with the remaining peel segments. Put the rolls into a large saucepan, cover with cold water, bring to a boil, and drain. Repeat this boiling and draining process 2 more times to remove bitterness from the peel. Cover the rolls with cold water again and bring to a boil. Boil gently about 30 minutes or until tender. Drain and place on paper towels to dry.

In a large enameled or stainless steel saucepan combine the sugar and 3 cups water. Bring to a boil over moderate heat, stirring constantly until the sugar dissolves. Add the lemon juice and boil the syrup, uncovered and undisturbed, 5 minutes. Add the necklaces of orange peel and simmer about 45 minutes or until the syrup is thickened. Remove from the heat and cool slightly. Carefully remove the threads and place the rolls in sterilized canning jars. Pour the syrup over the rolls, covering them completely. Seal the jars with the lids and store in a cool, dark place.

Serve the rolls with a little of their syrup, or roll them in sugar and offer them as crystallized fruit.

Makes about 2 pints

Rose Petal Jam
Murabba al-Ward

> Tarablus, or modern Tripoli, is often mentioned by Arab writers, who speak with enthusiasm of its wealth and the beauty of its gardens, surpassed only by those of Damascus. Then, as now, it abounded in extensive gardens of orange, lemon, apricot, pear, plum, apple, and other fruit trees; but it is, by way of eminence, the city of roses.[9]

Rose petal jam is a specialty of Tripoli, as are orange blossom and pumpkin jams. It is a great favorite among Armenians. I remember it being served in Aleppo, not only in Armenian homes but at the legendary Baron Hotel.

Hedges of highly perfumed pink roses (both eglantine and dog roses) often served as boundaries between vegetable gardens in Syria and Lebanon. In the Bekaa, peasant women used to pick the flowers, stuff them into sacks, and load them onto the backs of donkeys. Returning to their villages, the women would use the petals to make jam or rose essence.

Our property in Shtora was bordered on two sides by bushes of eglantine roses. If we were lucky, spring vacation would coincide with their brief period of bloom, and their strong, heavenly scent would greet us long before we reached our house.

Not all roses are suitable for making this jam. Try the recipe outlined below if you have access to pink or red roses whose petals are soft and delicate, unblemished, and free from chemicals or pesticides.

> **4 cups packed fresh rose petals (must be nontoxic and pesticide-free)**
>
> **3 cups sugar**
>
> **2 cups water**
>
> **2 tablespoons freshly squeezed and strained lemon juice**
>
> **1 tablespoon rose water, or to taste**

Cut off the white base of each petal with kitchen scissors and discard. Wash the petals carefully in cold water and drain. Arrange the rose petals in 4 layers in a large noncorrosive bowl, sprinkling each layer with 1/4 cup sugar. Let stand overnight. The following day combine the remaining 2 cups sugar and the water in a large, heavy enameled saucepan. Bring to a boil over moderate heat, stirring constantly until the sugar dissolves. Add the lemon juice and simmer, uncovered and undisturbed, 5 minutes. Remove from the heat and let the syrup cool to lukewarm. Stir in the rose petals and their liquid and bring the mixture slowly to a boil. Simmer about 15 minutes or until the syrup thickens, adding the rose water a few minutes before the end of cooking. Ladle the jam into sterilized canning jars and seal the jars with the lids. Store them in a cool, dark place.

Makes about 1 pint

The world is a rose; smell it and pass it on to your friends.
(Kurdish saying)

CHAPTER 15

Breads and Savory Pastries

Street fountain and bread seller in Damascus. *From Charles William Wilson, ed.,*
Picturesque Palestine, Sinai and Egypt, *vol. 1 (New York, D. Appleton, 1881)*

> For if you bake bread with indifference, you bake a bitter bread that feeds half man's hunger.
> Kahlil Gibran, *The Prophet* (1923)

There is a story about a woman named Hochmaea, who was a priestess of a Roman temple dedicated to the Syrian god Hadaranes in the Lebanese village of Niha, which overlooks the central Bekaa. In fulfillment of a vow she made to Hadaranes, Hochmaea abstained from eating bread for twenty years. Considering the important role bread has always played in the eastern Mediterranean diet, the priestess imposed a tremendous burden upon herself. An inscription in the temple states that as a reward for her sacrifice she lived to be one hundred years old.

Passing through the crowded bazaars of nineteenth-century Damascus, Thomson was fascinated by the number and variety of street cries that assailed his ears, among them "*Ya Karim, ya Karim,*" shouted by two boys as they carried a large tray of bread between them. "That is not the name for bread," he wrote, "but one of the attributes of God, and signifies the bountiful or generous; and since bread is the staff of life, the name implies that it is the gift of the Bountiful One."[1]

Bread is traditionally never cut with a knife, for that would be lifting up a sword against the blessing of God. Instead it is broken by hand, hence the expression "to break bread." Should a bit of bread accidentally fall on the floor, it is picked up gently and brought close to the lips and forehead in a symbolic gesture of atonement before being respectfully put aside. Leftover or stale bread is not discarded but is used in a number of dishes such as *fattush* and *fatta*.

Breads of the Middle Ages

For the majority of people in the medieval Islamic Empire, bread made from wheat was the foundation of daily sustenance. In the towns bread dough was usually kneaded at home and taken to a communal oven (*furn*), which produced the intense heat necessary for baking good bread, thus giving rise to the well-known Arab maxim, "Bring your bread to the baker, even if he eats half of it." Bread was also baked in a *tannur,* a beehive or cylindrical clay oven; in a *tabun,* a small jar-shaped oven dug in the ground and lined with pebbles, which was prevalent in rural districts; and on a convex iron plate, or *saaj.* Two main varieties of wheaten bread existed, one made from finely ground and sieved white flour (*khubz huwwara*) and the other, from coarse, unhusked flour (*khubz khushkar*). A third type, *khubz samidh,* was made from semolina.

Bread was made in various shapes and thicknesses. A thin, wide flatbread known as *riqaq* (similar to Mountain Bread, page 316) was baked in a *tannur.* Sometimes bread was made so thin and with such skill that it could be mistaken for a fine cloth. The social historian al-Isfahani (c. 897–967) relates how the poet al-Kilabi was deceived by the appearance of this kind of bread while attending a wedding banquet in a village near Aleppo. Al-Kilabi was about to ask the host to favor him with some pieces of it so that he could make a shirt out of them when, much to his surprise, the guests began eating them![2] In contrast, al-Jahiz tells us of a thick, coarse bread called *jardhaq,* which was consumed mainly by the common people.[3]

Medieval breads made use of a wide range of ingredients. The *Wusla* contains a recipe for one made by Franks and Armenians called *aflaghun* (from the Armenian *pgagund*). Three versions are given, the first of which is spread with an egg topping incorporating salt, pepper, ginger, aniseed, hempseed, sesame seeds, caraway seeds, cumin seeds, poppy seeds, *atraf al-tib* (page 64), and saffron, as well as wild rue, grated cheese, and pistachio nuts! Bread was often stuffed with sweet fillings, an example being a long loaf called *khushknanaj,* which contained a filling of ground almonds and scented sugar mixed with rose water.

Bread made from barley, millet, and, where plentiful, rice was consumed chiefly by people of lesser means. Bread was also made with ingredients other than cereals, such as lentils.

The Ottoman Era

Many Western travelers to the region have described the diverse breads made during this period, from the most primitive ones to the more modern European-type loaves. As in the Middle Ages, bread was usually made from wheat, with barley or millet being used only by the very poor. According to nineteenth-century writers, in some Syrian villages bread was also made with Indian corn. Mary Eliza Rogers has left us an account of breadmaking among the Beduin:

> Two women were skilfully stirring and spreading burning embers on the ground with their hands, as freely as if fire had no power to hurt them; another was kneading some paste. . . . [O]n a small circular hearth, formed of smooth round stones, spread evenly and close together on the ground, a brisk wood fire was kindled. When the stones of this prim-itive hearth were sufficiently heated, the embers were carefully removed, and the well-

Woman grinding at a handmill.
From Cunningham Geikie, The
Holy Land and the Bible *(London,
Cassell, 1891)*

kneaded paste thrown on to the hot stones, and quickly covered with the burning ashes. In this way several cakes of unleavened bread were soon made ready. . . . [T]he flat cakes of bread were served quite hot. They had received the impression of the pebbles of which the hearth was composed.[4]

The Beduin also made use of the *saaj* to bake their bread. This slightly less elementary method was observed by Meryon while he was accompanying Lady Hester Stanhope on her journey to Palmyra:

Opening a sack of flour, [the women] kneaded a certain quantity with water; and, without the aid of rolling-pins, by a rotatory motion of the left arm, they flattened the paste into a thin circular shape, about one foot and a half in diameter.[5] They then laid it on an iron plate, placed over a fire made in a hole in the ground, and in three minutes it was baked. Lastly, they threw it on the ashes to keep it warm, until a sufficient number of these cakes were prepared: and, this done, supper was served up.[6]

The settled population in rural areas often baked its bread (as well as some prepared dishes) in the *tannur*.[7] Thomson, who noted that the bread thus produced was thinner than that baked upon the *saaj,* has faithfully recorded this process as it was carried on in the Biskinta Valley in Lebanon:

Yusuf . . . has purchased a large quantity of that wonderfully thin and tough bread, which so much resembles sheets of brown paper cut round. . . .

He says the loaves are fresh baked, and that the oven is close by. I hear the pat, pat, patting of the women around the tannur of this small hamlet connected with the mill. There we will find a merry group busy in achieving a baking.

The tannur . . . is merely a hole in the ground, about three feet deep and two feet in diameter, lined with cement and smoothly polished. It is filled with thorn bushes, dry grass, and weeds when it is to be heated, or with any kind of fuel that will make a sudden and fierce blaze; and the heat is kept up by throwing in a fresh supply, as occasion requires. Three women are necessary to carry on the operation of baking to advantage. One to roll or pat the dough into comparatively thin loaves; another to manipulate each loaf, tossing it from hand to hand, and over her arms, so as to expand regularly when thrown upon a round cushion made for the purpose; and the third woman to clap the loaf on the cushion upon the heated interior side of the tannur, and tear off the one which is sufficiently baked. A shed is generally built over the tannur, or it is excavated in the floor of a small room, open in front, by which it is made easy of access, and sufficiently protected from the rain and the snow during the winter.

The loaves are not as thick as ordinary pasteboard, and are from one foot to a foot and a half in diameter. The bread is called markuk, that is, "rolled," or made thin; and when the tannur is quite hot two loaves can be thus baked "in a minute," and it is no unusual thing to see a pile of one hundred and fifty of these thin loaves by the side of the women baking at the tannur. Fresh, hot, and crisp, this bread is excellent eating . . . [8]

Other ovens of ancient origin, also called *tannur* or *tabun,* were used for baking bread as well, a popular one in the countryside being dome-shaped and made of clay, with openings both on the side and top that were covered during the baking process. The flat cakes of dough, one-fourth to one-half inch thick and the size of a dessert plate or larger, were laid on small stones placed on the floor of the oven, and the fire was built around the outside so that it did not come in contact with the interior. The hot stones gave a bubbly surface to the loaves, which, when baked, possessed an agreeably spongy texture and a delicious whole wheat flavor.

As in former times, towns were furnished with public ovens (*furn*s). Henry J. van Lennep has provided us with a description of these ovens, where bread was made and sold:

These ovens are built of baked bricks in the large towns, and occupy the innermost part of the little shop, whose street front consists of a large counter upon which the bread is sold. The oven itself is a chamber whose smooth floor, some four feet in diameter, is covered with flat bricks, and stands three feet above the ground. The sides and roof are arched, and the flue of the chimney is at the inner end. . . . The operation of baking begins by lighting a brisk fire all over the floor of the oven, and when its surface has become sufficiently heated the embers are raked out through the opening in the front, and the loaves of bread are laid and arranged on the floor of the oven with a long-handled wooden shovel. An iron door closes the oven until the baking is completed. [9]

The *furn* was also utilized for baking various prepared dishes brought to it by the people in the neighborhood.

The two most common types of town bread were both leavened and usually made

Breadmaking utensils.
1. Wheat bin. 2. Stone
mill. 3. Fine sieve.
4. Wooden bread bowls.
5. Straw mat used as a
tray or as a bread bowl
cover. 6 and 7. Clay
ovens, the fire for which
is to be built around the
outside. 8. Metal cooking
plate. 9. Tiny basket for
dry flour. (From the
Hartford Theological
Seminary Collection.)
From Elihu Grant, The
People of Palestine
(Philadelphia, J. B.
Lippincott, 1921)

of white flour. One was round, somewhat flat, and about six inches in diameter; the other was round or oval, half an inch thick, and twelve inches in diameter (this second type was often used instead of a dish or platter, with other food being placed upon it). According to Russell, most Aleppans made their bread at home and sent it to a *furn* to be baked. He also records that ring-shaped loaves sprinkled with sesame seeds or nigella (*ka'k*), as well as other breads, were sold in the bazaars and streets of the city.[10] In addition, Europeans were supplied with excellent French bread. Interestingly, from the middle of the seventeenth century until well into the twentieth, the sale of wheat, the milling of flour, and the baking and distribution of bread and pastry in Aleppo were virtually monopolized by Armenians who emigrated there from the town of Sasun in the heartland of historical Armenia.

Excellent bread could also be had in Damascus. According to Alphonse de Lamartine, the nineteenth-century French poet and author of the celebrated *Voyage en Orient,* various kinds of flatbreads were offered for sale, still hot from the oven, in the city's bazaars. "Nowhere else," he writes, "have I seen bread of such perfection, and it costs almost nothing."

A public oven. *From Henry J. van Lennep,* Bible Lands: Their Modern Customs and Manners Illustrative of Scripture *(New York, Harper, 1875)*

Breadmaking in Modern Times

Today bread continues to be an essential part of every meal, consumed in enormous quantities and in a number of varieties, leavened and unleavened, thick and thin. Good-quality bread is available from bakeries in cities and towns, and people generally go out to purchase it, fresh and warm, twice a day. When I was a child it was still common practice for many Beirut families to prepare their own bread at home and send it to be baked at the neighborhood *furn.* These were generally wood-burning and produced superlative results. Such ovens are far less prevalent today and are giving way to ones heated with gas or oil.

The best-known bread of the region is *khubz arabi* (or, simply, *khubz*), a round, flat, slightly leavened loaf about one-fourth inch thick and with a pocket inside. It is made in three different sizes: large (eight or more inches in diameter), medium (six to eight inches), and small (about five inches). In America, where it has become very popular, this bread is known as pita. A pocketless version is also available. In some Arab communities *khubz arabi* is called *kmaj* (from the Persian *kumaj*), while in others, *kmaj* refers only to the pocketless type. Recipes employing *kumaj* (*kmaj*) are found in both the *Wusla* and the *Kanz.* A thicker bread is *talami,* which is round and has no pocket.

In Lebanon pita is often referred to as town bread as opposed to the quite different bread of the countryside, known as *khubz marquq* or *khubz al-jabal* (mountain bread), although both are made from the same dough recipe. It is this latter, thinner bread (the making of which was described by Thomson) rather than pita that is generally considered by Lebanese and Syrians to be their national bread. Up until the 1940s *marquq* was still being baked by many villagers in a *tannur.* Because this method was very uncomfortable for the baker, forcing her to bend continuously toward the oven, the *tannur* was gradually replaced by the *saaj* of the Beduin (for a description of making *marquq* on a *saaj,* see page 316). *Saaj* bread is called *shrak* by Palestinians and Jordanians.

Fortunately the *tannur* has made a comeback after having been redesigned. The modern version is installed in a raised and horizontal position and is fueled with oil, facilitating its operation and making it possible to produce *khubz marquq* commercially.[11] Similarly, the *saaj* has been modernized so that it sits waist-high on a portable stand fired from below, and these days one can see mountain bread being made on this new type of *saaj* on the streets of Beirut. Pita continues to dominate in the towns and, being easier to market on a large scale, has recently spread into the countryside.

Other breads that I remember from my years in Lebanon include *bumwayya,* literally "father of water," a large bread resembling *talami* that was sprinkled with water before being baked; *meshta,* a thick, oblong flatbread that was also sprinkled with water and then indented with the fingers before being baked; *malkuma,* a bread similar to *meshta* but circular in shape; *qers bayd,* a small, round egg bread; and *manaqish,* a round bread with small indentations that were filled with extra-virgin olive oil before baking.

A classic snack eaten by generations of schoolchildren is *ka'k bi simsim,* sold by street vendors. It is a hollow bread that is coated with sesame seeds and looks like a crescent-shaped pocketbook with a handle. I recall looking forward impatiently to recess time, when a horde of students would descend upon the *ka'k* seller, who would be waiting faithfully at our school gate, displaying his breads on a large wooden tray resting on a three-legged stool. He would pinch a hole in the crisp, brown crust of each *ka'k* and sprinkle *za'atar* inside just before serving it to one of his eager young customers. When he had completed his business at the school, he would hoist the tray onto his head, grab the stool in his other hand, and stroll to his next location in the unlikely event that he had not sold out. Some *ka'k* sellers threaded their breads on long poles hung over their shoulders and traveled around on bicycles.

Another snack I recall that was especially popular with children is *ka'k kurshalli,* a dry, crisp bread that is munched on as zwieback is in the West. It is made in a number of variations and may incorporate such ingredients as nuts, raisins, and sesame seeds.

In the cities certain bakeries feature Western-style breads, two examples being a long, rectangular butter loaf and a crusty French bread known as *khubz franji* (European bread). In some areas one also finds *khubz tawil* (long bread), which is somewhat shorter than a baguette.

SAVORY PASTRIES

Virtually all cuisines boast some kind of savory pastry, but few can offer the remarkable variety found in the eastern Mediterranean. Such standbys as *lahm bi ajeen, fatayer, sambusak,* and *boerek* all belong to a time-honored repertoire of irresistible pastries that come in numerous shapes and lend themselves to a wide assortment of fillings. Most often formed into rounds, half-moons, triangles, or fingers, they are sometimes baked, sometimes fried. There is considerable confusion regarding these preparations, for the same pastry can turn up under different names in different communities, and, to complicate matters further, the same name can apply to two or more different pastries.

Savory pastries provide delightful buffet and party fare. Small ones make outstanding appetizers, while larger versions can be served as main courses. Whether slim and elegant or hearty and substantial, these treats are an integral part of the region's culinary tradition.

∽

Is it wheat or barley?

(Good or bad news?)

∽

Pita Bread

Khubz Arabi

∽

O Allah, send customers!

(Street cry of Damascus bread sellers of former times.)

∽

Baking pita at home conjures up vivid memories of the neighborhood bakery in Beirut that I used to patronize as a child. Using a long-handled wooden board, the baker would deftly place loaf after loaf on the floor of the furnacelike brick oven through the opening at the front. As I looked on spellbound, the loaves would inflate, now this one and now that one, in a continuous ballet. When each loaf was done, the baker would nimbly toss it with his board into a nearby bin. His air of confidence notwithstanding (even though his honor was surely on the line), I could not help but show apprehension that not all of the loaves would balloon up, which used to amuse him greatly. To my relief, they always did and, with a performer's pride, he would give me a knowing smile and a big wink as if to say, "I told you so!"

The following recipe, like that of the baker, has never failed me. If followed carefully, it should also work well for you.

1½ cups warm water (about 110°F)

1¼ teaspoons active dry yeast

1½ teaspoons sugar

4½ cups all-purpose flour

1½ teaspoons salt

1½ teaspoons olive oil or vegetable oil

Additional all-purpose flour for kneading (if necessary)

Pour ½ cup of the water into a small bowl and sprinkle it with the yeast and sugar. Let the mixture stand about 3 minutes, then stir to dissolve the yeast completely. Place the bowl in a warm, draft-free spot for 5 minutes or until the mixture becomes foamy.

In a large bowl combine the flour with the salt. Make a well in the center and add the remaining 1 cup water, the yeast mixture, and the oil. Blend the mixture until it forms a dough. Turn the dough out onto a lightly floured surface and knead about 10 minutes or until smooth and elastic, sprinkling with just enough of the additional flour, if necessary, to keep it from sticking. Form the dough into a 10-inch log and cut the log crosswise into 1-inch pieces. Knead each piece a few times and form it into a smooth ball. Arrange the balls 2 inches apart on trays lined with kitchen towels. Let the balls rise, covered with a kitchen towel, in a warm, draft-free place 1 to 1½ hours or until doubled in bulk.

On a lightly floured surface gently flatten each ball of dough and roll it out until it is ¼ inch thick and about 6 inches in diameter. Arrange the rounds 1 inch apart on a floured wooden surface or on floured kitchen towels. Let the rounds rise, covered with a floured kitchen towel, in a warm, draft-free place 1 hour or until they are puffed slightly.

Put a large, ungreased baking sheet on the lowest rack of the oven and heat the oven to 500°F. Remove the baking sheet from the oven and invert 2 or 3 of the rounds of dough 1 inch apart onto it, being very careful not to dent or stretch the dough. Bake the rounds on the lowest rack of the oven 4 to 5 minutes or until they are puffed and the bottoms are lightly browned. Turn the oven to broil and broil the rounds 4 inches from the heat 30 seconds to 1 minute or until the tops are very lightly browned.

Transfer the pita breads to racks and let them cool. Bake and cool the remaining rounds in the same manner. To store the pita breads, flatten them gently, stack them, and wrap them well in plastic wrap. Refrigerate for 2 days, or freeze. Thaw frozen loaves and reheat, uncovered, in a 300°F oven 5 to 10 minutes before using.

Makes 10

VARIATIONS:

Whole Wheat Pita Bread

Substitute whole wheat flour for 2¼ cups of the all-purpose flour.

Sesame Pita Bread
Khubz bi Simsim

Follow the recipe for Pita Bread (above) to the point at which you are ready to bake the loaves. Sprinkle the top of each loaf evenly with 1 tablespoon sesame seeds and bake as directed.

Makes 10

What the bread can carve, the sword cannot. *(A)*

Za'atar Bread
Manaqish bi Za'atar

A popular breakfast food and a tempting snack at any time, this bread is sold in cafés, sandwich bars, take-out shops, and by street vendors. Small versions make excellent appetizers to serve with cocktails.

Follow the recipe for Pita Bread (page 314) to the point at which the first rising of the balls of dough is almost completed.

In a small bowl combine ½ cup plus 2 tablespoons *za'atar* with ⅓ cup extra-virgin olive oil and mix well. On a lightly floured surface gently flatten each ball of dough and roll it out until it is ¼ inch thick and about 6 inches in diameter. Arrange 2 or 3 of the rounds of dough slightly apart on a large, ungreased baking sheet. Place about 1 tablespoon of the *za'atar* mixture in the center of each round, then spread it evenly to about ¼ inch of the edge. Bake the breads in a preheated 450°F oven 10 minutes or until very lightly browned.

Transfer the breads to racks and let them stand until they are cool enough to handle. Bake and cool the remaining rounds in the same manner. Serve warm or at room temperature.

Makes 10

To eat a morsel of bread for a meal in peace is better than having a chicken with quarreling.

Mountain Bread
Khubz Marquq *or* Khubz al-Jabal

When I was growing up, breadmaking in the Lebanon Mountains was a weekly ritual that took place outdoors. The village women were highly skilled at this art, which was passed from mother to daughter and took years of practice to master. The bread was baked on a *saaj* placed on stones about six inches above the ground over a wooden fire. Our summer home in Shtora had a stone hearth in a special area of the backyard that was shielded from excessive wind and sun, making the weekly baking of this bread a pleasant task. Its method of preparation fascinated me as a youngster. Seated cross-legged before a low wooden table, the breadmaker, a local villager, would shape small balls of dough into rounded loaves. Taking one loaf at a time, she would pat and press the dough between her palms as she shifted it from hand to hand and then, as it became thinner and thinner, rolled it from arm to arm with increasing speed until the dough was almost the size of the *saaj,* at least two feet in diameter and no thicker than wrapping paper. Next, she would drape it over a round pillow (*kara*), stretching the dough taut to an even, circular shape. Then she would flip the sheet of dough from the pillow onto the *saaj,* where it would bake until lightly golden but still soft and pliable (about one minute), after which she would carefully but quickly peel off the bread and stack it on a cloth-covered wicker mat woven especially for this purpose.

When the French first came to Lebanon they mistook loaves of *khubz marquq,* neatly folded beside their plates, for table napkins and proceeded to tie them around their necks! The American missionary Henry Harris Jessup was similarly fooled on first encountering this bread in 1856:[12]

> In Ain Zehalteh I . . . took my first meal in a Syrian home, that of Mr. Khalil Maghubghub, the teacher. As I had never seen the thin Arab bread called "markoak," which is baked in round sheets about fifteen or eighteen inches in diameter, I took a loaf and spread it on my lap supposing it to be a napkin. On my asking Mr. Lyons why they had no bread, he replied with a smile, "Because they eat their napkins!" I exclaimed, and the teacher on hearing of my mistake joined us in a hearty laugh. On every visit since that time to Ain Zehalteh during these fifty-three years, I am reminded of my eating my napkin.[13]

You can, without a *saaj* or years of practice, make an acceptable *khubz marquq* in the oven or on an inverted wok (see *Note,* below). While this bread is excellent made with all-purpose flour, it is often made partially or entirely with whole wheat flour. A delicious variation, which I discovered on a childhood visit to Damascus, is to sprinkle sesame seeds and nigella over the bread before baking. Today a bakery in the Damascus suburb of al-Mazzah specializes in this version.

Follow the recipe for Pita Bread (page 314) to the point at which the first rising of the dough is completed. Put a large ungreased baking sheet on the lowest rack of the oven and heat the oven to 425°F. Working with one ball of dough at a time (keeping the remaining dough covered), place the ball on a lightly floured surface and roll out as thinly as possible into a circle, sprinkling lightly with flour only if needed to keep it from sticking. Remove the baking sheet from the oven. Carefully roll the circle of dough on the rolling pin and unroll onto the baking sheet. Prick the surface of the dough in 3 or 4 places with a fork.

Bake the bread in the oven 3 to 4 minutes or until lightly golden but still soft and pliable. Roll out and bake the remaining balls of dough in the same manner. Wrap the hot breads in a kitchen towel to keep them soft. Serve warm or at room temperature. For a crisper texture, bake the breads 1 to 2 minutes longer or until blistered and golden, watching closely to prevent burning. Cool the breads briefly on racks,

***Women rolling out dough into thin loaves and baking them on a* saaj.** *From* National Geographic, *October, 1915*

then stack. To store, wrap the cooled breads tightly in plastic bags. If they lose their crispness, heat them in a preheated 300°F oven about 5 minutes or until crisp.

Makes 10

Note: To bake the breads on a wok, invert a well-cleaned, flat-bottomed wok with handles over medium-high heat and brush the outside lightly with vegetable oil. When the wok is hot, unroll a circle of dough onto it and bake about 30 seconds or until the underside of the bread is lightly browned. With tongs, carefully turn and brown lightly on the other side. Bake the remaining circles of dough in the same manner.

To give advice there will be many; to give bread very few. *(A)*

Mountain Bread Sandwich
Zuwedi

In rural Lebanon women would frequently get together to bake mountain bread. Sometimes, after the baking was completed, they would all enjoy a *zuwedi* (provision), an improvised sandwich composed of *marquq* bread and cheese, olives, raw or cooked vegetables, or jam. Often a *zuwedi* was eaten at breakfast, and it made a popular "lunch on the run" as well. A favorite *zuwedi* of mine consisted of mountain bread wrapped around thinly sliced or crumbled cheese (*hallum, kashkawan,* or *akkawi*) and minced scallions and baked on a *saaj* until lightly browned on both sides. This simple but appealing snack can easily be made using a sandwich grill or griddle. Other cheeses such as Cheddar, Gouda, or Gruyère will also work well for this sandwich.

The *zuwedi* has sustained farmers and shepherds in this part of the world for many centuries. Thomson mentions both the most common ingredients for this type of sandwich and the goatskin bag (*jarab*) in which they were carried to the fields:

> The peasants we meet along our path . . . carry no cooking utensils, and we should think they had little or nothing to eat.
>
> They, however, have a quantity of their thin, tough bread, a few olives, and perhaps a little cheese in that leathern bag which hangs from their shoulders—the "scrip" of the New Testament—and with those they are contented. When hungry, they sit by the fountain, or the brook, and eat. . . . At night they . . . kindle a fire of thorn-bushes, warm over it their stale bread; and, if they have shot a bird, they broil it on the coals, and thus dinner and supper in one are achieved with the least possible trouble.[14]

The "Bride"
ʿArus

This sandwich has long been a standard after-school snack for Arab children. In the Lebanon of my childhood, when a young bachelor was handed an ʿ*arus* by a village elder, it was a not-so-subtle hint that he should find a wife!

Spread freshly made soft and pliable Mountain Bread (page 316) with Yogurt Cheese (page 143) and extra-virgin olive oil. Sprinkle evenly with *zaʿatar* or cover with fresh spearmint leaves. Roll up and eat.

∾

The poor long for bread, the rich for everything. *(A)*

∾

Armenian Peda Bread

A close relative of Iranian *barbari* and its smaller cousin, the Iraqi *samun,* this delightfully chewy bread resembles a padded quilt. In Shtora I used to buy this kind of bread from a bakery owned by Aleppo Armenians whose forebears came to Syria from the Armenian town of Sasun (see page 311).

Peda is best eaten warm and goes especially well with stews, shish kebab, or cheese.

2 cups warm water (about 110° F)
2 packages active dry yeast
2 tablespoons sugar
1 tablespoon salt
3 tablespoons unsalted butter, melted, or olive oil
5 1/4 cups all-purpose flour plus 2 teaspoons for glaze
Additional all-purpose flour for kneading
1/2 cup cold water
1 tablespoon sesame seeds or nigella (optional)

Pour the warm water into a large mixing bowl and sprinkle with the yeast. Let the mixture stand 5 minutes, then stir in the sugar, salt, and melted butter or oil. Add 4 cups of the flour, about a cup at a time, beating thoroughly with a large wooden spoon or a heavy-duty electric mixer at medium speed. Continue beating about 5 minutes or until the dough is smooth. Gradually mix in the remaining 1 1/4 cups flour.

Turn the dough out onto a lightly floured surface and knead until it is smooth, sprinkling with just enough additional flour to keep it from sticking. Transfer the dough to a lightly oiled bowl, turning to coat with the oil. Cover loosely with a kitchen towel and let rise in a warm, draft-free place about 1 hour or until doubled in size.

Lightly grease 2 large baking sheets and dust with flour. Punch down the dough and divide it into 2 equal parts. Shape each part into a smooth ball and place it on a baking sheet. Cover lightly with clear plastic film and let rest at room temperature 30 minutes. Form each loaf into an 11-by-14-inch oval by pressing, stretching, and pounding the dough with your fist. Cover with clear plastic film and let rise in a warm, draft-free place 45 to 55 minutes or until doubled in size. With a soft brush dipped in cool water, lightly moisten the top and sides of each raised loaf. Dip your fingertips in water and, lining up the four fingertips of each hand, press down to the baking sheet, making a 1-inch-wide rim all around the edge of the oval. Then make crosswise and lengthwise lines about 2 inches apart. Let the loaves rise, uncovered, about 45 minutes or until almost doubled in size.

Bake one loaf at a time in the center of a preheated 450° F oven about 15 minutes or until golden brown. Meanwhile, in a small saucepan blend the remaining 2 teaspoons flour with the cold water until smooth. Cook over moderate heat, stirring constantly, until the mixture comes to a boil and thickens. Remove the flour glaze from the heat, cover, and set aside.

As each loaf is baked, remove it from the oven and immediately brush the top and sides lightly with the flour glaze. If you would like to put on the seeds, brush the loaf again lightly with the glaze and immediately sprinkle with the seeds. Let cool slightly on wire racks and serve warm. Or cool the loaves completely, wrap well in aluminum foil, and freeze. Reheat the loaves, uncovered, in a 350° F oven 5 to 8 minutes before using.

Makes 2 large loaves

Sesame Rings
Kaʿk

Recipes for *kaʿk* are found in al-Warraq's culinary manual and in the *Wusla*. The modern recipe outlined below produces crisp and chewy rings that make a good between-meal snack, or you can serve them with soups and salads.

> 1¼ cups warm water (about 110°F)
> 1 package active dry yeast
> Pinch sugar
> 4 cups all-purpose flour
> 2 teaspoons ground cumin
> 2 teaspoons ground coriander
> 2 teaspoons salt
> ⅔ cup unsalted butter, melted and cooled to lukewarm
> 1 egg, lightly beaten with 2 teaspoons water
> ½ cup sesame seeds
> Additional all-purpose flour for kneading (if necessary)

Pour the water into a small bowl and sprinkle it with the yeast and sugar. Let the mixture stand about 3 minutes, then stir to dissolve the yeast completely. Place the bowl in a warm, draft-free place 5 to 10 minutes or until the mixture becomes foamy.

In a large bowl combine the flour, cumin, coriander, and salt. Make a well in the center and add the melted butter and yeast mixture. Blend the mixture until it forms a firm dough. Turn the dough out onto a floured surface and knead 5 to 10 minutes or until smooth and elastic, sprinkling with just enough of the additional flour, if necessary, to keep it from sticking. Transfer the dough to a lightly oiled bowl, turning to coat with the oil. Cover loosely with a kitchen towel and let rise in a warm, draft-free place 1½ to 2 hours or until doubled in bulk.

Punch down the dough and, on a lightly floured surface, divide it in half. Form one half into a log about 2 inches in diameter. Cut the log crosswise into ½-inch-thick slices. Roll each slice into a 6-inch rope and press the ends together to form a ring. Brush one side of each ring with the egg and water mixture and dip that side into the sesame seeds. Arrange the rings, seeded side up, about 1 inch apart on a large, lightly greased baking sheet. Repeat this procedure with the remaining dough.

Bake the rings in a preheated 400°F oven 10 minutes. Reduce the heat to 325°F and bake 20 to 30 minutes or until they are lightly golden and crisp. Let the rings cool on wire racks.

Makes about 48

VARIATIONS:

Use only ½ teaspoon each cumin and coriander and add 4 teaspoons aniseed, crushed.

Substitute 4 teaspoons aniseed, crushed, and ¾ teaspoon each caraway seeds and *mahlab* for the cumin and coriander.

Open-Faced Meat Pies (M)
Lahm bi Ajeen *or* S'fiha

Reading Russell's description of a typical meal in a well-to-do eighteenth-century Aleppan household (page 30), I was delighted to come across "minced meat with pomegranate grains, spread upon thin cakes, and baked on an iron plate," which are none other than my all-time childhood favorite, *lahm bi ajeen* (meat with dough), or, as the good doctor called them, *"lahem ajeen."*

These time-honored pies are consumed with as much gusto on their home ground as pizza is in America. It is quite likely that the two share a common origin, with the latter possibly being the descendant of the former. Moreover, the name pizza may well be related to the word pita.

There are several theories as to how this type of pie reached the shores of Italy. One is that it was brought by the many Middle Eastern Jews who settled south of Rome long ago. Another suggests that it traveled with Greek-speaking Anatolians who emigrated to Naples after the fall of Byzantium. Some people trace the actual invention of open-faced meat pies not to the Jews, Arabs, or Byzantines but to the Armenians. It is true that Armenians are inordinately fond of *missahatz* (meat with bread, as the pies are known in Armenian) and that Armenian bakers in Beirut and, especially, in Aleppo are known for their expertise in making them. Given the fact that the bread and pastry trade in Aleppo was in the hands of Armenians for nearly three hundred years, there may be some truth to this assertion. It should be mentioned that the term *lahmajoon,* a corruption of the Arabic, is used by the Turks and many Armenians. I hasten to add, however, that an Arabic name for a dish does not necessarily indicate Arab provenance. Invariably a minority uses the language of the majority in whose country it lives for purposes of communication outside its own group. Similarly, this explains why many Armenian dishes are known by Turkish names. For most Armenians, who like the Arabs were for centuries a subject people in the Ottoman Empire, Turkish was the primary language of communication, sometimes being imposed by force, to the detriment of the Armenian language.[15]

Since home kitchens of former times were not equipped with ovens, people either purchased *lahm bi ajeen* from bakeries or made their own meat topping and sent it to the neighborhood bakery, where it was spread on dough supplied by the baker and cooked in his intensely hot oven. Today the pies enjoy tremendous popularity, not only in the Middle East but in many Armenian, Lebanese, and Syrian communities abroad.

Lahm bi ajeen are delicious whether served as a luncheon or supper main course or as a buffet or picnic dish. Cocktail-sized pies make excellent appetizers.

DOUGH

1 cup warm water (about 110°F)

1 package active dry yeast

¼ teaspoon sugar

3 cups all-purpose flour (approximately)

1 teaspoon salt

2½ tablespoons olive oil

Additional all-purpose flour for kneading (if necessary)

MEAT TOPPING

2 tablespoons olive oil

3 medium onions, finely chopped

1½ pounds lean ground lamb or beef

2 large tomatoes, peeled, seeded, finely chopped, and well drained

3 tablespoons tomato paste

⅓ cup finely chopped flat-leaf parsley

2 tablespoons finely chopped fresh spearmint leaves

¼ cup pine nuts, lightly toasted

1 tablespoon Pomegranate Molasses (page 57)

1 tablespoon freshly squeezed and strained lemon juice

1½ teaspoons Mixed Spices I or II (page 66)

Salt, freshly ground black pepper, and Middle Eastern red pepper to taste

To make the dough, pour ½ cup of the water into a small bowl and sprinkle it with the yeast and sugar. Let the mixture stand about 3 minutes, then stir to dissolve the yeast completely. Place the bowl in a warm, draft-free place for 5 minutes or until the mixture becomes foamy.

In a large bowl combine the flour and salt. Make a well in the center and add the remaining ½ cup water, the yeast mixture, and the oil. Blend the mixture until it forms a dough. Turn the dough out onto a floured surface and knead about 10 minutes or until smooth and elastic, sprinkling with just enough of the additional flour, if necessary, to keep it from sticking. Transfer the dough to a lightly oiled bowl, turning to coat with the oil. Cover loosely with a kitchen towel and let stand in a warm, draft-free place 1 to 1½ hours or until doubled in size.

Meanwhile, prepare the meat topping. In a medium, heavy skillet heat the oil over moderate heat. Add the onions and cook, stirring frequently, until soft but not browned. Remove from the heat and set aside. In a large mixing bowl combine the lamb or beef, tomatoes, and tomato paste and mix well. Add the parsley, mint, pine nuts, Pomegranate Molasses, lemon juice, Mixed Spices, and salt, black pepper, and red pepper. Drain the onions of oil and add to the meat mixture. Knead the mixture until it is thoroughly blended. Taste and adjust the seasoning. Divide the mixture into 16 equal portions and set aside.

Punch down the dough and divide it into 16 equal pieces. Form each piece into a smooth ball and arrange the balls 2 inches apart on a lightly floured board. Cover with a kitchen towel and let rest about 15 minutes.

On a lightly floured surface roll out each of the balls into a circle that is no more than ⅛ inch thick. Arrange the circles slightly apart on large, lightly greased baking sheets. Top each circle with a portion of the meat mixture and spread the mixture evenly to the edge. Bake the pies in a preheated 450°F oven about 10 minutes or until lightly browned. Serve hot (preferably) or at room temperature, accompanied with lemon wedges, Drained Yogurt (page 142), or Cucumber and Yogurt Salad (page 143).

Makes 16

Note: To store, place 2 pies together with the meat sides against each other. Stack 2 or 3 pairs together, wrap securely in aluminum foil, and refrigerate or freeze. To reheat the pies, bring to room temperature if frozen and place the pies, still with meat sides together, on a baking sheet. Heat, uncovered, in a preheated 450°F oven about 5 minutes or until hot.

VARIATIONS:

Add 1 tablespoon tamarind concentrate, or to taste, to the cooked onions and mix well. Omit the Pomegranate Molasses.

Garnish the pies with fresh sour pomegranate seeds (page 56), if available.

Substitute 1 cup Yogurt Cheese (page 143) for the tomatoes and tomato paste. (I first tasted this variation in Baalbek, where *lahm bi ajeen* is a local specialty.)

For a simplified version of these pies, substitute 16 flour tortillas (each about 6 inches in diameter) or 8 six-inch pita breads, halved horizontally to form 16 rounds for the circles of dough.

This dough will absorb lots of water. *(A)*
(This problem will require much time and effort to be solved.)

Spinach Pies (M)

Fatayer bi Sabanikh

Other greens such as Swiss chard, sorrel, dandelion, and purslane leaves are sometimes substituted for the spinach in this popular pastry. *Fatayer* can also be made with a filling of cheese or meat.

Dough for Open-Faced Meat Pies (page 323)

SPINACH FILLING

2 pounds spinach

1/4 cup olive oil

1 large onion, finely chopped

1/3 cup freshly squeezed and strained lemon juice, or more to taste

**1/2 cup fresh pomegranate seeds (page 56), or 2 tablespoons currants or raisins
   (optional)**

1/2 cup toasted pine nuts or coarsely chopped walnuts

1/2 teaspoon Mixed Spices I (page 66) (optional)

Salt and freshly ground black pepper to taste

Prepare the dough and let rise as directed. Meanwhile, prepare the filling. Remove the coarse stems and wilted leaves from the spinach. Wash the spinach well in several changes of cold water, squeeze dry, and chop finely.

In a large, heavy skillet heat the oil over moderate heat. Add the spinach and cook, stirring, until it is wilted. Remove from the heat, add the remaining ingredients, and mix well. Taste and adjust the seasoning and set aside.

Punch down the dough and divide it into 30 equal pieces. On a lightly floured board roll out each piece into a 4-inch circle. Place a heaping tablespoon of filling in the center of each circle. Bring up the sides from 3 equidistant points to make a triangular-shaped pie. Press the edges together firmly to seal the pie completely. Arrange the filled pies on lightly greased baking sheets and bake in a preheated 400°F oven 15 to 20 minutes or until lightly browned. Serve warm.

Makes 30

VARIATIONS:

Sauté the onion in the oil, then add the spinach and proceed as above.

Add 1/2 teaspoon ground sumac, or to taste, with the seasonings.

Cheese or Meat Turnovers (M)

Sambusak *or* Sanbusak

That is a *sambusak,* but we are not fit to be its filling.
(A fine affair, but not one in which we can participate.)

Here is a modern version of a time-honored classic whose virtues were extolled in poems recited at the courts of Abbassid caliphs in Baghdad.

PASTRY

½ **cup vegetable oil or olive oil**
½ **cup unsalted butter**
½ **cup water**
1 teaspoon salt
3 ½ **cups all-purpose flour (approximately)**

Cheese filling (page 327), or 2 recipes meat filling (page 234)
1 egg, lightly beaten
Sesame seeds (optional)

Prepare the pastry: Combine the oil and butter in a small saucepan and heat over low heat until the butter melts. Stir in the water and salt and pour the mixture into a large mixing bowl. Gradually add enough flour, mixing with a wooden spoon to make a very soft dough. Gather the dough into a ball, wrap it in plastic wrap, and let rest at room temperature 15 minutes.

On a lightly floured surface roll out the dough thinly, and with a 3-inch cookie cutter cut out circles. Place 1 heaping teaspoon filling in the center of one half of each circle. Moisten the edges of the circle with a finger dipped in cold water. Fold over the other half to make a half-moon shape and pinch the ends together to seal. Brush the surface with the beaten egg and sprinkle lightly with the sesame seeds, if desired.

Arrange the pastries slightly apart on a lightly greased baking sheet. Bake in a preheated 350°F oven about 30 minutes or until golden. Serve hot.

Makes about 36

VARIATION:

Omit the egg and sesame seeds. Instead of baking the pastries, fry them slowly in Clarified Butter (page 148) until golden on both sides and cooked through, or deep-fry in olive oil or vegetable oil.

Filo Pastry Triangles (M)

Boerek

These golden glories can easily induce unbridled gluttony! Before rushing to make this recipe, however, please read the entry for filo on page 74.

> 12 sheets filo pastry (about ½ pound), each 12 by 16 inches
> ¾ cup unsalted butter, melted
> Cheese Filling (below), or 2 recipes Meat Filling (page 234)

Cut the filo sheets into 4 strips, each 16 by 3 inches. Stack and cover the strips with a barely dampened kitchen towel to prevent drying. Remove the top strip of filo and brush it with melted butter. Place 1 generous teaspoon filling on a bottom corner and fold over to form a triangle. Continue folding in triangles the length of the strip. Secure the seam by brushing with melted butter. Place seam side down on a lightly buttered baking sheet. Repeat this procedure with the remaining filo strips and filling. Brush the tops of the triangles with melted butter. Bake in a preheated 350° F oven 15 to 20 minutes or until golden brown. Serve hot.

Makes 48

CHEESE FILLING

> 2 eggs
> 1 cup drained small-curd cottage cheese or ricotta
> 4 ounces feta cheese, finely crumbled or grated
> 2 tablespoons finely chopped flat-leaf parsley
> 1 teaspoon finely chopped fresh spearmint leaves (optional)
> Salt to taste

In a mixing bowl beat the eggs lightly with a fork. Add the cheeses and beat vigorously with a spoon until the mixture is well blended and smooth. Stir in the parsley and mint (if used). Taste and add salt, if needed. Cover and refrigerate.

CHAPTER 16

Desserts

Reception room of a house in Damascus. *From Charles William Wilson, ed.,* Picturesque Palestine, Sinai and Egypt, *vol. 1 (New York, D. Appleton, 1881)*

Money often has little attraction for a Bedawy, but when all efforts to obtain his assistance fail, one out of many means may yet be tried, and that is by offering to give him sweetmeats. "Helu" (sweet) is the attractive word for which the Bedawy always has an open ear; open a sack of dried figs, of dates, of candies, or, last but not least, of "Halawy" (that is, cooked sugar, or molasses, mixed with nuts), and see what a wonderful effect it produces! Antiquities are brought to you, parts of jewels even, anxiously hidden by a young Bedawi woman, are offered to you for some "Helu." It is the most favourite dainty the Bedawy knows . . . [1]

Sweets in Former Times

Medieval Syrians were inordinately fond of sweets and often indulged in them after their principal meals. Even those in modest circumstances concluded their repasts with some simple sweet such as dates, figs, *dibs,* or oilcakes. The affluent classes could choose from a wide variety of sweet dishes, among them *faludhaj, lawzinaj, zalabiyya, sabuniyya, sanbusak, taratir al-turkman, ma'muniyya, kinafa, qatayif, kul wa-shkur, mushabbak,* and *luqam al-qadi;* recipes for these and many more sweet dishes are found in the early cookery manuals.

Damascus was renowned for its sweets. Arab writers of the period refer to the northern gate of the city's Great Mosque as "the Gate of the Sweetmeat Sellers." Nabulus was known for a sweetmeat made with carob fruit and Baalbek, for one made with grape molasses, pistachios, and almonds called *al-mulabban.*

Many of the medieval sweets and ones descended from them were popular throughout the Ottoman era. Everyone, it seems, was enamored of sweets, as illustrated by the following account of Lady Hester Stanhope's pastry cook:

> He was an Arab, and spoke French remarkably well. He served his mistress to the utmost of his culinary as well as interpreting talents, during half the year or more, and was allowed for the remainder to wander forth, and turn them to account wherever his fancy chose. He was now established for some weeks with his son, a fine little boy, on this part of Lebanon, where

he supported himself, and made profit besides, by making and selling sweetmeats and pastry. His skill in this branch was by no means ordinary, if one might judge by the specimens he always took occasion to bring with him. . . . When he had ended his term of residence among the Druses, whose fondness for cakes and sweets is as great as all the rest of the Eastern people, his intention was to shift his quarters to another spot, where fresh customers as well as change of scene were to be found. The man was a true Arab in his penchant for wandering: the few materials and implements of his trade were easily transported on the back of a donkey, while he himself and his son walked on foot. On his arrival in the place where he intended to fix for a time, his small shop was soon hired, the fire of charcoal kindled, and pastry of various and excellent kinds was soon ready to be devoured by Christian, Druse, Moslemin, or Maronite mouths, for all were to be found in the course of half an hour; and his little boy was useful in carrying them about to those who did not take the trouble to seek them.[2]

Since the presence of a pastry cook of this caliber in the Syrian countryside was undoubtedly an extraordinary occurrence, most villagers had to content themselves with some *halawi* (sesame candy) and *mulabbas* (sugar-coated roasted chickpeas). On the other hand, the confectioner, or *halawani,* was known in all the towns. Besides baklava and *knafi,* he sold

> . . . pies and sweets as *mutababak,* made of a thin paste, almonds, and nuts, sweetened with honey or sugar, and folded together several times, as the name indicates, and forming a thick, luscious cake. The fellahin also make such sweets, but of coarser kind. . . . The *tamriyeh* is, as the name shows, made of dates, and is sold in small square cakes. . . . The *ma'mul* is a dry, conical cake, made of semolina, stuffed with pistachios, and sprinkled with dry sugar. This is also made at home, and figures at the meal of the principal feasts, especially at Easter. The *hallawy* is made of honey and sesame flour in large masses, and cut with large knives for sale by weight. There are different kinds of this *hallawy,* made with sesame seeds, and called *hallawy simsomiyeh,* or with nuts and called nut *hallawy,* &c. The *karabeej halab,* as the name indicates, are an Aleppo invention: oval cakes, about the size of an egg, made of semolina stuffed with nuts and pistachios, and drowned in a thick semi-liquid white sugar cream. It . . . is amongst the dearest of these sweets. The well-known *rahat el-halkom,* of Damascus manufacture, renowned as "Turkish delight," is sold in round wooden boxes. . . . Though most of those sweets are sold in the shops, all in one street, they are also retailed in the streets by men carrying them on copper trays, especially during the long Ramadan evenings, when night is almost turned to day, and when the savings of the whole year are so readily spent.[3]

All of the sweets mentioned above have remained favorites down to the present time.

Ottoman Damascus was a sweet lover's paradise. Skinner has described a popular Damascene confection, which was produced near *Bab Tuma* (The Gate of Thomas) and which is still eaten today:

> Among the whimsical works in the city and its neighbourhood, there is one carried on at this gate to a great extent: several men, with their arms bare, are pulling with all their strength,

for several hours a day, at what appear at first unusually long hanks of white yarn. I stood some time observing this scene, before I discovered that the cables were made of flour and sugar, which, when well kneaded together in this manner, is allowed to grow crisp, and sold as the favourite sweetmeat of the bazar.[4]

After a visit to Damascus shortly before World War I, an American professor who lived and worked in Beirut wrote:

> The intricate maze of the [city's] bazaars . . . presents scenes of marvelous variety and endless fascination. . . .
>
> As we pass along one street after another, we see . . . confectioners' booths filled with all manner of sherbets and jellies and delicious preserved fruits and the infinite variety of sweet . . . pastry in which the Syrians delight. In one little square there are great piles of thin apricot paste which look exactly like bundles of brown paper.[5]

Aleppo was also celebrated for its pastries and confections, with Armenians playing a major role in both their manufacture and distribution. Two of the city's numerous specialties were *karabij halab* and a soft, sweet, white almond paste imbedded with pistachio nuts. Among the many confections for which Tripoli was famous were candied fruits (especially oranges) and *jazariyya,* a sweet made with carrots. Today the best *jazariyya* in Lebanon is still made in Tripoli. European sweets must have been available in at least one Syrian city, for in 1861 Dr. Jessup writes of a Beirut confectionery shop owned by a Frenchman named Troyet.[6]

The Modern Era

Present-day Syrians, Lebanese, and Jordanians possess a vast collective sweet tooth and pride themselves on a dazzling repertoire of pastries, cakes, cookies, puddings, ices, ice creams, compotes, and candies. It has been said that for every candy shop elsewhere, there is a pastry shop in the Middle East. The Beirut of my childhood abounded in both Oriental and European *pâtisseries* boasting sweets of such exceptional quality that there was no real need for people to make them at home.

As a rule, rich pastries and confections are not eaten at the conclusion of a meal but are prepared for holidays, special occasions, and guests. The usual dessert is fresh fruit in season. In hot weather an array of iced fresh fruit is offered; during the winter months a compote of dried fruit or a bowl of dried fruits and nuts is frequently served, even in areas where fresh fruit is not scarce. Dried fruits and nuts may also appear as mid-evening refreshments along with coffee or tea.

Puddings based on rice, cornstarch, farina, or semolina are very popular. Fragrant with such flavorings as orange flower water, rose water, mastic, aniseed, or cinnamon and beautifully ornamented with nuts and fruits, they are not necessarily intended as a conclusion to a meal but are enjoyed when one is in the mood for a snack. They make excellent desserts, however, and some are even eaten at breakfast.

The population is passionately fond of ice creams and ices. The Arabs learned the art of creating iced desserts many centuries ago from the Chinese and, in turn, taught the Italians. Today superb French and Italian ice creams are produced in the region along with the local version, made with salep and mastic, which has a distinctive flavor and a consistency that is lusciously smooth, elastic, and chewy. I can still remember the sound of this ice cream being beaten during my childhood visits to the Suq al-Hamidiyya in Damascus.

In Beirut ice cream was avidly consumed at all times of the year. When I was growing up, the acknowledged stars of the city's ice cream scene were two sundaelike treats: a sublime *crème à la fraise* made with exquisitely flavorful strawberries and a "black and white" known as *chocolat mou* (not to be confused with chocolate mousse), a concoction adored by everyone I know who has ever tasted it. Many years ago an Italian friend of mine who was a brilliant cook and restaurateur in New York always used to listen politely whenever I exalted the virtues of this lavish temptation, although he was unable to disguise his suspicion that it could not possibly approach the standard set by his countrymen. Much later, upon his return from a business trip that had included a few hours' stopover in Beirut, he called me long distance to say that he too had become a convert to *chocolat mou*. It turned out that he had dashed from the airport into the city for the sole purpose of sampling this by-now-legendary creation and had found that it indeed lived up to its reputation! I have never come across anything to rival the *chocolat mou* of my childhood.

Superb ice cream could also be had in Tripoli, the sweets capital of Lebanon. Ice cream parlors, confectionery shops, and *pâtisseries* beckoned passersby with a galaxy of local specialties: alluring ices, including lemon, orange, black mulberry, mango, melon, apricot, and rose water; sublime ice creams, among them pistachio, chocolate, banana, apricot, fig, and prickly pear; tempting, opulent-looking chocolates, sugared fruits, and nougat-type candies in various flavors; exotic jams such as rose petal, bitter orange blossom, and pumpkin studded with blanched almonds; and tray after tray of *jazariyya, halawat al-jibn,*[7] *aysh al-saraya,*[8] and baklava, *knafi,* and other glorious pastries. The sweets of Tripoli were a delight to both residents and tourists, except for the agonies of indecision they provoked when it came time to make a selection!

One of my earliest memories of Tripoli (and an indelible one) has to do with the dark days of World War II, when British troops were stationed in Lebanon. I was only a small child at the time and had gone there with my mother to visit friends. After dinner we were taken out for a special treat of ice cream. Our hosts were about to order a second serving for me, whereupon my mother intervened, saying that since I had eaten enough sweets for the day and it was long past my bedtime, it would be inappropriate for me to indulge further. Just as I was resigned to my fate and had begun to lose interest in the evening, the waiter placed before me a tall glass of what must surely have been one of the fanciest productions in all of the Levant. This sudden and wholly unexpected improvement in my fortunes immediately banished my drowsiness, and I was about to pick up my spoon and dive in when my mother asked the waiter if there might be a mistake since we had not ordered anything additional. The waiter answered in hushed tones that it was not a mistake at all and that it had been ordered for me by a British soldier sitting a few tables away, who had a daughter my age back home. He did not know if he would ever see her again, and it would therefore give him great pleasure if I were to accept his small gift. "Madame, please do not refuse," the waiter urged my mother. On hearing the circumstances, she assured him that we indeed understood the soldier's feelings and would of course accept his gift. The waiter left our table, but in the meantime I had grasped the significance of the soldier's act. Overcome with emotion, I put down my spoon, my eyes filled with tears, and I refused to touch the celestial offering that lay in front of me. My mother now found herself in the awkward position of having to convince me to look happy and start eating when only a few minutes before she had so strongly forbidden me to have a second helping of ice cream! She gently explained that although she would have preferred that I not have any more, it was some-times necessary to do things that were less than ideal in order to lighten the pain of another person. This made good sense to me and alleviated my distress enough to enable me to comply with her wishes. Before leaving I was taken over to the table where the soldier was sitting with his comrades, shook his hand, and thanked him (not in English since I did not yet speak the language) for such a wonderful present. Although he could not make out my words, I felt certain that he fully understood the message that came from my heart.

PASTRIES, COOKIES, AND CAKES

Baklava
Baqlawa

A Bedouin, wild and fresh from his nomadic tribe, found himself once in Beyroot, and as he sauntered through the streets he passed a confectioner's shop, and stopped to gaze on it; the master invited him to enter and partake of some of the dainties. Nothing loth, he complied, and the master set before him a dish of *Baklawa* (Oriental sweetmeats). He ate and ate, and after thoroughly making way with the contents of the dish, he looked askance in the shopowner's face; the shopowner asked him if he knew what he had been eating. "No, *ya effendi*," says he, "but I suppose this is what I heard my father speak of as being the greatest luxury in the world, a *hummam*," i.e., a bath!!! [9]

When properly made, this most celebrated of Middle Eastern pastries is light and crisp, never soggy or cloyingly sweet. Despite its seeming complexity, baklava is in fact simple to prepare and makes an ideal dessert for entertaining since it can be made in advance.

Before proceeding with this recipe, please read the entry for filo on page 74.

NUT FILLING

2 cups finely chopped walnuts, blanched almonds, or blanched unsalted pistachio nuts,
    or 1 cup each walnuts and almonds
2 tablespoons superfine sugar
1 teaspoon ground cinnamon

PASTRY

1 cup melted Clarified Butter (page 148)
1 pound filo pastry sheets

SYRUP

1 1/2 cups sugar
3/4 cup water
1 tablespoon freshly squeezed and strained lemon juice
1 tablespoon orange flower water or rose water, or 1 1/2 teaspoons of each

Combine the filling ingredients in a bowl. Mix well and set aside.

To assemble the pastry, brush a 9-by-13-by-2-inch baking pan with some of the melted butter. Line it with half of the pastry sheets (trimming to fit, if necessary), brushing each with butter. Spread the nut mixture evenly over the entire surface. Top with the remaining pastry sheets, brushing each with butter. With a sharp knife, make vertical cuts in the pastry 2 inches apart and then cut diagonally into diamond shapes. Bake in a preheated 350°F oven 30 minutes. Reduce the heat to 300°F and bake 1 hour and 15 minutes or until the pastry is light gold, crisp, puffed, and baked through.

Meanwhile, prepare the syrup: In a small saucepan combine the sugar, water, and lemon juice. Bring to a boil over moderate heat, stirring constantly until the sugar dissolves. Simmer, uncovered and undisturbed, about 10 minutes or until the syrup reaches a temperature of 220°F on a candy thermometer. Stir in the flower water and remove from the heat. Cool and chill slightly.

When the baklava is done, remove it from the oven and spoon the chilled syrup over the hot pastry. Let cool to room temperature. Just before serving, cut out the pieces of baklava along the original lines and arrange them on a serving dish.

Makes about 40

How could a Beduin sleep with something sweet hanging over his head?
(The Beduins' love of sweets is proverbial throughout the Arab world.)

'Id al-Adha

> This being the vigil of the *Korban Byram,* or the Mahometan Easter . . . Lady Hester . . . despatched at twelve at night three servants, each with a *sennyah,* or round tray, on which they were to bring back from Sayda by daylight the *baklaawy, mamool,* and *karyby,*[10] three delicious sorts of sweet cakes, which are scarcely exceeded in delicacy by the choicest pastry of Europe.
>
> At noon, the servants, dressed in all their new finery, sat down to a copious dinner composed of the most luxurious Eastern dishes. . . . The day was literally abandoned to pleasure.[11]

This three-day celebration, the "Great Feast" or "Feast of Sacrifice," marks the end of the *hajj* (pilgrimage) season and is the last major festival of the Muslim year. Islam requires that all believers journey to Mecca at least once in their lifetime if they have the means and are physically able to do so. While there they must sacrifice a live animal, traditionally a sheep, hence the term *adha* (sacrifice). It is also customary for every other Muslim who can afford it to sacrifice a sheep, although a goat, cow, or even a camel may be offered instead. One-third of the animal is donated to the poor, one-third is served to friends and neighbors, and one-third is eaten by the family.

It is said that the caliph Harun al-Rashid and his wife Zubayda once made the long pilgrimage from Baghdad to Mecca entirely on foot. A castle with splendidly furnished apartments awaited them at every station of their caravan, and each day the road on which they walked was covered with carpets. For most everyone else in former times, the *hajj* was arduous and often fraught with peril, and many people who attempted the journey perished along the way. Now the faithful frequently make the trip by plane, but even this convenient mode of transportation can be subject to unforeseen delays and frustrations. During one sultry August in the early 1950s thousands of elderly pilgrims en route to the Holy City were stranded at the Beirut airport. Their travel arrangements, on which many of them had expended their life savings, had suddenly vanished into thin air at this point, and there seemed to be no hope of their being able to arrive in Mecca in time for the Great Feast. Then, almost miraculously, huge American C-54 military cargo planes appeared on the horizon, having been dispatched to the Lebanese capital from bases in Germany and Africa. Soon the pilgrims were invited to board these modern-day flying carpets and were transported safely to their destination.

Shredded Pastry with Nut Filling
Knafi bi Jawz

This stellar dessert is nearly as renowned as baklava and every bit as popular. In Amman one pastry shop alone bakes and sells some five hundred pounds of it daily! Like baklava, it is much easier to prepare than its elegant appearance suggests.

The merj *(meadow) by the Barada River, where pilgrims encamped before departing for Mecca. From* John Carne, Syria, the Holy Land, Asia Minor, &c., *vol. 1 (London, Fisher, Son, 1836)*

NUT FILLING

**2 cups finely chopped walnuts, blanched almonds, or blanched unsalted pistachio nuts,
    or 1 cup each walnuts and almonds**
3 tablespoons sugar
1 teaspoon ground cinnamon

PASTRY

1 pound *knafi* pastry
1 cup melted Clarified Butter (page 148)
Syrup (page 334)

Combine all the filling ingredients in a small bowl. Mix well and set aside.

Place the *knafi* in a large bowl and separate the strands with your fingers. Drizzle the melted butter over the pastry and toss and fluff with your hands until all the strands are evenly coated with the butter. Divide the *knafi* into two equal parts. Place one part in a buttered 9-by-13-by-2-inch baking pan. Spread the filling evenly over the pastry. Cover with the remaining pastry and press lightly with your palms to smooth the top. Bake in a preheated 350°F oven 45 minutes or until golden brown.

Meanwhile, prepare the syrup and let chill until ready to use.

When the *knafi* is done, remove it from the oven and spoon the chilled syrup evenly over the hot pastry. Serve warm or cold, cut into small (about 2-inch) squares.

Serves 12

Antioch and the Valley of Daphne

Knafi has long been a specialty of Antakya (historical Antioch), a town in the Hatay region of Turkey near the Mediterranean coast. Part of Syria for many centuries and Arab in atmosphere, the Hatay has belonged to Turkey only since 1939. With its pleasant location and climate, Antakya was the British consul Frederic Arthur Neale's favorite town. Its excellent fruits and vegetables, good mutton and fowl, delicious fish (especially eels) from the Orontes, and abundance of game from the nearby plain must have provided ample inspiration for the gourmet. In classical times Antioch was the third city of the Roman Empire after Rome and Alexandria and was renowned as a center of art and learning.

Only a few miles from Antakya lies the famous Valley of Daphne, described by ancient writers as the most delightful place on earth. In this small natural amphitheater between two high mountains, springs of cold, clear water burst forth from rocks and

View of Antakya (Antioch). From John Carne, Syria, the Holy Land, Asia Minor, &c., *vol. 1 (London, Fisher, Son, 1836)*

Site of Daphne near Antakya (Antioch). *From John Carne,* Syria, the Holy Land, Asia Minor, &c., *vol. 1 (London, Fisher, Son, 1836)*

run through lush verdure before coming together in two beautiful cascades, which fall into a torrent that rushes away to the Orontes. Aptly named *bayt al-ma'* (home of water) by the Arabs, this cool and refreshing spot was graced in antiquity with a magnificent temple consecrated to Apollo. Daphne was a sensual paradise where pleasure cloaked in the guise of religion exercised an almost irresistible temptation; Roman soldiers were forbidden even to approach the place! Although fire, earthquakes, and pillage have destroyed virtually all traces of Daphne's former splendor, much of its natural beauty still remains. Today there are a number of restaurants near the waterfalls, where one can savor *knafi* and conjure up images of the long-vanished Temple of Apollo,

> . . . its flights of columns casting their long shadows on the stream, the smoke of its sacrifices and clouds of perfume rising slowly over the groves, while over the cataracts slowly floated the music of many instruments, and the voices of invisible women.[12]

Shredded Pastry with Cheese Filling
Knafi bi Jibn

A great favorite throughout the region, this pastry is perhaps the most popular sweet in Jordan. It is a specialty of the Palestinian town of Nabulus on the West Bank, where it is made with the local sheep's milk cheese. Some people, however, prefer to use two or three kinds of cheese in its preparation. In Lebanon *knafi bi jibn* is frequently eaten for breakfast inside loaves of sesame bread *(ka'k bi simsim)*. It also makes an outstanding dessert.

Follow the recipe for Shredded Pastry with Nut Filling (page 335) with these changes: Instead of the nut filling, use 1½ pounds thinly sliced desalted *akkawi,** fresh unsalted mozzarella, or Monterey Jack; 1½ pounds ricotta; or ¾ pound grated fresh unsalted mozzarella mixed with ¾ pound ricotta. Serve the *knafi* warm, sprinkled with chopped unsalted pistachio nuts.

Serves 12

*To desalt *akkawi,* soak the slices in cold water 2 to 3 hours, changing the water frequently.

∾

To eat pastries, he is a camel; to carry loads, he is an ass. *(A)*
(Used to describe a lazy person.)

∾

Pancakes
Qatayif

Qatayif are small pancakes made with a yeast batter and dipped in syrup, spread with clotted cream, and sprinkled with chopped pistachios, almonds, or walnuts; or, they are stuffed with nuts, unsalted white cheese, or clotted cream and then dipped in syrup. Sometimes the stuffed *qatayif* are deep-fried in very hot oil before being dipped in the syrup.

These pancakes have been popular throughout the Middle East for centuries. Recipes for them are found in the medieval culinary manuals. The Abbassid poet Ibn al-Rumi (835–896) has compared the satisfaction he felt when eating *qatayif* stuffed with walnuts to that which his fellow poet and contemporary Abbas experienced when he found himself near his beloved Fawz.[13]

Qatayif are traditionally eaten by Muslims during 'Id al-Fitr (page 343) and by Christians during the Feast of St. Barbara in December. They are also a favorite wedding sweet. In the Middle East *qatayif* are almost always prepared with commercially made pancakes, which are purchased from bakeries and stuffed at home, and recipes in Arabic cookbooks usually call for these rather than homemade ones. Since I have yet to come upon a recipe that will produce pancakes that even begin to approach those I used to have in Beirut, you will not find a recipe for *qatayif* in this book. I have, however, included below a wonderful one for yogurt pancakes, which I think would meet with Ibn al-Rumi's approval.

Yogurt Pancakes

Lizzaqiyat al-Laban

In her memoir, *Legacy to Lebanon* (1984), Grace Dodge Guthrie reminisces about eating mouthwatering blackberry and yogurt pancakes made by her family's cook during summer holidays near the town of Dhur Shuwayr. I too find yogurt pancakes delicious and recall breakfasting on them during a stay at that well-known mountain resort. When I was a child yogurt pancakes were usually accompanied with honey, grape molasses, or jam, as they are today, but I preferred mine with pomegranate, quince, or sour cherry syrup, which must have seemed rather daring in such a tradition-bound society.

> 4 egg yolks
> ¼ cup sugar
> 2 cups plain yogurt
> 4 tablespoons unsalted butter, melted
> 1½ cups all-purpose flour
> 2 teaspoons baking powder
> 1 teaspoon baking soda
> 1 teaspoon salt
> 4 egg whites, beaten until stiff
> Honey or a fruit syrup (see Chapter 17)

In the large bowl of an electric mixer beat the egg yolks well. Stir in the sugar, then the yogurt and butter. Sift together the flour, baking powder, baking soda, and salt. Add to the yogurt mixture and blend until smooth. Fold in the beaten egg whites. Drop by tablespoons onto a hot, lightly greased griddle or heavy skillet, turning to brown on both sides. Serve at once with honey.

Serves 6

Fritters in Syrup

Awwaymat

Variations of this age-old favorite are found all over the Middle East and along the Mediterranean. Similar fritters, known as *zalabiyya* and *mushabbak,* are also popular. Different batters and flavorings exist for these crisp and puffy treats, which are made in a variety of shapes, including strips, rosettes, pretzels, or little balls as described below.

Awwaymat and its relatives are cooked to order by street vendors and in many shops which specialize in them. Although avidly consumed throughout the year, they are particularly favored during Muslim festivals. Among Christians they are traditional for the Feast of Epiphany (*al-Ghtaas*). In the past, grape molasses was sometimes substituted for the syrup called for in modern recipes. In his moving autobiography, *A Far Journey*

(1914), the Reverend Abraham Mitrie Rihbany has recorded his enthusiasm for these fritters:

> The material feast of Epiphany was *zulabiah* (fried cakes of the doughnut variety). I do not remember that I ever was unwilling to do any errand for my mother which served to further the cause of "frying" on that sacred occasion. The *zulabiah* must be fried in pure olive oil over a fire of olive wood, whenever it could be obtained, for the olive is the most sacred among the trees. It was supreme joy to me to feed the fire while my mother fried the cakes, to see the bars, coils, and balls of dough swell and sizzle in the hot oil, and to watch my mother take them out of the frying-pan, brown and hissing, and drop them into a large basin of grape molasses. A choice quantity of *zulabiah* we gave to the priest, when he came with his attendant on Epiphany day and sprinkled holy water at the door and in the four corners of the house, with an olive branch tied to a small cross.

2 recipes Syrup (page 334)

1 package active dry yeast

Pinch sugar

1½ cups warm water (approximately) (about 110° F)

3 cups all-purpose flour, sifted with 1 teaspoon salt if desired

½ cup milk

Olive oil or vegetable oil for deep-frying

2 tablespoons confectioners' sugar

½ teaspoon ground cinnamon, or to taste

Prepare the syrup and let chill until ready to use. In the large bowl of an electric mixer dissolve the yeast and sugar in ¼ cup of the water. Set aside in a warm, draft-free place about 5 minutes. Add the flour alternately with the milk and 1 cup of the remaining water and beat vigorously until the mixture forms a thick liquid batter (a little thicker than pancake batter) and is well blended and smooth. If it is too thick, add the remaining water, a tablespoon at a time, until the desired consistency is reached. Cover the bowl and let stand in a warm, draft-free place 30 minutes. Beat the batter vigorously again and let it rest for another 30 minutes.

In a deep-fryer or heavy saucepan heat 2 inches of oil over moderate heat to 375° F. Beat the batter once again. Drop 1 teaspoon of the batter at a time into the hot oil, being careful not to crowd the pan. Fry the fritters, turning them, until they are golden brown on all sides. As each batch is done, transfer the fritters with a slotted spoon to paper towels to drain. Dip them in the cold syrup while they are still very hot. Mound on a platter, sift the confectioners' sugar mixed with the cinnamon evenly over the tops, and serve.

Serves 8

Stuffed Cookies
Ma'mul

For Marcel Proust it was madeleines; for me it is these splendid cookies, dearly loved throughout the region. *Ma'mul* can have a variety of shapes and fillings, and the dough is sometimes made with semolina instead of flour, or a combination of both may be used.

For many Christians Easter would not be complete without a tray of nut-filled *ma'mul*. These cookies also reign supreme during the Muslim *Ramadan* and *'Id al-Fitr*. When I lived in Lebanon excellent *ma'mul* could be bought from bakeries and pastry shops, as it can be today. There was, in fact, a bakery that specialized in *ma'mul* close to our apartment, and I would often be dispatched to fetch a supply. Upon entering the premises I would be enveloped by the irresistible aroma of the cookies baking in the large oven, a pleasure that was surpassed only by their flavor. The beguiling appearance of the *ma'mul* was an event in itself, for each cookie was pressed into a decorative wooden mold called a *tabi* before baking, giving the cookie an ornate surface design. If you do not own one of these molds, you can decorate the tops of the cookies with tweezers or the tines of a fork.

> 3 ⅓ cups all-purpose flour
>
> 2 tablespoons superfine sugar
>
> 1 cup unsalted butter, at room temperature
>
> 2 tablespoons orange flower water or rose water, or 1 tablespoon of each
>
> 1 tablespoon milk or water, or as needed
>
> Nut Filling or Date Filling (below)
>
> Confectioners' sugar

In a large bowl mix the flour and sugar and rub in the butter. Add the flower water and just enough milk to make a soft and pliable dough.

Prepare each cookie as follows: Pinch off a walnut-sized piece of dough and roll it into a ball. Press your index finger into the ball to make a hollow and spoon a little filling into it. Bring the edges of the dough together and seal, making a ball shape. Gently flatten the ball slightly with the palms of your hands. Arrange the cookies on ungreased baking sheets and decorate the tops with tweezers, or gently indent with the tines of a fork (this will help the confectioners' sugar adhere to the cookies when they are baked). Bake in a preheated 350° F oven about 25 minutes or until the bottoms of the cookies are pale gold. Do not allow the cookies to brown.

With a metal spatula, carefully transfer the cookies onto wire racks set over wax paper and let cool. Just before serving, sift the confectioners' sugar liberally over the cookies.

Makes about 36

Note: To shape the *ma'mul* in a *tabi,* dust the mold with flour. Invert the mold and tap gently to remove any excess flour. Make a filled ball of dough that will be large enough to fit snugly inside the mold and press it in gently, leveling it off evenly with the lip. Invert the mold over an ungreased baking sheet and tap it to release the cookie, design side up.

Nut Filling

1 ½ cups finely chopped walnuts, blanched almonds, or blanched unsalted pistachio
   nuts
⅓ cup superfine sugar
2 tablespoons orange flower water or rose water

In a bowl combine all the ingredients and mix well.

VARIATION:

Use walnuts rather than almonds or pistachio nuts and add ¾ teaspoon ground cinnamon.

Date Filling

¾ pound pitted dates (a soft variety), chopped
2 tablespoons water, or as needed
1 tablespoon orange flower water
½ teaspoon ground cinnamon

In a food processor blend all the ingredients to a paste, adding more water if necessary.

VARIATION:

In a small, heavy saucepan combine the dates, water, and 2 tablespoons unsalted butter. Cook over low heat, stirring and mashing the dates until they form a paste. Stir in the orange flower water and cinnamon. Allow to cool.

Ramadan and 'Id al-Fitr

Writing about *ma'mul* brings back memories of a visit I made as a teenager to Tripoli, Lebanon's second city, while the fast of *Ramadan* and *'Id al-Fitr,* one of Islam's most important festivals, was in progress. I must have consumed more of these cookies on that particular occasion than at any other time in my life!

Ramadan is the ninth month of the Muslim calendar, in which Muhammad experienced the revelation of the Koran. During this month Muslims must abstain completely from food and drink between dawn (according to the Koran, when a white thread can be clearly distinguished from a black one) and sunset. In the past, cannons were fired to signal the beginning and end of each day's fasting period. Today the times are more likely to be announced on radio and television.

Since the Muslim calendar is a lunar one, the Fast of *Ramadan* falls eleven days earlier in each successive year of our Western (Gregorian) calendar. When it occurs during the summer it places a great strain on the population, owing to the increased hours of daylight and, in parts of the region, the very hot temperatures. The routine during *Ramadan* is to take a meal, the *suhur*, before dawn. In summer the fare is light and simple, but in winter it tends to be more substantial. When the signal to break the fast is heard at sunset, the cravings of hunger can at last be satisfied. The streets, no longer quiet, bustle with activity, shops and restaurants stay open late into the night, and people eat and drink heartily with their families and friends. Especially nourishing and filling dishes, all washed down with thirst-quenching beverages, make their appearance at the *iftar*, or evening meal. Sweets such as fruit compotes, puddings, baklava, *killaj*,[14] *qatayif*, *zalabiyya*, and, of course, *ma'mul* are enjoyed following the daylong fast.

For devout Muslims the Fast of *Ramadan* serves very clear purposes. One is to inculcate self-discipline, which is deemed necessary for proper submission to the will of God. Another is to engender in all Muslims, including those who are rich and powerful, a sense of compassion for the poor, who suffer from the pangs of hunger year-round. By having to experience similar, though mercifully more finite, deprivation, pious persons are reminded that they must show kindness and generosity to those less fortunate and express gratitude for the good things they have.

With the sighting of the next new moon the population breathes a collective sigh of relief. *Ramadan* is finally over, and the new month begins with general rejoicing. This is the time of *'Id al-Fitr* (the Feast of the Breaking of the Fast), a three-day holiday given over to celebrating, exchanging presents, wearing new clothes, and visiting and receiving friends and relatives. Among the well-to-do the afternoon meal on the first day of this *'Id* is a sumptuous affair starring a whole stuffed lamb or stuffed chickens. *Qatayif*, baklava, *knafi*, and *ma'mul* are just some of the traditional sweets enjoyed during this holiday.

Unlike larger and more heterogeneous Beirut, predominantly Muslim Tripoli underwent pronounced changes in its lifestyle during *Ramadan* and *'Id al-Fitr*. Throughout the daylight hours of *Ramadan*, the normally ubiquitous vendors who dispensed street foods seemed to have vanished, and the usually crowded coffeehouses were practically empty, with no *narghileh*s in sight. Following the *iftar* many stores reopened and conducted a roaring trade. The cinemas and coffeehouses were now full, and pastry and confectionery shops were overflowing with customers eagerly purchasing quantities of *ma'mul* and other sweets. Hawkers of *ka'k*, roasted nuts, cold drinks, and the like were vigorously making up for their earlier forced inactivity. It was as if, for these few hours, night had been turned into day. Inevitably one's thoughts were drawn back to that "Merchant from Mecca" who, more than thirteen centuries ago, first set this process in motion.

On the last day of *Ramadan* the signal cannon was fired at sunset announcing the end of the monthlong fast and heralding the arrival of *'Id al-Fitr*. Clothing stores, restaurants, cafés, ice cream parlors, *pâtisseries,* and candy shops were all thronged with customers long after their regular closing hours, and there seemed to be no letup in activity either on the streets or in most homes. If not out celebrating, many people were staying up all night cooking and making preparations to enjoy the holiday to the fullest. Getting any sleep was out of the question, and well before dawn the signal cannon was fired yet again to remind the citizenry that it was time to prepare to visit the mosques and cemeteries early in the morning before embarking on holiday festivities.

By dawn there were huge traffic jams as motorists and pedestrians made their way toward the cemeteries. Vendors selling *ka'k* were ready for them, as were those of greenery and flowers for the graves. A smartly dressed military band had stationed itself outside the Great Mosque to provide a ceremonial welcome for local and provincial dignitaries. For the next several hours it seemed as though half of Tripoli was heading toward the cemeteries and the other half heading away from them. By midmorning the cemeteries were deserted. The cinemas, with "Happy *'Id*" proclaimed on their marquees, were already open and filling up rapidly. Swings had been set up around town for the amusement of children, and the streets were alive with vendors peddling fresh fruit, confections, and sweet drinks. Around midafternoon whole families streamed out onto the city's boulevards to promenade in their new clothes. The feasting, visiting, and merrymaking continued for two more days in an atmosphere not unlike that of the Christian Carnival, before life in Tripoli resumed its normal course.

∾

The most delicious dish is "Fast and then eat."

∾

Stuffed Cookies with Natif Cream
Karabij Halab

The thick white cream (*natif*) for this Aleppan specialty is made with the dried root of the soapwort plant (*Saponaria officinalis,* also called "bouncing Bet"; see page 79). According to Dr. George E. Post, a professor at the Syrian Protestant College (now the American University of Beirut) during the latter part of the nineteenth century, soapwort grew near Aleppo and was cultivated for its saponaceous root, which was used in washing woolens (since it did not cause them to shrink) and in the manufacture of sweets. Besides being the foremost surgeon in the Near East, Dr. Post was recognized as the world's leading authority on Syrian botany. His classic work, *Flora of Syria, Palestine and Sinai,* seems to be unfamiliar to most writers on eastern Mediterranean cookery.

Although *bois de Panama,* the bark of the soapbark tree (*Quillaja saponaria*), can be used to make *natif* cream, soapwort root gives a superior result.

Prepare 1 recipe Stuffed Cookies with Nut Filling (page 342) with these changes: Leave out the orange flower water from the dough and omit decorating the cookies with tweezers or a fork. Instead of covering them with confectioners' sugar, serve them with a bowl of Natif Cream (below) on the side. Alternatively, just before serving, frost each cookie with a little of the cream and arrange the cookies on a platter. Present the remainder of the cream separately for those who wish to have more.

Makes about 36

NATIF CREAM

3 ounces soapwort root

2 cups water

1¼ cups sugar

1 tablespoon freshly squeezed and strained lemon juice

4 teaspoons orange flower water or rose water, or 2 teaspoons of each

3 egg whites

Rinse the soapwort root under cold running water. In a bowl soak the root in 1½ cups of the water 12 hours or overnight. In a saucepan boil the root in the same water over medium heat until the liquid is reduced to one-fourth its original volume (¼ cup plus 2 tablespoons). Remove the reduced soapwort liquid from the heat and discard the soapwort root. Strain the liquid through a fine sieve into a large mixing bowl and set aside.

In a small saucepan combine the sugar, remaining ½ cup water, and the lemon juice. Bring to a boil over moderate heat, stirring constantly until the sugar dissolves. Simmer, uncovered and undisturbed, about 10 minutes or until the syrup thickens sufficiently to coat a spoon. Stir in the flower water, remove from the heat, and keep warm.

With an electric mixer, beat the soapwort liquid until it becomes very frothy. Gradually stir the warm syrup into the frothy liquid until the mixture is well blended. Let cool to room temperature.

In a bowl, with cleaned beaters, beat the egg whites until very stiff. Add the cold syrup mixture very gradually, beating constantly until a thick, shiny, snowy white cream is formed.

VARIATION:

You can substitute this cream for the *natif* if neither soapwort root nor *bois de Panama* is available: Make a syrup as above, using only ¾ cup sugar and 2 teaspoons flower water. Combine 1 egg white and a tiny pinch salt in a bowl and beat until stiff.

Prosperous residents of eighteenth-century Aleppo. *From Alexander Russell,* A Natural History of Aleppo, *vol. 2 (London, G. G. and J. Robinson, 1794)*

Add the warm syrup very gradually, beating constantly until a thick, fluffy cream is formed.

Butter Cookies
Gh'rayba

> This was the last day I passed with Lady Hester Stanhope . . . and I drank tea with her. . . . There were three sorts of excellent rich cakes . . . *mamool, gharyeby,* and *baklaawy.* She asked me how I liked them, and, on my answering that they were delicious, she said I should find a chest of each sort prepared for the use of my family on the passage . . . [15]

These meltingly rich cookies may be shaped into diamonds, crescents, fingers, triangles, or, as suggested below, rounds or rings. The dough for *gh'rayba* is also used to make *sanyura,* a diamond-shaped cookie filled with unsalted pistachios. *Sanyura* is a specialty of Sidon, which is famous for *barazik* and orange flower water as well.

1 cup unsalted butter
1 cup confectioners' sugar
1 teaspoon orange flower water
2 ¼ cups all-purpose flour
Whole blanched almonds or shelled and blanched unsalted pistachio nuts

Jun, residence of Lady Hester Stanhope.

[Lady Hester] thought she would remain some time longer in Syria, where, looking down on the world from the top of Mount Lebanon, she might calmly contemplate its follies and vicissitudes, neither mixed up with the one, nor harassed by the other.

[*Charles Meryon*], Travels, *vol. 2.*

From John Carne, Syria, the Holy Land, Asia Minor, &c., *vol. 2 (London, Fisher, Son, 1836)*

In the large bowl of an electric mixer beat the butter, sugar, and orange flower water until the mixture is light and fluffy. With a wooden spoon, gradually mix in the flour.

Pinch off walnut-sized pieces of dough and roll them into balls. Arrange the balls 2 inches apart on ungreased baking sheets. Gently press to flatten each ball to make round cookies about 1 ½ inches in diameter and ½ inch thick. Press a blanched almond into the center of each. Bake the cookies in a preheated 325° F oven 20 to 25 minutes or until they are firm to the touch. Do not allow them to brown.

Remove from the oven and let the cookies cool on the baking sheets 5 minutes; then, using a metal spatula, carefully transfer them to wire racks to cool completely.

Makes about 24

VARIATION:

Instead of forming the dough into round cookies, roll into 6-inch-long ropes about ½ inch thick and join the ends to form rings. Decorate the tops with chopped rather than whole almonds or pistachios.

Sesame Cookies

Barazik

Both Damascus and Sidon are known for these addictive sesame-covered rounds, which can bring out the child in the most sophisticated cookie connoisseur.

> 1 cup unsalted butter
>
> 1 cup plus 4 teaspoons sugar
>
> 2 $\frac{1}{3}$ cups all-purpose flour
>
> 1 cup sesame seeds
>
> 1 tablespoon plus 1 teaspoon lightly beaten egg white

In the large bowl of an electric mixer beat the butter and 1 cup sugar until the mixture is light and fluffy. With a wooden spoon, gradually mix in the flour.

In a small bowl combine the sesame seeds, 4 teaspoons sugar, and the beaten egg white and mix well.

Roll the dough into balls the size of marbles and arrange them on lightly greased baking sheets. Press each ball into a thin round with the flat bottom of a drinking glass dipped in flour. Cover the top of each round with a layer of the sesame seed mixture, pressing gently so that the seeds adhere to the dough. Bake the cookies in a preheated 350°F oven about 10 minutes or until they are golden.

Remove the cookies from the oven and let them cool on the baking sheets 5 minutes; then, using a metal spatula, carefully transfer them to wire racks to cool completely.

Makes about 5 dozen

VARIATION:

Add ground cinnamon to taste to the sesame seed mixture.

According to the 1876 edition of Baedeker's *Palestine and Syria,* another version of *barazik* was offered for sale in the bakers' shops of the Damascus *suqs*:

> The *berazik* is thin wheaten bread, slightly covered with butter and grape syrup and sprinkled with sesame. The seller shouts "*Allah er-razik, ya berazik*" ("God is the nourisher, buy my bread"), or "*akel es-snunu*" ("food for the swallows," i.e. for delicate girls).

Wedding Cookies

> In summer time, when the marriages generally take place, the courtyards are illuminated at night with different coloured lamps, and nightingales in cages are hired and placed among the shrubs and trees . . . The dazzling diamonds of the ladies, and the various colours of their dresses, the lights, the singing of the birds, and the trickling of the water falling on the marble basins, make one fancy it to be Fairyland.
>
> . . . [D]uring the whole time sweetmeats and refreshments are passed round by the attendants, consisting of sherbets composed of syrup of roses, syrup of violets, syrup of cherries,

Roadside café in Damascus. The man in the foreground is selling the type of barazik *described by Baedeker, above.* From Charles William Wilson, ed., Picturesque Palestine, Sinai and Egypt, *vol. 1 (New York, D. Appleton, 1881)*

Eighteenth-century Aleppan musicians. From Alexander Russell, A Natural History of Aleppo, *vol. 1 (London, G. G. and J. Robinson, 1794)*

orgeat, lemonade, liqueurs, sugar plums, rahetlahalkoom, etc.; and following them come all sorts of Oriental cakes, differing from those in Europe.[16]

These heavenly cookies are very similar to ones offered at an Armenian wedding reception I was invited to in Aleppo, which took place in a beautiful courtyard not unlike the one described above.

1 cup unsalted butter, at room temperature

1 ½ cups confectioners' sugar

2 egg yolks

1 teaspoon vanilla extract

½ teaspoon almond extract

2 cups all-purpose flour, or more if needed

1 teaspoon ground cinnamon

½ teaspoon ground cloves

½ teaspoon baking powder

⅛ teaspoon salt

1 cup grated fresh coconut

1 cup coarsely ground walnuts

In the large bowl of an electric mixer beat the butter and ½ cup of the sugar until light and fluffy. Beat in the egg yolks and vanilla and almond extracts. Sift together the flour, ½ teaspoon of the cinnamon, ¼ teaspoon of the cloves, baking powder, and salt into a medium bowl. Gradually blend the flour mixture into the butter mixture. Stir in the coconut and walnuts and beat until the mixture is well blended. If necessary, beat in a little more flour to make a dough that is firm enough to shape.

Pinch off pecan-sized pieces of dough and form them into finger shapes, or flatten them into rounds. Arrange the cookies 1 inch apart on ungreased baking sheets. Bake in a preheated 300°F oven about 25 minutes or until barely golden. Do not allow them to brown. Remove from the oven and let the cookies cool on the baking sheets 3 or 4 minutes.

Meanwhile, in a small bowl mix together the remaining 1 cup sugar, ½ teaspoon cinnamon, and ¼ teaspoon cloves. Sift a ⅛-inch-thick layer of the mixture onto a large piece of wax paper and, using a metal spatula, carefully transfer the cookies to it. Sift half of the remaining sugar mixture evenly over the cookies and let them cool to room temperature. Sift the remaining sugar mixture over the cookies.

Makes about 60

∽

The man who is not hungry says coconut has a hard shell.

∽

The Ritual Bridal Bath

During the nineteenth century a bridal bath was a most important affair in the lives of Syrian women, being announced a fortnight beforehand, just as a ball was in Europe. In the year 1832 Madame de Lamartine, wife of the celebrated poet, was invited to spend an entire day with a group of two hundred ladies at such an occasion in Beirut honoring the impending nuptials of a young woman. Following is a rough and partial translation of her description:

> When the whole party was assembled, a wild music struck up. Women . . . uttered shrill and wailing cries, and played the fife and tambourin. This music never ceased throughout the day . . .
>
> The betrothed girl made her appearance, accompanied by her mother and her young friends. She was decked with such magnificence that her neck, arms, and bosom were completely concealed by strings of gold coins and pearls. . . . The fair bathers immediately fastened on her and stripped her one by one of all her ornaments and garments. Meanwhile, the rest of the ladies had been undressed by their slaves, and the different ceremonies of the bath commenced. . . . After the ladies had been steamed and washed . . . perfumed waters were poured over them, and then began the grand fun of the day. All at once the women began to splash about, throw water in each others' faces, and plunge each others' heads in the water, laughing and squealing like a troop of schoolchildren let loose to frolic in the

Levantine women. From Louis Charles Lortet, La Syrie d'aujourd'hui *(Paris, Librairie Hachette, 1884)*

water. . . . At last the watery diversions of the day were ended. The slaves and servants arranged the moist tresses of their mistresses, put on their necklaces and bracelets, and their silk robes and velvet jackets, spread cushions on mats placed on the wiped floor, and produced their baskets and silk wrappings containing refreshments. These consisted of all sorts of pastry and confections . . . with sherbet, orange flower water, and all those iced beverages profusely consumed by the people of the East. . . . Coffee, served in small cups enclosed in filigree vases of gold and silver, were passed round continuously, and there was animated conversation. The women dancers were now admitted and performed Egyptian dances and the monotonous evolutions of Arabia, to the same music as before. Thus passed the whole day; and it was not until nightfall that the revelers escorted the betrothed back to her mother's house.[17]

Almond Cookies
Kaʿk bi Lawz

In the past these cookies were among the sweets offered at the ritual bridal bath. They also were and still are enjoyed on holidays and special occasions.

1 ¼ cups ground blanched almonds

½ cup sifted confectioners' sugar

1 tablespoon orange flower water or rose water, plus additional flower water for shaping
    the cookies

In a medium bowl combine the almonds, sugar, and 1 tablespoon flower water until the mixture is well blended. Moisten your hands with additional flower water, pinch off pecan-sized pieces of the mixture, and form them into balls. Arrange the balls 1 inch apart on a lightly buttered and floured baking sheet. Gently press to flatten each ball to make round cookies that are about ½ inch thick. Bake the cookies in a preheated 350°F oven about 15 minutes or until they are set and barely golden. Do not allow them to brown. With a metal spatula, carefully transfer the cookies onto wire racks to cool.

Makes about 24

VARIATION:

Sift confectioners' sugar liberally over the cookies before serving them.

Orange Cake with Pomegranate Syrup ❧

This unusual recipe could be called a culinary hybrid since the cake is based on a recipe I developed for my yogurt book and the pomegranate syrup is descended from one found in my Armenian book.

½ cup unsalted butter, at room temperature

1 ½ cups sugar

2 eggs

2 tablespoons grated orange peel

2 tablespoons freshly squeezed and strained orange juice

2 ½ cups all-purpose flour

½ teaspoon baking soda

¼ teaspoon salt

1 cup plain yogurt

1 cup Pomegranate Syrup (page 384, Variation)

½ cup finely chopped toasted blanched almonds or hazelnuts

In the large bowl of an electric mixer beat the butter and sugar until light and fluffy. Add the eggs, one at a time, beating well after each addition. Stir in the orange peel and orange juice. Sift together the flour, baking soda, and salt into a medium bowl. Add the flour mixture to the butter mixture alternately with the yogurt, mixing until well blended. Turn the batter into a buttered and floured 9-inch-square baking pan and spread it out evenly. Bake in a preheated 375°F oven about 40 minutes or until the top is golden brown and a wooden pick inserted in the center of the cake comes out clean.

Remove the cake from the oven, let it cool about 5 minutes in the pan, then turn it out onto a rack. Pierce the top all over with a small skewer and slowly spoon the syrup evenly over it. Sprinkle the cake with the almonds and let it cool to room temperature.

Serves 8

Orange Coconut Cake
Gato al-Burtukal wa Jawz al-Hind

> My present residence . . . is situated in a very pretty garden filled with orange-trees, whose golden fruit I can pluck by merely stretching out my hand from the sitting-room windows.[18]

This is my version of a Lebanese cake, a childhood favorite of mine, that we used to make in Beirut.

½ cup unsalted butter, at room temperature

½ cup sugar

½ cup regular (not quick-cooking) farina

3 eggs

½ cup all-purpose flour

2 teaspoons baking powder

¾ teaspoon ground cinnamon

¼ teaspoon salt

¼ cup freshly squeezed and strained orange juice

1 tablespoon grated orange peel

⅔ cup grated fresh coconut

¼ cup chopped walnuts

¼ cup slivered blanched almonds

SYRUP

1½ cups water

1½ cups sugar

1 lemon slice

In the large bowl of an electric mixer beat the butter and sugar until light and fluffy. Gradually beat in the farina. Add the eggs, one at a time, beating well after each addition. Sift together the flour, baking powder, cinnamon, and salt into a medium bowl. Add the flour mixture to the butter mixture alternately with the orange juice, mixing until well blended. Stir in the orange peel, ⅓ cup of the grated coconut, and walnuts. Turn the batter into a buttered 9-inch-square baking pan and spread it out evenly. Sprinkle the top with the almonds. Bake in a preheated 350°F oven about 30 minutes or until the top is golden brown and a wooden pick inserted in the center of the cake comes out clean.

Meanwhile, prepare the syrup: In a small saucepan combine the water, sugar, and lemon slice. Bring to a boil over moderate heat, stirring until the sugar dissolves. Simmer, uncovered and undisturbed, 15 minutes. Remove from the heat and let cool slightly.

When the cake is done, remove it from the oven and prick in several places with a small skewer. Slowly spoon the syrup over the cake and sprinkle the top with the remaining ⅓ cup grated coconut. Let the cake cool to room temperature.

Serves 8

VARIATION:

Stir 1 tablespoon rose water into the syrup before spooning it over the cake.

PUDDINGS

Rice Flour Pudding
Muhallabiyya

> At about three o'clock . . . some black women . . . brought in dinner. . . . The tray was soon quite covered with the following dishes:—A small metal dish of fried eggs. A wooden bowl of lebben, or sour milk. A bowl of sweet cream made of goat's milk. A dish of very stiff starch, like *blanc mange,* sweetened with rose-leaf candy, with almonds and pistachio nuts chopped up in it. A large dish of rice boiled in butter, with little pieces of fried mutton all over the top. A plate of walnuts, dried fruits, and sugared almonds and lemon-peel.[19]

This classic pudding is distinguished by an elegant simplicity.

6 tablespoons rice flour
4 cups milk
½ cup sugar, or to taste
1 to 2 tablespoons orange flower water or rose water, or ½ to 1 tablespoon of each
Chopped blanched almonds and/or blanched unsalted pistachio nuts

In a small bowl dissolve the rice flour in ½ cup of the milk. In a medium, heavy saucepan combine the remaining 3½ cups milk and the sugar and bring to a boil over moderate heat, stirring until the sugar dissolves. Reduce the heat to low, add the dissolved rice flour, and simmer, stirring constantly, about 10 minutes or until the mixture is thick enough to coat the spoon heavily. Stir in the flower water and remove from the heat. Let the pudding cool slightly, then pour it into a large, heatproof glass serving bowl or small individual dessert bowls and let cool to room temperature. Cover and refrigerate at least 3 hours or until well chilled. Serve garnished with the nuts.

Serves 6

VARIATIONS:

Add 1 or 2 small crystals mastic, crushed to a powder with ½ teaspoon sugar, during the last few minutes of cooking.

Garnish the pudding with crystallized rose petals or violets.

Cornstarch Pudding

Baluza

Follow the recipe for Rice Flour Pudding (above), substituting cornstarch for the rice flour and water for the milk. Stir in ⅓ cup chopped walnuts, blanched almonds, or blanched unsalted pistachio nuts with the flower water.

Serves 6

VARIATION:

Cornstarch Pudding with Milk

Baluza Muhallabiyya or Muhallabiyya bil Nasha

Substitute cornstarch for the rice flour.

Fountain in a Lebanese village. From William McClure Thomson, The Land and the Book, *vol. 3 (New York, Harper, 1885)*

Spicy Rice Pudding
Mughli

Throughout Greater Syria the birth of a son has always been greeted with jubilation. In Lebanese villages of former times the news of this happy event would often be proclaimed by a drummer stationed at the front door of the lucky family's house. He would soon be joined by other villagers playing reed flutes, and the music would quickly fill the neighborhood, causing everyone within earshot to hurry over and congratulate the family on its good fortune. The more excitement the musicians could generate, the larger the tip they could expect.

The family would prepare great quantities of *mughli* in anticipation of a steady stream of well-wishers. They would also send generous portions to relatives and neighbors as a sign of thanksgiving to God for blessing them with a son.

The arrival of a newborn daughter, on the other hand, would not normally be met with the same enthusiasm except among the more broad-minded, as illustrated by the following account:

> A husband, anxious to be the father of a son, solemnly vowed that he would divorce his wife if she had a girl. Unfortunately, she had twin daughters. The poor fellow, however, really loved his wife, and racked his brains to get out of his oath. At last he solved the difficulty. "I said I would divorce her if she had a daughter, but not if she had two;" and so he kept her.[20]

The long-ingrained attitude of undisguised partiality to male offspring, exemplified by such Arab sayings as "Quiet reigns as though a daughter were born" and "May Allah be kinder to you next time," is still encountered and may be at least partially explained by the fact that a son carries on the family name while a daughter grows up to marry, leave her family, and take the name of another. Despite the outward preference expressed for boys, all children are cherished and regarded with affection, and a daughter is often referred to as "the flower of the house." The idea that a girl is capable of bringing as much glory to a family as a boy if only given the opportunity is a comparatively recent one and is far from being fully accepted. In the meantime, the drummer has disappeared and daughters have begun to make considerable headway.

In the past visitors who came to see a newborn baby girl were usually welcomed not with *mughli* pudding but with a humbler though no less delicious offering of *mughli* tea (page 399). Nowadays, however, depending on the community, either *mughli* pudding or *mughli* tea may be served to celebrate the birth of any baby, whether boy or girl.

1 piece dried gingerroot, about 1 inch long

7 cups water

1 cup rice flour

1 cup sugar, or more to taste

1 teaspoon ground caraway seeds

1 teaspoon ground aniseed

1 teaspoon ground cinnamon

1 teaspoon ground fennel seeds, or ½ teaspoon ground cloves (optional)

Mixed nuts (choose from blanched almonds, hazelnuts, walnut halves, unsalted
    pistachio nuts, and pine nuts)

Shredded fresh coconut

In a small saucepan bring the gingerroot and 1½ cups of the water to a boil over high heat. Reduce the heat, cover, and simmer 30 minutes. Remove from the heat and discard the gingerroot. Set aside.

In a small bowl mix the rice flour to a smooth paste with the gingerroot tea. Add the sugar, caraway seeds, aniseed, cinnamon, and fennel seeds or ground cloves (if used) and blend well. In a large, heavy saucepan bring the remaining 5½ cups water to a boil over moderately high heat. Gradually add the rice flour paste, stirring constantly with a wooden spoon. Bring to a boil again, then reduce the heat and simmer, stirring frequently, about 45 minutes or until the mixture is thick enough to coat the spoon. Let the pudding cool slightly, then spoon it into a large, heatproof glass serving bowl or small individual dessert bowls and let cool to room temperature. Cover and chill. Serve garnished with the nuts and coconut.

Serves 10

∾

Your son is yours, your daughter not.

∾

Whole Wheat Pudding
Qamhiyya

While encamped on the Syrian coast near Latakia, the Reverend Vere Munro was welcomed by a local sheikh, who furnished him with an excellent repast that included a pudding similar to this one.

> A large wooden tray . . . displayed an excellent pilau of kid, dressed vegetables of the size and form of "squash," a dish of sour curds, and a delicious sort of frumenty of well boiled wheat and raisins, sweetened with sugar, and flavoured with spice, in so judicious a proportion that the compote would have done credit to a scientific artist.[21]

Qamhiyya is traditionally served on the Sign of the Cross Day, St. Barbara's Day, and New Year's Day, as well as on the occasion of a baby's first tooth, when it is instead called sneniyya (teething).

1 cup skinless whole-grain wheat, soaked overnight and drained

5 to 7 cups water, or as needed

$\frac{1}{2}$ cup sugar, or to taste

1 tablespoon orange flower water

1 tablespoon rose water

$\frac{1}{4}$ teaspoon ground aniseed

$\frac{1}{2}$ cup raisins

$\frac{1}{2}$ cup coarsely chopped blanched walnuts

$\frac{1}{4}$ cup coarsely chopped blanched almonds

$\frac{1}{4}$ cup pine nuts

In a large, heavy saucepan combine the wheat and 5 cups of the water. Bring to a boil over high heat, then reduce the heat to low. Cover and simmer about 1 hour or until the grains burst open and become tender, adding more water if necessary. Add the sugar and cook, stirring, a few minutes until the sugar is completely dissolved. Stir in the remaining ingredients and remove from the heat. Spoon the pudding into a large, heat-proof serving bowl or individual heatproof dessert bowls. Serve hot or cold.

Serves 4

A peasant came down to the city. The only thing he wanted to eat was *dibs bi tahini.*

(In former times molasses mixed with *tahini* was practically the only dessert the peasant had at home.)

Semolina Pudding
Ma'muniyya

This pudding was a consistent winner with me as a child. I adored its homespun goodness and would request it for breakfast on chilly mornings. Medieval versions of *ma'muniyya* (probably named after the ninth-century caliph al-Ma'mun) are found in al-Warraq's cookery manual as well as in the *Wusla* and the *Kanz.*

1 cup sugar

2 cups water

2 teaspoons freshly squeezed and strained lemon juice

$\frac{1}{3}$ to $\frac{1}{2}$ cup unsalted butter

1 cup semolina or regular (not quick-cooking) farina

1 teaspoon ground cinnamon, or to taste

Clotted Cream (page 149) or whipped cream

In a medium, heavy saucepan combine the sugar, water, and lemon juice. Bring to a simmer, stirring constantly until the sugar dissolves. Simmer 10 minutes, uncovered and undisturbed. Remove the syrup from the heat and set aside.

In a large, heavy skillet melt the butter over moderate heat. Add the semolina or farina and cook, stirring with a wooden spoon, about 5 minutes. Gradually add the syrup, stirring vigorously, until it is absorbed and the pudding is thickened. Remove from the heat, place a kitchen towel over the skillet to absorb the steam, and cover with the lid. Let stand about 15 minutes. Spoon into a serving dish and sprinkle with the cinnamon. Serve warm with the cream.

Serves 6

VARIATION:

Substitute milk for 1 cup or all of the water and omit the lemon juice. Garnish the pudding with chopped toasted unsalted pistachios or toasted pine nuts and chopped toasted blanched almonds and walnuts.

Semolina Pudding with Cheese
Halawat al-Jibn

This sweet exists in several versions and is especially popular in Tripoli, Hama, and Aleppo.

Follow the recipe for Semolina Pudding (above) with these changes: Stir 2 teaspoons each orange flower water and rose water into the syrup. Have ready 1 cup mashed or finely diced desalted *akkawi* cheese (page 339) or fresh unsalted mozzarella. Add a large handful of cheese and some of the syrup to the semolina and butter mixture and stir vigorously until the syrup is absorbed. Continue until all the cheese and syrup have been added (end with syrup since it will help the cheese melt) and the pudding is thickened. Serve at once, garnished with toasted blanched almonds, walnut halves, or unsalted pistachios. Omit the cream and cinnamon.

Serves 6

FROZEN DESSERTS

Milk Ice Cream
Buza al-Halib

This snow-white ice cream, made with salep and mastic, has a distinctive flavor and delightfully chewy texture. It is also known as *buza bil mistki* (mastic ice cream) and, when it includes cream, *dondurma kaymak* (from the Turkish *kaymaklı dondurma*), a term in common use when the region was part of the Ottoman Empire. A Damascus ice cream manufacturer recently told me that requests for *dondurma* are now quite rare, coming mainly from old-timers, and that they invariably elicit smiles from his employees.

When I was growing up, the tinkling bell of the *buza* vendor was just as welcome a sound to Lebanese children as that of the ice cream man to the children in America. The functional "cone" into which he packed his superb handmade ice cream did not look like ours but was rectangular in shape, making a filled pocket that was just as convenient to eat as a small pita sandwich.

Try this recipe, which is my own, if you can find pure, unadulterated salep. *Do not* substitute either cornstarch or arrowroot for salep in this type of ice cream, as some cookbooks recommend, since they will not produce an acceptable result.

> 1 tablespoon Turkish salep (*sahlab stambuli*)
> 1 cup plus 2 tablespoons sugar
> 4 cups whole milk
> ¼ teaspoon mastic,* or to taste, pounded with ½ teaspoon sugar
> 1 tablespoon orange flower water, or to taste
> Finely chopped blanched unsalted pistachio nuts

In a small bowl combine the salep and 6 tablespoons of the sugar. Mix well and set aside. In a large enameled or stainless steel saucepan combine the milk and 6 tablespoons of the remaining sugar. Bring to a boil over moderate heat, stirring until the sugar dissolves. Reduce the heat to low. Sprinkle the salep and sugar mixture over the milk, a little at a time, stirring constantly. Add the remaining 6 tablespoons sugar and simmer gently, stirring, 10 minutes. Add the pounded mastic and simmer, stirring constantly, 1 minute. Stir in the orange flower water and remove from the heat. Cool the mixture to room temperature, stirring constantly. Transfer to an ice cream maker and freeze, following the manufacturer's instructions. Serve sprinkled with the pistachio nuts.

Serves 6

*Mastic is *not* the same thing as gum arabic, with which it is often confused.

VARIATIONS:

Substitute 3 cups whole milk and 1 cup heavy cream for the 4 cups milk.

Substitute 1 tablespoon rose water or 1½ teaspoons each orange flower water and rose water, or to taste, for the orange flower water.

∾

He who has money can eat ice cream in hell.

∾

Pomegranate Ice

> Sometime along in the autumn there is often noticed a warm spell of weather which natives call *Sayf Saghir,* or *Sayf Rumman,* that is, *Little Summer* or *Pomegranate Summer.*[22]

A recipe for pomegranate ice in my *International Appetizer Cookbook* (1984) proved to be so popular with readers that I have included one here as well. This tangy, crimson ice can begin, end, or come between courses of a meal and will provide a dazzling accent to a holiday table.

> ½ cup plus 1 tablespoon sugar
> ⅓ cup water
> 4 cups Pomegranate Juice (page 54)
> ⅓ cup freshly squeezed and strained lemon or lime juice
> Fresh pomegranate seeds (page 56)

In a medium enameled saucepan combine the sugar and water. Bring to a boil over moderate heat, stirring constantly until the sugar dissolves. Remove from the heat and let the syrup cool to room temperature. Stir in the Pomegranate Juice and lemon or lime juice. Transfer the mixture to an ice cream maker and freeze, following the manufacturer's instructions. Serve sprinkled with the pomegranate seeds.

Serves 4 to 6

FRUIT AND VEGETABLE DESSERTS

Fresh Fruit Compote
Kumbut al-Fawaki

> Here is a modern Lebanese dessert.

> 2 cups water
> 1 cup sugar
> 1 tablespoon freshly squeezed and strained lemon juice
> 2 teaspoons orange flower water
> 2 teaspoons rose water
> 1 large eating apple, peeled, cored, and sliced
> 1 cup cubed fresh pineapple
> 2 small bananas, peeled and sliced
> 2 tablespoons raisins
> 1 cup fresh strawberries, hulled and halved lengthwise
> 2 tablespoons toasted pine nuts or blanched almonds

In a small saucepan combine the water, sugar, and lemon juice. Bring to a boil over moderate heat, stirring constantly until the sugar dissolves. Simmer, uncovered and undisturbed, 25 minutes. Stir in the orange flower water and rose water and remove from the heat.

In a large, heatproof serving bowl combine the apple, pineapple, bananas, and raisins. Pour the hot syrup over the fruit and let the mixture cool to room temperature. Stir in the strawberries and pine nuts or almonds. Cover and chill before serving.

Serves 6

❧

He lies under the tree and expects the fruit to fall into his mouth.
(Said of a lazy or inactive person.)

❧

Quince Compote
Kumbut al-Safarjal

If you have a passion for quince as I do, here is a splendid way to indulge it.

2 pounds quinces
2 cups sugar
2 cups water
1 cinnamon stick, about 3 inches long
2 whole cloves
1 slice lemon or lime
1 slice orange
Clotted Cream (page 149), Sweetened Yogurt Cream (page 144), or whipped cream

Scrub the quinces well. Peel, quarter, core, and cut into ¾-inch-thick slices. In a large enameled or stainless steel saucepan combine the sugar and water. Bring to a boil over moderate heat, stirring constantly until the sugar dissolves. Add the quinces, cinnamon stick, cloves, and lemon or lime and orange slices. If necessary, add just enough water to cover the mixture. Reduce the heat to low, cover, and simmer 1 hour or until the quinces are tender. Remove from the heat and let the mixture cool. Discard the cinnamon stick, cloves, and the lemon or lime and orange slices and transfer the quinces with a slotted spoon to a serving dish. Pour the cooking liquid over the quinces and serve hot, or cover and chill thoroughly before serving. Accompany with the cream.

Serves 6

Baked Stuffed Apples
Tuffah bil Furn

According to medieval Arab writers, the finest apples came from Syria. A recipe in al-Warraq's manual calls for Syrian apples, while another specifies apples from Lebanon.

Apples have long been a Lebanese specialty. The illustrious Abbassid poet Abu

Nuwas compared the bouquet of the wine he drank in Baghdad to the aroma of succulent apples from the Lebanon Mountains. Another great Arab poet, al-Mutanabbi (c.915–c.965), who resided at the court of the amir of Aleppo, cites three luxuries he enjoyed most: "her cheeks, Lebanon's apples, and Homs's wine." [23] When I was growing up, the towns of Meyruba, Bikfaya, and Ain Zhalta in the Lebanon Mountains, and Kassab and al-Zabadani in Syria, were all famous for their apples. Concerning the last, the American John D. Paxton writes:

> The town of Zebdane . . . is a most lovely spot . . . its flowing waters and rich gardens had powerful inducements to stop us . . . we met several muleteers with mules loaded with fruit . . . I was casting in my mind how we could induce them to let us have some . . . when the foremost muleteer . . . put his hand into his bosom, took out a handful of apples, and with a kind salutation handed them to me . . . I know that I have seldom eaten apples with a finer relish . . . [24]

Here is an adaptation of a dessert I sampled in Bludan that was prepared with apples from nearby al-Zabadani.

6 large tart or sweet baking apples

2 tablespoons freshly squeezed and strained lemon juice

6 tablespoons finely chopped blanched almonds or walnuts

⅓ cup raisins or chopped dried apricots

1¼ cups sugar

½ teaspoon ground cinnamon

1¼ cups water

1 tablespoon Pomegranate Molasses (page 57) (optional)

2 teaspoons orange flower water or rose water, or 1 teaspoon of each

Whipped cream or Sweetened Yogurt Cream (page 144) (optional)

Core each apple to within ½ inch of the bottom. Pare off 1 inch of the peel around the upper part of the apples. Brush the inside and pared sections of the apples with the lemon juice. Arrange the apples in a large shallow baking dish.

In a small bowl combine the nuts, raisins or apricots, ¼ cup of the sugar, and cinnamon. Spoon the mixture into the apple cavities. Set aside.

In a small saucepan combine the water, Pomegranate Molasses (if used), and remaining 1 cup sugar. Bring to a boil over moderate heat, stirring constantly until the sugar dissolves. Pour the syrup into the baking dish around the apples. Bake in a preheated 350°F oven, basting occasionally with the pan juices, about 45 minutes or until the apples are tender when pierced with a small skewer but still hold their shape. Carefully transfer the apples to individual dessert dishes.

Pour the pan juices into a small saucepan and boil over moderate heat until reduced by half. Stir in the flower water and pour over the apples. Serve warm or at room temperature with the cream, if desired.

Serves 6

Apricot Dessert
Mishmishiyya

> The air was loaded with perfume. The groves in which the apricot abounded were gay with blushing blossoms. The whole scene was one of fairy land bowers for princesses and gardens of delight for kings. Now we began to realize some of the stories of the Arabian Nights, and appreciate the descriptions of Oriental gardens. . . . [W]ithin the houses themselves, and outside the walls of the city, Damascus is magnificence.[25]

Many of the older homes in Damascus have inner courtyards containing fountains, gardens, and pools. Tranquillity reigns within these enclosures, where families take pleasure in the songs of birds, the gentle murmur of water, the rustling leaves of fruit trees, and the scents of jasmine, damask roses, and carnations. It was in just such a lovely courtyard that I had my most memorable encounter with this refined and delicate dessert. On that particular occasion it was made with apricot leather (page 371), but is also delicious made with dried apricots, as suggested below.

    1 pound dried tart apricots
    ¼ to ½ cup sugar, or to taste
    1 cup heavy cream, chilled
    2 tablespoons confectioners' sugar
    1 tablespoon orange flower water or rose water
    ½ cup finely chopped toasted blanched almonds or unsalted pistachio nuts

In a medium enameled or stainless steel saucepan combine the apricots with water to cover and bring to a boil over moderately high heat. Reduce the heat, cover, and simmer 25 minutes. Stir in the sugar and cook 5 minutes or until the apricots are very tender. Purée the mixture in a blender or food processor and pour into individual dessert dishes. Cover and chill.

In a chilled bowl whip the cream until it begins to thicken. Add the confectioners' sugar and flower water and continue to whip until the cream holds stiff peaks. Garnish each serving with a dollop of the cream and sprinkle with the nuts. Serve at once.

Serves 6

Dried Fruit Compote
Khushaaf

I have long harbored a special fondness for this compote.

    4½ cups water
    ½ to ⅔ cup sugar, or to taste
    1 cup dried tart apricots
    ¾ cup dried pitted prunes

Inner court of a house in Damascus. From Henry J. van Lennep, Bible Lands: Their Modern Customs and Manners Illustrative of Scripture *(New York, Harper, 1875)*

¾ cup dried peaches or pears, cut into bite-sized pieces

½ cup raisins

1 cinnamon stick, 2 inches long

3 whole allspice

¼ cup split blanched almonds

¼ cup blanched unsalted pistachio nuts

¼ cup pine nuts

½ cup fresh pomegranate seeds (page 56) (optional)

2 tablespoons chopped toasted walnuts

Whipped cream or Sweetened Yogurt Cream (page 144) (optional)

In a large enameled or stainless steel saucepan combine the water and sugar. Bring to a boil over moderate heat, stirring constantly until the sugar dissolves. Simmer, uncovered, 5 minutes.

Add the dried fruits, cinnamon, and allspice to the saucepan. Cover and simmer 15 minutes. Stir in the almonds, pistachio nuts, and pine nuts. Cover and simmer about 5 minutes more or until the fruits are tender. Remove from the heat and let cool to lukewarm. Remove the spices and stir in the pomegranate seeds, if desired. Spoon the mixture into individual compotes or dessert bowls. Cover and chill. Sprinkle with the chopped walnuts and top each serving with a dollop of cream, if you like.

Serves 6

VARIATION:

Substitute 1 teaspoon each orange flower water and rose water for the cinnamon and allspice.

Note: Dried fruits that have been macerated rather than cooked are also popular. For a recipe, see my *Book of Salads,* page 119.

Pumpkin Dessert with Walnuts
Shirini

Among my most vivid childhood memories are those of visiting friends whose large, two-story nineteenth-century stone house stood on spacious grounds atop a hill in an old residential section of Beirut. These friends actually consisted of two families; one, Armenian and the other, American. The Americans, Dr. and Mrs. Jessup, lived on the second floor of the house. Dr. Jessup was a descendant of none other than Henry Harris Jessup, author of *Fifty-Three Years in Syria,* to which I refer throughout this volume. Behind the house was a children's playground with swings and a slide set between a formal garden on one side and, on the other, a citrus grove that included citron, tangerine, sweet lemon, and blood orange trees. It was a delight to play there, especially in the spring when the sun-swollen air would be laden with the intoxicating fragrance of flowers and citrus blossoms. The grounds also contained a lonely *hammam* that had long fallen into disuse. Its empty chambers, pervaded by a soft greenish light from colored glass set in domed ceilings, bore silent witness to the gracious leisure of a bygone era.

It was not only the fine old house and its surroundings that made every visit to these friends an event. Nearby lay a walled Kurdish settlement encircling a large, open area. Looking down at this enclave was like viewing the set of a Hollywood "Arabian Nights" movie, so vibrant was its atmosphere and so picturesque were its inhabitants dressed in their colorful traditional costumes. Depending on the time of day, the courtyard was the scene of children playing, women cooking, and men singing, dancing, feasting, and fighting, for these were simple, ebullient folk who had migrated from their ancestral home in the wild uplands of Kurdistan to work as laborers in Beirut. The window from which I used to observe them was also a window into the past, for life in this camp still moved largely to a rhythm established in former times.

Although Muslims, the Kurds are not Arabs and possess their own distinct language and culture. The most famous Kurd in history was the gallant and chivalrous Saladin (1138?–1193), who grew up in Baalbek and Damascus and later became sultan of Egypt and Syria and the admired enemy of Richard the Lion-Hearted.

Here is a classic Kurdish dessert, which I first tasted in Beirut.

$1\frac{1}{2}$ **cups sugar**

1 cup water

1 teaspoon freshly squeezed and strained lemon juice

2 pounds pumpkin, peeled, seeded, and cut into 1-inch cubes

½ cup coarsely chopped toasted walnuts

Ground cinnamon to taste

Clotted Cream (page 149), Sweetened Yogurt Cream (page 144), or whipped cream

In a medium enameled or stainless steel saucepan combine the sugar and water. Bring to a boil over moderately high heat, stirring constantly until the sugar dissolves. Add the lemon juice and simmer, uncovered and undisturbed, about 10 minutes or until the syrup coats the back of a spoon. Stir in the pumpkin and simmer gently until it is tender and has absorbed almost all of the syrup. Transfer the pumpkin to a serving platter. Garnish with the walnuts and sprinkle with the cinnamon. Serve warm or at room temperature with the cream.

Serves 6

CANDIES

Childhood Excursions to Damascus

Lying between the Anti-Lebanon and the Syrian Desert, Damascus is set like a pearl in an expansive emerald oasis called al-Ghuta, a fertile plain whose luxuriant gardens and orchards are the gift of the Barada River, which springs from the mountains and flows through the city. According to legend, when Muhammad laid eyes on Damascus from a distance, he was so overcome by its beauty that he refused to pass through its gates, declaring that only one Paradise was allowed to man and that he chose not to take his in this world.

Like many travelers before and after him, Charles Greenstreet Addison was enraptured when he first beheld this most fascinating of Muslim capitals:

> One of the most magnificent prospects in the world suddenly burst upon my sight. . . . [I]t is unique, and will bear comparison with no other that I have seen. I called up my companions, and one after another as they arrived, they stood electrified by the charming prospect.
>
> Conceive our sensations . . . suddenly to find ourselves . . . looking down . . . upon a vast plain, bordered in the distance by blue mountains, and occupied by a rich luxuriant forest, of the walnut, the fig, the pomegranate, the plum, the apricot, the citron, the locust, the pear, and the apple, forming a waving grove more than fifty miles in circuit . . . to see grandly rising in the distance, above this vast superficies of rich, luxuriant foliage, the swelling leaden domes, the gilded crescents, and the marble minarets of Damascus, while, in the centre of all, winding towards the city, ran the main stream of the river Barrada . . .
>
> We feasted our eyes, as we descended, on the lovely prospect, and we all agreed that we had never beheld a view more striking . . . [26]

View of Damascus. *From John Carne,* Syria, the Holy Land, Asia Minor, &c., *vol. 2 (London, Fisher, Son, 1836)*

Damascus is one of the oldest, if not the oldest, continuously inhabited cities in the world. The proximity of Shtora to this legendary metropolis, with its many historic landmarks and modern-day attractions, made it possible for me to visit it frequently. No trip to the Syrian capital was ever complete without spending a few hours exploring its bazaars, among them the Suq al-Bzuriyya. Damascus has been known throughout history for its confections, dried fruits, and nuts, all of which are found in profusion in this *suq.* During Roman times dried damson plums and figs from this area were considered epicurean treats and were widely distributed in cone-shaped baskets as far away as Britain! Present-day successors to the dried plums and figs are crystallized fruits—dates, figs, pears, plums, citron, apricots, and loquats—arranged like jewels in great circular painted boxes, which are exported to different countries. Although during my visits to Damascus I would indulge wholeheartedly in Turkish delight, halva, marzipan, nougat, Jordan almonds, sugar-coated roasted chickpeas, spun sugar (cotton candy) called *ghazl al-banat,* and a host of other confections whose names I no longer remember, it was a generous supply of crystallized fruits, sesame candy, and, especially, apricot leather that I never failed to take back with me to Shtora.

Apricot Leather

Amardine

> Tall mud-walls extended in every direction under the trees, and rich flowing streams of water from the Barada everywhere bubbled through the orchards, while all was alive with the song of birds and the hum of bees. The great apricot-trees were laden and bent down under strings of ripe, golden fruit. The lanes were strewn with apricots. Asses, mules, and camels in long strings carried heaped panniers of these "golden apples." Walnut, peach, plum, pomegranate, pear, olive, orange, and even apple trees, crowded the maze through which for an hour we wound, till we found our camping-ground in a garden, one tent shaded by an apricot, the other by a walnut-tree, surrounded by pomegranates in full blossom, while a rill from the Barada ran past to cool our water-bottles.[27]

Damascenes are justly proud of the fruits cultivated on the great garden oasis of al-Ghuta, which nurtures their city. The apricots that flourish in this area are renowned for their exquisite perfume and flavor. The Syrian capital is famous for the thin sheets of apricot leather known as *amardine* (*qamar al-din,* or "moon of the faith"), which have long been a popular sweet both at home and abroad. Burckhardt, who saw this delicacy displayed for sale in the markets of Mecca and Jidda, reports that it was exported from Damascus to all parts of Arabia, where it was considered a luxury, particularly among the Beduin.[28]

In former times, at the onset of summer, peasant women in the Ghuta would push up their pantaloons to their calves and crush the apricots underfoot in stone troughs. They would then remove the pits from the apricot pulp as it was spread out to dry in the sun. Nowadays the process of preparing the pulp is accomplished with modern machinery. First the fruit is washed and the pits are mechanically removed. Then the flesh is puréed and spread thinly on trays to dry outdoors.

In Damascus and elsewhere in the region, this type of confection is made from many different kinds of fruits besides apricots, such as apples, cherries, grapes, mulberries, peaches, and plums, but that made from apricots is the most popular. Although apricot leather imported from Damascus can be found in Middle Eastern groceries in this country, I have yet to find a brand that even begins to approach the *amardine* of my childhood. A similar domestic product known as fruit roll is available in a variety of flavors in many supermarkets and specialty foods shops. This age-old sweet can also be prepared at home. Make it in dry, sunny weather, preferably in the morning.

Amardine is delicious simply eaten on its own. It can also be soaked several hours in water, mashed or blended until dissolved, sweetened to taste, and chilled to make either a drink or a breakfast dish. Small pieces of *amardine* are sometimes used to flavor soups, stews, and ice cream. They are also good dipped in beaten egg and fried (see my *Cuisine of Armenia* for a recipe).

4 cups peeled, pitted, and sliced apricots (about 2 pounds)

¼ cup superfine sugar, or to taste

Line 2 large rimmed baking sheets with clear plastic wrap and secure the edges with tape. In a food processor or blender purée the apricots with the sugar until the mixture is very smooth. Pour half of the purée onto each baking sheet and spread it about $\frac{1}{8}$ inch thick. Cover the baking sheets with cheesecloth to protect the fruit from insects and dust while it dries and fasten with tape to prevent the cloth from touching the purée. Set the baking sheets outdoors in full sunlight until the purée is dry enough that it can be peeled off easily from the plastic wrap in one piece but not so dry that it cracks. The amount of time needed for drying depends on the sun's heat. If the purée is not dry by the end of the first day, bring the sheets indoors overnight and return to the sun the next morning to complete drying. Toward the end of drying, check frequently and do not allow the fruit to overdry. Roll up each sheet of apricot leather, still on the plastic wrap, and twist the plastic ends to seal. Wrap with an additional piece of plastic.

Apricot leather can be stored in a cool, dry, dark place at room temperature up to 1 month, in the refrigerator 3 to 4 months, or in the freezer up to 1 year.

Makes 2 sheets

Note: In humid climates it may be necessary to complete the drying indoors. Place the baking sheets in a preheated 150°F oven and leave the oven door ajar.

VARIATION:

For thinner apricot leather, spread the purée to $\frac{1}{16}$-inch thickness; for thicker leather, to $\frac{1}{4}$-inch thickness.

Apple Leather

North of the Syrian port of Latakia lies Jabal al-Aqra (Mt. Cassius), a beautiful spot with magnificent views. On its scenic slopes is the town of Kassab, inhabited by Armenians for over five hundred years. They raise livestock and cultivate cereals and fruits, especially sweet and succulent grapes and crisp apples that are among the finest I have ever tasted.

Apple leather was a specialty of an Armenian family of our acquaintance from Kassab.

Follow the recipe for Apricot Leather (above) with these changes: Substitute 4 cups cored, peeled, and sliced juicy apples, such as Gravensteins, for the apricots. Purée with 1 to 2 tablespoons freshly squeezed and strained lemon juice, $\frac{1}{4}$ cup superfine sugar, or to taste, $\frac{1}{4}$ teaspoon ground cinnamon (optional), and a little apple juice if the mixture is too thick to spread.

Makes 2 sheets

Jabal al-Aqra (Mt. Cassius), from the Mediterranean. From John Carne, Syria, the Holy Land, Asia Minor, &c., *vol. 1 (London, Fisher, Son, 1836)*

Plum Leather

The village and winter ski resort of Faraya is built on the slopes of Mt. Sannin in the Kisrawan region of Lebanon. Picturesque limestone outcroppings in the shapes of sugar loaves, mushrooms, half-domes, and other fantastic forms thrust themselves upward amid the houses, fields, and orchards of the surrounding countryside, giving it the appearance of a fairy wonderland. Among Faraya's attractions are a spectacular stone bridge that spans the Nahr al-Laban (River of Milk). The curve of this bridge is so regular and clean that one can scarcely believe that it is entirely natural.

Family friends in Beirut who spent their summers in Faraya used to make a confection much like this one with the excellent local plums.

Follow the recipe for Apricot Leather (page 371) with these changes: Substitute 3 cups sliced pitted plums (choose a variety with firm flesh such as Mariposa, Nubiana, or Santa Rosa) for the apricots. Purée with 1 to 2 tablespoons freshly squeezed and strained lemon juice and ¼ cup superfine sugar, or to taste.

Makes 2 sheets

With patience sour grapes become sweetmeat and mulberry leaves become silk.

The chasm of the Neba al-Laban. *From Charles William Wilson, ed.,* Picturesque Palestine, Sinai and Egypt, *vol. 2 (New York, D. Appleton, 1883)*

Stuffed Dates

Tamar Mahshi

> The many different uses to which almost every part of the date-tree is applied . . . render it as dear to the settled Arab, as the camel is to the Beduin. Mohammed, in one of the sayings recorded of him, compares the virtuous and generous man to this noble tree. "He stands erect before his Lord; in his every action he follows the impulse received from above, and his whole life is devoted to the welfare of his fellow-creatures."[29]

1 cup toasted blanched almonds or unsalted pistachio nuts

¼ cup confectioners' sugar

1 tablespoon rose water or orange flower water, or more if needed

8 ounces dried pitted dates

Combine the nuts and sugar in a blender or food processor and blend until the nuts are pulverized. With the back of a spoon, rub the mixture through a fine sieve into a small bowl. Stir in the rose or orange flower water and beat well until the mixture forms a smooth paste, adding more flower water if necessary.

With a small knife, cut a slit about 1 inch long and ½ inch deep in the side of each date. Stuff about 1 teaspoon of the nut paste into the slit and press the edges of the slit together to enclose the filling. Store the stuffed dates in an airtight container lined with wax paper, placing wax paper between the layers.

Makes about 24

Jews of Beirut. From Louis Charles Lortet, La Syrie d'aujourd'hui *(Paris, Librairie Hachette, 1884)*

Sesame Candies
Simsimiyya

In Beirut I used to buy this type of candy at a confectionery shop owned by a Jewish gentleman. It was not only the stupendous selection of both Middle Eastern and European sweets that made visiting his store so enjoyable. In addition to shelf after shelf of candies lining the walls, there stood on the floor a huge lazy Susan whose many compartments were filled with a myriad of mouthwatering temptations. I would point to whichever candy I wished to purchase and the owner, who sat at one side of the lazy Susan, would depress a pedal with his foot, causing the tray to revolve slowly. He would stop the tray so that my selection lay directly in front of him. Then, without leaving his seat, he would measure out my desired amount and weigh it on his scale.

It is interesting to note that Jews have historically been fond of sweets and have often pursued the trade of confectioner in Islamic lands. The introduction of sugarcane during the early Middle Ages gave rise to a great industry, in which Jews played a leading role; indeed some Jews today retain family names of Sugar and Sugarman. In the medieval Arab world Jews were known not only for their confectionery but for their cooking in general, as attested to by the well-known maxim, "Sleep in a Christian bed and enjoy Jewish food."

These candies are simple to prepare and are best attempted in cool, dry weather.

2 cups sesame seeds

$\frac{1}{2}$ cup chopped nuts (blanched almonds, walnuts, or raw peanuts)

$\frac{1}{2}$ cup honey

$\frac{1}{2}$ cup sugar

$\frac{1}{2}$ teaspoon ground cinnamon (optional)

Spread the sesame seeds and nuts in a single layer on a rimmed baking sheet. Toast in a preheated 350°F oven, stirring occasionally, about 15 minutes or until they are lightly golden. Transfer them to a bowl and set aside.

In a large, heavy skillet combine the honey, sugar, and cinnamon (if used). Bring the mixture to a boil over moderate heat, stirring constantly, and cook 2 minutes. Remove the skillet from the heat and stir in the sesame seeds and nuts. Mix well. Turn the mixture into a buttered 9-by-13-inch baking dish. Using a large buttered spoon, press the mixture firmly and evenly over the bottom. Let the candy cool in the pan until it is firm enough to be cut but is still warm and pliable. Run a spatula around the edge of the candy to loosen it, then lift it out of the pan onto a cutting surface. With a sharp knife, cut the candy into 1-by-2-inch rectangles. Let cool 2 hours or until very firm. Wrap in clear plastic film and store in an airtight container in a cool, dry place.

Makes 48 rectangles

VARIATION:

Use 2 ½ cups sesame seeds and omit the nuts and cinnamon. This version is forever linked in my mind with the candy vendor who used to station himself at the entrance to the Wadi in Zahleh. We would always buy some *simsimiyya* from him on our way out after feasting on *mazza.*

CHAPTER 17
Beverages

Waterfall of the upper Barada, near al-Zabadani. From Charles William Wilson, ed., Picturesque Palestine, Sinai and Egypt, *vol. 1 (New York, D. Appleton, 1881)*

Water

The water in Syria is for the most part excellent. That found at Baniyas, however, acts aperiently; and the water of Tyre causes constipation. At Baisan the water is heavy and bad; while verily we take refuge in Allah from that of Sughar! The water of Bait ar-Ram is execrable; but nowhere do you find lighter (better) water than at Jericho. The water of ar-Ramlah is easy of digestion; but that of Nabulus is hard. In Damascus and Jerusalem the water is not so hard, for the climate of these towns is less arid.[1]

Although the above was written by the eminent Syrian geographer al-Muqaddasi over a thousand years ago, I personally remember many people who were just as particular about the quality of their drinking water. Indeed, Arabs appreciate water as the French do wine.

Lebanon is a nation of water connoisseurs. Spring water is especially preferred, not only for drinking but also for cooking and baking, and it is not uncommon for people to travel a considerable distance to a particular spring noted for its excellent water in order to obtain their supply. Names such as "Spring of Milk" and "Spring of Honey" attest to the high regard in which such springs are held. A village blessed with a source of good water is justifiably proud of the fact, and one of the greatest compliments a visitor can pay its *mukhtar* is to tell him how delicious "his" water tastes.

When I was a youngster, women in rural communities were entrusted with the daily task of replenishing the family's water supply. A familiar scene was that of young girls on their way to and from a nearby spring in the early morning or late afternoon, carrying water in earthenware jars balanced on their heads or shoulders. This ritual was not lost on the young village bachelors, who would make sure they happened to be around as the girls walked along the path. The young men would endeavor mightily to attract attention to themselves, while the girls in turn would put on a great display of feigned indifference. When electricity and running water were introduced into some villages, the former was welcomed enthusiastically but the latter was not always as quick to gain acceptance. In one Syrian hamlet the women and young girls refused to use the tap water and continued to troop with their jars to the local well as before. After all, one cannot get either gossip or romance out of a faucet!

In addition to being a favorite social center and trysting place well into the first half of the twentieth century, the public well in a village could be a source of friction, if we are to believe the following tale about the residents of Aley, an important summer resort in prewar Lebanon:

> It seems that the only public well in the village used to be the subject of frequent quarrels between the inhabitants of the upper and lower quarters. So finally the sheikh stretched a slender pole across the middle of the opening and commanded that thenceforth each of the two opposing factions was to draw only from its own side. For a time all went peaceably; but one dark night a zealous partisan was discovered diligently at work dipping water from the farther side of the pole and pouring it into his half of the well![2]

As in former times, cold water is always served with meals, no matter what other beverages are present. It is traditionally stored in unglazed earthenware jars, which, being porous, keep the water pleasantly cool by evaporation even in the hottest weather. Water, especially in rural areas, is often drunk from an *ibriq,* an earthenware jug with a handle and a small spout (glass ones are also often seen these days). The *ibriq* is held in an upraised position, and the water flows directly into the mouth without the lips touching the spout. This method of drinking requires some practice to master, and I remember how proud I was as a small child when I first succeeded in this maneuver without subjecting myself to an unintentional shower. Watching foreigners' first attempts at drinking from an *ibriq* provides a source of amusement for longtime residents, who find it as reliable a method as any for identifying newcomers.

Bottled mineral water, both local and imported, is quite popular, and there is stiff competition among the various brands. One importer, concerned about losing market share, mounted a whisper campaign to spread the fame of his product's alleged aphrodisiac properties. Sales soared!

∾

He carries water in a basket.
(Meaning: He is a fool.)

∾

NONALCOHOLIC COLD BEVERAGES

Some people may be surprised to learn that it was in Syria during the period of the Crusades that Europeans first discovered iced soft drinks called sherbets (Arabic *sharbah,* "drink," from *shariba,* "to drink"). In the Middle Ages sherbets were commonly offered at convivial get-togethers held in the houses of the well-to-do. The favorite drink during evening gatherings at the court of the Umayyad caliph Mu'awiyya (reigned 661–680) was rose sherbet, which is still enjoyed in Damascus and other towns.

Woman carrying a water jar in Baniyas. *From Charles William Wilson, ed.,* Picturesque Palestine, Sinai and Egypt, *vol. 1 (New York, D. Appleton, 1881)*

Sherbets continued to be popular in Ottoman times. These beverages consisted of fruit or flower syrups diluted with water; fresh fruit juices sweetened with sugar or honey and flavored with flower waters and, perhaps, herbs such as mint; or water sweetened with sugar, flavored with fruit juices and/or flower waters, and sometimes perfumed with musk or ambergris. Sherbets were served at parties and wedding celebrations, in palaces and prosperous homes, and in cafés and public baths. They were also sold in the streets:

> The vendor of refreshments plies his trade in the streets, carrying a two-handled, wide jar, with a narrow neck, or a vessel made of glass, on his back. In his hands he holds brazen cups which he rattles, shouting—"*berrid ʿala kalbak*" ("refresh thy heart"), or—"*itfi el-harara*" ("allay the heat"). These are the cries of the dealers in lemonade and *eau sucrée*. The seller of *jullab*, or raisin water, shouts—"*muʿallal, ya weled*" ("well-cleared, my child"), etc., while the purveyor of *khushaf*, a beverage prepared from raisins, oranges, apricots, etc., extols its coolness . . . Liquorice water and plain water are carried about in goat-skins by other itinerant dealers.[3]

During my years in the Middle East, the streets were still alive with vendors of sherbets. Although a large selection of bottled syrups was available in shops, many people preferred to make their own. Popular flavors included almond, apricot, banana, carob, sour cherry, lemon, licorice, mulberry, orange, pomegranate, rose, tamarind, and violet. A perennial favorite was and still is apricot leather (*amardine*) soaked in water, mashed or blended until dissolved, sweetened to taste, and chilled. Freshly squeezed fruit juice was sold at stands everywhere. Today one can choose from a wide variety of seasonal fruits such as apple, banana, cantaloupe, grapefruit, orange, papaya, pineapple, and pomegranate. People are also fond of lemonade and carrot juice.

For many Middle Easterners the most refreshing and healthful beverage of all is *ayran* or *laban*, which is simply yogurt diluted with cold water and lightly salted. For pop lovers there is *gazuza*, a soft drink made with soda water and flavored with fruit, and a variety of other carbonated beverages. In addition, the advent of the electric blender has enabled hotel, restaurant, and home "mixologists" to devise new and exotic nonalcoholic drinks based on the many kinds of fruits available in markets.

A fool threw a stone into a well, but a thousand wise men could not remove it.

Mulberry Syrup
Sharab al-Tut

∾

He who refuses mulberries will accept their syrup.

∾

Unlike the white mulberry, which has historically been grown for silkworm culture, the black mulberry, or *tut shami* (Damascus mulberry), is cultivated for its pleasantly tart fruit. During summer outings in the Bekaa we would often rest in the shade of immense mulberry trees, whose fruit stained our hands as we ate it. A tall, wide-spreading black mulberry tree occupied a favorite spot in our Shtora garden, affording a dense and grateful shade on warm days. As a child I used to watch with increasing excitement as the fruits gradually developed from a pale green color into large red berries that finally turned a deep purple, indicating that they were ripe for eating. We enjoyed our mulberries in the garden or at table, and we used them to make fruit compotes, jellies, syrups, beverages, and fruit leather. Our single black mulberry tree yielded more berries than we could possibly consume, and we were only too glad to see friends and neighbors carry away basketfuls of the fruit for their own use.

Beverages made with mulberry juice have long been popular. A recipe for *sharab al-tut* appears in the medieval *Kanz*. I remember Lebanese villagers keeping bottles of mulberry syrup on hand to serve diluted with cold water to visitors on warm days. When we made this syrup in Shtora, instead of adding lemon juice we would squeeze a handful of unripe, tart red mulberries along with the black fruit.

Fully ripe black mulberries
Sugar
Freshly squeezed and strained lemon juice

Put the mulberries in a cheesecloth bag and, wearing rubber gloves, squeeze the juice from them through the bag into a ceramic or glass bowl. Alternatively, crush the mulberries with the back of a wooden spoon through an enameled colander lined with a double layer of dampened cheesecloth set in a nonmetallic bowl, pressing the fruit to extract as much juice as possible. Discard the mulberry pulp. Measure the juice, pour it into an enameled saucepan, and add 2 cups sugar and 1 tablespoon lemon juice for each cup of juice. Bring to a boil over moderate heat, stirring constantly until the sugar dissolves. Simmer uncovered, without stirring, until the syrup is thick enough to coat the back of a spoon, skimming off any foam as it rises to the surface. Let the syrup cool, pour it into sterilized bottles or jars, and seal. Store in the refrigerator.

To serve, place 1 or 2 tablespoons syrup in a glass and add ice cubes or crushed ice and cold water to taste. Stir gently to mix.

As he lay under a mulberry tree on a hot summer day, Joha contemplated some enormous watermelons that were growing nearby. "Why is it," he asked himself, "that such a huge tree as this produces only tiny and insignificant fruits while that lowly vine brings forth luscious, gigantic melons?"

As he was puzzling over this seeming contradiction, a mulberry fell down from the tree and struck him on the head. "Aha!" exclaimed Joha. "Now I understand!" [4]

Pomegranate Syrup
Sharab al-Rumman

Pomegranate syrup has been around for a very long time in the Middle East. A recipe for it is found in al-Warraq's tenth-century culinary manual. Writing in the 1850s, Sir Richard Burton relates that the city of Medina in Arabia was "celebrated for its thick pomegranate syrup, drunk with water during the hot weather, and esteemed cooling and wholesome."[5] In her book, *Domestic Life in Palestine* (1862), Mary Eliza Rogers describes her arrival at the home of the Governor of Arrabah in northern Samaria:

> My young guides, Selim and Saïd, ran before me, and cried out exultingly, "An English girl! an English girl! come! see!" I entered, and in a moment was surrounded by a little crowd of women, dressed in very brilliant costumes. . . .
>
> . . . They had never seen a European, and told me that no daughter of the Franks had ever entered their town before.
>
> They said, "Be welcome, oh sister from a far country, this house is yours, and we are your servants . . ."
>
> . . . One lady made some sweet sherbet of pomegranates and handed it to me.

This glistening, ruby red syrup possesses a very special flavor when made with the juice of sour pomegranates, sweet-sour pomegranates, or a combination of sweet and sour ones, all of which grew in our orchard. Pomegranate syrup imparts a lovely color and taste to a wide array of drinks, and I have discovered that fruits such as quinces, apples, and pears are enhanced when poached in it.

If the pomegranates you are using are very sweet, add enough freshly squeezed and strained lemon juice to achieve a sweet-tart flavor.

1½ cups fresh pomegranate juice (page 54)
¾ cup sugar

In a small enameled saucepan combine the pomegranate juice and sugar. Bring to a boil over moderate heat, stirring until the sugar is dissolved. Reduce the heat and simmer, skimming the froth, 5 minutes. Remove the syrup from the heat and allow it to cool. Pour into a sterilized bottle or jar, seal, and refrigerate up to 2 weeks.

To serve, place 2 tablespoons syrup in a glass and add ice cubes or crushed ice and cold water to taste. Stir gently to mix.

Makes about 1½ cups

VARIATION:

Use 1½ cups sugar and simmer 15 minutes. Stir in 4 teaspoons orange flower water or Grand Marnier to taste. This makes a splendid topping for pancakes, puddings, ice cream, cakes, and other desserts.

Rose Water Syrup
Sharab al-Ward

This syrup invariably reminds me of an afternoon visit to a fine old house in Damascus, where it was one of the refreshments served in exquisite crystal glasses that matched the elegant surroundings.

> **2 cups sugar**
> **1 cup water**
> **1 tablespoon lemon juice, freshly squeezed and strained**
> **Few drops red food coloring**
> **⅓ cup rose water**

In a medium enameled or stainless steel saucepan bring the sugar and water to a boil over moderate heat, stirring constantly until the sugar dissolves. Add the lemon juice and simmer uncovered, without stirring, 10 minutes, skimming off any foam as it rises to the surface. Add the food coloring and stir well. Add the rose water and simmer 3 minutes more. Let the syrup cool, pour it into sterilized bottles or jars, and seal. Store in the refrigerator.

To serve, place 2 to 3 tablespoons syrup in a glass and add ice cubes or crushed ice and cold water to taste. Stir gently to mix.

Makes about 1 pint

Pomegranate Lemonade
Laymunada bi Rumman

> In the cities of the coast, iced lemonade is sold for a cent a glass, cooled with snow from the summit of Mount Lebanon, 9,000 feet high.[6]

The Lebanese have a penchant for lemons, which thrive in groves along the Mediterranean, and are also very fond of lemonade, which is a favorite throughout the entire region. Over the years the coastal town of al-Batrun south of Tripoli has gained a considerable reputation for its excellent lemonade.

Lemonade is sometimes flavored with rose water or orange flower water and garnished with fresh spearmint leaves. We often flavored it with fresh pomegranate juice or strawberry, sour cherry, or pomegranate syrup.

> **1 cup freshly squeezed and strained lemon juice**
> **½ cup superfine sugar, or to taste**
> **4 cups cold water**
> **¾ cup Pomegranate Syrup (page 384), or to taste**
> **Ice cubes**
> **Lemon or orange slices**
> **Fresh spearmint sprigs (optional)**

In a pitcher combine the lemon juice and sugar and stir until the sugar dissolves. Add the water and Pomegranate Syrup and mix well. Serve in chilled glasses over ice cubes and garnish each drink with a lemon or orange slice and a mint sprig, if desired.

Makes about 5 cups

Iced Minted Orange Tea

> The Lebanese are excellent cooks . . . and their sweet desserts are notable. But there was something about New England pie crust and mince meat that my grandmother felt she had to do herself, and she did them to perfection. There was even a secret ingredient, and I was made a partner to the conspiracy. When the pie was ready for the oven, my grandmother would take me into the pantry, unlock a special cabinet, and take a black bottle from the shelf. She would pour a few dollops onto the pie, and turn to me and whisper, "This is from the medicine bottle for Mr. Bliss." . . . "Every day," she would explain, "I give Mr. Bliss a few drops of 'B' for his stomach." I always thought that the "B" stood for "Bliss medicine." Much later I learned that it stood for brandy, good medicine for my Puritan New England forebears, but it made wonderful mince pie, and supposedly prolonged my grandfather's life to almost 93.[7]

This passage, penned by Daniel Bliss II, grandson of the American University of Beirut's revered first president, provides us with some insight into the culinary habits of the Protestant missionary families who made up the American community of nineteenth- and early twentieth-century Beirut. These missionaries, who included Eli Smith, William Thomson, Daniel Bliss, Henry Jessup, George Post, and Bayard Dodge, were men of high intelligence and moral character who were graduates of prestigious New England colleges. They offered the local inhabitants the advantages of Western education and in so doing, made great and lasting contributions to the region. The Americans developed a genuine fondness for Lebanese food while retaining a love for the traditional dishes of their faraway homeland. For them breakfast would often be American; tea, British; and dinner, Arab.

Although in the Lebanon of my childhood the most popular beverage offered at garden parties was lemonade, I recall being served an iced tea similar to the one described below on more than one such occasion hosted by American residents of the city.

⅔ cup lightly packed fresh spearmint leaves, washed and drained

6 to 8 tablespoons sugar

Peel of 2 oranges

⅓ cup tea leaves (orange pekoe)

4 cups boiling water

1½ cups freshly squeezed and strained orange juice

2 tablespoons freshly squeezed and strained lemon juice

Ice cubes

Orange slices

Fresh spearmint sprigs

American Mission in Beirut. As a teenager I attended the American School for Girls.
From Henry Harris Jessup, Fifty-Three Years in Syria, *vol. 1 (New York, Fleming H. Revell Company, 1910)*

In a deep heatproof bowl toss the mint leaves with 6 tablespoons of the sugar and let stand at room temperature 20 minutes, stirring occasionally. Add the orange peel to the bowl and bruise the mint and the peel with the back of a spoon to release their flavor and aroma. Add the tea leaves and boiling water, cover, and let steep 5 to 7 minutes. Strain the mixture into a heatproof pitcher, discarding the spearmint leaves, tea leaves, and orange peel. Stir in the orange juice and lemon juice. Add some or all of the remaining sugar, if desired, and stir until it is dissolved. Let the mixture cool.

To serve, pour into chilled tall glasses filled with ice cubes and garnish each drink with an orange slice and a mint sprig.

Serves 6

Chilled Yogurt Drink
Ayran *or* Laban

Soothing and pleasantly tangy, this provides a perfect antidote to hot weather.

2 cups plain yogurt, drained to 1 cup (page 142)
2 cups ice-cold water, or to taste (depending on the consistency desired)
Salt to taste
Ice cubes
Fresh spearmint sprigs (optional)

In a deep bowl beat the yogurt until smooth. Gradually add the water, beating constantly. Add the salt and mix well. Alternatively, combine the yogurt, water, and salt in the container of a blender. Cover and whirl until the mixture is thoroughly blended and smooth. Serve chilled over ice cubes, garnishing each drink with a mint sprig, if desired.

Serves 3

VARIATION:

Add 2 teaspoons crushed dried mint, or to taste, with the salt. Omit the mint sprigs.

At home she has no tahn to drink, yet promenades in silk and mink. *(A)*
(Used to describe a vain woman. Tahn is the Armenian name for the above yogurt drink.)

HOT BEVERAGES

Coffee
Qahwa

> Over one of the dreariest wilds of Lebanon, the writer was one day passing, when a cloudy sky, a keen wind, and a miserable fog creeping upon every height, forest, and village, made the spirits sink and the blood run cold. The idea of comfort rose like that of an angel in the way. At last, a little hamlet presented itself near at hand; the path passed the door, and a young Syrian, in his light and graceful costume, came forth with a cup of excellent coffee: it was more precious than gold. He had probably descried us through the mist long ere we could discern his dwelling, and had instantly prepared the beverage: it was the berry of Mocha, hot, pure, inspiring, and quickly banished the misery from the frame, the sorrow from the mind: he smiled and wished us happiness, of which he was certainly the messenger at that moment.[8]

The coffee plant is native to Ethiopia, from which it was introduced into the Yemen, possibly in the fourteenth century. Just when it was discovered that a beverage could be made from roasted coffee beans is uncertain, but by the early 1400s coffee was being drunk by Yemeni Sufis to facilitate their religious devotions. Soon after, it began to come into general use in the Yemen, from which it spread north into Arabia and thence to Egypt and Syria.

THE COFFEEHOUSE, AN ARAB INSTITUTION

The growing popularity of coffee in the fifteenth and sixteenth centuries effected a marked change in Arab life that gave rise to a hitherto unknown institution, the coffee-

An Oriental café. From Henry J. van
Lennep, Bible Lands: Their Modern Customs and Manners Illustrative of Scripture (*New York, Harper, 1875*).

house (*bayt al-qahwa,* a "tavern without wine"), where the beverage was prepared and
sold. Although coffee was much consumed at home, where it became an important
element of certain social rituals, beginning in the early sixteenth century, the preferred
place to drink it was at a coffeehouse or coffee shop, and indeed it is likely that many
people first tasted it in a coffee shop. Taking coffee became a public pastime. (In traditional male-dominated Arab society, coffee shops and coffeehouses were the preroga-
tives of men, women being forbidden to be seen in such public places. Yet in the privacy
of homes, the consumption of coffee among women was as great as, if not greater than,
among men.)

   The Ottoman Turks embraced coffee with at least as much enthusiasm as the Arabs,
which has led some people to believe, quite erroneously, that the beverage was actually
invented by them. From all indications, however, one must conclude that both coffee
and the coffeehouse are institutions of Arab origin. According to the Ottoman chroni-
cler Ibrahim Paçevi (1574–1650), coffee, the coffeehouse, and all concomitant trappings
were introduced as a complete package to Istanbul around 1555 by two Syrians, Hakm
(from Aleppo) and Shams (from Damascus), who reputedly made a fortune in the
process.[9]

The setting of the coffeehouse was important. An attempt was made to create park- or gardenlike surroundings with flowers, trees, and running water. Some of the urban coffeehouses were built on a grand scale and were quite luxurious. Spacious coffeehouses were situated along major routes in the countryside as well, often shaded by great trees and trellises of vines and furnished with large benches. Russell relates that coffeehouses were found in all quarters of Aleppo, the better ones having a fountain in the middle and a gallery for musicians.[10] Beirut also boasted many coffeehouses, where the elite of the city would gather every evening to discuss the news of the day, smoke *narghileh*s, sip black coffee, and drink arak and sherbets. It was Damascus, however, that was celebrated for the number and elegance of its coffeehouses, the finest of which were situated along the Barada, with views of the river and adjacent gardens. The Damascene considered the coffeehouse an integral part of his daily life. It was

> . . . his opera, his theatre, his conversazione: soon after his eyes are unclosed from sleep, he thinks of his Café, and forthwith bends his way there: during the day he looks forward to pass the evening on the loved floor, to look on the waters, on the stars above, and on the faces of his friends; and at the moonlight falling on all.[11]

In the evenings some coffeehouses were enlivened by the performances of professional dancers, singers, and storytellers. These last, called *hakawati*s, would beguile their

Cafés along the Barada River in Damascus. *From John Carne,* Syria, the Holy Land, Asia Minor, &c., *vol. 1 (London, Fisher, Son, 1836)*

An Oriental orchestra. *From Henry J. van Lennep,* Bible Lands: Their Modern Customs and Manners Illustrative of Scripture *(New York, Harper, 1875)*

listeners with fantastic tales of ancient heroes and heroines. Russell has described the dramatic performance of the typical Aleppan storyteller of his time:

> He recites walking to and fro, in the middle of the coffee room, stopping only now and then when the expression requires some emphatical attitude. He is commonly heard with great attention, and, not unfrequently, in the midst of some interesting adventure, when the expectation of his audience is raised to the highest pitch, he breaks off abruptly, and makes his escape from the room, leaving both his heroine and his audience, in the utmost embarrassment. Those who happen to be near the door endeavour to detain him, insisting on the story being finished before he departs, but he always makes his retreat good; and the auditors, suspending their curiosity, are induced to return at the same hour next day, to hear the sequel. He no sooner has made his exit, than the company, in separate parties, fall a disputing about the characters of the drama, or the event of the unfinished adventure. The controversy by degrees becomes serious, and opposite opinions are maintained with no less warmth, than if the fate of the city depended on the decision.[12]

Today professional storytellers still ply their centuries-old art to rapt audiences in some eastern-style coffeehouses. I have heard of incidents where listeners were in such a state of suspense over the outcome of a tale that, being unable to sleep, they would go to a *hakawati*'s residence in the middle of the night and attempt to bribe him to give the story a happy conclusion the following evening!

In addition to traditional Arab coffeehouses, there are many French-style cafés. In prewar Beirut, the latter were found all along the Corniche overlooking the Mediterranean. Now one encounters hundreds of coffee vans on this seaside boulevard.

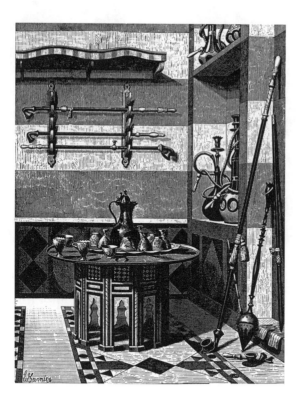

Pipes, narghilehs, *coffee cups, and trays. From William McClure Thomson,* The Land and the Book, *vol. 3 (New York, Harper, 1885)*

THE PREPARATION OF COFFEE

Much of the social life of Syria, Lebanon, and Jordan centers around the drinking of coffee. No one has been properly welcomed to a home until he or she has been offered this traditional sign of hospitality. Not to give coffee to guests would signify that they were unwelcome. That this custom was and is observed elsewhere in the eastern Mediterranean is attested to by the following incident related by Lewis Gaston Leary in his book, *Syria, the Land of Lebanon* (1913):

> Some years ago, our minister to Turkey, who had been promised an audience with [Sultan] Abdul Hamid, was made to wait half a day in an anteroom of the palace *without being offered coffee.* So far as I know, that fact was never published; for the American newspapers seem to have quite missed the significance of the omission, and our representative himself apparently did not realize that he had been publicly insulted. But the experienced diplomat who was then in charge of our Department of State cabled the minister, in case of further affront, to leave Constantinople immediately.

Visitors should not refuse coffee unless they are absolutely unable to drink it, in which case it may be declined gracefully and an alternative beverage accepted with thanks. This most esteemed of hot drinks is enjoyed at any time and provides the usual conclusion to a midday or evening meal. It is also frequently served by merchants to customers and by businessmen to visitors in offices.

Coffee is in such wide use among the Beduin that it is considered virtually a necessity of life. On a visit to a desert camp near Palmyra, Irby and Mangles observed:

> A black slave was perpetually pounding coffee from the moment we entered the tent till we went to sleep, and as he began in the morning at day-light, and was constantly employed, it would seem that the consumption in this article must be considerable.[13]

The Beduin, who are true connoisseurs of coffee, almost never add sugar to it, a point underscored by the following account:

> A group of Bedouins were disputing respecting the sanity of Lady Hester Stanhope; one party strenuously maintaining that it was impossible a lady so charitable, so munificent, could be otherwise than in full possession of her faculties; their opponents alleging that her assimilating herself to the Virgin Mary, her anticipated entry with our Saviour into Jerusalem, and other vagaries attributed to her, were proofs to the contrary. An old man with a white beard called for silence (a call from the aged amidst the Arabs seldom made in vain). "She is mad," said he; and, lowering his voice to a whisper, as if fearing lest such an outrage against established custom should spread beyond his circle, he added, "for she puts sugar in her coffee."[14]

Apparently it was not until the second half of the seventeenth century that townspeople in Syria began to add sugar to their coffee, for the practice is mentioned by

Beduin preparing coffee. From Charles William Wilson, ed., Picturesque Palestine, Sinai and Egypt, *vol. 2 (New York, D. Appleton, 1883)*

d'Arvieux as having recently been introduced. In contrast, Russell, writing in the late 1700s, states that it was "certainly not at present the custom." [15]

Today two styles of coffee, known as Turkish and Arabic, are made in the region. Turkish coffee, which is prevalent in urban areas, is brewed in and served from a long-handled, narrow-necked pot called a *rakwi* that comes in several sizes, the largest usually holding only about six servings. The *rakwi* is often made of tin-lined brass, but it may also be made of tin-lined copper or of enamelware. Its long handle protects the fingers from the fire, and its shape, which is narrower at the top than at the bottom, intensifies the foaming action as the coffee boils up. This type of coffee can be prepared either with or without sugar, which is stirred into it while it is being made rather than after it is poured into cups, since stirring at this point would disturb and raise the grounds that will have settled to the bottom. Normally guests are asked how they would like their coffee—sweet (*hilweh*), medium (*wassat* or *mazbuta*), or without sugar (*murra*)—but the amount of sugar can also depend on the occasion. Coffee served after dinner or with sweets is usually prepared with little or no sugar. For festive occasions such as weddings, birthdays, and parties, it is made with a generous amount of sugar, while during times of sorrow it is served bitter. (In Ottoman times, among some Armenians the serving of bitter coffee by a girl's family to the representatives of a boy's family during marriage negotiations signified that the proposal was being rejected.) When the coffee starts to boil and the foam begins to rise, the pot is removed from the heat to avoid boiling over. This procedure is repeated two more times to build up a foam that will stand up well (a good head of foam is a sign of properly prepared Turkish coffee). The foam is poured into each cup in equal amounts, followed by the rest of the brew, including the grounds, which soon settle to the bottom of the cup. Only the clear liquid is sipped, the remaining sediment being discarded when the cup is washed.

Arabic coffee, popular especially among the Beduin, is prepared in a single boil, almost always without sugar. Two pots (*dallahs*) are used; the brew is made in the first, from which it is poured into the second, leaving the sediment behind.

In the past, small pieces of ambergris were used by the rich to perfume coffee. A less

Brass mortar and pestle and coffeepot for preparing Arabic coffee. From Gottlieb Schumacher, The Jaulan *(London, Alexander P. Watt, 1889)*

Wooden coffee mortar and pestle. From Louis Charles Lortet, La Syrie d'aujourd'hui *(Paris, Librairie Hachette, 1884)*

costly flavoring was mastic. Other additives, still used today, are cinnamon, cloves, cardamom, rose water, and orange flower water. Milk or cream, however, is never added to Turkish or Arabic coffee.

Although many people purchase their coffee already roasted, pulverized, and packaged, the best coffee is made from freshly roasted beans that have been reduced almost to a powder. While beans from the Yemen are preferred, others from countries such as Brazil and Kenya are also used. The beans are roasted in a broad, long-handled iron ladle (*mihmas*) over a charcoal brazier (*kanun*) until brown and richly aromatic, after which they are cooled in a wooden shaker. They are then pulverized in a large stone, brass, or wooden mortar with a long iron or brass pestle. Roasted and cooled beans can also be ground in cylindrical coffee mills of chased brass such as those made in Damascus, but many people insist that coffee tastes best when prepared from pounded rather than ground beans, a conclusion reached by Carsten Niebuhr over two centuries ago:

> We carried a coffee-mill with us into Arabia, but soon found the taste of the pounded coffee much superior to that of the ground, and left off using our mill. The pounding seems better to express the oily parts of the bean, which give the coffee its peculiar relish.[16]

THE SERVING OF COFFEE

Because Middle Eastern coffee is strong, it is drunk from very small cups (*finjans*), which, depending on the region, may or may not have handles and saucers. Those without either are sometimes set in holders of filigreed brass (or, in wealthier homes, silver or even gold) that match an ornamented serving tray. Although Middle Eastern coffee cups appear diminutive to us, a Syrian may well find ours inordinately large, as Isabel Burton discovered soon after she arrived in Damascus to join her husband, Sir Richard, who was serving there as consul:

When I first came I brought English coffee-cups with me, which greatly amazed the servants. I had also a stable-mill to grind Indian corn, as that was what our horses lived upon in Brazil. The groom came to me one day, and asked if that was an English coffee-mill.

"No," I said; "Why do you ask?"

"Because I thought, O lady! that if those were the cups, this must be the coffee-grinder to fit them."[17]

Custom dictates a few rules for the serving of coffee. In the past men were served before women, but in areas where Western influence is strong, the opposite is now the norm. Guests are served first, with rank generally taking precedence over age. Coffee is traditionally served very hot:

It is a necessity as well as a sign of good breeding to keep the lips from quite touching the surface and to suck up the drink with a loud hissing noise. In a private house, this formality should by no means be neglected, even if the coffee has become cooled, as the omission would be equivalent to a criticism of the host.[18]

In some areas it is not customary for a guest to drink more than one cup of coffee. Among the Beduin, on the other hand, a visitor's cup is continuously filled until he jiggles it from side to side to indicate that he has had enough. It is not considered good form, however, to drink more than three cups in a row.

Coffee is often accompanied with a glass of cold water, which, if desired, is sipped afterward to clear the palate of grounds. This practice, however, has not always met with approval:

The Orientals often drink water before coffee, but never immediately after. I was once recognised in Syria as a foreigner or European, in consequence of having called for water just after I had taken coffee. "If you were of this country," said the waiter, "you would not spoil the taste of the coffee in your mouth by washing it away with water."[19]

It appears that during Ottoman times coffee sometimes played a sinister role in Eastern affairs:

Its heavy sweetness disguises varied and deadly poisons . . . drunk unsuspectingly by many a venturesome meddler in affairs of state. The death penalty is seldom inflicted in the Turkish Empire. Deposed ministers and irrepressible busybodies and troublesome reformers are merely imprisoned or exiled. Often they are sent to Damascus. Then, shortly, they die of indigestion or heart failure.[20]

A popular pastime is the reading of fortunes from the sediment in emptied coffee cups. Usually there is at least one member of a group who is adept at this type of fortune-telling. The cups are inverted onto saucers, and the grounds drip down and harden on the sides, forming patterns. The interpretations of these patterns are mostly bright and optimistic, but on occasion ominous, and frequently turn out to be surprisingly accurate. Now and then someone's cup will stick to its saucer, which is taken to mean that a person's wishes will be fulfilled, thus rendering a reading unnecessary.

Turkish Coffee

When I was growing up, Turkish, French, and American coffee were all consumed in Beirut. The first was by far the most popular, so much so that coffee meant Turkish coffee unless one specified French or American. This still holds true today.

Here is a recipe for Turkish coffee. For more than one cup, multiply the recipe by the number of servings you wish to make, keeping in mind that this coffee is best when made in small amounts, no more than four servings at a time.

> **1 demitasse fresh cold water**
>
> **1 teaspoon sugar, or to taste**
>
> **1 heaping teaspoon very finely pulverized dark roast coffee, or more for a stronger brew**

Combine the water and sugar in a *rakwi* (the coffee pot described on page 394) and bring to a boil, stirring constantly until the sugar is dissolved. Add the coffee, stir well, and bring the mixture to a boil. When the foam begins to rise, remove the pot from the heat to avoid boiling over. Repeat this procedure 2 more times. Pour off the foam as it forms into a demitasse cup (making a gently trembling motion with your hand will help to accomplish this), then slowly pour the hot coffee into the cup, being careful not to disturb the foam, which will rise to the surface. Serve at once.

Makes 1 demitasse cup

Note: Some people boil the water first and then add the sugar and coffee at the same time. Others combine all three from the start, but the above method is the most common.

VARIATION:

Add 2 or 3 cardamom seeds, or to taste, crushed, with the coffee.

Teas, Tisanes, and Other Hot Beverages

Although it lacks the historical significance of coffee and is surrounded by much less ritual, tea (*shay*) nevertheless occupies an important place in Syrian and Lebanese life. It is also popular in Jordan, where local legend has it that the Circassians were the first to bring it to that country. Tea is generally drunk sweetened with sugar and without milk and is often flavored with spearmint leaves or spices such as aniseed or cinnamon.

Tisanes made from various herbs, seeds, flowers, leaves, and roots survive from the past, when they were drunk for their beneficial medicinal properties. These aromatic infusions are still taken for the same reason, especially during the winter, but their comforting and refreshing qualities make them enjoyable beverages in themselves. They are made in much the same manner as regular tea. Boiling water is poured over the herb or other aromatic substance in a warmed teapot and is allowed to stand about 5 minutes to infuse. The resulting tisane is then strained into cups. It is drunk very hot, perhaps

Rosewater bottle. *From Henry J.*
van Lennep, Bible Lands: Their
Modern Customs and Manners
Illustrative of Scripture *(New York,*
Harper, 1875)

sweetened with sugar or honey, and with a slice of lemon or lime sometimes added to
each cup. Many different ingredients are used in preparing infusions. Lemon verbena,
black elder, jasmine, and rose petals are recommended for colds; and dried violets, hol-
lyhocks, and mallow flowers are suggested for coughs. A number of tisanes are thought
to relieve indigestion, for example, those made with mint leaves, aniseed, camomile
flower heads, and orange or lemon leaves. Another drink considered good for indigestion is *qahwa bayda* (*café blanc* or white coffee), which is made by adding a teaspoon of
orange flower water and, if desired, sugar to taste to a small coffee cup of boiling water.
Infusions of lemon balm and camomile are popular for their mild sedative effect. Tea
made with dried pomegranate flowers is believed to help relieve some intestinal com-
plaints, while tea made from dried sage leaves is deemed a cure for all sorts of ills.

A fragrant spice drink garnished with nuts and sweetened with sugar or honey is
mughli, which is traditionally served on the occasion of the birth of a baby. Also popular
is *sahlab,* a thick and warming wintertime beverage made with milk, sugar, and salep
and dusted with cinnamon. In Beirut this soothing drink is often served with sesame
bread (*ka'k*) or croissants, and in Shtora, steaming pots of it are on display in roadside
cafés during the cold months of the year.

Afifi, a petite, gentle widow from Shweir, cooked for us. . . . Once, when little David had
warts on his hands, Afifi brewed an herb tea; she swore that if David drank a bottle of it the
warts would disappear. He did, and they did.[21]

Spice Drink
Mughli *or* Ainar

Hot spiced beverages are much appreciated in Greater Syria, as Burckhardt discovered when he visited a Kurdish encampment near Aleppo:

> After dinner and coffee, Tshay[22] was served round, which the Aleppines and all Syrians esteem as one of the greatest dainties: it is a heating drink, made of ginger, cloves, rosewater, sugar and similar ingredients, boiled together to a thick syrup. Mursa Aga, the chief, a handsome young man, then took up his Tamboura or guitar, and the rest of the evening passed in music and singing.[23]

Here is a healthful, aromatic tea which, like *mughli* pudding (page 388), is by tradition served to visitors who have come to see a newborn baby. There is no reason, however, why one cannot enjoy this pleasant and warming beverage even if there are no babies due in the near future.

> **4 cups water**
> **1 cinnamon stick, about 3 inches long, broken into pieces**
> **1 piece dried gingerroot, about 1 inch long (available at Oriental markets)**
> **1 tablespoon aniseed, or more to taste**
> **1/2 teaspoon whole cloves**
> **1/4 cup or more split blanched almonds or a mixture of almonds, walnut halves, and
>   pine nuts**
> **Sugar or honey**

In a medium enameled or stainless steel saucepan bring the water and spices to a boil over moderate heat. Cover and boil gently about 15 minutes. Strain the mixture through a fine sieve into a heatproof pitcher. Pour into heated mugs or cups and garnish with the nuts. Serve hot with sugar.

Serves 4

Spiced Tea

Prepare Spice Drink (above) and bring to a boil. Place 2 teaspoons tea leaves (orange pekoe) in a teapot and pour the boiling spice drink over the tea leaves. Cover and let the tea steep 4 to 5 minutes. Strain it into heated mugs or cups and sprinkle with chopped walnuts. Or omit the nuts and serve with lemon wedges and sugar on the side.

Serves 4

VARIATIONS:

Anise Tea
Shay bi Yansun

Omit the cinnamon, gingerroot, and cloves.

Cinnamon Tea
Shay bi Darcin

Omit the gingerroot, aniseed, and cloves.

ALCOHOLIC BEVERAGES

Wine
Khamr

He can make a wine cellar out of one grape.
(Virtually a national motto in Lebanon.)

Excavations suggest that winemaking may have been carried on in Greater Syria as early as ten thousand years ago. Vineyards flourished there during the third and second millennia B.C., and the wines produced from them were much esteemed by the Egyptians, who imported them in great quantity. The Phoenicians exported wine from the Baalbek region, and the famous wines of Helbon were widely distributed from nearby Damascus. The Romans, who were fond of Lebanese wines, further encouraged the development of viticulture in the country. During Crusader times monastic orders planted vines in the Latin states of the Levant with as much dedication as they did in Europe, and wines from al-Batrun and Enfeh on the Lebanese coast attained a high reputation throughout these Christian kingdoms. Today in Lebanon one can still find huge vats hewn out of the rock, where the Phoenicians, Romans, and Crusaders crushed their grapes.

Wine had not always been forbidden to the Arabs, who had enjoyed it from earliest times. Pre-Islamic poets had sung the praises of wine imported from Lebanon and the Hauran. The excessive amount of drunkenness and gambling in Mecca and Medina, however, eventually led Muhammad to prohibit the consumption of alcohol, and thus "wine . . . and gambling—next to women the two indulgences dearest to the Arabian heart—were abolished in one verse." [24] Although the production of wine was severely curtailed by the establishment of Islam, the beverage did not completely disappear. Wines continued to be made and sold by Christians and Jews, and those of Tyre and Sidon were much in demand in Europe. The Muslim prohibition against intoxicating beverages was in reality no more successful than the Eighteenth Amendment was in the United States. So many caliphs, princes, wazirs, secretaries, and judges ignored the religious injunction that the Egyptian scholar, poet, and man of letters al-Nawadji (1386–1455) despaired of finding enough room to list them all in his anthology of wine, Halbat al-kumayt (1421).[25] The worst offender was the Umayyad caliph al-Walid II (reigned

***Monasteries in the Kisra-
wan.*** *From Walter Keating
Kelly,* Syria and the Holy
Land *(London, Chapman
and Hall, 1844)*

743–744), who reportedly delighted in swimming habitually in a pool of wine, gulping
enough to lower the level of the liquid considerably. When a nineteenth-century English
visitor to the Near East asked a Muslim why it was that the faithful abstained from pork
and indulged in wine when both were forbidden by his religion, the answer was, "Oh,
pig is filthy, and wine" (with a sigh) "is so nice."[26]

Wine was produced in many parts of Ottoman Syria. D'Arvieux praised the wine of
Aleppo, and his contemporary Thévenot, who visited the city, remarked that "every one
makes his own Wine in his own house."[27] Some of the best wine in Syria was made in
monasteries. Good wine was also produced by the Rothschild wine cellars, established
in the late 1880s near Jaffa in Palestine. By the early 1900s these had become the third
largest in the world.

It was Lebanon, however, with its large Christian population, that continued to
produce wine as celebrated for its quality as it had been in ancient times. In Colonel
Churchill's opinion, some of it could hardly be surpassed for richness of color and delicacy of flavor. Much of the wine was made in the mountainous Kisrawan region northeast of Beirut. Carne notes that "no less than twelve kinds are made on the range of
Lebanon; most of them are sweet, strong, and pleasant; two or three are excellent."[28] A
number of these were red, others white, the latter being considered superior. The finest
and most famous Lebanese wine was the *vino d'oro* (golden wine) made at the village of
Zuk in the Kisrawan. "It is the champagne of the East," exclaims Carne, "mousseux
when bottled, and inspiring."[29] Another spot in the Kisrawan where high-quality wine
was produced was the Armenian Catholic monastery of Bzummar. Carne, who was a
guest of the resident patriarch there, writes:

> In this noble establishment he entertains the traveller handsomely, and does the honors of
> his table with much taste: in proof of the excellence of his vintage, he has different kinds
> of wine, several of them of the choicest flavor, brought in succession.[30]

Excellent wine could also be had at the celebrated Maronite monastery of Cannobin in the Qadisha Valley and in the nearby village of Ehden, as well as at the monastery in Tripoli, which in Neale's words produced wine "equal to any claret that is imported into Syria."[31] Two other important wine-growing areas were Dayr al-Qamar and Zahleh, where the huge grape crop was the source of the town's pride and much of its wealth. Except for an occasional cask of *vino d'oro*, Syrian wines were rarely exported to Europe. French wine, on the other hand, was available in a number of towns, among them Aleppo, Beirut, Baalbek, and Shtora.

Among the Christian population, wine was either served during meals or brought out afterward on a tray in decanters along with glasses. Offered alone or with fruit, it was imbibed freely during wedding festivities and on holidays.

Lebanon continues to be known for its wines. Some vines can be traced back to the Crusaders or even earlier, and in more recent times various French and American strains have been introduced. As in the past, the area around Zahleh is still devoted principally to viticulture. The town's cherished traditions of wine and poetry are symbolized by a fig-leafed statue of Bacchus standing at its entrance, over which hangs a banner proclaiming "*Ville de vin et poésie.*"[32] A festival celebrating the vintage is held in Zahleh every September.

Less than five miles from Zahleh is the Ksara winery. Founded in 1857 by the Jesuits, it is the largest enterprise of its kind in the Middle East. Our summer house in Shtora was about a three-minute drive from the Ksara property and our own vineyard only a stone's throw away. The fathers produce good-quality, reasonably priced red, white, and rosé wines from their extensive, well-maintained vineyards. At the nearby village of Jdita are the cellars of Vin Nakad, while the southern Bekaa is home to Château Kefraya. Each of the above three wineries makes dry to medium-dry wines that can be drunk young. The world-class offerings of Château Musar are produced at an eighteenth-century castle in the village of Ghazir from excellent grapes grown in the Bekaa. This distinguished Château makes an elegant, fragrant, and full-bodied red wine reminiscent of fine Bordeaux, as well as outstanding white and rosé wines. Wine is also made at home and in monasteries for noncommercial use.

In Syria red, white, and rosé wines are produced in the environs of Aleppo and Homs, in the anti-Lebanon near al-Zabadani, and around the southern town of al-Suwayda, a region renowned for the quality of its grapes, which yield a full-bodied and fruity wine. As in Lebanon, wine is also made in monasteries.

Although vineyards flourished in ancient Jordan, the manufacture of wine is quite limited at the present time and is carried on almost entirely by Christian monks.

❧

May God guard the vineyard from its watchman.

❧

Watchman's booth.
From Henry J.
van Lennep, Bible Lands:
Their Modern Customs
and Manners Illustrative
of Scripture *(New York,*
Harper, 1875)

Beer

Bira

Although wine was the favorite beverage of ancient Syria, beer was also consumed. A stele from the second millennium B.C. unearthed at Byblos lists beer as one of the foodstuffs offered at a funerary repast. During medieval times beer was well known despite its inclusion in the category of fermented (and therefore forbidden) drinks. Recipes for a kind of barley beer are found in the culinary manuals under the heading of *fuqqaʿ*.

In the post-Ottoman period the relaxation of strict religious laws has led to the increased availability and consumption of beer, which goes well with many Middle Eastern dishes. Good light beers are now produced locally, and one can also purchase beer and ale imported from all over the world.

Arak and Other Spirits

The national apéritif of Syria, Lebanon, and Jordan is *arak,* a colorless, highly potent spirit distilled from grapes and flavored with aniseed. A close cousin of Turkish *raki* and Greek *ouzo,* it has been produced in the region since time immemorial. *Arak* is the traditional accompaniment to *mazza* and is usually served diluted with water and ice. A little is poured into a small glass, followed by up to an equal amount of water, with chipped ice being added as the mixture turns a milky white.

During Ottoman times this indigenous firewater was manufactured almost exclusively by Christians and Jews, ostensibly for their own consumption (according to Russell it was distilled in Aleppo by Muslims as well as Christians).[33] *Arak* was often taken before meals to stimulate the appetite and was considered indispensable at weddings to "rejoice men's hearts."

Muslims were not immune to the attractions of "lion's milk." Although the peasantry and middle class were comparatively untainted, the custom of drinking spiritous
liquors was in considerable evidence among the upper class, government officials, and
the poor. According to Neale, following afternoon prayers in the mosque, the *effendi*s of
Antioch would retire to a garden on the banks of the Orontes, where they drank *arak*
and nibbled cucumbers until almost sundown before making their way home to a hearty
dinner.[34] The degree to which drinking was repressed or tolerated in Aleppo depended
much on the attitudes of ruling officials:

> When a Bashaw, or other great man, is strictly abstemious, his dependants, or such as have
> business near his person, are afraid to approach, lest their breath should betray them; but
> where that restraint is once removed, it is not unusual to find half his retinue talking as
> familiarly of Rosolis, as they do of coffee.
>
> A story is told of a certain Sardar of Aleppo, much addicted to drinking, who used to
> retire to one of the gardens near town, in order to indulge more luxuriously in a Kiosk close
> to the river.
>
> Returning, one summer's evening, from a debauch of this kind, he observed, as he passed
> near the Christian burial ground, a Maronite sitting on a grave stone, and smoking his pipe,
> who, as soon as he perceived the Sardar at some distance, rose up, laid down his pipe, and at

Junction of a tributary stream with the Orontes. *From John Carne,* Syria, the Holy Land, Asia Minor,
&c., *vol. 1 (London, Fisher, Son, 1836)*

the same time attempted hastily to conceal something in his pocket. This the old Sardar suspected, and justly, to be arrack; therefore, stopping his horse, he despatched one of his attendants to bring the culprit before him.

The Christian was not only reproached for drinking thus publickly, but threatened with instant punishment for having aggravated the crime, by drinking on a tomb stone. Upon his swearing by the Gospel that he had tasted no strong liquor for a week, orders were given to search his pockets; but he had taken care no testimony should appear against him from that quarter, by dropping the empty bottle before he was seized. The Sardar then commanded another of his attendants to try whether the charge might not be proved from the criminal's breath. "Breathe ye, Giaur [Christian, infidel]," exclaims the Janizary, "breathe full in my face." The trembling culprit at first hesitated, but, knowing the consequences of refusal, was at last obliged to comply. "I knew very well" (said the Sardar) "I should detect this . . . Christian—does he not smell abominably Mustafa? Bring him nearer me—Don't you perceive his breath?" "Why really," (replies the half drunk Janizary) "that there is a strong smell of arrack among us, cannot be doubted, but whether it proceeds from you yourself Sir, from me, or from this damned Infidel, may I perish if I can justly determine." [35]

Whatever problems there may have been in the past, instances of drunkenness and alcoholism are uncommon today.

Although *arak* is produced in all three countries, some of the best in the world is said to come from Lebanon. When I was growing up, traveling distillers used to visit mountain villages during autumn, processing grapes into *arak*. Among the Lebanese towns long famous for the manufacture of *arak* are Ma'asir al-Shuf and, especially, Zahleh, where, as mentioned earlier, this heady *eau de vie* played a major role in establishing that flourishing resort and market center as a *mazza* lover's paradise.

In addition to *arak,* imported spirits—whiskey, gin, vodka, brandy, and the like—are widely available in the larger cities and towns of the region.

Vodka, Orange Liqueur, and Pomegranate Cocktail ❧
Abu Nuwas

This is my version of a drink that originated in Baghdad and eventually made its way to Beirut. It is named for Abu Nuwas, the dissolute court poet and boon companion of Harun al-Rashid, whose many verses on love and wine are among the finest examples of their kind in all of Arabic literature.

2 tablespoons vodka
2 tablespoons orange liqueur
1 tablespoon freshly squeezed and strained lemon juice
2 teaspoons Pomegranate Syrup (page 384)
1 tablespoon lightly beaten egg white
4 ice cubes
1 orange slice

In a cocktail shaker combine all the ingredients except the orange slice. Shake vigorously until the mixture is well chilled. Strain into a cocktail glass. Garnish the drink with the orange slice and serve at once.

Serves 1

❧

One drink can cure you, two can cheer you, three can kill you. *(A)*

❧

Plum and Wine Cooler

The combination of wine and fruit is a time-honored tradition in the Middle East. According to the Abbassid biographer Ibn Khallikan, the ninth-century Christian physician and translator Hunayn ibn Ishaq used to drink two quarts of wine daily, to which he sometimes added quinces and Syrian apples.[36] Russell tells us that wine with fruit formed part of Christian wedding celebrations in Ottoman Aleppo:

> Between eleven and twelve at night, the bridegroom accompanied by a few of the near relations, is introduced into the women's apartment, where a collation of fruit and wine is prepared. . . . [A]fter the young couple have drunk a glass to each other, the bridegroom drinks a bumper to the female guests, and then returns to the company, who are waiting without to receive him with loud acclamations.[37]

When the plums in our Shtora orchard were at their peak, we would often pack some in syrup to concoct warm-weather coolers much like this one. Mixed with a crisp, fruity wine from the nearby Ksara vineyards, the plums made a welcome beverage to sip and savor on summer afternoons.

Plums in Spiced Syrup (below)
Ice cubes
2 cups rosé or dry white wine, well chilled

Make the Plums in Spiced Syrup. For each serving, place 2 chilled plum halves in a wineglass partially filled with ice cubes. Mix 3 tablespoons plum syrup with 1/4 cup wine and pour the mixture over the plums. Serve at once with a spoon.

Serves 8

PLUMS IN SPICED SYRUP

8 large Santa Rosa plums
1 1/3 cups sugar
2 cups water
3 whole cloves
1 cinnamon stick, about 3 inches long

Dip the plums, a few at a time, in vigorously boiling water to cover about 1 minute or until the skins split. With a slotted spoon, remove the plums from the water, rinse them in cold water, and peel. Cut the plums in half, discarding the pits. Set aside.

In a medium enameled or stainless steel saucepan bring the sugar and water to a boil over moderate heat, stirring constantly until the sugar dissolves. Add the cloves and cinnamon stick and boil, uncovered, about 20 minutes or until the syrup is reduced to about 1½ cups. Remove from the heat, add the plums, and cool to room temperature. With a slotted spoon, transfer the plums to sterilized jars. Pour the syrup over the plums, seal the jars with the lids, and refrigerate up to 5 days.

Makes about 2 pints

The wine goes in, the secret comes out. *(A)*

Mulled Pomegranate Wine Punch

It was the custom in ancient times, as it still is in the East, to mix spices and other ingredients with wine, to give it a special flavour, or make it stronger, or the reverse.[38]

This drink is inspired by a punch we used to make in Beirut. I have served it during the Thanksgiving and Christmas holidays with much success.

A 750-ml bottle full-bodied Lebanese or other dry red wine
2 cups pomegranate juice (page 54)
½ cup sugar, or to taste
4 whole cloves
2 cardamom pods, lightly crushed (optional)
1 cinnamon stick, 2 inches long, broken into pieces
Peel of ¼ lemon
Thin unpeeled orange slices
¼ cup raisins
¼ cup split blanched almonds or walnut halves, or a combination of both

In a large enameled saucepan combine the first 7 ingredients. Bring the mixture just to the boiling point over moderate heat, stirring constantly until the sugar dissolves. Reduce the heat and simmer, uncovered, 15 minutes. Strain into a heatproof punch bowl (set, if desired, over a candle or on an electric warming tray) and float the orange slices on top. Ladle into cups, adding about 1 teaspoon each raisins and nuts to each cup. Serve hot.

Makes about ten 4-ounce servings
(about 5 cups)

VARIATION:

Substitute ⅓ to ½ cup Pomegranate Molasses (page 57) for the pomegranate juice. Use only 1 cardamom pod or omit it entirely. This will make about 6 servings.

∾

I sifted my flour; I hung up my sieve. *(A)*
(Meaning that one's work is done.)

∾

Sources for Ingredients

The following is a brief list of stores that carry eastern Mediterranean food products. Some will accept mail orders. For additional sources consult your telephone directory for Arab, Armenian, and Greek groceries and bakeries as well as natural foods stores and specialty foods shops. Also, Middle Eastern religious and cultural organizations in your area may be able to assist you in your search for ingredients.

ARIZONA

Hajji Baba Middle Eastern Food, 1513 East Apache, Phoenix 85281

CALIFORNIA

C & K Importing Co., 2771 West Pico Boulevard, Los Angeles 90006
G. B. Ratto & Co. International Grocers, 821 Washington Street, Oakland 94607
International Groceries of San Diego, 3548 Ashford Street, San Diego 92111
Haig's Delicacies, 642 Clement Street, San Francisco 94118
Samiramis Importing Co., 2990 Mission Street, San Francisco 94110

COLORADO

Middle East Grocery, 2238 South Colorado Boulevard, Denver 80222

CONNECTICUT

Shallah's Middle Eastern Importing Co., 290 White Street, Danbury 06810

DISTRICT OF COLUMBIA

Acropolis Food Market, 1206 Underwood Street N.W., Washington 20012

FLORIDA

Farah's Imported Foods, Inc., Town & Country Shopping Center, Jacksonville 32205
Eastern Star Bakery, 440 Southwest 8th Street, Miami 33130

GEORGIA

Middle Eastern Groceries, 22-50 Cobb Parkway, Smyrna 30080

ILLINOIS

Holy Land Grocery Inc., 4806 North Kedzie Avenue, Chicago 60625

Middle Eastern Bakery & Grocery Inc., 1512 West Foster Street, Chicago 60640

LOUISIANA

Central Grocery Co., 923 Decatur Street, New Orleans 70116

MASSACHUSETTS

Syrian Grocery Importing Co. Inc., 270 Shawmut Avenue, Boston 02118

Near East Baking Co., 5268 Washington Street, West Roxbury 02132

MICHIGAN

Kalil's Mediterranean Pastries and Gourmet Foods, 19872 Kelly Road, Harper Woods 48225

NEW JERSEY

George Hayek & Son Middle East Market, 368 Getty Avenue, Paterson 07503

NEW YORK

Oriental Pastry and Grocery, 170-172 Atlantic Avenue, Brooklyn 11201

Adriana's Bazaar, 2152 Broadway, New York 10023

Dean and DeLuca, 560 Broadway, New York 10012

Orient Export Trading Corp., 123 Lexington Avenue, New York 10016

OHIO

Middle East Foods, 19-57 West 25th Street, Cleveland 44113

Sinbad Food Imports, 2620 North High Street, Columbus 43202

PENNSYLVANIA

Mideast Grocery Store, 1014 Federal Street, Philadelphia 19147

Salim's Middle Eastern Food Store, 47-05 Center Avenue, Pittsburgh 15213

TEXAS

Phoenicia Bakery & Deli, 2912 South Lamar, Austin 78704

Khoury's Liquor Food & Imports, 3207 West Northwest Highway, Dallas 75220

Antone's Import Co., 807 Taft Street, Houston 77019

WASHINGTON

DeLaurenti Specialty Food Market, 1435 First Avenue, Seattle 98101

Notes

Introduction

1. A semolina dessert.

2. Constantin-François Volney, *Voyage en Egypte et en Syrie* (1787). In Volney's time Syria included Lebanon, which did not become a separate country until after World War I (see page 39).

3. Regrettably, the town is a very different place today.

4. Although professional cooks historically have generally been men, the preparation of family meals is normally the responsibility of women.

Historical Background

1. al-Tabari, *The History of al-Tabari*, vol. 13, translated by Gautier H. Juynboll (1989).

2. Despite the proscription against the consumption of pork in both Judaism and Islam, domestic as well as wild pigs were common articles of food among the pagan peoples of the Middle East from time immemorial.

3. This collection has been translated into English by Charles Perry in *Petits propos culinaires*, vol. 21 (November 1985).

4. Although writers have generally acknowledged the Persian and Greek contributions to Turkish cookery, they have consistently ignored or denied the important Armenian one, the word "Anatolian" often being used in an effort to avoid the word "Armenian."

5. This word actually means "stuffed" (from the Arabic *hasha*, "to stuff").

6. Russell's examples include baklava and *knafi* (see Chapter 16).

7. See page 366 for a modern version.

8. Josias Leslie Porter, *Five Years in Damascus*, vol. 1 (1855).

9. Ibn Battuta, *The Travels of Ibn Battuta, A.D. 1325–1354*, vol. 1 (1956).

10. Thomas Skinner, *Adventures during a Journey Overland to India, by Way of Egypt, Syria, and the Holy Land*, vol. 2 (1836). The Arabs speak of a person who possesses anything peculiar as its father or mother, hence the terms "*abu*" or "*umm.*"

11. Laurence Oliphant, *Haifa, or Life in the Holy Land, 1882–1885* (1887).

12. James Lewis Farley, *Two Years in Syria* (1858).

13. Louis Charles Lortet, *La Syrie d'aujourd'hui* (1884). Apparently Beirut was ahead of Haifa in piano playing!

14. Frederic Arthur Neale, *Eight Years in Syria, Palestine, and Asia Minor, from 1842 to 1850*, 2d ed., vol. 1 (1852).

15. "The West Went Thataway—East," *Life*, vol. 60 (7 January 1966), 46–53.

16. Ann Zwicker Kerr, *Come with Me from Lebanon* (1994).

Markets

1. Howard La Fay, "Syria Tests a New Stability," *National Geographic*, vol. 154, no. 3 (September 1978): 333.

2. Nasir-i-Khusrau, *Book of Travels*, translated by W. M. Thackston, Jr. (1986).

3. William McClure Thomson, *The Land and the Book*, vol. 2 (1882).

Ingredients

1. The small, sweet fruit of the Syrian Christ-thorn (*Zizyphus spina-christi*).

2. A sweetmeat made with carob molasses, almonds, and pistachio nuts.

3. A city in southwestern Persia. The lettuce referred to is romaine.

4. al-Muqaddasi, quoted in Guy Le Strange, *Palestine under the Moslems: A Description of Syria and the Holy Land from A.D. 650 to 1500* (1890).

5. An area in southernmost Lebanon.

6. Charles Henry Spencer Churchill, *Mount Lebanon: A Ten Years' Residence from 1842 to 1852*, vol. 1 (1853).

7. Henry Harris Jessup, *Fifty-Three Years in Syria*, vol. 1 (1910).

8. Oliphant, *Haifa*.

9. Edward Robinson, *Later Biblical Researches in Palestine, and in the Adjacent Regions* (1856).

10. Philip Khuri Hitti, *Lebanon in History* (1957).

11. Schlomo Dov Goitein, *A Mediterranean Society: The Jewish Communities of the Arab World as Portrayed in the Documents of the Cairo Geniza*, vol. 1 (1967).

12. Russell identifies this herb in Arabic as *zatre (za'atar)*.

13. Harim, a town located west of Aleppo.

14. Alexander Russell, *The Natural History of Aleppo*, vol. 1 (1794).

15. Broulos (Burullus), a lagoon on the Nile Delta, produces the finest watermelons in Egypt.

16. Volney, *Voyage*.

17. Charles Greenstreet Addison, *Damascus and Palmyra: A Journey to the East*, vol. 2 (1838).

18. [Charles Meryon], *Memoirs of the Lady Hester Stanhope*, vol. 2 (1845). Meryon was the personal physician of Lady Hester Stanhope (1776–1839), the extraordinary niece of William Pitt the Younger. She settled in Lebanon and became a legend there.

19. Russell, *Aleppo*, vol. 1.

20. Rafik Schami, *Damascus Nights*, translated by Philip Boehm (1993).

21. Churchill, *Mount Lebanon*, vol. 1.

22. Thomson, *The Land*, vol. 1 (1880).

23. Thomson, *The Land*, vol. 3 (1885).

24. Charles Thomas Wilson, *Peasant Life in the Holy Land* (1906).

25. During my years in Lebanon *dibs* was actually made in *four* different consistencies: (1) a thin syrup such as that described by Wilson, used to make fig jam; (2) a somewhat thicker one used as a dip for bread and for cooking; (3) the thicker beaten type described by Thomson, which was often eaten with bread in winter; and (4) a very thick concentrate that could be eaten out of hand like nougat.

26. Laurent d'Arvieux, *Mémoires du Chevalier d'Arvieux, envoyé extraordinaire du roy*, with commentary by R. P. Jean Baptiste Labat, vol. 5 (1735).

27. Thomson, *The Land*, vol. 1.

28. Abu'l-Fida', quoted in Le Strange, *Palestine under the Moslems*.

29. This of course holds true not only for eastern Mediterranean / Middle Eastern recipes but for Caucasian (eastern Armenian, Georgian, and Azerbaijani) recipes as well.

30. Although I have come across recipes for *hummus bi tahini* (page 106) published in this country that call for a garnish of pomegranate seeds (and sweet ones at that!), this is not traditional and I do not recall ever seeing such a thing in the eastern Mediterranean.

31. Russell, *Aleppo*, vol. 1.

32. Ibn Battuta, *Travels*, vol. 1.

33. Neale, *Eight Years*, vol. 2.

34. Ibn Sayyar al-Warraq, *Kitab al-tabikh*, edited by Kaj Öhrenberg and Sahban Mroueh (1987).

35. Thomson, *The Land*, vol. 3.

36. Wilson, *Peasant Life*.

37. Taqui Altounyan, *Chimes from a Wooden Bell* (1990).

38. Russell, *Aleppo*, vol. 1.

39. David Urquhart, *The Lebanon (Mount Souria): A History and a Diary*, vol. 1 (1860).

40. Schami, *Damascus Nights*.

41. David Waines, *In a Caliph's Kitchen* (1989).

42. Some sources give lavender for spikenard and the fruit of the elm or beechnut for ash fruit and include mulberry and black pepper.

43. Churchill, *Mount Lebanon*, vol. 3.

44. Robert Alexander Stewart Macalister, "Food," in *Dictionary of the Bible*, edited by James Hastings, vol. 2 (1899–1904), 38.

45. John Carne, *Syria, the Holy Land, Asia Minor &c.*, vol. 3 (1836).

46. A village in northern Lebanon.

47. Jessup, *Fifty-Three Years*, vol. 1.

48. Wilson, *Peasant Life*.

49. Johann Ludwig Burckhardt, *Travels in Syria and the Holy Land* (1822).

50. A similar product known as *targhana* is sold in Armenian groceries. A recipe for a simplified version of *targhana* is found in my *Cuisine of Armenia*.

The Modern Kitchen

1. Adapted from James Edward Hanauer, *Folk-Lore of the Holy Land* (1935).

A Tradition of Hospitality

1. [Josias Leslie Porter], *A Handbook for Travellers in Syria and Palestine* (1875).

2. al-Muqaddasi, quoted in Le Strange, *Palestine under the Moslems*.

3. Ibn Battuta, *Travels*, vol. 1.

4. Walter Keating Kelly, ed., *Syria and the Holy Land: Their Scenery and Their People* (1844).

5. Excessive generosity, however, is discouraged, as illustrated by the Arab proverb, "He who makes peoples' stomachs his earthen jars will be ruined."

6. Churchill, *Mount Lebanon*, vol. 1.

Meals and Menus

1. Jacqueline Carol, *Cocktails and Camels* (1960).

2. Joanne Smith, *Cuisine, Texas: A Multiethnic Feast* (1995). This is, of course, equally true of Syrians and Jordanians!

Chapter 1

1. Robert Hichens, *The Holy Land* (1910).

2. Kerr, *Lebanon*.

3. Adapted from Idries Shah, *The Pleasantries of the Incredible Mulla Nasrudin* (1971).

4. Kelly, *Syria*.

5. The Festival was revived in July 1997, after a twenty-three-year hiatus.

6. Hichens, *Holy Land.*

7. Ibn Battuta, *Travels,* vol. 1.

8. Isabel Burton, *The Inner Life of Syria, Palestine, and the Holy Land* (1884).

9. During Bashir's reign no less than three hundred visitors were served lunch daily in the court-yard of his palace at Bayt al-Din. The prospect of chopping onions for so many people, probably for the rest of her life, could not have failed to make a deep impression when compared with her other choice!

10. Churchill, *Mount Lebanon,* vol. 1.

11. Muhammad R. Ghanoonparvar gives two Iranian versions in his *Persian Cuisine, Book Two* (1984).

Chapter 2

1. Taqui Altounyan, *In Aleppo Once* (1969).

2. Thomas Jenner, *That Goodly Mountain & Lebanon* (1874).

3. [Charles Meryon], *Travels of Lady Hester Stanhope,* vol. 2 (1846). The author is describing the variation of this recipe.

4. Thomson, *The Land,* vol. 3.

Chapter 3

1. Adapted from Shah, *Pleasantries.*

2. Eliot Warburton, *Travels in Egypt and the Holy Land; or, the Crescent and the Cross* (1859). The author is describing the bazaars of Damascus.

3. [Meryon], *Travels,* vol. 3. This conversation took place in Baalbek, Lebanon.

Chapter 4

1. In modern Lebanon a curd cheese known as *qambaris* is traditionally made with cow's milk, goat's milk, and salt, by a process that takes several months.

2. The skin or hide of an animal, such as that of an ox, buffalo, or goat.

3. Jean de Thévenot, *Travels into the Levant,* Part 2 (1687).

4. Actually, it is of pre-Arab origin; Aleppo appears under the name of Khalpu in documents from the third millennium B.C.

5. d'Arvieux, *Mémoires,* vol. 6.

6. Russell, *Aleppo,* vol. 1.

7. Charles Montagu Doughty, *Travels in Arabia Deserta,* vol. 2 (1888).

8. The term *jibna bayda,* or white cheese, can also be applied to other cheeses such as feta and *akkawi.*

9. Skinner, *Adventures,* vol. 1.

10. Burckhardt, *Syria.*

11. During the nineteenth century clarified butter and cheeses made from goat's milk were important commodities in Zahleh, which was the center of commercial activity for a broad area.

12. [Meryon], *Travels,* vol. 2. The Belaz is an area southeast of Hama.

13. Russell, *Aleppo,* vol. 2.

Chapter 5

1. Mary Winifred Bushakra, *I Married an Arab* (1951).

2. Waines, *In a Caliph's Kitchen.*

3. Warburton, *The Crescent.*

4. Elihu Grant, *The People of Palestine* (1921).

Chapter 6

1. Russell, *Aleppo,* vol. 2.

2. Neale, *Eight Years,* vol. 2.

3. Burckhardt, *Syria.*

4. Vere Munro, *A Summer Ramble in Syria, with a Tartar Trip from Aleppo to Stamboul,* vol. 2 (1835).

5. [Meryon], *Travels,* vol. 3.

6. Russell, *Aleppo,* vol. 2.

7. Thévenot, *Travels,* Part 2.

8. Henry J. van Lennep, *Bible Lands: Their Modern Customs and Manners Illustrative of Scripture* (1875).

9. Freya Stark, *Letters from Syria* (1942). The author is describing the Bekaa.

10. al-Dimashqi, quoted in Le Strange, *Palestine under the Moslems.*

11. Volney, *Voyage.*

12. Skinner, *Adventures,* vol. 2.

13. Thomson, *The Land,* vol. 2.

14. Ernest Renan, *Mission de Phénicie* (1864).

Chapter 7

1. Charles Edward Irby and James Mangles, *Travels in Egypt and Nubia, Syria, and Asia Minor; during the Years 1817 & 1818* (1822).

2. Burckhardt, *Syria.*

3. Neale, *Eight Years,* vol. 2.

4. Ibid.

5. Philip Ward, *Touring Lebanon* (1971).

6. Herbert van Thal, ed., *Edward Lear's Journals: A Selection* (1952).

7. John Sykes, *The Mountain Arabs: A Window on the Middle East* (1968). The author is describing a meal he had in a Beirut restaurant.

8. Isabel Burton, *Inner Life.* Mashgharah, located in the southern Bekaa, is famous for its water, vineyards, and gardens.

9. Alexis Soyer (1810–1858), a French chef who achieved fame in England.

10. Farley, *Two Years.*

11. Kelly, *Syria.*

Chapter 8

1. Van Lennep, *Bible Lands.*

2. Irby and Mangles, *Travels.*

3. Russell, *Aleppo,* vol. 2.

4. Abraham Mitrie Rihbany, *A Far Journey* (1914).

5. Russell, *Aleppo,* vol. 1.

6. Addison, *Damascus and Palmyra,* vol. 2.

7. Isabel Burton, *Inner Life.* The author is describing a meal at a Beduin camp near the former Lake Hulah.

8. Isaac Riley, comp., *Syrian Home-Life* (1874).

9. The keeper of Tripoli's Great Mosque at the time.

10. Jessup, *Fifty-Three Years,* vol. 1. A "Philadelphia lawyer" is an attorney skilled in taking advantage of legal technicalities.

11. Nasir-i-Khusrau, *Book of Travels.*

12. Urquhart, *The Lebanon,* vol. 1.

13. Burckhardt, *Syria.* The author is describing a meal he had in a Damascus home.

Chapter 9

1. Riley, *Syrian Home-Life.*

2. [Meryon], *Travels,* vol. 1.

3. Many of these Maronites are descendants of Armenians who settled there and in other Lebanese towns in the latter part of the fourteenth century.

4. Thomson, *The Land,* vol. 3.

Chapter 10

1. Kelly, *Syria.*

2. Grant, *Palestine.*

3. Urquhart, *The Lebanon,* vol. 1.

4. Alphonse de Lamartine, *Voyage en Orient, 1832–1833* (1876). The author is describing a meal he had at the palace of Bayt al-Din.

5. Ibn Battuta, *Travels,* vol. 1.

Chapter 11

1. al-Muqaddasi, quoted in Le Strange, *Palestine under the Moslems.*

2. [Meryon], *Travels,* vol. 1. Although the author mentions rice being used in three of the dishes, both the vine leaves and the lamb may have had a stuffing that included it.

3. Burckhardt, *Syria.*

4. Thomson, *The Land,* vol. 2. See also Historical Background, page 17.

5. See page 175 of my *Best Foods of Russia* for a recipe.

6. Mary Eliza Rogers, *Domestic Life in Palestine* (1862). The author is describing a meal in Nabulus.

7. Urquhart, *The Lebanon,* vol. 1. The author's assertion that bulgur had escaped the observation of travelers is not entirely true. Europeans such as Russell, Burckhardt, Meryon, and Neale had in fact mentioned it in their writings.

Chapter 12

1. John D. Paxton, *Letters on Palestine and Egypt. Written during Two Years' Residence* (1839).

2. Addison, *Damascus and Palmyra,* vol. 2.

3. Skinner, *Adventures,* vol. 2.

4. Paxton, *Letters.*

Chapter 13

1. The terms "eastern" and "western" refer to historical Armenia and not to the present country, whose much smaller territory encompasses only a majority of what was the eastern section of Armenia.

2. Russell, *Aleppo,* vol. 1.

Chapter 14

1. I recall some Turkish-speaking Armenians who lived in northwestern Syria referring to pomegranate molasses by this term. As mentioned on page 252, most villagers in that part of the country are of Armenian descent.

2. Neale, *Eight Years,* vol. 2.

3. Rogers, *Domestic Life.*

4. Some Lebanese villagers preserved tomatoes by a method mentioned on page 157.

5. Addison, *Damascus and Palmyra,* vol. 2. The author is describing a meal he was served at the palace of Bayt al-Din in Lebanon.

6. Karl Baedeker, ed., *Palestine and Syria. Handbook for Travellers* (1876). From a description of the Damascus bazaars.

7. Grant, *Palestine.*

8. Neale, *Eight Years,* vol. 1.

9. Thomson, *The Land,* vol. 3.

Chapter 15

1. Thomson, *The Land,* vol. 3.

2. Muhammad Manazir Ahsan, *Social Life under the Abbasids* (1979).

3. Ibid.

4. Rogers, *Domestic Life.* This type of bread is sometimes called *khubz tabun.* It is still made, especially in Jordan.

5. In some areas the dough laid on the *saaj* was not circular in shape but formed into thin rectangular strips approximately four by eight inches.

6. [Meryon], *Travels,* vol. 2.

7. Today at least one restaurant in Amman, Jordan, specializes in local dishes cooked in a clay *tannur.*

8. Thomson, *The Land,* vol. 3.

9. Van Lennep, *Bible Lands.* This oven is similar to the kind used to bake the bread I purchased as a child in Beirut.

10. Russell, *Aleppo,* vol. 1.

11. It has been heartening for me to observe how *marquq* and its Armenian counterpart *lavash* are becoming increasingly popular in this country.

12. Such an assumption was not entirely erroneous, considering the fact that flatbread was often used to wipe one's mouth at mealtimes, especially in rural areas.

13. Jessup, *Fifty-Three Years,* vol. 1.

14. Thomson, *The Land,* vol. 2.

15. Dora Sakayan, *Armenian Proverbs* (1994).

Chapter 16

1. Gottlieb Schumacher, *Pella* (1895).

2. John Carne, *Recollections of Travels in the East* (1830).

3. Philip G. Baldensperger, "The Immovable East," *Palestine Exploration Fund Quarterly Statement* (January, 1903): 75–76.

4. Skinner, *Adventures,* vol. 2.

5. Lewis Gaston Leary, *Syria, the Land of Lebanon* (1913). For more on apricot paste, including a recipe, see page 371.

6. Jessup, *Fifty-Three Years,* vol. 1.

7. Cream-filled semolina and cheese rolls with syrup. For a simpler version of this sweet, see page 361.

8. Syrup-soaked bread baked to a cakelike texture and topped with clotted cream. This famous sweet, which some people believe was created by Ottoman Turkey's most celebrated chef, an Armenian named Tokatlian, is known as *ekmek kadayif* among Turks and Armenians.

9. Gregory M. Wortabet, *Syria, and the Syrians*, vol. 1 (1856). The bath referred to is a so-called Turkish bath.

10. See pages 333, 342, and 347 for recipes.

11. [Meryon], *Travels*, vol. 2. The author, writing in Ottoman Lebanon, is referring to this 'Id by its Turkish name.

12. Carne, *Syria*, vol. 1.

13. Fayez Aoun, *280 Recettes de cuisine familiale libanaise* (1980).

14. This pastry, which is made with a very thin dough that is also called *killaj*, usually has a cream filling and is fried and dipped in syrup before being served.

15. [Meryon], *Travels*, vol. 1.

16. Edward B. B. Barker, ed., *Syria and Egypt under the Last Five Sultans of Turkey*, vol. 1 (1876). The quotation is taken from a description of wedding celebrations in nineteenth-century Aleppo.

17. Lamartine, *Voyage*, vol. 1.

18. Farley, *Two Years*. The author is referring to his house in Beirut.

19. Rogers, *Domestic Life*.

20. Cunningham Geikie, *The Holy Land and the Bible* (1891).

21. Munro, *Summer Ramble*, vol. 2.

22. Grant, *Palestine*.

23. Hitti, *Lebanon in History*.

24. Paxton, *Letters*.

25. William C. Prime, *Tent Life in the Holy Land* (1857).

26. Addison, *Damascus and Palmyra*, vol. 2.

27. Canon Tristram, quoted in Thomson, *The Land*, vol. 3. The English naturalist is describing the Ghuta, which rings Damascus.

28. Johann Ludwig Burckhardt, *Travels in Arabia* (1829).

29. Ibid.

Chapter 17

1. Al-Muqaddasi, quoted in Le Strange, *Palestine under the Moslems*.

2. Leary, *Syria*.

3. Baedeker, *Palestine and Syria*.

4. Adapted from Shah, *Pleasantries*.

5. Richard Francis Burton, *Personal Narrative of a Pilgrimage to El Medinah and Meccah* (1856).

6. Riley, *Syrian Home-Life*.

7. Carleton S. Coon, Jr., ed., *Daniel Bliss and the Founding of the American University of Beirut* (1989).

8. Carne, *Syria*, vol. 1.

9. Ralph S. Hattox, *Coffee and Coffeehouses: The Origins of a Social Beverage in the Middle East* (1985).

10. Russell, *Aleppo*, vol. 1.

11. Carne, *Syria*, vol. 1.

12. Russell, *Aleppo*, vol. 1.

13. Irby and Mangles, *Travels*.

14. James Raymond Wellsted, *Travels in Arabia*, vol. 1 (1838).

15. Russell, *Aleppo*, vol. 1.

16. Carsten Niebuhr, *Travels through Arabia, and Other Countries in the East,* translated by Robert Heron, vol. 2 (1792).

17. Isabel Burton, *Inner Life.*

18. Leary, *Syria.*

19. Burckhardt, *Arabia.*

20. Leary, *Syria.*

21. Grace Dodge Guthrie, *Legacy to Lebanon* (1984). David was the author's younger brother.

22. The word *tshay* (or *shay*) is derived from the Chinese word for tea. In the Syria of Burckhardt's time, *tshay* often referred to herbal or spiced tea, while real tea was generally distinguished by the name *tshay hindi* (tea of India).

23. Burckhardt, *Syria.*

24. Philip Khuri Hitti, *History of the Arabs,* 10th ed. (1970). The quotation refers to the Koran 5:92. The wine available in Medina at the time was made from dates rather than grapes.

25. Wine was, however, never drunk by Muslims at meals, even in the most dissolute period, but was often enjoyed at convivial parties.

26. Henry C. Barkley, *A Ride through Asia Minor and Armenia* (1891).

27. Thévenot, *Travels,* Part 2.

28. Carne, *Syria,* vol. 1.

29. Carne, *Syria,* vol. 2.

30. Carne, *Syria,* vol. 3.

31. Neale, *Eight Years,* vol. 1.

32. Zahleh claims to have turned out more poets per capita than any other place in Lebanon.

33. Russell, *Aleppo,* vol. 1.

34. Neale, *Eight Years,* vol. 2.

35. Russell, *Aleppo,* vol. 1.

36. Hitti, *History of the Arabs.*

37. Russell, *Aleppo,* vol. 2.

38. Geikie, *Holy Land.*

Selected Bibliography

During the course of writing this book, I consulted a great many sources in several languages. The list below includes, in addition to those mentioned in the text, some others that were especially useful.

Addison, Charles Greenstreet. *Damascus and Palmyra: A Journey to the East.* 2 vols. Philadelphia: E. L. Carey & A. Hart, 1838.

Ahsan, Muhammad Manazir. *Social Life under the Abbasids.* London and New York: Longman Group, 1979.

Altounyan, Taqui. *Chimes from a Wooden Bell.* London: I. B. Taurus, 1990.

———. *In Aleppo Once.* London: John Murray, 1969.

Aoun, Fayez. *280 Recettes de cuisine familiale libanaise.* Paris: Jacques Grancher, 1980.

Arberry, Arthur J. "A Baghdad Cookery-Book." *Islamic Culture* 13, nos. 1 (January 1939) and 2 (April 1939): 21–47, 189–214.

d'Arvieux, Laurent. *Mémoires du Chevalier d'Arvieux, envoyé extraordinaire du roy.* 7 vols. With commentary by R. P. Jean Baptiste Labat. Paris: Charles-Jean-Baptiste Delespine, 1735.

Baedeker, Karl, ed. *Palestine and Syria. Handbook for Travellers.* Leipzig: Karl Baedeker, 1876.

Baghadadi, Nadin, and Hamdi Zamzam. *Atbaq shaheh* (Delicious Dishes). Damascus: Dar al-iman, 1986.

Baldensperger, Philip G. "The Immovable East." *Palestine Exploration Fund Quarterly Statement* (January 1903): 75–76.

Barker, Edward B. B., ed. *Syria and Egypt under the Last Five Sultans of Turkey.* 2 vols. London: Samuel Tinsley, 1876.

Barkley, Henry C. *A Ride through Asia Minor and Armenia.* London: John Murray, 1891.

Bodenheimer, F. S. *Animal Life in Palestine.* Jerusalem: L. Mayer, 1935.

Bottéro, Jean. "The Cuisine of Ancient Mesopotamia." *Biblical Archaeologist* 48, no. 1 (March 1985): 36–47.

Burckhardt, Johann Ludwig. *Travels in Arabia.* London: Henry Colburn, 1829.

———. *Travels in Syria and the Holy Land.* London: John Murray, 1822.

Burton, Isabel. *The Inner Life of Syria, Palestine, and the Holy Land.* London: Kegan Paul, Trench, 1884.

Burton, Richard Francis. *Personal Narrative of a Pilgrimage to El Medinah and Meccah.* New York: G. P. Putnam, 1856.

Bushakra, Mary Winifred. *I Married an Arab.* New York: John Day, 1951.

Carne, John. *Recollections of Travels in the East.* 3 vols. London: Henry Colburn and Richard Bentley, 1830.

———. *Syria, the Holy Land, Asia Minor, &c.* London: Fisher, Son, 1836.

Carol, Jacqueline. *Cocktails and Camels.* New York: Appleton Century Crofts, 1960.

Christensen, Arthur. *L'Iran sous les Sasanides.* 2d ed. Copenhagen: Ejnar Munksgaard, 1944.

Churchill, Charles Henry Spencer. *Mount Lebanon: A Ten Years' Residence from 1842 to 1852.* 3 vols. London: Saunders and Otley, 1853.

Coon, Carleton S., Jr., ed. *Daniel Bliss and the Founding of the American University of Beirut.* Washington, D.C.: The Middle East Institute, 1989.

Darby, William J., Paul Ghalioungui, and Louis Grivetti. *Food: The Gift of Osiris.* 2 vols. New York: Academic Press, 1977.

al-Din, Batul Sharaf. *Fann al-tabkh* (The Art of Cooking). Beirut: al-Maktaba al-hadith, 1984.

Doughty, Charles Montagu. *Travels in Arabia Deserta.* 2 vols. Cambridge: Cambridge University Press, 1888.

Farley, James Lewis. *Two Years in Syria.* London: Saunders and Otley, 1858.

Fedden, Robin. *Syria and Lebanon.* London: John Murray, 1965.

Feghali, Michel. *Contes, légendes, coutumes populaires du Liban et de Syrie.* Paris: Librairie d'Amérique et d'Orient, 1935.

Frayha, Anis. *Modern Lebanese Proverbs.* Beirut: American University of Beirut, 1953.

Geikie, Cunningham. *The Holy Land and the Bible.* London: Cassell, 1891.

George, C. J., V. A. Athanassiou, and I. Boulos. *The Fishes of the Coastal Waters of Lebanon.* Miscellaneous Papers in the Natural Sciences, no. 4. Beirut: American University of Beirut, Publication of the Faculty of Arts and Sciences, 1964.

Ghanoonparvar, Muhammad R. *Persian Cuisine. Book Two: Regional and Modern Foods.* Lexington, Ky.: Mazda Publishers, 1984.

Goitein, Schlomo Dov. *A Mediterranean Society: The Jewish Communities of the Arab World as Portrayed in the Documents of the Cairo Geniza.* Vol. 1. Berkeley: University of California Press, 1967.

Grant, Elihu. *The People of Palestine.* 2d ed. Philadelphia: J. B. Lippincott, 1921.

Guthrie, Grace Dodge. *Legacy to Lebanon.* Richmond, Va.: N.p. 1984.

Hanauer, James Edward. *Folk-Lore of the Holy Land.* New and enl. ed. London: The Sheldon Press, 1935.

Hastings, James, ed. *Dictionary of the Bible.* Rev. ed. by Frederick C. Grant and H. H. Rowley. New York: Scribner's, 1963.

Hattox, Ralph S. *Coffee and Coffeehouses: The Origins of a Social Beverage in the Middle East.* Seattle: University of Washington Press, 1985.

Hichens, Robert. *The Holy Land.* New York: The Century Co., 1910.

Hitti, Philip Khuri. *History of the Arabs.* 10th ed. London and New York: Macmillan and St. Martin's Press, 1970.

———. *Lebanon in History.* London and New York: Macmillan and St. Martin's Press, 1957.

———. *Syria: A Short History.* London and New York: Macmillan and St. Martin's Press, 1959.

Ibn al-'Adim, Kamal al-Din. *Kitab al-wusla ila'l-habib fi wasf al-tayyibat wa'l-tib* (The Book of the Link with the Beloved). 2 vols. Edited by Sulayma Mahjub and Durriya al-Khatib. Aleppo: Ma'had al-turath al-'ilmi al-'arabi, 1988.

Ibn Battuta. *The Travels of Ibn Battuta, A.D. 1325–1354.* Vol. 1. Translated and edited by Hamilton A. R. Gibb. London: The Hakluyt Society, 1956.

Irby, Charles Edward, and James Mangles. *Travels in Egypt and Nubia, Syria, and Asia Minor; during the Years 1817 & 1818.* 1822. Reprint, London: Darf Publishers, 1985.

Jenner, Thomas. *That Goodly Mountain & Lebanon.* 2d ed., rev. London: Hamilton, Adams, 1874.

Jessup, Henry Harris. *Fifty-Three Years in Syria.* 2 vols. New York: Fleming H. Revell Company, 1910.

Kelly, Walter Keating, ed. *Syria and the Holy Land: Their Scenery and Their People.* London: Chapman and Hall, 1844.

Kerr, Ann Zwicker. *Come with Me from Lebanon.* Syracuse, N.Y.: Syracuse University Press, 1994.

Khawam, René R. *La Cuisine arabe.* Paris: Albin Michel, 1970.

Khayat, Marie Karam, and Margaret Keatinge. *Food from the Arab World.* Beirut: Khayats, 1959.

———. *Lebanon, Land of the Cedars.* 2d ed., rev. Beirut: Khayats, 1960.

Khuri, Fuad I. *From Village to Suburb: Order and Change in Greater Beirut.* Chicago and London: University of Chicago Press, 1975.

Kramer, Samuel Noah. *The Sumerians: Their History, Culture, and Character.* Chicago and London: University of Chicago Press, 1963.

La Fay, Howard. "Syria Tests a New Stability." *National Geographic* 154, no. 3 (September 1978): 326–361.

Lamartine, Alphonse de. *Voyage en Orient, 1832–1833.* 2 vols. Paris: Hachette—Furne, Jouvet, 1876, 1878.

Leary, Lewis Gaston. *Syria, the Land of Lebanon.* New York: McBride, Nast, 1913.

Le Strange, Guy. *Palestine under the Moslems: A Description of Syria and the Holy Land from A.D. 650 to 1500.* London: Alexander P. Watt, 1890.

Lortet, Louis Charles. *La Syrie d'aujourd'hui.* Paris: Librairie Hachette, 1884.

Macalister, Robert Alexander Stewart. "Food." In *Dictionary of the Bible.* Edited by James Hastings. Vol. 2. New York: Charles Scribner, 1899–1904: 27–43.

Marín, Manuela, and David Waines, eds. *Kanz al-fawaʿid fi tanwiʿ al-mawaʿid* (A Treasury of Varied and Wholesome Meals). Bibliotheca Islamica, vol. 40. Stuttgart: Franz Steiner Verlag, 1993.

[Meryon, Charles]. *Memoirs of the Lady Hester Stanhope.* 3 vols. London: Henry Colburn, Publisher, 1845.

[———]. *Travels of Lady Hester Stanhope.* 3 vols. London: Henry Colburn, Publisher, 1846.

Mouzannar, Ibrahim. *La Cuisine libanaise.* Beirut: Librairie du Liban, 1983.

Munro, Vere. *A Summer Ramble in Syria, with a Tartar Trip from Aleppo to Stamboul.* 2 vols. London: Richard Bentley, 1835.

Naff, Alixa. "A Social History of Zahle, the Principal Market Town in Nineteenth-Century Lebanon." Ph.D. diss., University of California, Los Angeles, 1972.

Nasir-i-Khusrau. *Book of Travels.* Translated by W. M. Thackston, Jr. Persian Heritage Series, no. 36. Albany: State University of New York Press, 1986.

Neale, Frederic Arthur. *Eight Years in Syria, Palestine, and Asia Minor, from 1842 to 1850.* 2d ed. 2 vols. London: Colburn, Publishers, 1852.

Niebuhr, Carsten. *Travels through Arabia, and Other Countries in the East.* 2 vols. Translated by Robert Heron. Edinburgh: N.p., 1792.

Oliphant, Laurence. *Haifa, or Life in the Holy Land, 1882–1885.* 1887. Reprint, Jerusalem: Canaan Publishing House, 1976.

Oppenheim, A. Leo. *Ancient Mesopotamia: Portrait of a Dead Civilization.* Rev. ed., completed by Erica Reiner. Chicago and London: University of Chicago Press, 1977.

Paxton, John D. *Letters on Palestine and Egypt. Written during Two Years' Residence.* Lexington, Ky.: A. T. Skillman, 1839.

Perry, Charles. "Kitab al-tibakhah: A Fifteenth-Century Cookbook." *Petits propos culinaires* 21 (November 1985): 17–22.

———. "Notes on Persian Pasta." *Petits propos culinaires* 10 (March 1982): 48–49.

———. "The Oldest Mediterranean Noodle: A Cautionary Tale." *Petits propos culinaires* 9 (November 1981): 42–45.

Porter, Josias Leslie. *Five Years in Damascus.* 2 vols. London: John Murray, 1855.

[———]. *A Handbook for Travellers in Syria and Palestine.* Part 2. New and rev. ed. London: John Murray, 1875.

Post, George E. *Flora of Syria, Palestine and Sinai.* 2d ed. Rev. and enl. by John Edward Dinsmore. 2 vols. Beirut: American Press, 1932.

Prime, William C. *Tent Life in the Holy Land.* New York: Harper, 1857.

Qudaama, Ahmad. *Qamus al-tabakh al-sahih* (Dictionary of Correct Cooking). Beirut: Dar al-nafaes, 1980.

Rayess, George N. *Art of Lebanese Cooking.* Beirut: Librairie du Liban, 1982.

Renan, Ernest. *Mission de Phénicie.* Paris: Imprimerie impériale, 1864.

Rihbany, Abraham Mitrie. *A Far Journey.* Boston and New York: Houghton Mifflin, 1914.

Riley, Isaac, comp. *Syrian Home-Life.* New York: Dodd & Mead, [1874].

Robinson, Edward. *Later Biblical Researches in Palestine, and in the Adjacent Regions.* Boston: Crocker & Brewster, 1856.

Rodinson, Maxime. "Ghida." In *Encyclopedia of Islam.* New ed. Vol. 2. Leiden: E. J. Brill, 1965: 1057–1072.

———. "Recherches sur les documents arabes relatifs à la cuisine." *Revue des études islamiques* 17 (1949): 95–165.

Rogers, Mary Eliza. *Domestic Life in Palestine.* 1862. Reprint, London: Kegan Paul International, 1989.

Russell, Alexander. *The Natural History of Aleppo.* 2 vols. 2d ed., rev., enl., and ill. with notes by Patrick Russell. London: G. G. and J. Robinson, 1794.

Saggs, H. W. F. *Everyday Life in Babylonia and Assyria.* New York: Dorset Press, 1987.

Sakayan, Dora. *Armenian Proverbs.* Delmar, N.Y.: Caravan Books, 1994.

Sanjian, Avedis K. *The Armenian Communities in Syria under Ottoman Dominion.* Cambridge, Mass.: Harvard University Press, 1965.

[Sarkis, Khalil]. *Ustad al-tabbakhin.* 6th ed. Beirut: [Sarkis], 1931.

Schami, Rafik. *Damascus Nights.* Translated by Philip Boehm. New York: Farrar, Straus & Giroux, 1993.

Schumacher, Gottlieb. *Pella.* London: Richard Bentley, 1895.

Shah, Idries. *The Pleasantries of the Incredible Mulla Nasrudin.* New York: E. P. Dutton, 1971.

Siurmeian, Artavazd. *Patmutʻiun Halepi Hayotsʻ* (History of the Armenians of Aleppo). Vol. 2. Beirut: Dbaran M. Maksudian, 1946.

Skinner, Thomas. *Adventures during a Journey Overland to India, by Way of Egypt, Syria, and the Holy Land.* 2 vols. London: Richard Bentley, 1836.

Smith, Joanne. *Cuisine, Texas: A Multiethnic Feast.* Austin: University of Texas Press, 1995.

Stark, Freya. *Letters from Syria.* London: John Murray, 1942.

Sykes, John. *The Mountain Arabs: A Window on the Middle East.* London: Hutchinson, 1968.

al-Tabari. *The History of al-Tabari.* Vol. 13. Translated by Gautier H. A. Juynboll. Bibliotheca Persica. Albany: State University of New York Press, 1989.

Thévenot, Jean de. *Travels into the Levant.* Part 2. English ed. 1687. Reprint, Westmead, England: Gregg International Publishers, 1971.

Thomson, William McClure. *The Land and the Book.* 3 vols. New York: Harper, 1880, 1882, 1885.

Urquhart, David. *The Lebanon (Mount Souria): A History and a Diary.* 2 vols. London: Thomas Cautley Newby, 1860.

Uvezian, Sonia. *The Best Foods of Russia* (paperback ed. title *Cooking from the Caucasus*). New York: Harcourt Brace Jovanovich, 1976, 1978.

———. *The Book of Salads.* San Francisco: 101 Productions, 1977.

———. *The Book of Yogurt.* San Francisco: 101 Productions, 1978. Reprint, Ecco Press, 1999.

———. "Bulgur." *Gourmet* 42, no. 4 (April 1982): 46, 80, 82, 84.

———. *The Complete International Sandwich Book.* New York: Stein and Day, 1982.

———. *The Cuisine of Armenia.* New York: Harper & Row, 1974. Reprint, Hippocrene Books, 1996, 1998.

———. *The International Appetizer Cookbook.* New York: Ballantine/Fawcett Columbine, 1984.

———. "Pita." *Gourmet* 43, no. 10 (October 1983): 48, 152–155, 158–161.

———. "Pita—the Bread with a Pocket—to Fill in Surprising Ways." *Vogue* 169, no. 2 (February 1979): 168, 171, 174, 176.

Van Lennep, Henry J. *Bible Lands: Their Modern Customs and Manners Illustrative of Scripture.* New York: Harper, 1875.

Van Thal, Herbert, ed. *Edward Lear's Journals: A Selection.* New York: Coward McCann, 1952.

Volney, Constantin-François. *Voyage en Egypte et en Syrie.* 2 vols. 1787. Reprint, Paris: Mouton, 1959.

Waines, David. *In a Caliph's Kitchen.* London: Riad el-Rayyes Books, 1989.

Warburton, Eliot. *Travels in Egypt and the Holy Land; or, the Crescent and the Cross.* Philadelphia:
    H. C. Peck & Theo. Bliss, 1859.
Ward, Philip. *Touring Lebanon.* London: Faber and Faber, 1971.
al-Warraq, Ibn Sayyar. *Kitab al-tabikh* (Cookery Book). Edited by Kaj Öhrnberg and Sahban Mroueh.
    Studia Orientalia, vol. 60. Helsinki: Finnish Oriental Society, 1987.
Wellsted, James Raymond. *Travels in Arabia.* 2 vols. London: John Murray, 1838.
"The West Went Thataway—East." *Life* 60 (7 January 1966): 46–53.
Wilson, Charles Thomas. *Peasant Life in the Holy Land.* London: John Murray, 1906.
Wortabet, Gregory M. *Syria, and the Syrians.* Vol. 1. London: James Madden, 1856.
Yassine, Sima Osman, and Sadouf Kamal. *Middle Eastern Cuisine.* Beirut: Dar el-ilm lil-malayin, 1984.

Index